Basic Real Estate
and Property Law
for Paralegals

ASPEN PUBLISHERS

Basic Real Estate and Property Law for Paralegals

Third Edition

Jeffrey A. Helewitz
Adjunct Professor of Law
City University of New York
School of Law
Touro College Law Center

 Wolters Kluwer

Law & Business

AUSTIN   BOSTON   CHICAGO   NEW YORK   THE NETHERLANDS

Aspen Publishers
Attn: Permissions Department
76 Ninth Avenue, 7th Floor
New York, NY 10011-5201

To contact Customer Care, e-mail customer.care@aspenpublishers.com,
call 1-800-234-1660, fax 1-800-901-9075, or mail correspondence to:

Aspen Publishers
Attn: Order Department
PO Box 990
Frederick, MD 21705

Printed in the United States of America.

1 2 3 4 5 6 7 8 9 0

ISBN 978-0-7355-7631-5

Library of Congress Cataloging-in-Publication Data

Helewitz, Jeffrey A.
    Basic real estate and property law for paralegals / Jeffrey A. Helewitz. — 3rd ed.
        p. cm.
    Includes index.
    ISBN 978-0-7355-7631-5
1. Real property — United States. 2. Conveyancing — United States. 3. Vendors
and purchasers — United States. 4. Legal assistants — United States — Handbooks,
manuals, etc. I. Title.

    KF570.H45 2009
    346.7304'3 — dc22
                                                                            2009011798

About Wolters Kluwer Law & Business

Wolters Kluwer Law & Business is a leading provider of research information and workflow solutions in key specialty areas. The strengths of the individual brands of Aspen Publishers, CCH, Kluwer Law International and Loislaw are aligned within Wolters Kluwer Law & Business to provide comprehensive, in-depth solutions and expert-authored content for the legal, professional and education markets.

CCH was founded in 1913 and has served more than four generations of business professionals and their clients. The CCH products in the Wolters Kluwer Law & Business group are highly regarded electronic and print resources for legal, securities, antitrust and trade regulation, government contracting, banking, pension, payroll, employment and labor, and healthcare reimbursement and compliance professionals.

Aspen Publishers is a leading information provider for attorneys, business professionals and law students. Written by preeminent authorities, Aspen products offer analytical and practical information in a range of specialty practice areas from securities law and intellectual property to mergers and acquisitions and pension/benefits. Aspen's trusted legal education resources provide professors and students with high-quality, up-to-date and effective resources for successful instruction and study in all areas of the law.

Kluwer Law International supplies the global business community with comprehensive English-language international legal information. Legal practitioners, corporate counsel and business executives around the world rely on the Kluwer Law International journals, loose-leafs, books and electronic products for authoritative information in many areas of international legal practice.

Loislaw is a premier provider of digitized legal content to small law firm practitioners of various specializations. Loislaw provides attorneys with the ability to quickly and efficiently find the necessary legal information they need, when and where they need it, by facilitating access to primary law as well as state-specific law, records, forms and treatises.

Wolters Kluwer Law & Business, a unit of Wolters Kluwer, is headquartered in New York and Riverwoods, Illinois. Wolters Kluwer is a leading multinational publisher and information services company.

Summary of Contents

Contents

CHAPTER 5: REAL ESTATE CLOSING PROCEDURES   153

CHAPTER 6: CONDOMINIUMS, COOPERATIVES, AND COMMERCIAL PROPERTY   189

Contents

Preface

This text is designed to assist legal professionals in understanding and effectuating real estate and personal property transactions. The term "legal professional" includes legal assistants, attorneys, law clerks, legal secretaries, and all other persons whose day-to-day activities involve real estate and law. The principles, forms, and tasks discussed in the text are applicable to anyone in the legal profession who deals with these matters. In any given transaction the totality of the work may be accomplished by a lawyer or a paralegal or legal secretary working under the lawyer's supervision. However, in almost no other area of law is the non-lawyer legal professional called upon to perform such independent work.

Basic Real Estate and Property Law for Paralegals provides an analysis of the basic legal principles involved in real and personal property law, as well as practical guidance in creating, organizing, and completing real estate transactions. Furthermore, by links to Loislaw, state-specific forms and materials are accessible to conform the material to the rules of a given jurisdiction. This text provides a complete and comprehensive guide to all aspects of property law—real estate, landlord-tenant, land use, and personal property. These topics form the mainstay of almost every general practice law office in the country, and understanding them is a fundamental skill required of all legal professionals.

Jeffrey A. Helewitz

February 2009

Basic Real Estate and Property Law for Paralegals

1 Estates in Land and Future Interests

LEARNING OBJECTIVES

After studying this chapter you will be able to:

- Distinguish between real and personal property
- Differentiate between freeholds and leaseholds
- Discuss the vesting and divesting of fee estates
- List the five types of concurrent fee ownership
- Understand how to create a tenancy in common
- Indicate the requirements to create a joint tenancy
- Discuss how to establish a tenancy by the entirety
- Know the effect of holding community property
- Define a tenancy in partnership
- Explain the concept of a life estate
- Identify future interests in estates
- Define and apply the Rule Against Perpetuities
- Apply the salvage doctrines to the Rule Against Perpetuities
- Apply some practical tips in a real property practice

CHAPTER OUTLINE

Overview: Real v. Personal Property
Classifications of Estates
    Freeholds
      Fees
        Fee simple absolute
        Fee simple determinable
        Fee simple subject to a condition subsequent
        Fee simple subject to an executory interest
      Concurrent Ownership
        Tenancy in common
        Joint tenancy
        Tenancy by the entirety
        Community property
        Tenancy in partnership
      Life Estates
    Leaseholds
Future Interests
    Indefeasibly vested remainder
    Vested remainder subject to open
    Vested remainder subject to complete divestment
    Contingent remainder
The Rule Against Perpetuities
    Salvage doctrines
Practical Tips

CHAPTER OVERVIEW

The law of property has often been referred to as a "bundle of rights." This designation underscores the fact that property law encompasses more than just one simple legal concept. Rather, the law of property concerns a person's ability to possess, transfer, and access both real and personal property.

Real property is defined as land, vegetation growing on the land, structures permanently affixed to the land, and mineral resources that are located beneath the soil. **Personal property** is all property that is not classified as real property, such as clothing, furniture, electronic equipment, and so forth. An individual's ability to use, possess, and transfer real and personal property is dependent upon the legal title to that property that is vested in that individual. **Title** is the legal term indicating rights to property, and **vesting** refers to a person's ability to enforce such rights in the courts. To understand the law of property, one must first understand the different categories of title to property that a person may hold.

This chapter explores this basic legal concept with respect to property—title. When referring to the title that a person has in real property, such title is called an **estate.** However, the same title attaches to personal property as well. The rights (and obligations) incident to a specific title to property are identical regardless of whether the property is **realty** (real property) or **personalty** (personal property). For the purposes of this initial explanation, these titles are exemplified by estates in land.

Classifications of Estates

All estates, or titles, in land are divided into two broad categories: freeholds and leaseholds. A **freehold** is an estate in land that a person has for an indefinite period of time. A **leasehold** is a possessory interest in land that a person has for a period of time specified in a contract called a **lease.** The holder of a freehold estate has rights and obligations created by the law, both common and statutory. The holder of a leasehold has rights and obligations dictated by the provisions of the lease.

Freeholds

Fees

Freehold estates are divided into two sub-categories: fees and life estates. A **fee,** or **fee simple absolute,** is the largest estate in land recognized by the law. The holder of a fee interest can sell, gift, devise, and encumber that interest, and holds that interest for an indefinite period of time.

 EXAMPLE:

A woman purchases a house that rests on one-half acre of land. There are no restrictions on her title, so she holds the property as a fee simple absolute. If she wishes to sell off a portion of the land, rent her house, or use her interest in the property as collateral for a loan, she may do so, because her interest is absolute and unrestricted.

Not all fee interests are absolute. The law recognizes two types of fee simple estates that may terminate upon the happening of a particular event. Note that this interest is still indefinite, because the event may or may not occur, and the time of such possible occurrence is unknown. However, this interest does impose a certain limitation on the titleholder.

The two types of fees that may terminate at the happening of a specified event are called a fee simple determinable and a fee simple subject to a condition subsequent. These two types of terminable fees are referred to as **defeasible fees,** meaning that the interest of the titleholder may be cut off, or defeated, if the event occurs.

A **fee simple determinable** is a fee that terminates upon the happening of a specified event, at which time the title to the property is automatically transferred back to the person who created the interest, known as the **grantor,** or transferor, of the interest in the realty.

 EXAMPLE:

> Grantor, who holds a fee simple absolute title to a parcel of property called Blackacre, transfers the title to his son "for so long as the property is used for residential purposes." This restriction on the use of the property creates a fee simple determinable. If the son, or anyone to whom the son transfers his interest, decides to use the property for commercial purposes, the title to Blackacre automatically reverts back to the grantor or the grantor's heirs if such use occurs after the grantor's death. This automatic reversion to the grantor of a fee simple determinable is called a **possibility of reverter,** indicating that there is a possibility that title will revert to the grantor.

A **fee simple subject to a condition subsequent** is created when the grantor transfers title to the property but reserves the right to regain the title upon the happening of an event specified in the transfer.

 EXAMPLE:

> Grantor, who holds a fee simple absolute title to a parcel of property called Whiteacre, transfers title to his daughter "but if the property is ever used for commercial purposes, then Whiteacre will go back to Grantor." If the property is subsequently used for commercial purposes, the grantor may reclaim the property provided that he has specifically reserved a **right of re-entry** in the transferring document (which he has). This right, unlike the possibility of reverter, is not automatic under the law, and the grantor or his heirs may decline to exercise this right.

A fee simple determinable and a fee simple subject to a condition subsequent are very similar, and the distinguishing characteristic lies in the words used by the grantor in the transferring document. Phrases such as "for so long as," "during," "while," and so forth indicate a fee simple determinable, whereas the phrase "but if" or "upon the happening of" creates a fee simple subject to a condition subsequent. With the former, the prohibited use must be mentioned; with the latter any use except for the one specified is permitted. The consequence of this linguistic use is crucial.

With a fee simple determinable the title may revert back automatically; with a fee simple subject to a condition subsequent the grantor or the grantor's heirs must actually exercise the right of re-entry or such right is lost. Also, the limitations on the use of the property extend to all persons to whom the property is transferred by and through the original transferee.

EXAMPLE:

A grantor creates a fee simple subject to a condition subsequent. Five years after the transfer the transferee uses the property in a manner that gives rise to the condition. The grantor is aware of the change in use, but does not exercise the right of re-entry. This right of re-entry, if not exercised, will be lost, and the transferee now has a fee simple absolute. If the title had been a fee simple determinable, the title would have automatically reverted to the grantor regardless of the grantor's action or inaction.

If, when creating the title, the grantor decides that he or she does not wish to regain the title but, if the specified event occurs, wishes a third person to be entitled to the property, the grantor may so indicate. The title thus created in the transfer is referred to as a **fee simple subject to an executory interest.** This simply is either a fee simple determinable or a fee simple subject to a condition subsequent in which the reversionary interest passes not to the grantor but to a third person so designated by the grantor.

EXAMPLE:

A grantor transfers title to Greenacre to his son provided that it is used only for recreational purposes, then to his daughter. The son has a fee simple subject to a condition subsequent, and the daughter has an executory interest, in this case a right of re-entry, which she may exercise if the son uses the property for non-recreational purposes.

Historically, a type of limited fee simple existed known as a **fee tail,** meaning that the property could only pass to lineal descendants of the titleholder. Almost every jurisdiction in the country has abolished this type of title.

EXAMPLE:

A grantor transfers his property to his son and "the male heirs of his body." This creates a fee tail in the son's male descendants, referred to as a *fee tail male.*

A fee simple estate may be held by just one person, or by two or more persons collectively. If one person holds the title, it is called a **tenancy in severalty.** The word "tenancy" comes from the French word "tenir," meaning "to hold": the person holds the title individually. If the title is held by two or more persons, the title is referred to as **concurrent ownership.** The United States recognizes five types of concurrent title to property:

1. tenancy in common
2. joint tenancy
3. tenancy by the entirety
4. community property
5. tenancy in partnership

1. Tenancy in common.   A **tenancy in common** is an estate in property in which two or more **co-tenants** (titleholders) own a concurrent, but not necessarily equal, title to the property. This interest is deemed to be separate but undivided from the other tenants' interests. Each tenant in common, regardless of her percentage of ownership, is entitled to possess the entire property, but has no right to the exclusive possession of any portion of the property. Each tenant in common is free to **alienate** (transfer) her interest in the property, and there is no right of survivorship in the remaining tenants of a deceased tenant's interest. The interest of a deceased tenant in common passes to her heirs.

EXAMPLE:

> A woman inherits a summer home from her great-aunt. She decides that she does not want to use the home all the time, and to raise capital she sells a one-quarter interest to each of two friends. The three friends are now tenants in common, with the first woman owning a 50 percent interest and the two friends owning a 25 percent interest each. Despite the unequal ownership percentages, each friend has the right to possess the entire house—for example, none of them can lay claim to exclusive use of the "best" bedroom (absent an agreement to that effect).

Any co-tenant who is in actual possession of the property has the right to retain any profit derived from his or her own use of the property, and is not required to share those profits with the co-tenants who are not actually in possession. However, if the tenant in possession realizes profit from an agreement with a third person for the use of the property, this profit must be shared with co-tenants in proportion to their ownership interest.

EXAMPLE:

> Two brothers buy a parcel of real estate as tenants in common. One brother lives on the property where he grows vegetables. The

second brother lives in a city 100 miles away from the property. The brother in possession does not have to share the profit he derives from the sale of the vegetables he grows on the property. However, if the brother in possession rented the property to a neighboring farmer, the brother would have to share the rent with the urban brother. The difference involves income derived from a tenant's own efforts versus income derived from leasing the possessory interest.

Each tenant in common has the legal right to **encumber** her interest, meaning that she may mortgage that interest or have that interest subject to mechanic's liens, but no one tenant may encumber the interests of the other co-tenants without their consent. If the creditor of the tenant in common who encumbered her interest forecloses because the tenant failed to meet the credit obligation, the foreclosure, in most states, acts to sever the title into tenancies in severalty, proportionate to the co-tenants' interests.

 EXAMPLE:

A tenant in common wants to raise some cash to buy some corporate shares as an investment. To raise this capital, she mortgages her one-half interest in the subject property. The price of the shares falls and the woman loses her entire investment and cannot repay the loan. The creditor to whom she mortgaged the property forecloses on the realty (see Chapter 4). After foreclosure the creditor now owns a fee simple absolute in one-half of the property, while the former co-tenant now owns a fee simple absolute in the other one-half of the property.

If the co-tenants want to terminate the tenancy in common, they have three options:

(a) they can collectively transfer their title, transferring to each a fee simple absolute in his or her proportionate share;
(b) a tenant in possession may go to court to seek an **ouster**, a court-ordered termination of a co-tenant's rights because of the co-tenant's failure to meet some specified legal obligation or abandonment of the property; or
(c) if the parties cannot agree to a suitable division, they may seek a court-ordered **partition** of the property in which the court will determine the portion each co-tenant will receive.

A tenant in common may seek contribution from the other co-tenants for all repairs, taxes, and mortgage payments made on the property that exceed the percentage interest of the paying tenant in common, but the tenant is not entitled to be reimbursed for improvements made to the property absent an agreement by the other co-tenants or pursuant to a court order.

EXAMPLE:

Four cousins inherit a home from their grandmother as tenants in common. Two cousins want to rent the property to produce an income. Prior to such rental, one cousin pays for necessary repairs to the roof and the installation of a new boiler, and then decides to have the property artistically landscaped. This cousin may seek reimbursement for the roof repairs and the boiler but not for the landscaping, which was not a necessary repair.

Whenever two or more **grantees** acquire concurrent title to property and they are not married to each other, the law assumes that they hold title as tenants in common unless a different title is specified in the conveyance.

2. Joint tenancy. A **joint tenancy** is a form of concurrent ownership of property in which each joint tenant has an undivided interest in the whole estate, and there is a **right of survivorship** in the remaining joint tenants upon the death of each of them. To create a joint tenancy, the conveyance must contain what is referred to as the **four unities** of time, title, interest, and possession. In other words, unlike a tenancy in common that may be created by several conveyances and in which each tenant in common may own a different percentage of the whole, to create a joint tenancy all of the joint tenants must acquire the same title by the same instrument at the same time, and the title must be equal with respect to each tenant.

EXAMPLE:

Three sisters decide to purchase some land together as an investment, and decide to hold the title as joint tenants. To create the joint tenancy, the grantor must convey this interest in the property in one document in which each sister is given a one-third interest in the realty. The document must also specify that a joint tenancy is being created.

Unlike a tenancy in common in which a co-tenant may alienate his or her interest in the property without destroying the title, with a joint tenancy, because each joint tenant owns an undivided interest, any attempt to alienate his or her interest in a joint tenancy during his or her life acts to destroy the joint tenancy. This alienation will create a tenancy in common. If more than two people hold title as joint tenants, the result would be fairly convoluted: the joint tenant who alienated her portion now holds title as a tenant in common with the former joint tenants who are collectively a tenant in common holding that interest as joint tenants.

**EXAMPLE:**

Abel, Baker, and Carr acquire some property as joint tenants. Abel decides to sell his interest to Dorrance. Once the sale is consummated, Abel's alienation has severed the joint tenancy. The property is now held as a tenancy in common. Dorrance holds title as a tenant in common for a one-third interest, and Baker and Carr, holding title as joint tenants, are the tenant in common for a two-thirds interest in the property. If Baker dies, the title to the joint property devolves on Carr, and the property is now a tenancy in common with Dorrance being a tenant in common for a one-third interest, and Carr being a tenant in common for a two-thirds interest. Carr received Baker's interest by right of survivorship.

As indicated by the above example, upon the death of a joint tenant his interest passes automatically to the surviving joint tenants. Any attempt by a joint tenant to transfer his interest by means of a will fails. Note that an inter vivos transfer destroys the joint tenancy and creates a tenancy in common, whereas testamentary transfers are ineffective and title passes by right of survivorship to the surviving joint tenants.

If a joint tenant encumbers his interest, this also may act to sever the joint tenancy in many jurisdictions. Furthermore, some jurisdictions have held that even entering into a contract for the sale of an interest in a joint tenancy, without the actual sale being consummated, is sufficient to destroy the joint tenancy and create a tenancy in common. Many states prohibit a joint tenant from acquiring a title by right of survivorship if the surviving joint tenant was responsible for the death of the deceased joint tenant.

Joint tenancies are not favorable to the tenants because of the restriction on the alienation of interest, and most jurisdictions require that a joint tenancy be specified as the title in the conveyance for it to be created.

3. Tenancy by the entirety.   A **tenancy by the entirety** is a form of joint tenancy recognized by many states for legally married couples. A tenancy by the entirety is created with the four unities of a joint tenancy plus a fifth unity of a valid marriage.

A tenancy by the entirety cannot be encumbered or conveyed by one spouse alone; any transfer without the consent of both spouses is ineffective. As with a regular joint tenancy, there is an automatic right of survivorship in the surviving spouse, and a tenancy by the entirety may only be severed by divorce, mutual agreement, or a foreclosure by a creditor of *both* parties.

**EXAMPLE:**

A married couple purchases a house as tenants by the entirety. As a couple they borrow a portion of the purchase price from a bank and give the bank a mortgage on the house to secure the loan. Several years later, the wife, an inveterate gambler, borrows money to pay her gambling debts and gives her creditor a mortgage on the house. When both of the loans are in default, only the bank can foreclose because both spouses signed the mortgage; the wife's creditor is unable to foreclose because he is the creditor of the wife alone.

A tenancy by the entirety affords protection to the married couple because neither spouse alone has the legal ability to destroy the title, and the right of survivorship will remain intact. This provides more benefits to a couple than a regular joint tenancy.

4. Community property.   Nine jurisdictions in the United States currently recognize community property as a title for married couples. **Community property** is a title to property given to property acquired by a married couple during the marriage if no other title is specified on the conveyance, or if that title is specifically selected. With community property, each spouse is deemed to be the outright owner of one-half of the property, meaning that each is able to alienate his or her portion, and there is no automatic right of survivorship.

EXAMPLE:

A married couple in New Mexico, a community property state, purchases a parcel of undeveloped real estate as an investment. The wife is killed in a car accident, and in her will she leaves all of her real property to her sister. Because the couple did not specify a different title when purchasing the land, the property is considered to be community property, and the wife was free to will her interest to whomever she wished. Consequently, the property is now held by the husband and the sister as tenants in common.

5. Tenancy in partnership.   For business partners, the law has described a fifth type of concurrent ownership known as a tenancy in partnership. A **tenancy in partnership** is only available to persons operating a business as a general or a limited partnership. All of the business property, unless otherwise designated, is deemed to be held as a tenancy in partnership. The attributes of such title are:

(a) no one partner may possess the partnership property for other than partnership purposes without the other partners' consent;

(b) no one partner may sell the property, otherwise than in the regular course of business, without the other partners' consent;

(c) the personal creditors of the individual partners may not attach this property to satisfy the personal debts of the individual partners; and

(d) the heirs of a deceased partner are only entitled to receive the value of the deceased partner's interest in the property—the title to the property itself passes to the surviving partners by operation of law.

The purpose behind the creation of a tenancy in partnership is to assure business partners that the property that is acquired by and for the business will remain the property of the collective partners to be used exclusively for business purposes.

EXAMPLE:

Three friends decide to go into business together to buy and sell gemstones. Each partner contributes a certain amount of capital, and they purchase a quantity of colored gemstones for the business. Later, one of the partners defaults on a loan that he had taken out to go on a vacation. This partner's creditor cannot attach the gemstones to satisfy the debt because they are held in tenancy in partnership. Conversely, if the three partners collectively borrowed the money to buy gemstones, this creditor could attach the gemstones because it is a debt of the partnership, not the individual partner.

Life Estates

The second subset of freehold is known as a **life estate,** whereby a person holds title for a "lifetime," which is deemed to be an indefinite period. At the termination of the "life," title to the property will automatically pass to someone else whose identity is specified in the conveyance that created the life estate.

EXAMPLE:

In her will a woman leaves a house, which she owned as a tenancy in severalty, to her "beloved husband for life, then to our children." The husband has inherited a life estate, meaning that he has a possessory interest in the property only during his lifetime, and on his death the children will inherit the property as tenants in common (the woman did not specify any type of title for the children so the law will assume a tenancy in common).

The person whose life determines the duration of the estate is referred to as the **measuring life.** In the most common situation, the grantee is the measuring life, as exemplified above. However, under certain circumstances the holder of the life estate may only hold this possessory interest during another person's life. This type of estate is referred to as a **life estate pur autre vie.**

EXAMPLE:

In the previous example, assume that the widower does not wish to live in the house but wants to travel. To raise capital he conveys his interest in the property to a third person. This person now has a life estate pur autre vie, holding title only so long as the widower, the measuring life, lives. At the widower's death, the title passes to the children according to the terms of their mother's will.

The **life tenant,** the person who holds title to the life estate, is entitled to the ordinary use and profits from the property, but is precluded from doing anything that would injure or reduce the interests of the person who will ultimately acquire the fee estate. The person who eventually receives the fee interest in the property after the termination of the life estate is referred to as the **remainderman** (the children from the previous example). To determine whether the use of the land is considered ordinary or detrimental to the remainderman, see Chapter 2.

Leaseholds

The second broad category of estates is the leasehold. As the term would imply, a leasehold is an interest in property that a person holds pursuant to a contract known as a **lease.** A person who has a transferable interest in property may grant the use of that property to some one. If this transfer is accomplished by means of a lease, the transferor is called the **lessor,** or **landlord,** and the person who acquires the right pursuant to the lease contract is called the **lessee** or **tenant.** A leasehold differs from a freehold interest in that it is a possessory interest only, and it terminates at a set period of time as determined by the lease.

A leasehold is formed by contract, in which the lessor gives the lessee possession of the property for a specified period of time, and the lessee agrees to pay the lessor a fee for such use known as **rent.** Leasehold rights and obligations are determined by the contract between the parties as well as statutory and common law. These legal rights and obligations come under the heading of **landlord-tenant law,** which is fully discussed in Chapter 7.

 EXAMPLE:

The widower from the previous example decides that, rather than conveying his entire interest to a third person, he will just rent the house for one year and use the rent to travel. He contracts with the third party to rent the property, and then leaves on a trip. The third person now has a leasehold rather than a life estate pur autre vie. *Query:* What would happen if the widower died in a plane crash two days after the lease was executed? See Chapter 4.

Future Interests

One of the primary concerns of property law is to ensure that at some point one person (or a collective group) has a sufficient interest in the property to be able to exercise all rights of a fee holder. This legal ability to exercise rights of ownership and possession is called *vesting*. The area of property law known as future interests is concerned with seeing that all property titles are vested within a reasonable period of time. In the example above, the widower has a presently vested life estate and the children have vested remainder interests in fee, which take effect in the future, at the death of their father.

Earlier in the chapter the concept of the possibility of reverter, the right of re-entry, and reversions were all introduced. Each of these estates is a future estate because even though the holder of such right has a property interest, the ability to exercise that right is delayed until some point in the future.

Classifications

The law recognizes four classifications of future estates:

1. **Indefeasibly vested remainder:** This type of estate is created in a person who is both in existence and ascertainable at the time the conveyance creating such interest comes into existence. The interest is indefeasibly vested because it occurs automatically at the natural termination of a previous estate.

EXAMPLE:

In her will a woman conveys her house to her niece Betty for life, then to Betty's daughter Joan. Betty has a life estate and her daughter Joan has an indefeasibly vested remainder. When Betty dies, title automatically passes to Joan. Joan's right is currently vested because she can stop Betty from doing anything that would injure or diminish the value of the property.

2. **Vested remainder subject to open:** This estate is created when a vested remainder is given not to a named person but to a class of persons and that class may be added to. "Subject to open" means that the title is shared by persons who may be added to the class.

EXAMPLE:

In the preceding example, assume that the woman's will leaves the property to "my niece Betty for life, then to Betty's children." At the date of the woman's death, Betty has one child, Joan. However, because Betty may have more children before she dies, Joan's interest is subject to being proportionately diminished by the addition of more siblings to the class. Joan's interest is a vested remainder subject to open.

3. **Vested remainder subject to complete divestment:** This is a **vested remainder that is subject to a condition subsequent** as discussed above. The interest may be totally lost (divested) if the condition occurs.

EXAMPLE:

A man conveys his house to his wife for life, then to his son provided that the son always uses the property for residential purposes, otherwise to his daughter. The son has a vested remainder in fee subject to a condition subsequent. If he uses the property for non-residential purposes, he will be divested and the title will pass to his sister.

4. **Contingent remainder:** This is a remainder interest that may or may not vest — it is conditioned upon either a condition precedent or is created in a person who is unborn or unascertainable at the time of the conveyance.

A remainder subject to a condition precedent is exemplified by a conveyance that gives a remainder interest provided that some condition is met before the remainder becomes a present estate.

EXAMPLE:

A man conveys his house to his wife for life, then to his son provided that the son becomes a priest. The son's interest is contingent upon his taking orders, which means that it may never vest in him if the condition is not met.

A contingent remainder created in unborn or unascertained persons occurs when the person who will hold the eventual title is not in existence at the date of the conveyance creating the interest.

EXAMPLE:

A woman conveys her house to her sister for life, then to the children of her brother. If the brother has no children at the time of the conveyance, the interests of the unborn children are deemed to be contingent (upon their birth). Note that if the brother had at least one child at the time of the conveyance, the child's interest would be a vested remainder subject to open.

Any time a future interest either cuts off an earlier estate or only comes about after a gap following the natural termination of an earlier estate, it is referred to as an **executory interest.** These interests are not considered vested, and therefore are treated under the law in the same fashion as a contingent remainder.

EXAMPLE:

Grantor to *A* for life, then two years after *A*'s death to *C*'s children. *C*'s children's interest is executory because it follows a gap (two years) after the termination of the preceding estate.

The Rule Against Perpetuities

In order to avoid the situation in which vested titles to land are held up indefinitely because of contingent remainders, the law mandates that, for a transfer of property to be valid, all interests created by the transfer must vest (be legally enforceable) within a predetermined period of time from the date of the instrument creating those interests. This legal doctrine is called the **Rule Against Perpetuities,** and its application has worried and confused legal professionals for centuries. Simply stated, the Rule mandates that all interests must vest, if at all, within 21 years after the death of the lives in being at the effective date of the initial conveyance, plus the period of gestation (pregnancy). In order to understand how the Rule affects estates, each component of the Rule must be analyzed.

"All interests" refers to every interest, vested, contingent, or executory, that is created by the document of conveyance.

"Must vest" means the vesting of each of these interests is required to be legally enforceable.

"If at all" means that if any one of these interests, regardless of how remote, fails to vest within the stated period, none of the interests vests because the transfer is considered invalid.

"Within 21 years after the death of the lives in being at the effective date of the conveyance" refers only to those persons who are alive at the date the instrument becomes effective and who, either directly or indirectly by being the progenitor of an interest taker, acquire some interest in the conveyance. These persons also include anyone who is *in utero* at that date. Persons who do not fall into this discrete grouping are not considered to be lives in being. This provision of the Rule sets the maximum time period for the vesting of all interests created by the conveyance.

EXAMPLE:

In his will a man leaves his property to his "wife for life, then their children for life, then to their grandchildren." In this example the effective date of the conveyance is the day of the man's death when the will takes effect. The wife has an immediately vested life estate. The children are all lives in being because all of a person's children must be either alive or in utero at the date of the person's death, and all of them have vested life estates. The man's grandchildren, who are uncertain at this date, have contingent remainders, but they will all be ascertained at the date of his children's death and their interests vest immediately upon the death of those children who are all lives in being. Consequently, this transfer does not violate the Rule Against Perpetuities.

 EXAMPLE:

A man makes an inter vivos transfer, as an anniversary gift, to his "wife for life, then to our children for life, then to our grandchildren." In this instance the transfer is invalid according to the Rule. The transfer takes effect immediately. The man and his wife can have a new child two years after this conveyance. Assume that the man, his wife, and their children who were alive at the date of the conveyance are all subsequently killed in a car accident, only leaving the afterborn child alive. According to the transfer, this child takes a life estate, and after his death the property would go to his children. The baby is not a life in being, and if he lives more than 21 years before dying and leaving a child, this grandchild's interest will vest more than 21 years after the death of the lives in being — the man, his wife, and the children alive at the date of the conveyance.

As demonstrated above, the date of the conveyance is the crucial aspect of applying the Rule. In its classical application, the provisions of the transfer are determined by looking at all possibilities, regardless of how improbable, to ascertain whether the provisions of the Rule will be violated. If, under any conceivable scenario, an interest would vest beyond the period of the Rule, the entire transfer fails. To determine whether this might occur, follow these steps:

1. determine the effective date of the transfer;
2. determine who are the lives in being at that date;
3. create an afterborn child;
4. assume all lives in being then die; and
5. using the afterborn, follow through with the provisions of the transfer. If it is possible that an interest will vest more than 21 years after all lives in being die, the entire conveyance fails and the property reverts to the grantor or the grantor's heirs.

Several states have enacted **salvage doctrines** to save conveyances from being found invalid for possible violation of the Rule Against Perpetuities. The most common of these doctrines are:

1. Age contingency: If the transfer would be invalid because a person's interest is delayed until after the person's twenty-first birthday, the transfer is read as though the person would take an interest at age 21.
2. Administrative contingency: If the transfer would violate the Rule because some contingent event is mentioned in the transfer, the doctrine assumes that the contingency will take place within the period of the Rule.
3. Gifts to person by title rather than by name: The traditional example of this was a gift that wills to "my son for life, then to his widow for life, then to her children." It is conceivable that the woman the son is married to at the testator's death will die, and the son will remarry a woman who was not alive at his parent's death. This man's second wife will be the "widow," and she is not a life in being. The last gift will be to her child who takes after her death, and so the Rule may be violated. This salvage doctrine states that the term "widow" is deemed to refer to the person who meets that description at the time the transfer takes effect, not anyone who may subsequently meet that designation.
4. Wait and see: Many jurisdictions have enacted statutes that will only apply the provisions of the Rule if a violation actually occurs. This means that the court will not look prospectively to improbable situations, but will let the transfer take effect until an actual violation of the Rule occurs. If the "improbable" does take place, the transfer is only deemed ineffective from that point forward.
5. Year limitation: Many states have bypassed the Rule entirely by enacting statutes that permit transfers to continue for a specified number of years (usually 90) at which point the last interest must vest.

When drafting or analyzing a conveyance that purports to create successive estates, the legal professional must perform the following steps:

1. examine the provisions to determine whether the transfer may violate the Rule; and
2. determine whether the state in control of the conveyance has provided for any salvage doctrine that will save the transfer from violating the Rule.

Practical Tips

- To determine the title, obtain an **abstract of title** from the county recorder's office that provides a detailed indication of how the property has been transferred over the years.
- Keep a receipt for the abstract, which is an expense.
- If there is a break in the chain of the title, advise the attorney immediately.

- Review the transfer documents to make sure the Rule is not violated.
- Make a summary of all key documents for easy review.
- Create an information sheet for missing information that must be obtained.
- Review the property descriptions to make sure there are no discrepancies in the different transfers.

Chapter Review

The purpose of this chapter is to introduce the various types of titles to property that a person may possess. Although the discussion generally is focused on titles to realty, it must be remembered that these same titles, rights, obligations, and restrictions apply to personalty as well.

Interests in real property are known as estates, and the law divides estates into two broad categories: freeholds and leaseholds. Freehold estates are those interests in property that the tenant holds for an indefinite and uncertain period of time. Freeholds are subdivided into fee estates and life estates. These titles may be held by one person or by a group of persons collectively.

The second classification of estates, the leasehold, is an interest in property that is created by contract. The rights and obligations of the parties are determined by the provisions of the lease entered into by them. A complete discussion of the law of leaseholds appears in Chapter 7.

Not all estates in property are presently exercisable. Some interests are created to take effect in the future, known as future interests. These future interests can have an important effect on a person's estate, and, to this end, several legal theories have come into existence over the years to clear titles to property.

The Rule Against Perpetuities was enacted to mandate that all transfers of property will create vested (i.e., legally enforceable) rights within a period of time specified in the Rule. Traditionally, if any future interest would vest beyond the period of the Rule, the entire conveyance was deemed invalid. To avoid invalidating conveyances, many jurisdictions have enacted salvage doctrines to bypass the dictates of the Rule. Further, any attempt to restrict the transferability of legal interests in property is deemed invalid in many states if such restriction extends beyond a statutorily determined period of time.

The law of property is one of the bulwarks of the U.S. legal system, and legal professionals must be conversant with the rights, duties, and liabilities imposed on titles to property.

Ethical Concern

All legal professionals who are not attorneys must be careful not to give legal advice. In the case of real property law, because so much of the work is performed by legal assistants, it is very tempting for the paralegal to provide advice to clients. This is an ethical violation for the legal assistant and for the attorney who supervises the legal assistant.

Key Terms

Abstract of title
Alienate
Co-tenant
Community property
Concurrent ownership
Contingent remainder
Defeasible fee
Encumber
Estate
Executory interest
Fee
Fee simple absolute
Fee simple determinable
Fee simple subject to a condition
  subsequent
Fee simple subject to an executory
  interest
Fee tail
Four unities
Freehold
Grantee
Grantor
Indefeasibly vested remainder
Joint tenancy
Landlord
Landlord-tenant law
Lease
Leasehold
Lessee
Lessor

Life estate
Life estate pur autre vie
Life tenant
Measuring life
Ouster
Partition
Personal property
Personalty
Possibility of reverter
Real property
Realty
Remainderman
Rent
Right of re-entry
Right of survivorship
Rule Against Perpetuities
Salvage doctrines
Tenancy by the entirety
Tenancy in common
Tenancy in partnership
Tenancy in severalty
Tenant
Title
Vested remainder subject to
  complete divestment
Vested remainder subject to a
  condition subsequent
Vested remainder subject to open
Vesting

Exercises

1. Research how your state applies the Rule Against Perpetuities and whether it has any salvage doctrines.

2. Discuss the advantages of holding title to property as a tenant in common, a tenant by the entirety, and community property.
3. Give three examples by which a life estate pur autre vie may be created.
4. Discuss the difference between a contingent and an executory interest.
5. Discuss several problems that may occur if a conveyance is made to a class of persons rather than to named individuals.

Situational Analysis

A couple has lived together for eight years but has not married. They decide to purchase a home together and want to make sure that each one's rights are protected. The woman is providing the bulk of the purchase price. How should the couple be advised to protect their interests? What factors must be considered?

Edited Cases

The first case discusses the partition of property owned by tenants in common. The second case highlights the problems involved in the construction of a grantor's wishes with respect to the nature of the title he wishes to convey.

Witt v. Sheffer
6 Kan. App. 2d 868; 636 P.2d 195 (1981)

This is an action for partition of oil, gas and other minerals in place under a quarter section of land in Russell County. The trial court granted partition. This appeal followed.

The facts are undisputed. Appellees own a total of 220/320ths of the mineral estate in fee and have the reversionary right to the other 100/320ths. Appellants own a total of 100/320ths of the minerals for a primary term of fifteen years from September 15, 1935, and so long thereafter as oil or gas is produced from the premises. Appellants' term minerals were perpetuated by production of oil on the northeast ten acres of the quarter section. Appellees sought partition of only the non-producing 150 acres. The appellants asked that the other ten acres be included. The court ordered partition of the entire 160 acres. This appeal is from that order.

The first issue on appeal is: Did the court err in granting partition where appellees, as tenants in common of oil, gas and mineral interests in land, own an undivided portion thereof in fee simple, together with all reversionary rights, and the appellants own term interests therein?

Three different qualities of the mineral estate are involved here: 1) the appellees' fee simple interests; 2) the appellants' term interests, and 3) the appellees' reversionary interests. Appellants contend partition of these three qualities of mineral estate is inequitable as a matter of law.

Some background regarding the nature of partition will be helpful in understanding this issue. In *Miller v. Miller, 222 Kan. 317, 320, 564 P.2d 524 (1977)*, the court stated:

> "Partition provides a method whereby two or more persons who own property together may put an end to the multiple ownership, so that each may own a separate portion of the property or, if a division in kind is not feasible, the property may be sold and each owner given an appropriate share of the proceeds. It is said to be a right much favored in the law because it secures peace, promotes industry and enterprise, and avoids compelling unwilling persons to use their property in common. *59 Am. Jur. 2d, Partition, sec. 3*, p. 773. The right of partition is said to be an incident of common ownership. 68 C.J.S., Partition, sec. 21, p. 33."

The same general idea was earlier set forth in *Holland v. Shaffer, 162 Kan. 474, 480, 178 P.2d 235 (1947)*:

> "Ordinarily ... a cotenant ... is entitled to partition, as a matter of right. The right of partition is considered an incident of common ownership. It is based on the equitable doctrine that it is better to have the control thereof in one person than in several who may entertain divergent views with respect to its proper control and management. The general rule therefore is that all property capable of being held in cotenancy is subject to partition by judicial proceedings, the partition being either in kind or by appraisal and sale."

Thus, partition proceedings contemplate an absolute severance of the individual interests of each joint owner and after partition each has the right to enjoy his estate without supervision, let, or hindrance from the other. Since an interest in oil and gas in place constitutes an interest in real estate, partition of a mineral estate is proper.

What then of partition in a case such as this, where appellees own a part of the mineral estate in fee and have reversionary rights to the other part and the appellants own term interests in part of the mineral estate?

Again it must be emphasized that the issue before the court is one of law and not fact. If it is at all possible to equitably partition such interests in a mineral estate this court must disregard the particular facts of this case and assume the trial judge will adapt the judgment to the facts. In a partition action the trial court, sitting as a court of equity, has the discretion to adapt its judgment to the particular circumstances presented and to prevent the remedy from becoming an instrument of fraud or oppression.

It is the cotenancy in the property that gives the right to compulsory partition. Thus there must be unity of possession and each tenant must have the right to occupy the whole with his cotenants. Because of this, a person will not be allowed to maintain partition proceedings unless he has an estate in possession. Clearly appellees here have a possessory estate, the fee simple title to 220/320ths of the mineral interest. Appellees also have a non-possessory estate in the reversionary rights to the other 100/300ths, but the fact that appellees have an indefeasible estate in fee simple in one undivided share allows them to subject all interests in the estate to partition.

Appellants are mainly concerned that the parties involved have different qualities of interest in the mineral estate. According to 59 Am. Jur. 2d, Partition § 31, p. 794:

> "It is not essential to the right to partition that the cotenants shall have estates that are equal. One may have a term, another an estate for life, and another an estate in fee. All that is necessary is that they shall be cotenants of what is proposed to be partitioned."

The same qualities of interests held by the parties to this action were involved in the Seeligson case. Although it did not deal with the precise issue involved here, the court found no impediment to partition in the fact that plaintiffs' interest was a term mineral interest rather than a mineral interest in fee simple absolute. Similarly, there should, in theory, be no such impediment in the instant case since the "thereafter" clause in appellants' term interests indicates appellants each own an interest in fee simple defeasible. See 2 Williams & Meyers, Oil and Gas Law § 506.7, p. 618 (1981).

Appellants point to several Kansas cases for their proposition that mineral estate interests of the type involved here can never be subject to partition. Heaviest reliance is placed on Fry v. Dewees, 151 Kan. 488, Syl. para. 6:

> "Where owners of an entire estate convey to others for a limited term an interest in oil, gas and minerals in place, and in such as may be produced under oil and gas leases to which the conveyances are subject, and there has been exploration for and production of oil under such leases, the rights in and to production are inextricably bound up with the mineral rights, and one tenant in common may not compel partition of the mineral interests as a matter of right."

Appellants' reliance on this case is misplaced. Fry involved two separate and distinct estates. There, the court denied partition because the title to the oil and gas in place as well as title to the lease and royalty interests were involved, the later interests being treated as personal property and not subject to partition. See Fry v. Dewees, 151 Kan. at 496. This was before the enactment of K.S.A. 60-1003, which allowed partition of royalty and lease interests. The court did not consider the difficulty of making a fair division of the oil and gas in place in the land as a reason for denying partition. See also Spikes v. Magnolia Petroleum Co., 158 Kan. 659, 149 P.2d 348 (1944). Strait v. Fuller, 184 Kan. 120, 334 P.2d 385 (1959), is mentioned by appellants. That case merely involved the pleading requirements in a partition action.

The final issue is whether the trial court erred in including the leased ten acres in its order of partition. Fry v. Dewees is authority for the trial judge's excluding the ten acres covered by the oil and gas lease in order of partition. The inclusion of the leased ten acres brings two separate and distinct estates into the suit—the mineral estate and the leasehold estate.

The holding in *Fry* disallows this. The court's concern in that case was the fact that rights in both real and personal property were involved and that the code of civil procedure did not control partition of personal property. See *Fry at 496-97*.

Although interests in an oil and gas lease are still considered personal property, *Reese Enterprises, Inc. v. Lawson, 220 Kan. 300, 310, 553 P.2d 885 (1976)*, subsequent developments arguably distinguish *Fry v. Dewees*. The Kansas Code of Civil Procedure now governs partition of oil and gas leases. *K.S.A. 60-1003(a)* states that the petition in such a partition action shall have the same requirements as a petition for partition of real estate. The purpose of this amendment, according to the court in *Strait v. Fuller* was to "make the rules pertaining to oil and gas interests as nearly similar to those pertaining to real property as possible." *184 Kan. at 125*. Thus, even though *Fry v. Dewees* has not been overruled, the basis for that decision has been removed. Personal and real property interests in oil and gas are now treated the same for the purposes of partition.

As a matter of law, partition of the mineral estates under the unleased 150 acres was proper without question. Including the ten leased acres in the interests partitioned may have been error under the old Code of Civil Procedure and the rule in *Fry v. Dewees*. Now, however, for the purposes of partition, interests in an oil and gas lease are treated the same as interests in real property under the Code. *K.S.A. 60-1003*. Thus, there is no reason the ten leased acres should not be included in this action. Indeed, the appellants asked for the inclusion of these ten acres in the court order. We hold it proper to include the entire 160 acres in the order of partition.

The judgment of the trial court is affirmed.

Case Questions

1. What is the import of the court's discussion of partition?
2. Why are oil and mineral rights considered personal property?

White v. Hayes
2003 Tenn. App. LEXIS 683 (2003)

This is a will construction case. The testator's will devised his estate to his children, then to his grandchildren, then to his great-grandchildren. When the great-grandchildren became of age, the estate was to be divided "as law directs." The plaintiffs, great-grandchildren of the testator, filed this action seeking interpretation of the will and a statement of each party's interests. The trial court found that the will in question violated the Rule Against Perpetuities and ordered that the estate be divided among the testator's living heirs as tenants in common and per stirpes. The plaintiffs appeal. We vacate the decision of the trial court and remand for consideration of the cause in light of the Tennessee Uniform Statutory Rule Against Perpetuities, *T.C.A. 66-1-201 to -208*.

Dr. Hillery W. Key ("Dr. Key") died testate in 1912. Paragraph six of his holographic will ("Will") devised the following:

> I desire and will that my real estate shall be enjoyed by my children during their lives as tenants in common; then by my grandchildren during their lives and then by my great-grandchildren until they become of age. Then said estate may be divided as the law directs. This bequest is of course subject to the bequests made above.

Dr. Key's children have died and his last living grandchild died in 1992. It appears from the record that he currently has twenty living great-grandchildren and twenty-nine living great-great-grandchildren.

In 1998, seventeen of Dr. Key's great-grandchildren (collectively, "the Plaintiffs"), asked the trial court to interpret Dr. Key's Will and state each party's interest in Dr. Key's estate. A hearing was held on November 4, 1999. Arguments were presented regarding application of the class gift doctrine and the Rule Against Perpetuities. The trial court found that the class gift doctrine did not apply to the Will, but that the Will violated the Rule Against Perpetuities. The trial court stated:

> It is argued by the plaintiffs that, because a great-grandchild was living at the time of Dr. Key's death, paragraph 6 of the will does not violate the Rule Against Perpetuities. However, it is clear that the test as to the Rule Against Perpetuities is not whether the property does vest within the time prescribed, but whether the interest must vest, if at all, not later than 21 years after some life in being at the creation of the interest. (Footnotes omitted.) Obviously, there is the possibility of grandchildren and great-grandchildren being born after the termination of the lives in being at the time of Dr. Key's death, and that there was a possibility that the property would vest in unborn children of unborn children. Thus, the provision is void for remoteness.

Therefore, the trial court found that the Will violated the Rule Against Perpetuities. Based on this holding, the trial court held that the property would vest in Dr. Key's children, and that "all living heirs of Dr. Key own the property as tenants in common and per stirpes." From this order, the Plaintiffs appeal.

On appeal, the Plaintiffs argue that the Will does not violate the common law or statutory Rule Against Perpetuities and that the property should vest solely in the great-grandchildren of Dr. Key.

In 1994, the Tennessee legislature adopted the Tennessee Uniform Statutory Rule Against Perpetuities. *Tenn. Code Ann. 66-1-201 to -206* (Supp. 2002). *Section 66-1-202 of the Tennessee Code Annotated* states in part:

> (a) A nonvested property interest is invalid unless one (1) of the following conditions is satisfied:
> (1) When the interest is created, it is certain to vest or terminate no later than twenty-one (21) years after the death of an individual then alive; or (2) the interest either vests or terminates within ninety (90) years after its creation.
> *Tenn. Code Ann. 66-1-202(a) (Supp. 2002).*

Thus, the statute incorporates a variation of the traditional common law Rule Against Perpetuities, stating that an interest in nonvested property can be valid if the interest vests or terminates within ninety years after its creation. See generally Amy Morris Hess, *Freeing Property Owners from the RAP Trap: Tennessee Adopts the Uniform Statutory Rule Against Perpetuities*, 62 *Tenn. L. Rev. 267 (1995)*. In addition, *section 66-1-204 of the Tennessee Code Annotated* provides that, under certain circumstances, the disposition of property may be reformed.

In the case at bar, the trial court correctly found that Dr. Key's Will violated the common law Rule Against Perpetuities. It appears from the record, however, that the Tennessee Uniform Statutory Rule Against Perpetuities was not argued to the trial court and was not considered by the trial court in its holding. Since the statute appears applicable, we must vacate the trial court's decision and remand the cause for consideration in light of the Tennessee Uniform Statutory Rule Against Perpetuities, including, but not limited to, *sections 66-1-202 and -204 of the Tennessee Code Annotated*.

The decision of the trial court is vacated and the cause remanded for further proceedings not inconsistent with this Opinion. Costs on appeal are taxed equally to the appellants, Lorenzo C. White and Vernon R. White, and their surety, for which execution may issue, if necessary.

Case Questions

1. Do you agree with the decision of the court?
2. Are there any salvage doctrines that would create a different result?

2 Rights Incident to Titles in Realty

LEARNING OBJECTIVES

After studying this chapter you will be able to:

- Define "adverse possession"
- Discuss the effect of adverse possession on title to realty
- Understand the legal implications of surface rights
- Explain what water rights are
- Differentiate between a watercourse, ground water, and surface water
- Define "nuisance"
- Indicate the difference between a public and a private nuisance
- Discuss the concept of a fixture
- List the four types of waste that may effect a person's rights to property
- Define "emblements"
- Apply some practical tips with respect to rights incident to real property titles

CHAPTER OUTLINE

Adverse Possession
    Statutory period

CHAPTER OVERVIEW

The preceding chapter introduced the various titles that may be acquired to create an interest in property. As discussed in that chapter, these titles apply to interests in all property, real or personal. This chapter and the five that follow focus on rights that are incident to a person holding a title in real property only.

Chapter 1 began with the adage that the law of property really concerns a "bundle of rights." This chapter underscores that axiom by discussing several different rights that are incident to owning or possessing realty in which the only common denominator is the realty itself. That is, for the most part, these rights and obligations are not conceptually related outside of their relationship to the land. The seven rights that are examined in this chapter are:

(a) adverse possession, the manner in which the owner of realty may lose his or her title to all or part of the land to an interloper;
(b) surface rights, the right of a landowner to have the land supported by the neighboring property;
(c) water rights, the right of a titleholder in realty to use and exploit the natural resources located beneath the land;
(d) nuisance, the right of the titleholder to the quiet enjoyment of the use of the property;
(e) fixtures, the manner in which personal property may become permanently affixed to and considered part of the land;
(f) waste, the right of the titleholder to prevent the reduction in value of the property; and
(g) emblements, the right to use and enjoy the vegetation that grows on the land.

Adverse Possession

Adverse possession is a method whereby a person may acquire title to all or part of another person's real estate by operation of law. Titles acquired by adverse possession arise when a person, not the titleholder, takes physical possession of the property for a statutorily determined period of time without the true owner attempting to oust the trespasser. To acquire title by adverse possession, certain requirements must be met:

(a) The statutory period: Each jurisdiction, by statute, specifies the time period for determining whether a person has acquired title by means of adverse possession. Typically, the period ranges between 10 and 20 years, depending upon the particular state.

EXAMPLE:

Blackacre is located in a state in which a person may acquire title by adverse possession after possessing the property for ten years. The owner of Blackacre, an undeveloped parcel, lives over 800 miles away and has never visited the site; the property was purchased as an investment for future development. An interloper comes onto the land in 1991 and puts up a shack on the property. The interloper uses the property as a residence. In 2001, after ten years have elapsed, the interloper may have the court declare him the owner of Blackacre by adverse possession.

(b) The possession of the property must be open and notorious: This requirement mandates that the interloper's possession be visibly apparent so that the true owner would be deemed to have notice of the fact that someone was in possession of the property.

EXAMPLE:

In the preceding example, the fact that the interloper constructed a shack on the lot and actually resided in the shack for the statutory period would be deemed sufficiently "open and notorious" to meet this requirement. If the owner had visited Blackacre the shack and the evidence of habitation would have been obvious.

(c) Actual and exclusive possession: This requirement indicates an actual use and possession of the property in question. If the interloper only occupies a small part of the property, he or she may only acquire title by adverse possession to the part actually used. However, if the interloper occupies a reasonable portion of the property, and has some colorable title to the rest of the land, it will be considered as actual possession of the entire lot.

EXAMPLE:

Whiteacre is a ten-acre tract of undeveloped land. An interloper comes onto the property and builds a small house with a flower and vegetable garden on one-half acre of the property. The interloper then constructs a small and simple stone fence around all of Whiteacre. This use of the property would probably be considered possession of all of Whiteacre.

The fact that two or more people may be taking possession does not destroy the requirement of "exclusive" use, provided that one of the persons is not the true owner.

EXAMPLE:

A brother and sister find an abandoned house on an acre of property. They take possession of the house for the statutory period. The siblings may acquire title by adverse possession as tenants in common. Conversely, if the house had been inherited by the sister from their father and the brother resented that fact and continued to reside in the house along with the sister, he would not acquire title by adverse possession because he is residing with the true owner.

(d) Continuous possession: To acquire title by adverse possession, the interloper must possess the property for the entire statutory time limit in one continuous period — unconnected periods of possession cannot be totaled together to meet the statutory period. However, the use of the property by the interloper does not have to be continuous if such use would be inconsistent with the nature of the property in question. Also, an interloper may tack his possessory period to another's period, provided that there is privity between the interlopers.

EXAMPLE:

An interloper obtains possession of a run-down beachfront house that she uses for vacations during the warm weather periods and for holidays during the winter months. This use of the property is consistent with the nature of the property, and therefore this use would be deemed continuous.

EXAMPLE:

An interloper has lived on a parcel of land for seven years when he dies. He wills his interest to the property to his daughter who continues to live on the land for the remainder of the statutory period (ten years). Because there was privity between the parties, the seven years can be tacked on to the three years for the full possessory period of ten years.

(e) Hostile possession: The person who is claiming title by adverse possession must evidence that he or she possessed the property without the permission of the true owner. If the true owner agrees to the possession, explicitly or implicitly, the possession is not considered to be hostile and the statutory period will not run.

EXAMPLE:

In the earlier example in which a house was inherited by a sister but was inhabited by the brother as well as the sister, as long as the sister permits the brother to reside with her, the brother's possession is not considered to be hostile. Whenever the owner remains in possession of the property, all other persons are legally considered to be in possession with the owner's permission.

If the property in question is held by two or more people as co-tenants (see Chapter 1), the possession by one tenant is never considered to be adverse to the other co-tenant because all co-tenants have equal rights of possession. For a co-tenant to be in possession adverse to the interests of the other co-tenants, the tenant-in-possession must attempt to oust the co-tenant by a court order or by an explicit assertion that he or she is claiming exclusive title.

EXAMPLE:

Two brothers inherit a farm as tenants in common. One brother decides to live on the farm and work the land while the other brother returns to the city. Merely leaving the farm and going to the city does not constitute an abandonment of the property by the urban brother, thereby making the farming brother's possession adverse; the urban brother must make an affirmative act of abandonment in order to start the other brother's period of adverse possession.

Once all of the statutory requirements have been met, the claimant interloper may go to court for an order to **quiet title** in which the court will vest title in the claimant by adverse possession (see Chapter 5). The adverse possessor has now become the true owner of the property.

Surface Rights

Surface rights refer to a property owner's right to have the land supported in its natural state by all adjoining land (**lateral support**). This means that if one landowner uses his property in a manner that causes a neighbor's land to subside, the landowner will be held strictly liable for the resulting injuries to the land. Being held **strictly liable** means that the person who causes the injury is held legally responsible for the injury regardless of how careful he was in performing the action that caused the injury.

EXAMPLE:

A young couple have just purchased their first house and are remodeling the property. They want to create a small ornamental pond, and hire a landscaper to excavate the pond on a corner of their property. Unbeknownst to the parties, there is a fault beneath the surface, and when the landscaper digs down a few feet a portion of the land collapses, including a part of their neighbor's garden. The couple is strictly liable for the injuries resulting from the collapse of the land to the neighbor's garden.

If the property that is injured has buildings constructed on it, and the damage to the surface causes injury to the structures, the landowner who caused the damage will be held liable if the collapse would have occurred to the property in its natural state. Otherwise, the person who caused the damage to the lateral support will only be liable if he or she acted negligently.

**EXAMPLE:**

A woman is remodeling her townhouse. The townhouse shares a wall with the house next door. While the digging is taking place the work causes the neighbor's wall to collapse two feet. If the neighbor can prove that the land would have collapsed even if no house were on it, the woman will be held strictly liable for the damage to the house. If the damage to the wall was only occasioned because of the weight of the house built on the land the woman will only be held liable if the digging was done in a negligent manner.

In addition to lateral support, a property owner is entitled to **subjacent support,** meaning that anyone who is occupying the area beneath the property must support the surface and all buildings on the property that existed when the use commenced. The underground user will be held strictly liable for any resultant injuries to the land and the buildings on it. If a building is erected after the underground use began, the underground user will only be liable for damage to that structure if the user was negligent and that negligence caused the injury.

EXAMPLE:

A landowner permits an oil company to drill for oil on his property. The property in question has a house located on it. After the drilling has begun, the landowner uses some of the money he received from the oil company to build a garage. Two months later, due to a weakness in the underground rock that could not have been discovered prior to the drilling, the land gives way and damages the house and the garage. The oil company will be held strictly liable for any resulting injury to the house, but will only be liable for injury to the garage if it can be shown that the company was negligent in its work and that negligence caused damage to the garage. The house was on the property when the use began, but the garage was added after the work had started.

Water Rights

The owner of land has certain rights of use, and limitations of use, of the water located on the land. These rights depend upon whether the water is a watercourse, ground water, or surface water.

(a) Watercourse: A **watercourse** is a stream, a river, or a lake, and four separate legal concepts have developed with respect to the rights incident to these types of waters:
   i. The riparian doctrine. The **riparian doctrine** holds that a landowner has the unfettered right to use all watercourses that abut or are surrounded by his or her land. The person who holds riparian rights may use the water only for the land that gives

rise to this right, but this use may be limited by the particular jurisdiction.

ii. Natural flow theory. Pursuant to the **natural flow theory,** the landowner may only use the water in a manner that does not damage the quality, quantity, or velocity of the water for adjoining landowners.

EXAMPLE:

A farmer owns a parcel of land through which a small river flows. In order to irrigate the land, the farmer constructs dykes in the river to direct the water. This causes a tremendous diminution in the amount of water that flows onto his neighbor's property. The neighbor can enjoin the farmer from such use because it destroys the natural flow of the river.

iii. **Reasonable use.** This doctrine, which is the most prevalent, states that riparian owners may make a reasonable use of the water, meaning that all use is permissible provided that it does not substantially interfere with the rights of other riparian owners. To determine whether the use is "reasonable," the courts consider six factors:

- the amount of the alteration in the flow of the water
- the purpose for which the water is being used
- whether the use causes any pollution to the water
- the amount and extent of the use
- the flow of the water
- any other factors that the court deems significant

Under this theory, permissible use is determined on a case-by-case basis.

EXAMPLE:

A landowner constructs a waterwheel to harness the flow of a river on her property to generate electricity. This use causes a reduction in the flow of the river, and some downstream neighbors complain that this use has caused some pollution and a reduction in the amount of water that flows onto their property. The court will consider all factors to determine whether the landowner's waterwheel is a reasonable use of her riparian rights.

In determining whether the use of the watercourse by the riparian owner is permissible, the courts will always look to see whether such use furthers a natural or artificial purpose. Natural use is always favored over an artificial use.

iv. **Prior appropriation doctrine.** Under this theory landowners acquire use of the watercourse by historical actual use.

Provided such use does not cause a natural decline in the flow of the water, the courts allocate priority by the time of the appropriation of the watercourse. Under this theory, an appropriated right may be lost by the abandonment of the use by the landowner.

EXAMPLE:

In 1985 a landowner diverted a stream that runs on his property to create an ornamental pond. This diversion caused a minor reduction in the velocity of the water. Later, the adjoining property is purchased by a couple who want to use the stream for irrigation but cannot because of the decrease in velocity. The court may consider that the first landowner has prior rights to the stream, under the prior appropriation doctrine, or may decide that such use causes a significant reduction in the velocity of the water for the neighbors.

(b) Ground water: **Ground water,** also called **percolating water,** refers to underground water. Four different theories have developed with respect to the rights to this water, depending upon the particular jurisdiction:
   i. **Absolute ownership doctrine.** Twenty eastern states adhere to this doctrine, which permits the landowner to all unrestricted use of such water.
   ii. **Reasonable use doctrine.** Twenty-five states favor this concept, which permits the owner of the land all use of such water except for export.
   iii. **Correlative rights doctrine.** This doctrine is favored in California; it permits all the owners of overlying land reasonable use of the ground water.
   iv. **Appropriation rights doctrine.** This doctrine, followed by several states in the west, allows use based on the historical use of such water, in the same manner as the prior appropriation doctrine for watercourses.

(c) Surface water: **Surface water** is defined as water that accumulates on the land, such as rainfall, that does not flow by means of a river or stream. About half of the states consider surface water to be a **common enemy,** meaning that the landowner may do anything he or she wishes to cause drainage and removal of surface water. The other states permit landowners to use only reasonable methods of draining the surface water.

The legal problems associated with surface water only concern drainage rights.

EXAMPLE:

During the fall rains, a small river tends to overflow, causing surface water on the property through which it flows. One landowner has created a system of canals to run off the water, which causes a higher level of surface water on his neighbor's land. Another neighbor has constructed a channel to drain the surface water into a storage tank. The landowner who has constructed the canals may be liable to his neighbors for the increase in the surface water on the neighboring property, depending upon the jurisdiction in which the land is located. The landowner who stores the water would be totally free to make such storage use of surface water.

Nuisance

Nuisance is a theory that is based in tort law that affects a person's property rights. The law distinguishes two types of nuisance: public and private.

> **Public nuisance.** A **public nuisance** is any act that unreasonably interferes with the health, safety, or property rights of the community at large. This injury can only be asserted by the government on behalf of the community; a private property owner may only assert a claim based on a public nuisance if the property owner can demonstrate some particular individual injury to his or her property. An example of a public nuisance would be using a building for hazardous waste detention that affects the property rights of the surrounding property owners.

> **Private nuisance.** A **private nuisance** is a substantial and unreasonable interference with another person's use or enjoyment of property that he or she possesses. "Substantial interference" refers to any act that is offensive to the average person. The law does not consider the action to cause a substantial interference if the interference arises because of a person's hypersensitivity or the particular use to which the subject property is put.

 EXAMPLE:

A nightclub has just opened on a residential street. The couple who own the house directly opposite the club are constantly awakened by the noise from the nightclub and the increased traffic from the club's patrons. The couple may be able to enjoin the club from operating if they demonstrate that the noise generated by the club creates a substantial interference with the enjoyment of their property.

If the basis of the claim of nuisance is the "unreasonable interference" with the use or enjoyment of the property, the claimant must be able to demonstrate that this interference with use or enjoyment of the property outweighs the utility of the defendant's conduct. In making its decision, the court will always bear in mind that a person is entitled to the reasonable use of his or her property, considering:

- the neighborhood in which the property is located;
- the effect on the land value to the property in question; and
- the ability of the defendant to use a different method of operation.

 EXAMPLE:

A revivalist church has just opened in a residential neighborhood. The person who lives next door to the church asserts that the Sunday morning services are so loud that they interfere with the quiet enjoyment of his property. In determining whether the church's activities are a nuisance, the court will look at the actual amount of noise generated and the particular characteristics of the neighborhood.

Note that the right against interference from nuisance attaches not only to the owners of the property, but also to anyone who has the lawful possession of the property, such as a tenant.

Fixtures

A **fixture** is defined as a chattel that has been so affixed to real property that it is deemed to have become a part of the realty. A **chattel** is simply an item of personal property.

The determination as to whether a chattel has retained its identity as personal property or has become incorporated into the realty depends on two factors:

1. whether the intent of the party affixing the chattel was to make it a permanent part of the real estate; and
2. whether the chattel has been affixed in such a manner that its removal would be inconsistent with its use or would damage the structure to which it has been attached.

 EXAMPLE:

A landowner decides to construct a house on a vacant lot. The bricks, tiles, cement, and so forth, all of which are chattel, are incorporated into the structure during the construction of the building and they are totally incorporated as real property. Other chattels, such as water pipes, are so integral to the structure that their removal would cause severe damage to the structure; they are thereby deemed fixtures, permanently attached to the land.

EXAMPLE:

A homeowner is decorating her new house. She has wall-to-wall carpeting installed in the dining room, whereas in the living room she decides to use area rugs. The wall-to-wall carpeting has become a fixture because it was installed for a particular use with the house. Conversely, the area rugs are not fixtures because area rugs are intended to be moved around.

In situations in which title to the realty is divided among two or more persons, such as a life estate followed by a remainder interest or a tenant's possessory title in the landlord's property (see Chapter 7), the law assumes, absent an agreement to the contrary, that the person with the possessory interest lacks the intent to have a chattel permanently affixed to the realty because he or she has a terminable interest.

EXAMPLE:

A couple rent an apartment for a two-year period and decide to put linoleum on the kitchen floor. The linoleum is considered to be personal property, not a fixture, unless the lease specifies a different result.

Many problems are encountered when homeowners attempt to sell their property and the prospective buyer assumes certain items, such as chandeliers, switch plates, and so forth, are fixtures, whereas the sellers consider the items as personal property that they intend to take with them. To avoid conflicts, whenever property is sold the seller should indicate at the outset which items will not be deemed fixtures.

Waste

Waste is the damage caused to real property by a person who does not have a fee simple title to the property that affects the value of the property for the successor fee holder. The doctrines associated with waste apply to life tenants and lessees because their interests terminate in favor of the holder of a fee title.

The law classifies four different types of waste:

1. **Voluntary waste:** This type of waste occurs when the tenant intentionally or negligently damages the property, or extracts its natural resources in a manner inconsistent with the rights of a life tenant or a lessee.

EXAMPLE:

A life tenant decides that he does not want the two-car garage that is on the property. He calls a construction company and has the garage demolished. The tenant's voluntary action has diminished the value of the property and therefore constitutes voluntary waste.

EXAMPLE:

A woman inherits a life estate in a diamond mine. As a life tenant of such property she is entitled to engage in ordinary mining activities. However, the woman decides to hire miners to extract the diamonds 24 hours a day, 7 days a week, to extract all the diamonds in the mine. This use is beyond the ordinary and reasonable use of the mine and may be considered waste to the interests of the remainderman.

2. **Permissive waste**: This type of waste results when the tenant fails to protect the property from damage from the elements. The life tenant is expected to make ordinary repairs on the property to maintain it in the same condition it was in when he or she acquired possession of the estate.

EXAMPLE:

A couple inherit a life estate in a brick house. They only use the house periodically, and when water starts seeping in they simply mop up the floor. Brickwork needs to be pointed every few years, but the couple are unwilling to go to the expense of maintaining the brickwork. When the damage from the water becomes so severe that the bricks start falling out, the couple will be held liable for permissive waste.

3. **Ameliorative waste:** This category of waste is distinguishable from the other forms of waste because the action of the tenant increases rather than decreases the value of the property. Historically, a remainderman was entitled to receive the property in the same state it was in when the earlier estate took possession, thereby including all changes to the property within the category of waste. The modern trend of the court is to deny the remainderman any action for ameliorative waste, unless the remainderman can demonstrate that the "improvement" in fact lessens the value of the property to him.

 **EXAMPLE:**

A life tenant of a house decides that he wants to add a two-car garage to the property. The garage increases the value of the property. Historically, this construction would be considered waste to the remainderman. Today, such construction would not be considered waste, unless the remainderman could show that the building was an eyesore that will have to come down or that it was constructed in a manner that violates the zoning laws of the community.

4. **Equitable waste:** This type of waste concerns land that is used for agricultural purposes and arises when the life tenant fails to exercise good husbandry thereby causing decreased production value of the land. It is fairly close to voluntary waste, but attaches to this particular type of property.

 EXAMPLE:

A man inherits a life estate in a farm. During his tenancy he only grows corn on the land and fails to rotate crops. This causes depletion in the mineral content of the soil, lessening the value of the land. The remainderman could sue on a claim of equitable waste.

If a tenant has committed waste on the property, the remainderman has a cause of action. The remainderman may either seek **damages,** a monetary amount to compensate the remainderman for the degree of injury sustained by the waste, or an **injunction,** a court order requiring that the tenant stop the action that constitutes waste to the property.

Emblements

Emblements are the resources incident to the land, such as crops, minerals, timber, and so forth. All persons with a possessory interest in real property are entitled to take and use the profits, or emblements, on the land, provided that such use does not go beyond an ordinary and reasonable use that would adversely affect the interests of the remainderman or the owner.

Emblements fall into two broad categories:

1. **fructus naturales** — these are items naturally growing or living on the land that can be used by the possessor during the period of lawful possession.
2. **fructus industriales** — these are items that are specifically planted by the possessor; the fruits growing on the land as the result of the

possessor's own efforts. The possessor is entitled to one final taking of such fruit after the termination of the tenancy, provided that the fruit was growing on the land at the time of the termination of the tenancy.

 EXAMPLE:

A woman acquires a life estate in a small house situated on a few acres of land. The land has several cherry trees growing on it, as well as wild flowers. The woman decides to create an herb garden for vegetables and herbs. During the tenancy the woman may use all of the cherries, flowers, vegetables, and herbs that grow on the land. On her death, her heirs may enter the land to remove the vegetables and herbs that were planted and growing at the time of her death, but have no right to the cherries or the wildflowers.

Practical Tips

- Determine the appropriate law in the jurisdiction with respect to surface and water rights before making any changes to the land.
- If representing a landowner, make sure that the owner visits the land periodically to prevent squatters from taking adverse possession.
- If representing a squatter, make sure that he or she has stayed on the land in an open and notorious manner.
- If representing an adverse possessor, make sure that the title is affirmed by a court and recorded with the county recorder's office.

Chapter Review

Any person who acquires an interest in realty also acquires certain other specific rights that automatically attach to the title in land. This is true regardless of whether the title was acquired by sale, inheritance, lease, or adverse possession. Conversely, the titleholder may lose his or her title if a third person obtains possession of the property for a statutory period in a manner that is open, notorious, continuous, and adverse to the rights of the true owner.

The rights that are incident to titles in realty fall into two broad categories: those that permit the titleholder to exert dominion over the land itself, and those that provide the titleholder with freedom from interference with his or her enjoyment or use of the property.

The rights that permit the titleholder to exert dominion over the land are water rights (the right to use watercourses that run on the property and surface water), the right to extract minerals, and the right to fixtures, which are chattels that become permanently affixed to the land.

The rights that afford the titleholder protection from interference with the use and enjoyment of the property include the right to be free from nuisance and the right to seek judicial relief from waste to the property caused by a life tenant or lessee.

A title in realty affords the holder not only the ability to use the land, but also a bundle of other rights that permit her to protect that interest and exert control over actions that affect the land itself.

Ethical Concern

Law and interpersonal relationships often conflict. This is especially true with respect to water and surface rights. The owner of real property must be aware of the impact that asserting these rights for his or her land may have on the neighboring land. Even though the right may be legal, it may cause many personal problems between neighbors.

Key Terms

Absolute ownership doctrine	Percolating water
Adverse possession	Permissive waste
Ameliorative waste	Prior appropriation doctrine
Appropriation rights doctrine	Private nuisance
Chattel	Public nuisance
Common enemy	Quiet title
Correlative rights doctrine	Reasonable use
Emblements	Reasonable use doctrine
Equitable waste	Riparian doctrine
Fixture	Strict liability
Fructus industriales	Subjacent support
Fructus naturales	Surface rights
Ground water	Surface water
Lateral support	Voluntary waste
Natural flow theory	Waste
Nuisance	Watercourse

Exercises

1. Research the statutory period for adverse possession in your state.
2. Research which of the water rights doctrines applies in your state.

3. List several factors that you would use to determine whether a particular chattel is a fixture or removable personal property.
4. Differentiate and give your own examples of the different types of waste.
5. Briefly discuss the factors that a court might use to determine whether a given action constitutes nuisance to a property owner.

Situational Analysis

A brother and sister inherit a large farm from their grandfather. The sister is an attorney who works in a large city; the brother is unemployed. The brother takes up residence on the farm to till the soil. Because of the size of the farm, the brother only farms one-half of the property. Ten years later, a couple claim title to the other half of the property by adverse possession, stating that they have lived in a cabin on the land for ten years. What evidence would be needed to support the couple's claim? What impact does this claim have on the sister's rights? What other information do you need?

Edited Cases

The first case, *The Prudential Ins. Co. of Am. v. Spencer's Kenosha Bowl, Inc.*, discusses the concept of waste, and the second decision, *Fraley v. Minger*, analyzes the doctrine of adverse possession.

The Prudential Insurance Company of America v. Spencer's Kenosha Bowl Inc.
137 Wis. 2d 313, 404 N.W.2d 109 (1987)

Spencer's Kenosha Bowl, Inc. (Spencer's) appeals from a judgment awarding $369,188.21 in damages to the Prudential Insurance Company of America (Prudential). The award is for waste committed by Spencer's upon real estate against which Prudential holds a mortgage. Spencer's raises four issues on appeal: (1) whether Spencer's, as a successor owner which did not assume the mortgage indebtedness, may be held liable for waste, including passive or permissive waste; (2) whether Prudential's waste claim was properly included in a foreclosure action; (3) whether the trial court properly calculated the amount of the waste judgment against Spencer's; and (4) whether the waste finding is sufficiently supported by the evidence. Because we resolve all of the issues against Spencer's, we affirm.

The property involved in this litigation is a commercial building constructed in 1970 and situated on real estate located in the city of Kenosha.

Spencer's purchased the property in 1975 from Delco Development Co. (Delco) which had previously mortgaged the property to Prudential. It is undisputed that Spencer's did not assume Delco's mortgage indebtedness when it purchased the property. Prudential subsequently foreclosed on the property after the mortgage note was in default.

In April, 1983, the Honorable Frederick Kessler, the judge then assigned to the case, granted Prudential's request for foreclosure of the property. The amount owed on the mortgage note at the time of the sheriff's sale was fixed at $994,497.80. The property sold for $635,000 in May, 1984. Following the sale, the Honorable Richard G. Harvey, Jr., the judge subsequently assigned to the case, held a hearing on Prudential's claim that Spencer's had committed waste upon the property. In his decision on the waste issue, Judge Harvey found that Spencer's had committed waste in the following amounts:

Property Taxes	$198,743.34
Roof	37,890.00
Ceiling Tile and Grid	103,064.52
Electric Facilities	14,647.16
Drywall-wood	36,251.85
Restroom	766.66
Exterior Canopy	13,090.83
Cleanup Costs	16,381.00
Floor Tile Damage	24,000.00
	$444,835.36

However, because the amount of the waste exceeded the amount of the debt less the foreclosure sale proceeds, Judge Harvey lowered Prudential's waste award so that it equaled the amount of the debt deficiency.

Spencer's initially argues that a grantee who does not assume the mortgage of a grantor-mortgagor cannot be held liable for any waste committed on the mortgaged property. Whether a mortgagor has a cause of action for waste is a question of law. See *Williams v. Security Savings & Loan Ass'n*, 120 Wis. 2d 480, 482, 355 N.W.2d 370, 372 (Ct. App. 1984). As a result, we review this question independently of any conclusions made by the trial court. Id.

Waste is a species of tort. See *Jaffe-Spindler Co. v. Genesco, Inc.*, 747 F.2d 253, 256 (4th Cir. 1984). It is defined as "the unreasonable conduct by the owner of a possessory estate that results in physical damage to the real estate and substantial diminution in the value of the estates in which others have an interest." *Pleasure Time, Inc. v. Kuss*, 78 Wis. 2d 373, 381, 254 N.W.2d 463, 467 (1977). Although a mortgagee only has a lien on the mortgaged property, see sec. 708.01, Stats.; *State v. Phillips*, 99 Wis. 2d 46, 50, 298 N.W.2d 239, 241 (Ct. App. 1980), he or she is entitled to maintain a legal action for waste against a mortgagor. See *Jones v. Costigan*, 12 Wis. 757, 760–65 (1860).

We conclude that the waste doctrine permits a mortgagee to maintain an action for waste against a nonassuming grantee of a mortgagor. In *Scott v. Webster*, 50 Wis. 53, 6 N.W. 363 (1880), the supreme court held that senior mortgagees in possession of property were accountable to a junior mortgagee for waste committed on the property. Id. at 64, 6 N.W. at 365. There, the senior mortgagees removed a large amount of timber from the property which substantially diminished its value. Id. at 60–61, 6 N.W. at 363. Prior to the timber removal, the senior mortgagees purchased an equity of redemption which entitled them to possession of the property. Id. at 62, 6 N.W. at 364. Consequently, the senior mortgagees were both owners and mortgagees of the property. Id. at 63, 6 N.W. at 364–65. The court reasoned that with respect to the junior mortgagee, the senior mortgagees were mortgagees in possession and as such must be held liable for the waste they committed while in possession of the property. Id. at 63–64, 6 N.W. at 365.

Here, as in *Scott*, Spencer's legally had possession of the property and, under the trial court's findings, committed acts which resulted in a substantial diminution in the property's value. It is undisputed that Prudential, as a mortgagee, had an interest in the property. See *Phillips*, 99 Wis. 2d at 50, 298 N.W.2d at 241. As a result, all of the essential ingredients for a waste cause of action as set out in *Pleasure Time* are met. See *Pleasure Time*, 78 Wis. 2d at 381, 254 N.W.2d at 467. Moreover, we consider the court's reasoning in *Scott* as an indication of the liberality to be allowed a mortgagee when enforcing or protecting the lien interest. See also *Atkinson v. Hewett*, 63 Wis. 396, 23 N.W. 889 (1885) (mortgagee allowed to recover for wasteful conduct of trespasser). We do not deem the nonassuming grantee's status so unique that it warrants insulation from a waste action and prevents the mortgagee from preserving and protecting a security interest.

Our conclusion is also supported by the supreme court's language in *Edler v. Hasche*, 67 Wis. 653, 659–61, 31 N.W. 57, 59–61 (1887). There, Edler and Brandt were mortgagee and mortgagor, respectively. As in this case, Hasche purchased the mortgaged property from Brandt "subject to the mortgage." Id. at 659, 31 N.W. at 59. While the court left for a later proceeding the question of Hasche's liability for the mortgage debt and strongly suggested that the evidence might not support a finding that Hasche had assumed the mortgage, the court nonetheless recognized that Hasche's removal of a building was waste for which he was liable to Edler. The court stated that "Hasche's liability for waste . . . upon every principle of justice is clear and must be affirmed." Id. at 661, 31 N.W. at 60–61.

The import of *Edler* on this case is clear. Regardless of successor liability on the mortgage debt, the court in *Edler* affirms the principle that a nonassuming grantee can be liable to a mortgagee for waste committed to the secured property. Consequently, Spencer's nonassuming grantee status does not affect its liability for waste.

As an extension of this issue, Spencer's attempts to draw a distinction between its liability for active and passive waste. Passive or permissive waste results from negligence or omission to do that which would prevent injury. See *Finley v. Chain*, 374 N.E.2d 67, 79 (Ind. Ct. App. 1978) (overruled on other grounds by *Morris v. Weigle*, 383 N.E.2d 341, 345 n.3 (Ind. 1978)). Active or voluntary waste requires an affirmative act which results in the destruction or alteration of property. See *Jowdy v. Guerin*, 457 P.2d 745, 748 (Ariz. Ct. App. 1969). At common law, an individual could be held liable for waste only if the acts were tortious and intentional. See Leipziger, The Mortgagee's Remedies for Waste, 64 Cal. L. Rev. 1086, 1093–94 (1976). No waste cause of action lay for negligent waste. Id. at 1094, 1130–32.

Whether a particular act is waste depends upon the circumstances. *Pleasure Time*, 78 Wis. 2d at 381, 254 N.W.2d at 467. Modern Wisconsin law does not distinguish between passive and active waste. However, early Wisconsin law recognized that waste could "be either voluntary or permissive." *Melms v. Pabst Brewing Co.*, 104 Wis. 7, 9, 79 N.W. 738, 739 (1899). Moreover, Wisconsin law has dealt with fact situations where the actions characterized as waste can be described as either active or passive. See, e.g., *Scott*, 50 Wis. at 53, 6 N.W. at 363 (waste resulting from removal of timber); *Jones*, 12 Wis. at 757 (removal of doors and windows from house); *Pleasure Time*, 78 Wis. 2d at 381, 254 N.W.2d at 467–68 (waste alleged involved demolished and deteriorated buildings); *First Nat'l Bank v. Clark & Lund Boat Co.*, 68 Wis. 2d 738, 741, 229 N.W.2d 221, 223 (1975) (failure to pay taxes).

We conclude that the modern waste definition is broad enough in Wisconsin to include both active and passive waste. The common law "limitations are not well rationalized in the cases and seem to have come about largely by accident." *Leipziger*, supra, at 1094. Conduct which results either in active or passive waste "may injure or threaten property rendering the debt unsafe." *Finley*, 374 N.E.2d at 79. Consequently, the mortgagee's security may be impaired by either passive or active waste and the policy for allowing the mortgagee recovery is the same regardless of the type of waste involved.

Next, Spencer's argues that the entry of judgment was not warranted because the amount of the waste found to have been committed was less than the amount obtained from the sale of the property. Spencer's, however, cites no legal authority for this proposition and, as a result, we are not required to consider it. See *State v. Schaffer*, 96 Wis. 2d 531, 545–46, 292 N.W.2d 370, 378 (Ct. App. 1980). Moreover, Spencer's argument seems to be a distortion of the common law rule that, in lien jurisdictions, a mortgagee cannot recover until his security has been substantially impaired which occurs only when waste has reduced the value of the encumbered property to less than the unpaid balance of the debt. See *Leipziger*, supra, at 1097. It is undisputed in this case that the waste found by the trial court reduced the value of the encumbered property in the fashion required by this rule.

Spencer's also challenges the trial court's calculation of the damages based on the debt deficiency. Spencer's argues that this is in fact an award of a deficiency judgment on a mortgage which it never assumed. However, in lien jurisdictions, a trial court must determine the extent of reduction in the value of the security interest in the property, not just the amount of injury to the real estate. See *Finley*, 374 N.E.2d at 78. Where, as here, the amount of waste committed on the property is greater than the amount of the debt deficiency, the extent of reduction in the value of the mortgagee's security interest will always be equal to the debt deficiency. Consequently, we do not view the trial court's award as a deficiency judgment but, rather, as an independent award litigated within the context of a foreclosure proceeding.

Finally, Spencer's argues that the trial court's finding that Spencer's had committed waste by failing to maintain the property is not supported by the evidence. Whether a particular act constitutes waste is left to the trier of fact. *Pleasure Time*, 78 Wis. 2d at 382, 254 N.W.2d at 468. Factual findings will not be overturned unless clearly erroneous. Sec. 805.17(2), Stats.

We conclude that the trial court's finding that Spencer's failed to maintain the property is supported by the evidence. The record reveals that at the time of Spencer's occupancy in 1975, the building's roof was only five years into its twenty-year expected life span; that the roof was in full compliance with the state building code when Spencer's took occupancy in 1975; that an expert witness testified that the leaks in the roof had existed for some time and had resulted in extensive damage to the interior fixtures; that the roof was first cited for being in violation of the state building code in 1983; and that when this action was commenced the roof had completely deteriorated and needed total replacement. Consequently, the trial court concluded that most if not all of the roof's deterioration and subsequent damage to the building occurred while Spencer's had possession of the property. This finding is not clearly erroneous.

Judgment affirmed.

Case Questions

1. How does the court support the statement that "waste is a form of tort"?

2. What factors does the court rely on to determine that waste has occurred?

Fraley v. Minger
829 N.E.2d 476 (Sup. Ct. Ind. 2005)

In this quiet title action asserting adverse possession, the defendant Clarence E. Fraley appeals a judgment awarding fee simple title to approximately 2.5 acres of land to the adverse possessors, plaintiffs Clarence K. Minger and Eva Minger. The Court of Appeals reversed. *Fraley v. Minger, 786 N.E.2d 288 (Ind. Ct. App. 2003)*. We granted transfer, *804 N.E.2d 748*.

Upon examination of the common law concept of adverse possession in Indiana, we rephrase its essential elements and find those elements established here. In addition, however, renewing our fifty-year-old construction of the adverse possession tax statute, we conclude that this statutory additional adverse possession requirement is not satisfied in this case and reverse the judgment of the trial court.

This is an appeal from a bench trial final judgment following remand from the Court of Appeals, which in a memorandum decision had reversed the grant of summary judgment in favor of the Mingers. *Fraley v. Minger, 729 N.E.2d 614, 2000 Ind. App. Lexis 790 (Ind. Ct. App. 2000).* Upon remand, counsel for Fraley requested written findings of fact and conclusions of law, both parties submitted proposed findings and conclusions, and the trial court included findings of fact and conclusions of law with its judgment. Fraley does not challenge the trial court's findings of fact but argues that the facts explicitly found by the trial court and the uncontradicted trial evidence fail to establish adverse possession as a matter of law.

The dispute in this case involves a 2.5-acre tract of undeveloped rural land along the west side of and adjacent to a twenty-four-acre farm in rural Ripley County purchased by the Mingers from Raymond and Ada Chaney in 1955. At the time, the Chaneys denied owning the 2.5-acre tract and stated that they did not know who owned it. Trans. at 19-20. And Truman Belew, who in 1963 acquired the land that was eventually deeded to Fraley, told the Mingers that he did not own the tract. *Id.* at 35. The Mingers believed the tract was unclaimed. Truman died in 1994, and in 1996, this tract was included in land conveyed by deed to Fraley from Melvin Belew, Truman's son, as guardian of Luella Belew, Truman's widow. The trial court's judgment sets forth findings of fact and conclusions of law including in relevant part the following:

1. The Mingers acquired title to the land adjoining the disputed tract ... on May 21, 1955.
2. The Mingers have paid taxes on the real estate adjacent to the disputed tract.
3. The disputed tract consists of approximately 2.5 acres ...
4. [Fraley] received a deed to the disputed tract and other real estate ... on February 28, 1996.
5. The Minger children and their friends played on the disputed tract from 1970.
6. Friends and neighbors thought the Mingers owned the disputed tract.
7. Neither the Mingers or their friends and neighbors ever saw the Belews [the titled owners at the time] on the disputed tract.
8. The Mingers moved to their farm adjacent to the disputed tract on June 17, 1955.
9. The Mingers knew when they purchased their farm that the disputed tract was not described in their deed.
10. The Mingers believed the disputed tract was unclaimed in 1955.

11. The Mingers took possession of the disputed tract:
    a. One year after 1955, the Mingers regarded the disputed tract as theirs.
    b. By 1972, the Mingers had built a fence along County Road 625 East to fence the disputed tract.
    c. The Mingers pastured cattle on the disputed tract.
    d. The Mingers used wood from the disputed tract from the 1980's to as late as 1993.
    e. The Minger children camped and hunted on the disputed tract in the 1960s, 1970s, and 1980s.
    f. The Mingers sold timber from the disputed tract.
    g. Minger children and friends rode dirt bikes on the disputed tract.
    h. The Mingers installed a culvert in the ditch from County Road 625 East on to the disputed tract and used it as access to the disputed tract.
12. No evidence was offered by [Fraley] to refute the testimony of the [Mingers'] witnesses that the Mingers exercised possession and control of the disputed tract for more than the statutory time required for them to obtain title.
13. The Mingers had the actual possession of the disputed tract from 1956 to the date of trial.
14. The Mingers had visible possession of the disputed tract from 1956 to the date of trial.
15. The Mingers had notorious possession of the disputed tract from 1956 to the date of trial.
16. The Mingers had the exclusive possession of the disputed tract from 1956 to the date of trial.
17. The Mingers claimed ownership hostile to [Fraley and his] predecessors in title for more than ten (10) continuous years prior to February 29, 1996.

Conclusions of Law

1. The continuous use of the disputed tract by the Mingers for more than a continuous period in excess of ten years to pasture their cattle, cut wood, sell timber, and recreational activities constitutes the visible and exclusive possession of the disputed tract.
2. The common perception for more than ten years of the friends and neighbors of the Mingers that the Mingers were the owners of the disputed tract constitutes notorious possession of the disputed tract.
3. The common perception of the friends and neighbors of the Mingers that the Mingers were the owners of the disputed tract constitutes a claim of ownership hostile to [Fraley and his] predecessors in title.

4. The construction of the fence should have alerted any reasonable title owner that his property is being adversely claimed.
5. Open and visible possession has been stated in general terms, thus: it is necessary and sufficient if the nature and character is such as is calculated to apprise the world that the land is occupied and who the occupant is.
6. The Mingers exercised actual, visible, notorious and exclusive possession of the disputed tract of real estate under a claim of ownership hostile to [Fraley and his] predecessors in title for a continuous period of more than ten years prior to filing the law suit herein.
7. The Mingers had established that they were the owners of the disputed real estate many years prior to February 29, 1996.
8. [Fraley] failed to oust the Mingers from the disputed tract before the Mingers had exercised actual, visible, notorious and exclusive possession of the disputed tract of real estate under a claim of ownership hostile to [Fraley and his] predecessors in title for a continuous period of more than ten years.
9. The statute of limitations was not stayed even if the Belews and others in title were unaware of their ownership.
10. The Mingers are entitled to a judgment on their complaint against [Fraley] and against [Fraley on his] counterclaim against the [Mingers].

In the appellate review of claims tried without a jury, the findings and judgment are not to be set aside unless clearly erroneous, and due regard is to be given to the trial court's ability to assess the credibility of the witnesses. *Ind. Trial Rule 52(A)*. A judgment will be clearly erroneous when there is "no evidence supporting the findings or the findings fail to support the judgment," *Chidester v. City of Hobart, 631 N.E.2d 908, 910 (Ind. 1994)*, and when the trial court applies the wrong legal standard to properly found facts, *Yanoff v. Muncy, 688 N.E.2d 1259, 1262 (Ind. 1997)*. While findings of fact are reviewed under the clearly erroneous standard, appellate courts do not defer to conclusions of law, which are reviewed de novo. *Fobar v. Vonderahe, 771 N.E.2d 57, 59 (Ind. 2002); Bader v. Johnson, 732 N.E.2d 1212, 1216 (Ind. 2000); Menard, Inc. v. Dage-MTI, Inc., 726 N.E.2d 1206, 1210 (Ind. 2000)*. Where cases present mixed issues of fact and law, we have described the review as applying an abuse of discretion standard. *Forbar, 771 N.E.2d at 59* ("Although this is in some sense an issue of law, it is highly fact sensitive and is subject to an abuse of discretion standard."). In the event the trial court mischaracterizes findings as conclusions or vice versa, we look past these labels to the substance of the judgment. *Beam v. Wausau Ins. Co., 765 N.E.2d 524, 528 (Ind. 2002); State v. Van Cleave, 674 N.E.2d 1293, 1296*. "In order to determine that a finding or conclusion is clearly erroneous, an appellate court's review of the evidence must leave it with the firm conviction that a mistake has been made." *Yanoff, 688 N.E.2d at 1262*.

Suggesting that a heightened degree of proof is needed to establish adverse possession, Fraley argues that such claims require proof by strict, clear, positive, and unequivocal evidence. This assertion finds support in some prior opinions. *See, e.g., Panhandle Eastern Pipe Line Company v. Tishner, 699 N.E.2d 731, 736 (Ind. Ct. App. 1998)* ("Each of the elements of adverse possession must be strictly proved by evidence that is clear, positive, and unequivocal."); *Piel v. Dewitt, 170 Ind.App. 63, 73 n.10, 351 N.E.2d 48, 55 n.10 (1976)* ("The burden of establishing title by adverse possession falls affirmatively upon the asserter who must adduce proof which is strict, clear, positive, and unequivocal."); *Milhon v. Brown, 127 Ind.App. 694, 700, 143 N.E.2d 573, 576 (1957)* (Adverse possession "must be strictly proved" and supported by "competent and substantial evidence."); *Coal Creek Coal Co. v. Chicago, T.H. & S.E. Rte, 114 Ind.App. 627, 640, 53 N.E.2d 179, 184 (1944)* ("The burden of overcoming the presumptions which exist in favor of the holder of the legal record title rests upon the one claiming title by adverse possession and the proof must be strict, clear, positive and unequivocal."); *Philbin v. Carr, 75 Ind.App. 560, 582, 129 N.E. 19, 27 (1920)* ("Proof of all the essential facts must be clear and unequivocal."). At least one commentator observes that "American state courts are in general agreement" that the elements of adverse possession must be established "by clear and convincing evidence." 16 *POWELL ON REAL PROPERTY § 91.01[2]* at 91-6, 91-7 (1999). On the other hand, other relatively recent cases have omitted reference to any heightened standard of proof. Deferring to the majority of cases that have actually discussed the quantum of proof issue, we find that the heightened standard is appropriate. Employing current terminology, however, we believe that "clear and convincing" is a preferable way to describe the heightened standard needed to establish adverse possession, thus embracing and superseding the variety of terms previously used.

Where overcoming a presumption requires a heightened quantum of proof, however, such determination falls within the sound discretion of the fact-finder, whose discretion is afforded deferential review. *See In re Guardianship of B.H., 770 N.E.2d 283, 287 (Ind. 2002)*. In reviewing a judgment requiring proof by clear and convincing evidence:

> an appellate court may not impose its own view as to whether the evidence is clear and convincing but must determine, by considering only the probative evidence and reasonable inferences supporting the judgment and without weighing evidence or assessing witness credibility, whether a reasonable trier of fact could conclude that the judgment was established by clear and convincing evidence.

Id. at 288. We will likewise apply this standard of appellate review in the instant case and determine whether a reasonable trier of fact could conclude from the facts found by the trial court that the challenged elements of adverse possession were established by clear and convincing evidence.

Common Law Adverse Possession

The common law doctrine and application of adverse possession has a long history. As early as 2250 B.C. the Code of Hammurabi discussed adverse possession and the misuse of land, including provisions that

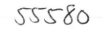

punished land waste, rewarded long-term development, and allowed one who worked the land of another for three years to take and keep the land. *See* Brian Gardiner, Note, Squatters' Rights and Adverse Possession, *8 Ind. Int'l & Comp. L. Rev. 119, 123 (1997)* (hereafter "Gardiner"); John G. Sprankling, An Environmental Critique of Adverse Possession, *79 Cornell L. Rev. 816, 821 n.17 (1994)* (hereafter "Critique"). In England, the history of adverse possession can be traced back to the Norman Conquest in 1066. *See Gardiner at 125.* The common law doctrine of adverse possession was applied to resolve land disputes between colonists in Virginia as early as 1646, where it was used "in an effort to help resolve the proverbial conflicts between speculators and squatters." *Critique at 823 n.29.* The first statutory recognition of adverse possession in the New World appeared in a 1715 statute of limitations in North Carolina. Jeffry M. Netter, et al., An Economic Analysis of Adverse Possession Statutes, 6 Int'l Rev. L. & Econ. 217, 219 (1986) (hereafter "Netter").

With the western migration of pioneers, the federal government initially prohibited settlement of the western lands unless purchased from the government, but that requirement was gradually relaxed; anti-squatting prohibitions were abandoned, recognition of preemptive purchase rights were extended, and land was distributed to military veterans. *See* John G. Sprankling, The Antiwilderness Bias in American Property Law, *63 U. Chi. L. Rev. 519, 528-29 (1996).* Eventually, with the 1852 passage of the *Homestead Act*, land was freely available to such settlers. *Id.* At the same time, whereas the courts had originally followed the English example of requiring that the adverse possesser engage in activities giving notice to an inspecting owner such as residence, cultivation, fencing, and other improvements, American courts began to focus upon acts by the adverse possessor in keeping with the nature and character of the land involved. *Id. at 538-39.* The policy behind favoring adverse possession was the same as that of land distribution: favoring the productive use of the land. *Id. at 534-40; see also* Netter at 219 (adverse possession rewards the use of land and punishes those who sit on their rights).

Claims of adverse possession were litigated in Indiana from the early years of statehood. In *Doe v. West, 1 Blackf. 133, 135 (Ind. 1821)*, the Court observed that "in England, and in some of our sister States, it has been decided that 20 years' peaceable possession gives a right which is sufficient to maintain ejectment." The common law doctrine of adverse possession received legislative approval in Indiana with the enactment of specific 20-year statutes of limitation in 1820 and again in 1823. *Id. at 136 ed. n.1.* In 1853, this Court stated that for a claim of title based in adverse possession to defeat a legal title to property, "strict proof must be made not only that the possession was, from its inception, under a public claim of title adverse to that of the real owner, but that both such claim and possession have been continuous and uninterrupted . . . through the full period of twenty years." *Doe v. Brown, 4 Ind. 143, 145 (Ind. 1853).* In 1951, the General Assembly demonstrated its continued approval of the doctrine by shortening the applicable statute of limitations from twenty years to ten years. *See* Acts of 1951, ch. 301, § 2; *see also Phar-Crest Land Corp. v. Therber, 251 Ind. 674, 683-684, 244 N.E.2d 644, 649 (Ind. 1969)* (Hunter, J., concurring); *Berrey v. Jean, 401 N.E.2d 102, 104-105 (Ind. Ct. App. 1980)*.

During the latter nineteenth century, many of the Indiana adverse possession cases began to articulate specific elements required to establish adverse possession. *See, e.g., Hargis v. Inhabitants of Congressional Township, 29 Ind. 70, 71 (Ind. 1867)* (requiring the claimant be "in actual, open, notorious, and exclusive possession thereof, claiming to be the owner in fee."). A relatively consistent list of similar elements of common law adverse possession developed and is found thereafter even in more recent cases. Citing *Penn Central Transportation Co. v. Martin, 170 Ind.App. 519, 353 N.E.2d 474 (1976)*, the parties each assert that to establish title by adverse possession, the claimant has the burden of proving the possession was: (1) actual; (2) visible; (3) open and notorious; (4) exclusive; (5) under claim of ownership; (6) hostile; and (7) continuous for the statutory period. Brief of Appellant Fraley at 5, Brief of Appellees Minger at 4. *See also Marengo Cave Co. v. Ross, 212 Ind. 624, 630, 10 N.E.2d 917 (Ind. 1937)*. Later cases from this Court have used a slightly different formulation that omits "visible" and "hostile" but adds "adverse," and substitutes "claim of right" for "claim of ownership." This Court's opinions in *Beaver v. Vandall, 547 N.E.2d 802, 804 (Ind. 1989)*, and *McCarty v. Sheets, 423 N.E.2d 297, 300 (Ind. 1981)*, state that adverse possession is established by "open, continuous, exclusive, adverse and notorious possession of property under a claim of right for the statutory period." As authority for this statement, McCarty cited *Worthley v. Burbanks, 146 Ind. 534, 45 N.E. 779 (1897)*. But Worthly lists the "five indispensable elements" of adverse possession as 1, It must be *hostile and under a claim of right;* 2, it must be *actual;* 3, it must be *open and notorious;* 4, it must be *exclusive;* and 5, it must be *continuous."* *146 Ind. at 539, 45 N.E. at 781* (emphasis in original). Emphasizing that the nature and situation of the disputed land must be taken into consideration, Worthly cites the following as a generally accepted proposition:

> An entry upon land with the intention of asserting ownership to it, and continuing in the visible, exclusive possession under such claim, *exercising those acts of ownership usually practiced by owners of such land, and using it for the purposes to which it is adapted, without asking permission and in disregard of all other conflicting claims,* is sufficient to make the possession adverse.

146 Ind. at 543, 45 N.E. at 782 (quoting *Collett v. Board, 119 Ind. 27, 34, 21 N.E. 329, 331 (1889)* (emphasis added in Worthly)).

In addition to Worthly, many other early Indiana cases recognized that a person may claim adverse possession based solely upon entry and actual possession of land, without any initial claim of color of title. *See Bell v. Longworth, 6 Ind. 273, 276-77 (1855); Vancleave v. Milliken, 13 Ind. 105 (1859); May v. Dobbins, 166 Ind. 331, 333-34, 77 N.E. 353, 354 (Ind. 1906); Martin, 170 Ind.App. at 524, 353 N.E.2d at 477; Swanson v. New York Central R.R. Co., 83 Ind.App. 580, 583, 149 N.E. 353, 354 (1925)*. It is not necessary that possession be under color of title; what is required is claim of right. In *May v. Dobbins,*

166 Ind. at 333, 77 N.E. at 354, this Court rejected an instruction "which stated that if appellant took possession of the land without color of title, and knew or had reason to believe who the rightful owner was, his occupancy would not be such good-faith occupancy under claim of ownership as would confer title, however long continued." *Id.* The Court recognized that such an instruction "accords with good morals, but it is not sound in law." *Id.* "The acquisition of title by adverse possession is predicated upon the statute of limitations, and the running of the statute may be instituted without even color of title, and without reference to the good or bad faith of the adverse claim asserted by the occupant." *Id.; see also Moore v. Hinkle, 50 N.E. 822, 824, 151 Ind. 343, 347-48 (1898).* Where one enters the land with the intention of asserting ownership and possesses the land openly and exclusively, exercising the usual acts of ownership upon the land for the full time under the statute of limitations, title will pass to the possessor. *May, 166 Ind. at 334, 77 N.E. at 354-55.* While cases listing the elements of adverse possession frequently recite that the adverse claimant must occupy the land under a claim of right, that claim of right can be established by entering upon and occupying land with the intent to hold the land as one's own. *See Martin, 170 Ind.App. at 524, 353 N.E.2d at 477.* The Martin court succinctly stated that a "claim of right may be inferred in favor of the party in possession" where the party uses the land "in the same manner that an owner ordinarily uses his land." *Id.* (citing *Swanson v. New York Central R.R. Co. , 83 Ind.App. 580, 583, 149 N.E. 353, 354 (1925);* and *Abel v. Love, 81 Ind.App. 328, 337, 143 N.E. 515, 518 (1924).*

Synthesizing and rephrasing these varying expressions to reflect a simplified articulation of the common set of shared concerns and the essence of the common law doctrine, we hold that the doctrine of adverse possession entitles a person without title to obtain ownership to a parcel of land upon clear and convincing proof of control, intent, notice, and duration, as follows:

> (1) Control — The claimant must exercise a degree of use and control over the parcel that is normal and customary considering the characteristics of the land (reflecting the former elements of "actual," and in some ways "exclusive," possession);
>
> (2) Intent — The claimant must demonstrate intent to claim full ownership of the tract superior to the rights of all others, particularly the legal owner (reflecting the former elements of "claim of right," "exclusive," "hostile," and "adverse");
>
> (3) Notice — The claimant's actions with respect to the land must be sufficient to give actual or constructive notice to the legal owner of the claimant's intent and exclusive control (reflecting the former "visible," "open," "notorious," and in some ways the "hostile," elements); and,
>
> (4) Duration — the claimant must satisfy each of these elements continuously for the required period of time (reflecting the former "continuous" element).

In the present case, Fraley does not challenge the basis of the Mingers' claim of ownership as lacking a sufficient basis. As to the historical common law elements of adverse possession, Fraley claims, rather, that the facts found by the trial court and shown by uncontradicted evidence fail to establish the requisite hostility and continuity needed for adverse possession.

He argues that the Mingers acknowledged uncertainty about who held title to the property and did not dispute the superior rights of the legal owners. Fraley contends that the Mingers neither communicated a claim of hostile ownership to the titled owners nor possessed the property adversely and to the exclusion of all others. He urges that the Mingers' activities such as pasturing cattle, cutting wood, and engaging in recreational activities on the disputed tract were sporadic and periodic activities and thus insufficient to establish that the Mingers possessed the property adversely. Fraley also argues that the Mingers' activities on the tract were insufficient to establish permanent continuous possession for the requisite ten-year period.

These claims essentially assert that the findings are insufficient to establish each of the requisite elements of control, intent, notice, and duration.

Fraley argues that the Mingers' possession was not hostile because Mrs. Minger "openly acknowledged the superior rights of the record title holder by making an inquiry about buying the parcel." Opp. to Pet. for Transfer at 5. Between the time of the death of Truman Belew in 1994 and the deed conveying the disputed tract to Keith Fraley in 1996, Eva Minger inquired about the possible purchase of about half of the tract from Melvin Belew. Fraley's contention that this inquiry disproves the Mingers' adverse possession is erroneous because title by adverse possession passes to the claimant by law at the end of the possessory period. *Kline v. Kramer, 179 Ind. App. 592, 597, 386 N.E.2d 982, 987 (Ind. Ct. App. 1979)*. Once title vests in a party at the conclusion of the ten-year possessory period, the title may not be lost, abandoned, or forfeited, even where the party pays rent to the titleholder (*Riggs v. Riley, 113 Ind. 208, 15 N.E. 253 (1887)*), agrees to a survey to attempt to find the true boundary line (*Fatic v. Myer, 163 Ind. 401, 72 N.E. 142 (1904)*), expresses satisfaction with a survey whose results are inconsistent with the property adversely possessed by him (*Grim v. Johns, 61 Ind.App. 514, 112 N.E. 13 (1916)*), or states that he does not claim the land and offers to buy it (*Rennert v. Shirk, 163 Ind. 542, 72 N.E. 546 (1904)*). *See also Marathon Petroleum Co. v. Colonial Motel Properties, Inc., 550 N.E.2d 778, 783 (Ind. Ct. App. 1990); Kline, 179 Ind.App. at 597, 386 N.E.2d at 987*. The ten-year possessory period required for the Mingers' adverse possession clearly expired long before Mrs. Minger's purchase inquiry after 1994 (which may have merely been an effort to avoid litigation), and her inquiry would not undermine any ownership by adverse possession that the Mingers had gained years earlier.

Fraley also argues that periodic or sporadic acts of ownership are not sufficient to establish adverse possession. While it is true that the land must be used continuously for adverse possession, the use required need only be in keeping with the ordinary uses of the land. In *McCarty*, 423 N.E.2d at 300, we held that "what constitutes possession of a 'wild' land may not constitute possession of a residential lot." In *Snowball Corp. v. Pope, 580 N.E.2d 733, 736 (Ind. Ct. App. 1991)*, the adverse claimant did little more with the land in question than treat it as an extension of his yard, but because the land was essentially a swamp, that use was held to be consistent with its character and sufficiently continuous to establish adverse possession.

Fraley describes the disputed tract as "undeveloped land in a rural portion of Ripley County." Br. of Appellant at 3. At trial, he depicted the tract as "rough, growed up, wooded hillside" with "a lot of scrub and brush that would take a number of years to grow," and as "rough ground" and "rough hillside." Trans. at 81, 82. The Mingers assert that the disputed tract "was a briar patch and grownup." Br. of Appellees at 2. There is no essential dispute between the parties as to the nature of the tract, and we conclude that the Mingers' use of the tract was consistent with its character throughout the possessory period.

Supporting its conclusions as to the element of control are the trial court findings that the Mingers took possession of the disputed undeveloped rural tract in 1956; fenced and pastured cattle upon it; used wood and sold timber from it; and camped, hunted, and rode dirt bikes on it. The intent element is also supported by findings that the Mingers believed the disputed tract was unclaimed when they acquired and began residing on the adjacent tract in 1955; that the Mingers used the tract as their own; that they claimed ownership hostile to Fraley's predecessors in title; and that the Mingers' friends and neighbors believed the Mingers owned the disputed tract. These findings, plus the fact that they installed a culvert in a ditch to enable their access to the tract, also provide support establishing the notice element. As to duration, the trial court found that the Mingers' actual, visible, notorious, exclusive, and hostile ownership of the disputed tract continued from 1956 to the date of trial in 2002, thus establishing control, intent, and notice during a continuous period exceeding the ten-year statute of limitations.

We hold that, considering the issues of law and the facts found by the trial court and the inferences reasonably drawn therefrom, a reasonable trier of fact could correctly conclude that the challenged common law elements of adverse possession were established by clear and convincing evidence.

Statute Requiring Payment of Taxes

In addition to challenging the elements of common law adverse possession, Fraley contends that the court erred in finding adverse possession despite absence of evidence that the Mingers complied with a statutory provision requiring payment of taxes during the period of adverse possession. The trial court found that the Mingers "have paid taxes on the real estate *adjacent* to the disputed tract," Appellant's App'x. at 6 (emphasis added), but made no findings regarding the payment of taxes on the disputed tract itself.

The Indiana adverse possession tax statute, enacted in 1927, followed "great agitation in the northern part of the state caused principally by 'squatters' who were obtaining original titles to land by adverse possession." James H. Neu, Adverse Possession in Indiana, 16 Notre Dame

Lawyer 216, 219 (1941) (hereafter "Neu"). A number of large corporations, which owned huge tracts of land and paid property taxes on them, were losing their land to "squatters" who settled on the land for the required twenty years and claimed the land by adverse possession. *Id.* at 219-20. To prevent these losses, the General Assembly enacted a statute providing:

> Hereafter in any suit to establish title to lands or real estate no possession thereof shall be deemed adverse to the owner in such manner as to establish title or rights in and to such land or real estate unless such adverse possessor or claimant shall have paid and discharged all taxes and special assessments of every nature falling due on such land or real estate during the period he claims to have possessed the same adversely: *Provided, however,* That nothing in this act shall relieve any adverse possesser or claimant from proving all the elements of title by adverse possession now required by law.

Acts 1927, ch. 42, § 1, p. 119 (currently codified, with minor changes, at *Ind. Code* § 32-21-7-1).

Some legal commentators expected that the adverse possession tax statute would "blow[] the lid off the kettle" with regard to the doctrine of adverse possession. Neu at 219. In the first twenty-four years after the adverse possession tax statute was enacted, however, this Court neither cited nor relied upon the adverse possession tax statute in seven decisions involving adverse possession. *See Hare v. Chisman, 230 Ind. 333, 340-41, 101 N.E.2d 268, 271 (Ind. 1951)* (noting adverse claimant paid property taxes but finding evidence insufficient to establish adverse possession); *Elkhart v. Christiana Hydraulics, Inc., 223 Ind. 242, 259, 59 N.E.2d 353, 359 (Ind. 1945)* (referring to adverse possession only summarily); *Draper v. Zebec, 219 Ind. 362, 372, 37 N.E.2d 952, 956 (Ind. 1941)* (referring to adverse possession only summarily), *overruled on other grounds by O'Donnell v. Krneta, 238 Ind. 582, 598, 154 N.E.2d 45, 52 (Ind. 1958)*; *Ft. Wayne Smelting & Refining Works v. Ft. Wayne, 214 Ind. 454, 459, 464, 14 N.E.2d 556, 559, 560-61 (Ind. 1938)* (summarizing findings that adverse claimant and predecessors paid property taxes but affirming judgment for adverse possession without mention of tax statute); *Marengo Cave Co. v. Ross, 212 Ind. 624, 628, 10 N.E.2d 917, 919 (Ind. 1937)* (noting adverse claimant paid property taxes but finding evidence insufficient to establish adverse possession); *Geiger v. Uhl , 204 Ind. 135, 180 N.E. 10 (Ind. 1932)* (finding adverse possession established but without mention of tax statute among elements); *Hitt v. Carr, 201 Ind. 17, 162 N.E. 409 (1928)* (same). Between 1927 and 1955, we find four Court of Appeals decisions mentioning adverse possession and the payment of taxes, two noting that the period of adverse possession preceded the statute, one affirming a judgment challenged on grounds unrelated to taxes, and one reversing a judgment because the findings were insufficient to establish compliance with the adverse possession tax statute.

In the first case in which the adverse possession tax statute was actually analyzed by this Court, *Echterling v. Kalvaitis, 235 Ind. 141, 126 N.E.2d 573 (Ind. 1955)*, the statute was found not applicable. This decision undertook to "examine the language of the act and look to the intention of the Legislature," explaining:

> The 1927 act was enacted to halt the pernicious effect of squatters upon lands where title holders had paid taxes on lands owned by them, but where possession of parts of the land was usurped by squatters for long years without claim of title or payment of taxes. These squatters eventually claimed they became seized with title through adverse possession.

Id. at 145, 126 N.E.2d at 575. But the Court proceeded to construe the adverse possession tax statute as "supplemental" to the adverse possession statute of limitations "and not as superseding it." *Id. at 146, 126 N.E.2d at 575.* This construction of the statute was premised on the policy that the intended effect of the adverse possession statute of limitations was "not to punish one who neglects to assert his right, but to protect those who maintained the possession of the land for the time specified by the statute." *Id.* (quoting *Craven v. Craven, 181 Ind. 553, 560, 105 N.E. 41 (1914)*). The disputed tract in Echterling resulted from a barbed wire fence constructed ten feet west of and parallel to a section line and running for 1320 feet along one side of a quarter of a quarter of a section. Noting that "complete legal descriptions of real estate are not present on the tax duplicates issued by county or city treasurers" and that instead they are "usually sketchy and inaccurate," the Court concluded:

> Where continuous, open, and notorious adverse possession of real estate has been established for twenty years to a contiguous and adjoining strip of land such as that here in question, and *where taxes have been paid* according to the tax duplicate, although said duplicate did not expressly include that strip, *adverse possession is established* to that strip *even though the taxes were not paid* by the adverse claimant.

235 Ind. at 146-47, 126 N.E.2d at 575 (emphasis added). The Court illustrated its intention regarding application of the tax statute with the following:

> An example might be where one has record title to Lot No. 1 and has erected a building on that lot, which, twenty years later, is found by some surveyor to be one foot over on an adjoining lot, No. 2-the fact that the owner of Lot No. 1 was assessed for improvements (the building) and real estate (Lot No. 1) would be sufficient to comply with the statute as to payment of taxes.

Id. at 147, 126 N.E.2d at 575-76.

Thus the Court essentially applied the statute to require the adverse claimant to *substantially* comply with the requirement for payment of taxes. Although the opinion did not expressly mention that the claimant's failure to pay taxes on the claimed boundary strip was inadvertent and unintentional, we believe that this is the clear implication.

Echterling's construction of the adverse possession tax statute has never been overruled or reconsidered by this Court. One case, *Mark v. H.H. Smith Co., 547 N.E.2d 796 (Ind. 1989)*, recites that, in addition to the elements of common law adverse possession, "the adverse claimant must pay real estate taxes on the property for the statutory period." *Id. at 799-800.* But Mark makes no mention of Echterling. The dispositive issue in Mark was not whether the claimant paid taxes but rather that the claimant never changed his permissive occupancy to that of adverse or hostile possession. *Id. at 801.*

The interpretation of the adverse possession tax statute in Echterling has been frequently followed during the ensuing fifty years of decisions by the Court of Appeals. *See Clark v. Aukerman, 654 N.E.2d 1183, 1187 (Ind. Ct. App. 1995); Greene v. Jones, 490 N.E.2d 776, 778 n.2 (Ind. Ct. App. 1986); Dowell v. Fleetwood, 420 N.E.2d 1356 (Ind. Ct. App. 1981); Colley v. Carpenter, 172 Ind.App. 638, 644, 362 N.E.2d 163, 167 (1977); Penn Cent. Transp. Co. v. Martin, 170 Ind.App. 519, 522, 353 N.E.2d 474, 477 (1976); Longabaugh v. Johnson, 163 Ind.App. 108, 112, 321 N.E.2d 865, 868 (1975); Nasser v. Stahl, 126 Ind.App. 709, 720, 134 N.E.2d 567, 572 (1956); Smith v. Brown, 126 Ind.App. 545, 556, 134 N.E.2d 823, 828 (1956).*

During the past twenty years, however, several decisions of the Court of Appeals have construed the adverse possession tax statute as interpreted in Echterling by viewing its purpose to be that of providing notice to the legal owner and concluding that, where clear notice was otherwise provided, courts could disregard the statutory requirement for payment of taxes by the adverse claimant. In *Kline v. Kramer, 179 Ind.App. 592, 600, 386 N.E.2d 982, 989 (1979)*, the court stated:

> Under the statute requiring the payment of taxes, the adverse claimant who had paid taxes for ten years would have good title against the recorded titleholder who took no action to oust the adverse claimant even though the recorded titleholder had paid taxes during the same ten year period. The intent of the legislature and the purpose of the statute is to give the recorded titleholder notice that someone is claiming an interest adverse to his. This notice may be in the form of a tax refund or a tax statement that the taxes are paid. Upon receiving this notice the recorded titleholder must take action to oust the adverse claimant within ten years or forfeit good title to the land described on the tax statement.
>
> Where the payment of taxes will not serve as notice to the recorded title holder that someone is in possession of his land and claiming an interest adverse to his interest in the land, the statute requiring the payment of taxes is not a supplementary element of adverse possession.

Id. at 600, 601, 386 N.E.2d at 989. The Kline court affirmed a determination of adverse possession for a strip of land 309 feet long and varying in width from one to four feet, where the adverse claimant believed his property extended to a boundary fence and assumed that he was paying taxes on the enclosed parcel. Rejecting the view of Judge Hoffman that Echterling "should be overruled and the plain and unambiguous meaning of the statute returned to it as was contemplated by the Legislature which adopted it," *Id. at 603, 386 N.E.2d at 990* (Hoffman, J., dissenting), the court majority stated:

> The holding in Echterling ... emphasizes the Indiana view of adverse possession and the practical need to cure defects in the recording of property descriptions and other defects of title. In circumstances where boundary disputes arise due to the erection of fences or other structures, the supplementary element of tax payments is inapplicable, since it does not serve as notice to the recorded titleholder that the identical described land on the tax statement is being adversely claimed by

another. The erection of the fence or other structure becomes the notice to the adjoining titleholder.

Kline, 386 N.E.2d at 990.

On this issue, *Kline* was followed or quoted with approval in *Williams v. Rogier*, 611 N.E.2d 189, 193 (Ind. Ct. App. 1993) (stating that payment of taxes is not necessary where erection of fence or other structure provides sufficient notice to adjoining titleholder); *Connors v. Augustine*, 407 N.E.2d 1186, 1189 (Ind. Ct. App. 1980); (finding adverse possession of 16-acre tract openly farmed by claimant for requisite period, thereby providing notice to titled owner, and thus payment of taxes by claimant not required); *Ford v. Eckert*, 406 N.E.2d 1209, 1211 (Ind. Ct. App. 1980); (finding for adverse claimant who exerted possession on boundary strip he believed was his and who paid taxes as billed); and *Berrey v. Jean*, 401 N.E.2d 102, 105 (Ind. Ct. App. 1980) (citing Kline with approval but deciding case on other grounds).

In several of its decisions since Kline, the Indiana Court of Appeals thus appears to have favored a policy preference that avoided full application of the language of the adverse possession tax statute. Some opinions have expressly acknowledged this choice. *See, e.g., Berrey*, 401 N.E.2d at 105 ("Cases construing [the adverse possession tax statute] have not demanded its rigid application in all situations."); *Ford*, 406 N.E.2d at 1211 ("This rule of reasonableness in applying the tax provision is a sound one.").

Such disregard of clear statutory language, however, should be avoided, and we disapprove of *Kline* and its progeny as to their understanding and application of the adverse possession tax statute. This Court has emphasized that "courts must be careful to avoid substituting their judgment for those of the more politically responsive branches," *Sanchez v. State*, 749 N.E.2d 509, 516 (Ind. 2001), and that "in our separation of powers democracy, the constitution empowers the legislative branch to make law. *Baldwin v. Reagan*, 715 N.E.2d 332, 337-38 (Ind. 1999). It is clear that "the legislature has wide latitude in determining public policy, and we do not substitute our belief as to the wisdom of a particular statute for those of the legislature." *State v. Rendleman*, 603 N.E.2d 1333, 1334 (Ind. 1992).

As a co-equal and independent branch of government, the judiciary must be empowered to interpret and apply the law. Public trust and confidence in an independent judiciary, however, is enhanced when judges exercise their authority with restraint and respect for the role and function of the legislative branch to decide questions of public policy. The judiciary must respect the fact that the General Assembly is likewise a co-equal and independent branch.

In addition to these important principles of judicial restraint, however, it is well-established that a judicial interpretation of a statute, particularly by the Indiana Supreme Court, accompanied by substantial legislative inaction for a considerable time, may be understood to signify the General Assembly's acquiescence and agreement with the judicial interpretation. In *Durham v. U-Haul Int'l.*, 745 N.E.2d 755 (Ind. 2001), this Court observed that "if a line of decisions of this Court has given a statute the same construction and the legislature has not sought to change the relevant parts of the legislation, the usual reasons supporting adherence to precedent are reinforced by the strong probability that the courts have correctly interpreted the will of the legislature." *Id. at 759. See also Robbins v. Baxter, 799 N.E.2d 1057, 1062 (Ind. 2003)* (applying legislative acquiescence where no legislative response for ten years); *Halteman Swim Club v. Duguid, 757 N.E.2d 1017, 1021 (Ind. Ct. App. 2001),* citing *Department of Revenue v. U.S. Steel Corp., 425 N.E.2d 659, 662 (Ind. Ct. App. 1981)* ("When the court interprets a statute and the legislature fails to take action to change that interpretation, the legislature is presumed to have acquiesced in the court's interpretation.").

Although our holding in Echterling has not been repeated in a series of cases from this Court, we have never repudiated it, and it has been applied for over fifty years in numerous Court of Appeals opinions, as discussed above. During this time, the legislature has not responded by making any changes to the operative language of the 1927 statute as construed in Echterling fifty years ago. That statute prohibited obtaining title by adverse possession "unless such adverse possessor or claimant shall have paid and discharged all taxes and special assessments of every nature falling due on such land or real estate during the period he claims to have possessed the same adversely." Such language was retained verbatim until minor verb tense and gender amendments were made in 2002, and even these changes do not manifest any legislative disagreement with the way Echterling understood and applied the statute. This provides strong evidence of current legislative intent to abide by the Echterling interpretation.

Recognizing our obligation to follow and enforce the adverse possession tax statute as enacted by our legislature, we take a restrained view of the legislative acquiescence in Echterling 's interpretation of the statute. We hold that *Echterling* permits substantial compliance to satisfy the requirement of the adverse possession tax statute in boundary disputes where the adverse claimant has a reasonable and good faith belief that that the claimant is paying the taxes during the period of adverse possession. But we decline to extend *Echterling* to permit total disregard of the statutory tax payment requirement merely on grounds that the legal title holder has other clear notice of adverse possession.

In the present case, as found by the trial court, the Mingers paid taxes on their land *adjoining* the disputed tract, but made no finding that the Mingers paid, intended to pay, or believed that they were paying, the taxes on the disputed tract. There is no finding that during the period of adverse possession the Mingers "paid and discharged all taxes and special assessments of every nature falling due on such land" as required by the adverse possession tax statute, nor is there a finding of substantial compliance. This is not a case of mistake due to imprecision in a tax duplicate or other assessment document. We therefore hold that, considering the issues of law and the facts found by the trial court and the inferences reasonably drawn therefrom, a reasonable trier of fact could not correctly conclude that compliance with the adverse possession tax statute was established, let alone by clear and convincing evidence.

Conclusion

We reverse the judgment of the trial court and remand with instruction to enter judgment for the defendant appellant, Clarence E. Fraley.

Case Questions

1. What does the court say is the standard for proving adverse possession?

2. What is the effect of the payment of taxes on adverse possession?

3 Land Use

LEARNING OBJECTIVES

After studying this chapter you will be able to:

- Define the concept of land use
- Discuss what is meant by a "covenant"
- List the requirements to create a valid covenant
- Distinguish between horizontal and vertical privity
- Explain how a covenant may be extinguished
- Differentiate between a covenant and an equitable servitude
- Define what is meant by an "easement"
- List the four types of easements recognized by law
- Discuss a license as it relates to land use
- Explain the different standards of care that the possessor of land owes to persons who enter onto the land
- Distinguish between trespasssers, licensees, and invitees
- Define an "attractive nuisance"
- Discuss the implications of zoning on land use
- Apply some practical tips to assist you in a land use practice

CHAPTER OUTLINE

Covenants
    Requirements
        Intent
        Notice
        Horizontal privity
        Vertical privity
        Touch and concern the land
    Equitable servitude
Easements
    Appurtenant
    In gross
    Creation
        Express grant
        By implication
        By necessity
        By prescription
Licenses
Duty of Care
    Trespassers
    Licensees
    Invitees
    Attractive nuisance
Zoning
Practical Tips

CHAPTER OVERVIEW

Land use refers to the right of enjoyment and access to land
that may be permitted to persons who are not the legal owners or possessors of the land. In this regard, this right to the use of the land affects both
the person with current legal title to the property as well as a person who
will eventually acquire that title.

Five major topics are discussed under the heading of land use. The
first concerns restrictions that may be placed on the titleholder with respect
to the nature of the use to which the property may be put. These restrictions
are known as covenants and they affect all persons who acquire title to the
property from the person who originally received the property subject to
the covenant.

An easement is the right of passage over or use of another person's
realty, which may be acquired in several ways. Once the easement is established, the easement holder has rights to such use that may be enforced
against the titleholder.

A license refers to the power a person may have to perform a particular act, or series of acts, on another person's property, such as having the right to receive the fruit from a neighbor's cherry tree.

Any person who has lawful possession of realty, by common and statutory law, owes certain duties of care to anyone who is physically present on the property, even if that person is considered to be a trespasser — a person who has no lawful authority to enter onto the land.

Finally, all owners of property may be subject to certain governmental restrictions. The government — federal, state, and local — has the legal authority to limit the nature of the use of geographic sections within their jurisdiction under the concept of zoning regulation.

This chapter continues the exploration of the "bundle of rights" associated with the law of property by examining these limitations imposed on a person's use of his or her own land.

Covenants

A **covenant** is a written promise to do or not to do something on or with the land. Covenants are often referred to as **real covenants** to imply their effect on realty. Most typically are found in the deed that conveys the property (see Chapter 4), and are considered to "run with the land," meaning that these provisions limit not only the person who originally acquired the deed that included the covenant, but to all subsequent titleholders as well.

EXAMPLE:

> A widow decides to generate some capital by selling off a large tract of undeveloped land that she inherited. She wishes to keep the area purely residential, and so in the deeds she executes as she parcels off the property she includes a covenant that the grantee will not construct a multi-family dwelling on the property. This restrictive provision creates a covenant that runs with the land, thereby ensuring that the property will remain residential.

As a general proposition, a person is not legally bound to any provision that he or she did not specifically indorse. However, under real property law, a person will be bound to a covenant that runs with the land regardless of his or her actual assumption of the provision if the following five requirements are met with respect to the creation of the covenant:

1. Intent: In order for the covenant to run with the land it must be evidenced that the grantor who created the covenant specifically meant that it bind the use of the property. This intent will usually

depend upon the exact wording of the covenant, but may be inferred as well.

EXAMPLE:

The widow from the previous example has divided her tract of land into 20 parcels. In 19 of her deeds she specifically includes the covenant with respect to single-family dwellings. This indicates her intent. On the last parcel she inadvertently neglects to insert the covenant. Her intent *may* be determined from the words of all the other deeds that created the subdivision.

2. Notice: This requirement means that, for a subsequent purchaser to be bound by a covenant, he or she must have notice of the existence of the covenant. This notice could either be actual, because it appears in the conveyance the purchaser acquires, or implied, because the covenant appears in the record books where title to real property is officially recorded (see Chapter 4).

EXAMPLE:

A young couple purchases a parcel of land from the widow in the preceding examples. Twenty-five years later they decide to sell their house. The conveyance to the man who purchases their house does not include the covenant, but the deed with the covenant was filed with the recorder's office when the widow first sold the property. The man is bound by the covenant because the recording of the covenant provides notice to him as a subsequent purchaser of the property.

3. Horizontal privity: **Horizontal privity** means that the original parties to the covenant must share some interest in the property (usually the covenant), such as being the buyer and the seller, the landlord and the tenant, or the mortgagor and the mortgagee. This common interest creates privity.
4. Vertical privity: **Vertical privity** means that the person who acquired the property from the person who first acquired the property with the covenant has acquired the entire interest of that original party.

EXAMPLE:

In the previous example, the widow and the young couple have horizontal privity because of the contract for the sale of the land. The man who buys the property from the couple has vertical privity because the couple owned a fee that they sold to the man—he acquired their entire interest.

5. Touch and concern the land: To create a covenant, the subject of the covenant must **touch and concern the land,** meaning that its provisions must restrict a person from doing something on the parcel of land (such as not constructing multi-family dwellings) or require that the person do something on the particular parcel (maintaining the land in its natural state).

If all of the preceding five requirements are established, a real covenant that runs with the land has been created. If this type of covenant exists, the successor in interest to the original party may enforce that covenant in a court of law. The original parties would be the persons who first created the covenant, such as the widow and the young couple from the preceding example. The successor in interest is anyone who acquired title from the person who first obtained the title subject to the covenant, such as the man who bought the house from the young couple in the preceding example. (See Chapter 1 for a discussion of a fee simple subject to a condition subsequent.) To enforce the covenant, the successor in interest must prove the following:

(a) the original parties intended that the covenant could be enforced by a successor in interest;
(b) there is privity with respect to the party seeking enforcement and the original party; and
(c) the covenant touches and concerns the land.

If all of these requirements are satisfied, the party seeking enforcement of the covenant may seek damages — monetary relief — for the injury caused by its breach.

 EXAMPLE:

The man who purchased the property from the young couple in the previous example decides to modify the house to make it a two-family dwelling. This construction would violate the covenant. The man's neighbor, who also purchased his property from the widow, may go to court to seek damages if such construction takes place because the man is subject to the covenant as is the neighbor whose deed from the widow contained the same provision.

The provisions of a real covenant may terminate if the person who could enforce the covenant executes a **release,** a document that relinquishes legal rights; the property is condemned by the government (see below); or the property is reacquired by the promissee or the promissee's successor in interest (the above-discussed widow). The reacquisition of the property by the original grantor is called a **merger** of the interests.

Closely associated with the concept of real covenants are equitable servitudes. An **equitable servitude** is a form of a covenant that is distinguished from real covenants by the remedy that is being sought by the party seeking to enforce its provisions. If the injury results from a covenant, the injured party may seek monetary damages; if the injury results from an equitable servitude, the injured party may only seek an injunction or specific performance — equitable rather than legal remedies.

As with covenants, an equitable servitude may be created by a writing, but unlike a covenant an equitable servitude may also arise by implication. Typically, equitable servitudes arise by implication when a common scheme for a subdivision can be discerned, as with the example of the widow's property discussed above. To be bound by an equitable servitude, any person who acquires a tract of land in a subdivision must have notice of the servitude. Such notice may be actual, by means of the deed of purchase; by record, if it appears in the county record books; or by inquiry, by visual inspection of the property.

To be bound, in addition to notice, the equitable servitude must "run with the land" in the same fashion as a covenant. The primary differences between a covenant and an equitable servitude are:

(a) a covenant *must* be created by a writing whereas an equitable servitude may arise by implication;
(b) no privity, horizontal or vertical, is necessary for an equitable servitude;
(c) notice for an equitable servitude may arise by inquiry; and
(d) the remedy for the breach of a covenant is money, whereas the remedy for the breach of an equitable servitude is an injunction.

Equitable servitudes terminate in the same manner as covenants.

Covenants and equitable servitudes may be viewed as limitations on the use of the land that create fees simple determinable or fees simple subject to a condition subsequent, depending on the wording (see Chapter 1).

Easements

An **easement** is the right of access or use of another person's realty and, unless otherwise terminated, is deemed to exist in perpetuity. Easements are divided into two broad categories: easements appurtenant and easements in gross.

Easements appurtenant are rights of access and use of adjoining property. The tract of land that has the right over the adjacent property is called the **dominant tenement,** and the property that is subject to the use of the easement holder is called the **servient tenement.** Easements appurtenant attach to the land and pass along with the transfer of the title to the land.

**EXAMPLE:**

Fred and Ricky own adjacent lots. Fred wants to extend his driveway, but the construction will encompass six inches of Ricky's property.

By agreement, Ricky permits Fred to use the six-inch strip but retains ownership of the area. Years later, Ricky sells his property to Lucy. Lucy acquires title to the property subject to the use by Fred of the six-inch strip for his driveway.

An **easement in gross** is an easement that is held by an individual for his or her own enjoyment over non-adjacent property. An example of an easement in gross would be the right a homeowner gives to children in the neighborhood to use his property to reach their school even though they do not live on the adjoining property. If the easement in gross is for non-commercial purposes it is not transferable by the easement holder (the children), but if it is for a commercial purpose it may be transferred.

 EXAMPLE:

A property owner has been approached by a cellular telephone company that wants to erect a pole on the property. For a fee the property owner agrees. Because the easement is commercial in nature, the telephone company may transfer its easement rights.

Easements may be created in one of four ways:

1. **Express grant**: The express grant is a writing that may appear in the deed conveying the property or by a separate document. The person who grants the easement must be the owner of the servient tenement upon which the right of the easement will attach. The grantor of the easement may only grant the easement for the period of his title, either fee, life estate, or by lease. The grantee is the owner of the dominant tenement that benefits from the easement. An example of an easement created by express grant would be the previous example involving Fred and Ricky in which Ricky agreed to let Fred use part of his land to build a driveway.

2. **By implication**: An **implied easement** arises by the actual use of the adjacent property without consent. This is created by operation of law and so no writing is necessary. The implied easement may arise by the continuous use of the property because such use is necessary for the enjoyment of the dominant tenement. An example would be a vacation home that has access to a lake either by public road that takes two miles or by a private road over a neighboring property that would take only half a mile. If the vacation home-owner uses this private road for a significant period of time, an implied easement will be created.

3. **By necessity**: An **easement by necessity** occurs when a tract of land has no access to a public road except by going over a neighboring property. In this "landlocked" situation, the dominant tenement has the easement right to gain access to the road, but the servient tenement can determine the exact route for this access.

EXAMPLE:

A tract of land is subdivided in a manner by which a property owner's access to the public road can only be gained by going over his neighbor's property. The neighbor must let the property owner have such access, but may limit that access to a particular strip of land. If access to the public road eventually extends directly to the dominant tenement property, the easement will terminate.

4. **By prescription**: An **easement by prescription** is an easement that is created in the same manner as acquiring full title to property by adverse possession (see Chapter 2). To acquire the right, the easement holder must use the adjoining property in manner that is:
   (a) open and notorious;
   (b) adverse to the interest of the servient property;
   (c) continuous and uninterrupted; and
   (d) for the statutory period mandated by the state statute.

An easement by prescription differs from adverse possession in that the person acquiring the easement is only acquiring the right of use and access rather than title to the property itself.

Easements may terminate in one of eight ways:

1. by the condition that was stated in the grant of the easement

EXAMPLE:

"You may use my property to gain access to the lake until the new public shortcut is constructed."

2. when the same person acquires title to both the dominant and servient tenements, thereby merging the titles
3. if the easement holder executes a release of his rights, which may be gratuitous or for consideration
4. if the easement holder abandons the easement, either for a statutory period or by a physical act such as constructing a fence surrounding the dominant tenement, thereby closing his access to the servient tenement
5. if the dominant tenement orally states his intention of abandoning the easement and the servient tenement relies on this oral expression to her detriment, the dominant tenement will be estopped from reclaiming the easement

EXAMPLE:

The dominant tenement says that he no longer wishes to use the easement. Based on this statement, the servient tenement constructs a wall around the property. The dominant tenement will be barred from claiming easement rights because the servient tenement constructed the wall based on those statements.

6. the servient tenement can terminate the easement by prescription—using the property in a manner that is inconsistent with the easement holder's rights for the statutory period
7. if the easement was created by necessity, the easement automatically terminates when the necessity no longer exists
8. the easement will terminate if the property is condemned by the government or is unintentionally destroyed

While an easement is in effect, the servient tenement is precluded from engaging in any activity that would interfere with the easement right of the dominant tenement.

EXAMPLE:

The owner of a servient tenement no longer wants his neighbor to trample over his property, so he constructs a wall around his land. The neighbor who has the easement right may sue the servient tenement to have the wall taken down so as not to interfere with his easement rights.

Easements create significant rights for the dominant tenement and impose significant liabilities on the servient tenement. Whenever a person acquires title to property she should determine whether any easement attaches to that property.

Licenses

A **license** is the right to do an act or a series of acts on another person's land. Unlike an easement that creates a perpetual right of use, a license arises at the pleasure of the property owner and may be rescinded by the property owner at any time. A license merely grants the **licensee,** the license holder, the permission to enter onto the other person's property, whereas an easement creates a property right in the easement holder.

EXAMPLE:

Blackacre borders a large lake. The owner of Blackacre let his neighbors use a path across Blackacre to get to the lake. The owner also lets his friend from the city use Blackacre to fish in the lake. The neighbors may have an easement over Blackacre, whereas the city friend merely has a license. The owner of Blackacre can stop his friend from using Blackacre but the neighbors may have acquired certain property rights to the use of Blackacre for access to the lake.

Duty of Care

Any person who is a lawful possessor of real property owes certain duties of care to third persons who come onto that property. The nature and extent of that duty depends on the category into which the third person may fall. Generally persons who enter onto the land fall into one of three categories:

1. **Trespassers** are those persons who enter onto realty without permission. Because these persons have no lawful right to be on the land, the person in possession only owes such people slight care. This means that the possessor must alert such persons only of artificial structures on the property, or natural circumstances that are not readily discernible, that may injure trespassers. An example might be the posting of a sign indicating that there are bear traps located on the property to alert the trespasser to a dangerous situation.

2. **Licensees** are persons who are permitted to enter the property with the possessor's permission for a purpose that generally benefits the licensees. This category would include all social guests of the property owner/possessor. Licensees are entitled to the ordinary standard of care, meaning that they must be warned about dangerous conditions, such as a loose step or a broken chair, that may or may not be readily apparent.

3. **Invitees** are persons who are asked onto the property to benefit the property owner/possessor's pecuniary interest, such as customers in a retail store. The property owner/possessor owes invitees the highest standard of care, which requires that the invitee be warned of all potential defects that might cause injury.

Despite these differences, the modern trend of the law is to require the ordinary standard of care to all persons who enter onto property, regardless of the nature and reason for that entrance.

There is one important exception to the foregoing, and that exception involves any situation that would cause children to be attracted to the property. In this instance, the property owner/possessor is held to the highest standard of care so as to protect children, and may be held strictly liable under a legal doctrine called **attractive nuisance**. This doctrine relates to situations that would lure children to the property, such as a swimming pool, construction site, natural gorge, and so forth. If the property owner/possessor knows or should know that children will be drawn to the property, she is expected to take all reasonable precautions to protect the children from harm.

**EXAMPLE:**

A property owner has just built a swimming pool on his property and the children in the neighborhood continually come onto the property to swim in the pool. It is dangerous for small children to swim unsupervised, and therefore the homeowner is required to construct a fence around the pool to keep the children away from the pool for their own good.

Zoning

The government is empowered to restrict land use for the purpose of protecting the general health and welfare of the public. To effect this mandate, local governments enact **zoning regulations** that restrict land use. Provided that there is some rational basis between the zoning regulation and the general welfare of the community, such government restrictions on land use are deemed to be constitutional, meaning that it is not considered to be a deprivation of property. However, to ensure the constitutionality of the zoning regulation, a proposed regulation is subject to a public hearing so that members of the community may present arguments for and against the proposed regulation. See Exhibit 3.1.

Exhibit 3.1: California Statutes

Zoning Statutes

§ 65854.2.1.   Single-family   residence zone; permit for dwelling unit for senior citizen occupancy; application of section

Notwithstanding Section 65906, any city, including a charter city, county, or city and county may issue a zoning variance, special use permit, or conditional use permit for a dwelling unit to be constructed, or which is attached to or detached from, a primary residence on a parcel zoned for a single-family residence, if the dwelling unit is intended for the sole occupancy of one adult or two adult persons who are 62 years of age or over, and the area of floor space of the attached dwelling unit does not exceed 30 percent of the existing living area or the area of the floor space of the detached dwelling unit does not exceed 1,200 square feet.

Basically, zoning consists of designating geographic areas for specific purposes, such as residential, commercial, public (parks, town halls), and mixed use. Furthermore, within these areas the zoning regulation may prescribe the nature of the buildings that may be constructed within the zone, such as single-family dwellings, multi-family dwellings, and so forth. Enforcement of the zoning regulations rests with a governmental body known as a **zoning board**.

Various problems may arise with respect to zoning regulations. First, if a particular use of the property has existed for a long period of time prior to the zoning regulation that would not permit such a use, the property owner may continue such use provided that it can be demonstrated that such use actually pre-dated the regulation.

EXAMPLE:

> At the turn of the twentieth century a farmer built a small shed next to the road to sell his farm produce. Over the years the entire area became residential, and most of the farms were sold off. The farmer's great-grandchild continues to use the shed, slightly enlarged, as a store. The area has just been re-zoned for residential use only, and the neighbors want the store to stop operating. The greatgrandchild may be able to continue running the store by documenting a preexisting use.

If a preexisting use has been established, that use may continue, but any change in the specific use would thereafter have to conform to the current zoning regulations.

Second, zoning regulations may also require certain architectural standards to maintain a uniform style in a community. Therefore, when a homeowner intends to make structural changes to his or her house, it may require prior approval of the zoning board.

EXAMPLE:

> A woman has just purchased a colonial house in a city's historical district. She wants to modernize the house for twenty-first century use. Before she may make any changes to the outside of the building, she must obtain approval of the zoning board.

Third, if a person wants to use his property in a manner inconsistent with current zoning regulations, he may be able to obtain a **variance** from the zoning board, giving him permission to use the property in this manner. Before permitting a variance, most boards require a public hearing so that members of the community may express concerns about the effect of the variance on the community.

Exhibit 3.2: California Statutes

Building Code

§ 65850.2. Use of regulated substances or sources of hazardous emissions; development projects or building permit applications for projects not requiring development permits; information lists and application forms; completion of application or approval; risk management plans; fees

(a) Each city and each county shall include in its information list compiled pursuant to Section 65940 for development projects, or application form for projects which do not require a development permit other than a building permit, both of the following:

    (1) The requirement that the owner or authorized agent shall indicate whether the owner or authorized agent will need to comply with the applicable requirements of Section 25505 and Article 2 (commencing with Section 25531) of Chapter 6.95 of Division 20 of the Health and Safety Code and the requirements for a permit for construction or modification from the air pollution control district or air quality management district exercising jurisdiction in the area governed by the city or county.

    (2) The requirement that the owner or authorized agent shall certify whether or not the proposed project will have more than a threshold quantity of a regulated substance in a process or will contain a source or modified source of hazardous air emissions.

(b) A city or county shall not find the application complete pursuant to Section 65943 or approve a development project, or a building permit for a project which does not require a development permit other than a building permit, in which a regulated substance will be present in a process in quantities greater than the applicable threshold quantity, unless the owner or authorized agent for the project first obtains from the administering agency with jurisdiction over the facility, a notice of requirement to comply with, or determination of exemption from, the requirement to prepare and submit an RMP. Within five days of submitting the project application to the city or county, the applicant shall submit the information required pursuant to paragraph (2) of subdivision (a) to the administering agency. This notice of requirement to comply with, or determination of exemption from, the requirement for an RMP shall be provided by the administering agency to the applicant, and the applicant shall provide the notice to the city or county, within 25 days of the administering agency receiving

Exhibit 3.2: *(Continued)*

adequate information from the applicant to make a determination as to the requirement for an RMP. The requirement to submit an RMP to the administering agency, shall be met prior to the issuance of a certificate of occupancy or its substantial equivalent. The owner or authorized agent shall submit to the city or county certification from the air pollution control officer that the owner or authorized agent is in compliance with the disclosures required by Section 42303 of the Health and Safety Code.

(c) A city or county shall not issue a final certificate of occupancy or its substantial equivalent unless there is verification from the administering agency, if required by law, that the owner or authorized agent has met, or is meeting, the applicable requirements of Section 25505 and Article 2 (commencing with Section 25531) of Chapter 6.95 of Division 20 of the Health and Safety Code, and the requirements for a permit, if required by law, from the air pollution control district or air quality management district exercising jurisdiction in the area governed by the city or county or has provided proof from the appropriate district that the permit requirements do not apply to the owner or authorized agent.

(d) The city or county, after considering the recommendations of the administering agency or air pollution control district or air quality management district, shall decide whether, and under what conditions, to allow construction of the site.

(e) Nothing in this section limits any existing authority of a district to require compliance with its rules and regulations.

(f) Counties and cities may adopt a schedule of fees for applications for compliance with this section sufficient to recover their reasonable costs of carrying out this section. Those fees shall be used only for the implementation of this section.

(g) As used in this section, the following terms have the following meaning:

   (1) "Administering agency," "process," "regulated substance," "RMP," and "threshold quantity" have the same meaning as set forth in Section 25532 of the Health and Safety Code.

   (2) "Hazardous air emissions" means emissions into the ambient air of air contaminants which have been identified as a toxic air contaminant by the State Air Resources Board or by the air pollution control officer for the jurisdiction in which the project is located. As determined by the air pollution control officer, hazardous air emissions also means emissions into the ambient air of any substance identified in subdivisions (a) to (f), inclusive, of Section 44321 of the Health and Safety Code.

(h) Any misrepresentation of information required by this section shall be grounds for denial, suspension, or revocation of project approval or permit issuance. The owner or authorized agent

Exhibit 3.2: *(Continued)*

> required to comply with this section shall notify all future occu-
> pants of their potential duty to comply with the requirements of
> Section 25505 and Article 2 (commencing with Section 25531) of
> Chapter 6.95 of Division 20 of the Health and Safety Code.

Zoning regulations are typically enforced by the government by seeking an injunction against any person who violates a zoning regulation without having obtained permission by means of a variance from the zoning board.

Closely associated with zoning regulations are **building codes** that mandate minimum requirements for construction, electricity, plumbing, and so forth, of all structures. See Exhibit 3.2. Such laws regulate the material and methods used in construction of a building, and buildings may not be occupied without obtaining a **permit** and inspection by the locality's governmental agency that oversees these laws. If a structure does not meet the standards of the building codes and is declared to be dangerous for occupancy, the government may be able to **condemn** the building, meaning that it may be destroyed for the welfare and safety of the public.

Probably the most dramatic governmental interference with land use is its ability to take over private property for public purposes, such as the construction of a road, under the doctrine of **eminent domain.** To meet constitutional guarantees, no private property may be taken by the government without adequate compensation. Questions may arise as to the adequacy of the proffered compensation, but the property owner has no choice but to sell the property to the government.

EXAMPLE:

A man purchased some undeveloped land ten years ago as an investment. At the time he paid $10,000 for the property. Over the years the surrounding area has become populated, and the man believes his investment is now worth $100,000. The local government informs him that they will need to acquire his property to create roads, utilities, and so forth, due to the new population in the area. The government only pays him $45,000 for the property. The man must transfer title to the government, but may challenge the adequacy of the consideration in court.

Practical Tips

- Check the title at the recorder's office to determine whether any easement exists on the land. If representing the easement holder,

make sure all easements are recorded; if representing the servient tenement, see if the easement can be removed.
- Make sure all valid easements and liens are recorded.
- Make no change to existing structures until all zoning requirements and restrictions have been determined.
- Prepare any documents that may be necessary to validate the need for a zoning variance.
- Maintain evidence of all licenses that may be granted to avoid any future problems.
- Become familiar with members of the local zoning board.

Chapter Review

The right to own and possess land is not absolute. Certain limitations and restrictions may be imposed on the use of realty that severely limit the titleholder's unfettered enjoyment of the property.

The most prevalent types of restrictions on land use are covenants and equitable servitudes, restrictions on the use of property that arise when the property is transferred. These limitations create rights in persons not the property owner to see that these restrictions are enforced, either by means of seeking monetary damages for violations of the real covenants or injunctions against violations of equitable servitudes.

Easements create rights of use of and access over one person's property by another, and this use and access can have important effects on what the property owner may or may not do to his or her own land. Unless specifically terminated, easements are deemed to exist forever, and the owner of the property that is subject to the easement cannot do anything that would interfere with the easement holders' rights.

Closely related to easements are licenses — permissions by the property owner/possessor to third persons to enter the land for a particular act or for a series of acts. However, unlike easements, licenses are not rights, and unless established by contract, are totally revocable by the property owner/possessor at will.

All persons in lawful possession of realty are required to maintain the property in a manner that renders it safe for third persons who enter onto the land. Historically, the law distinguished the standard of care owed by the property owner/possessor by the nature of the third person — trespasser, licensee, or invitee — but the modern trend of authority imposes the ordinary standard of care on the property owner/possessor regardless of the status of the third person. There is one exception to this modern trend that exists for attractive nuisances, hazardous situations that could cause children to wish to enter the property. In this instance the property owner/possessor is held to a standard of strict liability.

Finally, a person's ability to use his or her property may be restricted by several governmental regulations, such as zoning regulations, building codes, and the power of eminent domain.

Ethical Concern

Just because a trespasser is injured on the land does not mean that the landowner is in any way responsible. It is unethical to institute a legal claim against a landowner for injuries that a trespasser caused through his or her own fault. Such frivolous actions may result in sanctions imposed by the court.

Key Terms

Attractive nuisance	Implied easement
Building code	Invitee
Condemn	Land use
Covenant	License
Dominant tenement	Licensee
Easement	Real covenant
Easement appurtenant	Release
Easement by necessity	Servient tenement
Easement by prescription	Touch and concern the land
Easement in gross	Trespasser
Eminent domain	Variance
Equitable servitude	Vertical privity
Express grant	Zoning regulations
Horizontal privity	Zoning board

Exercises

1. Determine the statutory period for acquiring an easement by prescription in your jurisdiction, as well as the other requirements to create such an easement.
2. Briefly discuss the methods whereby an easement may be terminated.
3. Research the zoning regulations for your neighborhood. Determine the procedures for obtaining a variance from your zoning board.
4. How would you determine "reasonable compensation" for the taking of private property by the government in a case of eminent domain?
5. Research some cases of attractive nuisance decided in your state.

Situational Analysis

By agreement, Alan was given the right to use a portion of Betty's property as a driveway for a period of one year until he could construct a driveway of his own. The year ended four months ago and Alan continues to use Betty's property and has not constructed his own driveway. What are the respective rights of the parties? What information might you need to arrive at your conclusion?

Edited Cases

The following two judicial decisions underscore certain principles introduced in this chapter. Problems with easements are discussed in *Price v. McNeil*, and licenses are analyzed in *Wisconsin Bell, Inc. v. Sheffield Systems, Inc.*

Price v. McNeil
2001 Ala. Civ. App. LEXIS 221

Gary Price and Martha Price (the "servient estate") own real estate subject to an easement that is now owned by Deborah McNeil (the "dominant estate"). They are adjacent landowners. The servient estate sued the dominant estate, alleging that the dominant estate had wrongfully obstructed their use of the easement by erecting a locked gate. The trial court eventually ruled in favor of the dominant estate, concluding that the dominant estate had an "exclusive" easement that barred any use by the servient estate. The servient estate appealed to the supreme court, which transferred the case to this court, pursuant to Ala. Code 1975, Sec. 12-2-7(6). We reversed the trial court's judgment, holding that, as a matter of law, the easement was not "exclusive." See *Price v. McNeil*, 771 So. 2d 1054 (Ala. Civ. App. 2000) (*Price I*). We instructed the trial court on remand "to determine the extent to which the [servient estate is] allowed to use the easement." 771 So. 2d at 1057. On remand, the trial court ordered that the dominant estate can maintain the locked gate, but that the servient estate is to have a key and that they can use the key to open the gate and then lock it back after each use. The servient estate appealed to the supreme court, which again transferred the case to this court pursuant to Ala. Code 1975, Sec. 12-2-7(6).

In *Price I*, we instructed the trial court on remand to follow the principles set forth by our supreme court in *Blalock v. Conzelman*, 751 So. 2d 2 (Ala. 1999), and *Duke v. Pine Crest Homes, Inc.*, 358 So. 2d 148 (Ala. 1978), to determine to what extent the servient estate may use the easement. The *Duke* court stated that a servient estate may use an easement as follows:

> It is well settled in Alabama that the owner of the servient estate may himself use the land upon which an easement has been dedicated so long as [his use] does not conflict with the purpose and character of the easement. . . .
> . . . We wish to make it clear that the servient owner must not in any way interfere with or impinge upon the rights secured by the dominant estate under the express grant of the easement. . . . Nor must use by the servient owner create any such additional burden upon the easement as would interfere with those rights granted by the express terms of the easement.

358 So. 2d at 150, 151 (citation omitted).

The *Blalock* court stated:

> Moreover, pursuant to the general rule, the [dominant estate and servient estate] have concurrent rights to the use of the easement, and neither party can prevent the other from using the easement in a manner consistent with the purposes for which the easement was created. Thus, the existence of the easement creates mutual rights and obligations.
>
> "The landowner may not, without the consent of the easement holder, unreasonably interfere with the latter's rights or change the character of the easement so as to make the use thereof significantly more difficult or burdensome." Conversely, the easement holder "can not change its character, or materially increase the burden upon the servient estate."

751 So. 2d at 6 (citations omitted).

The servient estate argues that the placement of the locked gate across the easement, regardless of the fact that they now have a key to unlock the gate each time they want to cross the easement, is an "undue burden" on the servient estate. The evidence in the record indicates that the dominant estate placed the gate at the point where the easement accesses a public road. The dominant estate testified that she erected the gate in order to protect "her property" from trespassers. The easement crosses the servient estate for several hundred feet before entering the dominant estate. The servient estate argues that the locked gate should be placed at the point where the easement enters the dominant estate.

The dominant estate's easement is "[a] perpetual easement for ingress and egress." In *Blalock*, the dominant estate had an easement "for ingress and egress to and from said property." The dominant estate used the easement for a driveway. The servient estate altered the driveway and planned to remove trees and shrubbery along the easement. The dominant estate sued the servient estate, seeking to enjoin it from removing the trees and shrubbery. The trial court enjoined the servient estate from removing the trees and shrubbery. The supreme court reversed, stating:

> At its core, the [dominant estate's] action is about vegetation, that is, the [dominant estate] asserts a right to certain trees and vegetation growing in the area of the easement. However, the easement created by the deeds conveying lots 1 and 2 is only "for ingress and egress to and from [lot 1] as shown in [the resurvey]." Nothing in those deeds addresses vegetation. Thus, the [dominant estate] seeks to change the essential character of the easement from that of a right of way, to — in effect — one of shade and air. See *Metcalf v. Houk*, 644 N.E.2d 597, 600 (Ind. Ct. App. 1994) ("Generally an easement for ingress and egress confers only the right to pass over the land and not to control the real estate or install improvements"); see also *Upson v. Stafford*, 205 Ga. App. 615, 616, 422 S.E.2d 882, 884 (1992) (the holder of an access easement had no right to a "buffer of trees" between his easement and adjoining property); *Solow v. Liebman*, 175 A.D.2d 120, 121, 572 N.Y.S.2d 19, 20 (1991) (holder of an access easement "had no right, as a matter of law," to prevent the owner of the servient estate from removing trees from the easement).
>
> Moreover, the presence or absence of vegetation is not material to the [dominant estate's] ability to use the easement. It is, however, highly material to [the servient estate's] ability to use the easement.

751 So. 2d at 6.

The easement in this case is likewise limited to an easement for "ingress and egress." We hold that, just as the control over the vegetation was held not to be material to the use of the easement in *Blalock*, the placement of the gate across the easement for the protection of the dominant estate, regardless of whether the servient estate is provided a key to the gate, is not material, or reasonably necessary, to the use of this easement. See *Clark v. Kuhn*, 171 Ore. App. 29, 15 P.3d 37 (2000) (holding that the dominant estate's placement of a gate across the easement is not reasonably necessary for the purpose of using an easement for ingress and egress); and *Drew v. Sorensen*, 133 Idaho 534, 538, 989 P.2d 276, 280 (1999) (holding that the placement of a gate across the easement, which barricaded a significant area of the servient estate, is an "unreasonable burden" on the servient estate and is not "reasonable and necessary" to maintenance of the easement). See also *Ballington v. Paxton*, 327 S.C. 372, 488 S.E.2d 882 (S.C. Ct. App. 1997) (holding that the servient estate could maintain on the easement a locked fence that did not unreasonably interfere with the dominant estate's use of the easement).

Therefore, we reverse the trial court's judgment providing that the dominant estate may maintain a gate on the easement as long as the servient estate is provided a key to the gate. As stated above, the dominant estate, as a matter of law, cannot maintain a locked gate on the easement, because the gate imposes an unreasonable burden on the servient owners. On remand, the trial court is instructed to enter a judgment consistent with this opinion.

Case Questions

1. How are the rights of the dominant tenement infringed in this case?
2. How does the court conclude that both the dominant and servient tenement have concurrent rights?

Wisconsin Bell, Inc. v. Sheffield Systems, Inc.
222 Wis. 2d 622, 587 N.W.2d 456 (Wis. App. 1998)

I. Background.

On February 17, 1993, Pakhar Singh, then the owner of Stark Food Market, entered into a three-year contract with Wisconsin Bell, permitting Wisconsin Bell to install pay phones on his property in exchange for a percentage of the revenues generated by the pay phones. On May 5, 1994, Pakhar Singh leased the entire building to Gurpal Singh and sold him the business, Stark Food Market. None of the legal documents involving these transactions make any reference to the contract with Wisconsin Bell. Following the lease of the building and the sale of the business, Wisconsin Bell continued to pay revenues generated by the pay phones to Pakhar Singh.

Several months after buying the business and leasing the building, Gurpal Singh entered into a contract with Sheffield Systems for the installation of public pay phones. During the time Sheffield Systems and Gurpal Singh were negotiating their contract they asked for and received from Wisconsin Bell information which confirmed that Pakhar Singh and Wisconsin Bell had entered into a three-year contract placing phone equipment on Pakhar Singh's property. Nonetheless, the appellants demanded that Wisconsin Bell remove its phone equipment from the site, and when Wisconsin Bell failed to comply, Sheffield Systems removed Wisconsin Bell's equipment. Later, Wisconsin Bell picked up its equipment and, under protest, paid the fees demanded by Sheffield Systems.

Wisconsin Bell then commenced suit on June 30, 1995, against Gurpal Singh and Sheffield Systems, claiming, *inter alia*, in Counts II and III, that the appellants engaged in tortious interference with its contract with Singh. After the appellants filed an answer denying any wrongdoing, Wisconsin Bell filed a motion seeking summary judgment on these two counts. Following a hearing, the trial court granted Wisconsin Bell's summary judgment motion and this appeal follows.

II. Analysis.

A. There was a Valid Enforceable Contract.

The appellants concede that Pakhar Singh and Wisconsin Bell entered into an agreement. They assert, however, that this agreement did not bind Gurpal Singh when he bought the business and leased the building because the agreement between Pakhar Singh and Wisconsin Bell constituted a personal services contract, which under the law is treated as a revocable license, as it is simply a limited grant of access to the real estate, a grant that was revoked as a matter of law when the business was sold and the building was leased. Accordingly, since no valid contract existed between Pakhar Singh and Wisconsin Bell at the time the appellants contracted for the installation of Sheffield Systems's phone equipment, the appellants conclude the first element of tortious interference with a contract has not been met. The respondent disputes the characterization of the agreement as a license but asserts that regardless of what it is labeled, the contract created an irrevocable interest in Pakhar Singh's property for three years. We agree.

The appellants argue that the agreement between Pakhar Singh and Wisconsin Bell exhibits all the characteristics of a revocable license. The appellants rely on cases from other jurisdictions which have held that contracts similar to this one are revoked as a matter of law when the property is conveyed to another. There is, however, no Wisconsin law on point.

Thus, to resolve this issue, a survey of Wisconsin law is necessary. The appellants assert this contract is actually a license because licenses usually permit access to real property for a limited purpose such as servicing vending machines and when granting a license the parties ordinarily do not intend to create an interest in the land. Grappling with the related issue of whether a contract conveying hunting and fishing privileges is a revocable license or a contract establishing an "estate or interest in lands 'or real property,'" the supreme court in *Van Camp v. Menominee Enterprises, Inc., 68 Wis. 2d 332, 341-43, 228 N.W.2d 664, 669-70 (1975)*, concluded that hunting and fishing rights can constitute an interest in land. "We conclude, therefore, that the hunting and fishing rights do constitute an interest in land ...." *Id. at 344, 228 N.W.2d at 670*. Borrowing from a handbook on property rights, the court said: "A grant of a right to take and kill game on land or waters belonging to the grantor is a grant of an interest in the land itself within the Statute of Frauds." *Id. at 343, 228 N.W.2d at 670* (quoting 1 Thompson, Real Property, § 135, at 513 (1964 Replacement)) (ellipses omitted). In ruling in favor of the appellants, however, the supreme court noted that summary judgment was inappropriate because the original grantor failed to reduce the contract to writing. Thus, the holding in this case clarifies that in Wisconsin it is possible for contracts which allow limited access to property, similar to what licenses often do, to create an interest in property, but they must be written.

Another Wisconsin case lending support to the conclusion that the contract is not a revocable license is *Wisconsin Public Service Corp. v. Marathon County, 75 Wis. 2d 442, 249 N.W.2d 543 (1977)*. This is a case with a similar issue that was litigated for different reasons. The disputed issue in *Marathon County* was whether the utility had a sufficient interest in land where it maintained overhead power lines to require compensation when the authorities ordered the power lines removed.

The supreme court, in discussing the subtle differences between a conveyance granting an easement and a contract granting a license, recited portions of two earlier cases for its determination that the Wisconsin Public Service Corporation had an interest in the land:

> "An easement ... is a permanent interest in the land of another, with the right to enjoy it fully and without obstruction for the period of the easement. A license or contract right is a privilege to do one or more acts on the land of another without possessing an actual land interest."

Id. at 446, 249 N.W.2d at 545 (quoting *Schwartz v. Evangelical Deaconess Soc'y, 46 Wis. 2d 432, 438-39, 175 N.W.2d 225, 228 (1970))*. "If anything more than a revocable license is created it is an easement *or interest in the land* ...." *Van Camp, 68 Wis. 2d at 344, 228 N.W.2d at 670* (internal quotation marks omitted; citation omitted) (emphasis added). Thus, in Wisconsin, any contract which creates something beyond a revocable license has effectively created an interest in land.

The appellants contend that this contract was a revocable license and they rely on the definition of a license found in *Schwartz v. Evangelical Deaconess Soc'y, 46 Wis. 2d 432, 175 N.W.2d 225 (1970)*:

> A license in real property is defined as a personal, revocable and unassignable privilege, conferred either by writing or parol, to do one or more acts on land without possessing any interest therein. Indeed, the distinguishing characteristics

of a license in land are that it gives no interest in the land and that it may rest in parol.

Id. at 438, 175 N.W.2d at 227-28 (internal quotation marks omitted; citation omitted). They concede that the contract in question is written, but they argue that the agreement between Wisconsin Bell and Pakhar Singh meets all the other requirements because it is personal in nature, permitting only Wisconsin Bell to enter the property for the exclusive purpose of installing or maintaining the property and because it is not actually assignable as the contract is so restrictive that an assignment can only be made to a Wisconsin Bell affiliate. We disagree.

Two of the characteristics of a contract creating an interest in another's real estate are present here. The contract is written and despite the appellants' contentions to the contrary, it is assignable. In *Marathon County,* 75 Wis. 2d at 446, 249 N.W.2d at 544, the court reaffirmed the holding in *Schwartz* that the ability to assign the rights to another is a significant difference between a license and a contract creating an interest in the property. "A license is unassignable." *Id.* (citing *Schwartz, 46 Wis. 2d at 438-39, 175 N.W.2d at 227*). "Assignability is a characteristic of rights in or connected with property." *Id.* According to the appellants' interpretation, the contract is unassignable because it permits an assignment only to be made to a Wisconsin Bell affiliate which is the legal equivalent of Wisconsin Bell. We are not persuaded. The pertinent contract language reads:

> Successors, Assigns and Appointment of Agents- Wisconsin Bell may, at any time, assign this Agreement or any portion hereof, to any affiliate of Wisconsin Bell. This Agreement shall benefit and/or be binding upon the successors, assigns, lessees or beneficiaries of Space Provider Pakhar Singh. However, in no event may Space Provider Pakhar Singh assign this Agreement, or otherwise transfer its rights and obligations hereunder, without the express consent of Wisconsin Bell. Additionally, in no event shall Space Provider Pakhar Singh appoint an agent for the purpose of acting as Wisconsin Bell's sole and exclusive Space Provider Pakhar Singh contact for negotiating with Wisconsin Bell or receiving payments hereunder without the expressed consent of Wisconsin Bell. In the event Space Provider Pakhar Singh enters into such an agency agreement, without Wisconsin Bell's consent, its terms of agency shall be null and void with respect to Wisconsin Bell. At all times during the term or any Renewal Term of this Agreement, Wisconsin Bell shall retain the right to directly negotiate with and directly pay any commissions hereunder to Space Provider Pakhar Singh.

The contract language supports the assignability of the contract. The fact that Wisconsin Bell contracted to restrict its power to assign the contract to its own affiliates does not alter the fact that the contract is assignable. The contract also permits Pakhar Singh to assign his interest to another, as long as Wisconsin Bell consents.

Further, had the parties intended to create only a revocable license, revocable by law when the building changed hands, there would be no reason to regulate the rights of "successors, assigns, lessees, or beneficiaries" in the contract. The inclusion of the rights of these parties in the contract confirms that the parties intended something more than a revocable license.

As noted, a contract that purports to grant anything more than a revocable license is a contract which creates an interest in the land of another. Here, the parties have created a contract which grants more than a revocable license.

Consequently, we conclude that the contract created an interest in Pakhar Singh's land and the trial court correctly found that the contract was valid and enforceable at the time the appellants removed Wisconsin Bell's phone equipment. Having established that the contract was one which established an interest in property, we decline to address the arguments raised by the parties as to whether certain written leases are irrevocable in Wisconsin.

B. There is no Statute of Frauds Violation.

The appellants next argue that even if the contract between Wisconsin Bell and Pakhar Singh is interpreted to create an interest in the land which would survive the sale of the business and the lease of the building, it is unenforceable because it violates the Statute of Frauds. The appellants' argument is premised upon Chapter 706, Stats., which regulates conveyances of real property including leases of property which extend for more than one year. Their contention is two-fold. They claim that the contract is invalid because it fails to meet the formal requisites embodied in § 706.02, Stats., requiring the conveyance to identify the land and the interest being conveyed; and it violates § 706.03(2), Stats., because it was not executed by an officer of Wisconsin Bell. Although the respondents assert the appellants have no standing to attack the contract as they are not parties to it, we decline to address that issue because we conclude the appellants have misconstrued the statutes.

Chapter 706, Stats., governs all interests in land (other than some exclusions which are not relevant to this discussion), including limited rights in land such as that which was conveyed to Wisconsin Bell. Two of the requirements of § 706.02 are that the conveyance identify the land and the interest being conveyed. Here the contract language states that Pakhar Singh "hereby grants Wisconsin Bell permission to install, maintain, and collect public telephone service on the Space Provider's premises for a period of three years . . . ." Further, the contract contains the address of the store and identifies the owner as Pakhar Singh. Thus, the land and the interest being conveyed have been accurately identified.

With respect to appellants' argument that the contract is invalid because it is not "executed by an officer of Wisconsin Bell pursuant to 706.03(2)." we note that the appellants fail to acknowledge other subsections which give corporate agents the ability to bind their principals in contracts conveying interests in property. Specifically, § 706.03(1m) refutes the appellants' claim that the document can only be signed by a corporate agent who meets the qualifications of § 706.03(2), and the document must be in recordable form pursuant to § 706.03(3). Section 706.03(1m) reads:

> A conveyance signed by one purporting to act as agent for another shall be ineffective as against the purported principal unless such agent was expressly

authorized, and unless the authorizing principal is identified as such in the conveyance or in the form of signature or acknowledgment. The burden of proving the
authority of any such agent shall be upon the person asserting the same.

The contract contains the name of the purported principal, Wisconsin
Bell, and the contract is signed on behalf of Wisconsin Bell by "Ann Affeldt"
who identifies herself as a manager for Wisconsin Bell. Additional authority for the legality of Ann Affeldt's signature can be found in **R.C.R. Corp. v.**
Bank of Middleton, 58 B.R. 291, 294 (Bankr. W.D. Wis. 1986), where the court
found that an attack on a contract based upon the fact that the contract was
not properly executed by a corporate officer pursuant to § 706.03(2) was
meritless because agency authority is contained in § 706.03(1m). Section
706.03(2) merely "provides a method for meeting the burden of proof as to
agency authority contained in section 706.03([1m])." **Id.** (footnote omitted).
The court further noted that: "Section 706.03(2) may not be used by the
parties to a transaction or their successors in interest to attack an admittedly
authorized conveyance." **Id.** Obviously the inference from the holding is
that third parties may not attack the validity on this basis, either. Significant
to the issue here is the fact that there is no challenge to Affeldt's authority
by Wisconsin Bell or Pakhar Singh. Thus the appellants' attack on the
validity of the contract for its alleged failure to be signed by a corporate
officer or an authorized agent recorded with the register of deeds is
meritless.

By the Court. — Judgment and order affirmed.

Case Questions

   1. How does the court define "license"?
   2. What is the court's analysis with respect to the Statute of Frauds?

4

Conveyancing

LEARNING OBJECTIVES

After studying this chapter you will be able to:

- Define "conveyancing"
- Discuss a basic contract for the sale of realty
- Explain the requirements to create a valid contract
- Discuss the concept of equitable conversion
- Explain the implications of the Vendor and Purchaser Risk Act on real estate contracts
- List the methods for describing real property
- Indicate all of the clauses that should appear in a contract for the sale of realty
- Define "earnest money"
- Indicate what might place a cloud on a title to realty
- Discuss the various types of listing agreements that are used to sell realty
- List the different types of warranties that may appear in a contract for the sale of realty
- Discuss what is necessary to be considered a deed
- List the different types of deeds that may be used to transfer title to realty

- Explain the covenants that appear in the different types of deeds
- Discuss how a mortgage works
- Explain the mortgagee's rights in the case of default by the mortgagor
- Discuss the different types of foreclosure that may exist
- Understand the different types of recording statutes and the concept of priority
- Apply some practical tips to assist you in a real estate conveyancing practice

CHAPTER OUTLINE

Conveyancing Defined
Land Sales Contracts
    Requirements
    Breach
       Damages
       Specific performance
       Risk of loss
          Doctrine of equitable conversion
          Vendor and Purchaser Risk Act
    Contract provisions
       Parties
       Consideration
          Land description
             Plat
             Metes and bounds
             Rectangular survey
       Title
          Encumbrances
             Liens
       Closing
       Transfer of possession
       Risk of loss
       Earnest money
       Rights of the broker
          Open listing
          Exclusive listing
          Exclusive right to sell
       Assignments
       Warranties
       Time of the essence
       Conditions
       Notice

CHAPTER OVERVIEW

Conveyancing refers to the legal process whereby title to real estate is transferred from one person to another. Transfer of realty typically takes one of three forms: gifts, in which the titleholder, the **donor,** gives the property to another, the **donee,** without an exchange of consideration (for free); testamentary transfers, in which title is transferred pursuant to the titleholder's will or by operation of law on the titleholder's death; and by contract, the general bargain and sale exchange of property.

A detailed discussion of the law surrounding testamentary transfers is beyond the scope of this text, and a discussion of the law of gifts appears in the last chapter of this book. This chapter concentrates on the process involved in the sale of real property. The process of effectuating a sale of realty generally follows a simple four-step format:

1. The parties to the sale enter into a contract for the sale of the property that contains certain **warranties,** or guarantees, with respect to the nature of the interest being transferred.

2. After the contract is executed, the buyer checks the seller's title to the property and demands that any defects in the title (see below) be cured prior to the closing date. Also, during this period the buyer will enter into a mortgage agreement with a bank or financial institution if financing will be necessary to complete the purchase.

3. On the **closing date,** title passes from the seller to the buyer by the delivery to the buyer of a validly executed deed. The delivery of the valid deed extinguishes any contract rights that may have existed between the parties, and all legal rights of the buyer and seller are now based on the provisions of the deed.

4. The buyer records the deed in the county recorder's office in the county in which the property is located in order to protect his or her title against any subsequent transfer of the title by the former owner (seller).

This chapter explores each of these steps in the sale of realty in detail.

Contracts for the Sale of Realty

Land Sales Contracts

Pursuant to the Statute of Frauds, in order to be enforceable in a court of law, all contracts for the sale of an interest in realty must be in writing. This provision of the Statute of Frauds may also apply to the lease of property as well (see Chapter 7). To meet this statutory requirement, the document must

1. be an actual writing;
2. be signed by the party who is to be charged, i.e., the party against whom the document is attempting to be enforced; and
3. contain all of the essential terms of the agreement, including the parties to the contract, a legally sufficient description of the property being transferred, and the purchase price.

EXAMPLE:

A father wishes to sell his home to his son and daughter-in-law. To meet the provisions of the Statute of Frauds, the father drafts a contract in which he identifies himself as the seller and the son and daughter-in-law as the buyers; specifies the purchase price; and identifies the property by the description that appears in his deed to the land. This document contains sufficient information to make it enforceable under the Statute of Frauds.

A court may enforce a contract for the sale of real estate that is not in writing or sufficiently detailed if the parties to the agreement have completely or partially performed their obligations, such as paying the purchase price, living on the property for a significant period of time, or making substantial improvements on the land.

 EXAMPLE:

A father decides to sell his farm to his son. The father and son do not sign any contract, but the son takes possession of the land, farms the property for over five years, pays all property taxes on the land, makes payments to the father as part of the oral purchase agreement, and makes substantial improvements to the house and farm buildings. After five years the father decides to sell the farm to a third party. In this instance, based on the son's performance, the court would probably enforce the oral agreement between the father and son.

In addition to the provisions of the Statute of Frauds, a contract for the sale of realty must meet all of the requirements of every valid contract:

1. There must be a valid **offer,** which is defined as a proposal by one party, the **offeror,** to another to enter into a valid contract. The offer must contain all of the essential terms of what will be the contract—parties, price, description of the land, and so forth.
2. The person to whom the offer was made, the **offeree,** must agree to all of the terms of the proposal as specified by the offeror. An offeree may not vary any of the essential terms of the offer.
3. The agreement must be supported by legally sufficient **consideration.** Consideration is generally defined as a benefit conferred or a detriment incurred at the request of the other party. For contracts for the sale of realty, the consideration is the land and the purchase price. To have a valid contract, both parties must give and receive something of value (the land and the money).
4. The parties must actually intend to enter into the agreement. A presumed contract will fail if it can be demonstrated that one or another of the parties was forced into entering into the agreement, was mistaken as to the provisions of the agreement, or any other factor can be demonstrated that indicates a lack of intent to contract.
5. The parties must have **contractual capacity,** which is the legal ability to enter into a contract. Generally, this means that they must have attained the age deemed by the state statute to be a legally sufficient age to contract (18 years of age is considered to be legally sufficient in every state, but many jurisdictions provide for younger persons to enter into certain types of contracts—the provisions of each state statute must be individually analyzed). Also the person must have the mental ability to understand the nature of the agreement.
6. Finally, the contract provisions may not violate any law.

The moment at which the contract comes into effect is crucial in determining the parties' rights.

First, once the contract exists, if either side breaches the contract — fails to fulfill his or her contractual obligations — the other side is entitled to certain remedies in court. The non-breaching party may be entitled to **damages,** a monetary award based on the degree of financial injury the non-breaching party has suffered based on the breach, or the non-breaching party may be entitled to **specific performance,** a non-monetary remedy available pursuant to the court's equitable powers. Specific performance is generally only permitted for unique property, and all land, under the law, is considered to be unique. Therefore, the non-breaching party may be able to have the court order the breaching party to purchase or convey the realty in question.

Second, once the contract is validly formed, the risk of loss of the property may be transferred. In the United States there are two theories concerning the risk of loss or destruction of real property. The first is known as the **doctrine of equitable conversion.** Under this concept, once the contract is signed the buyer is considered to be the owner of the realty, and the seller is considered only to have the right to receive the purchase price. Consequently, if the property is damaged or destroyed after the contract is signed (but before title passes — see below) the resultant loss may be borne by the buyer. The second theory, more recently adopted, is called the **Vendor and Purchaser Risk Act.** Pursuant to this theory, the risk of loss remains with the seller until the buyer takes actual possession of the property and makes some improvement to the realty. Each state's statute must be examined to determine which theory is prevalent in a particular jurisdiction.

 EXAMPLE:

Buyer and seller enter into a valid contract for the sale of Blackacre. The seller remains in possession of the property until the closing date, which is set for six weeks after the contract is signed. Two weeks after the signing, a hurricane totally destroys Blackacre. If the jurisdiction follows the doctrine of equitable conversion, the risk was on the buyer and the seller has the right to receive the complete purchase price for the property. Conversely, if the jurisdiction has adopted the Vendor and Purchaser Risk Act, the risk remained with the seller and the buyer may either avoid the contract or demand a reduction of the purchase price to reflect the destruction of Blackacre.

The typical contract for the sale of real estate usually contains the following specific provisions in addition to the foregoing general contract requirements (see Exhibit 4.3 at the end of this chapter):

(a) *The parties:* The parties to the contract must be named, including their addresses and indicating the legal titles by which they are making the purchase and sale, such as the officer of a corporation, a partner, and so forth.

(b) *Consideration:* The contract must recite the consideration for the agreement—the purchase price, including any method of payment that will be made, such as an **installment sale** in which the purchase price is to be paid over a specified number of years. The recitation of the consideration should also include any and all financing provisions that have been made with respect to the sale of the property (see below). The consideration should also detail the description of the property. See Exhibit 4.1. Real property is described according to several methods:

   (i) **Plat description:** This method of land description is based on a **survey**, which is a written evaluation and description of real property. The plat indicates the dimensions and boundaries of the property, and is often used in a description of planned subdivisions. The plat will include the following information:
   • the state, county, and district in which the property is located,

---

Exhibit 4.1: Real Property Description

ALL that certain lot or piece of ground situated in the City of Pittsburgh, County of Allegheny, and Commonwealth of Pennsylvania, bounded and described as follows, to wit:

BEGINNING at a point on the Westerly line of South Graham (formerly Graham) Street distant 371.961 feet Northerly from the intersection of the Westerly line of South Graham Street and the Northerly line of Baum Boulevard as formerly located; thence along said line of South Graham Street in a Northeasterly direction, 40.00 feet to a point; thence extending back in a Northwesterly direction a distance of 150.00 feet to the Easterly line of Vintage Way; thence Southerly by said line of Vintage Way and parallel with South Graham Street, a distance of 40 feet to a point; thence in a Southeasterly direction and preserving the same width throughout of 40.00 feet, a distance of 150 feet to South Graham Street, at the place of beginning.

HAVING erected thereon a residential dwelling being municipally known and numbered as 432 South Graham Street.

BEING FURTHER DESIGNATED as Block & Lot 51-G-255 in the Deed Registry Office of Allegheny County, Pennsylvania.

BEING the same property which Susan E. Carr, unmarried by her deed dated October 15, 1993 and recorded in the Recorder's Office of Allegheny County, Pennsylvania, in Deed Book Volume 9205, Page 104, granted and conveyed unto Edward J. Petrick, Jr., unmarried, the grantor herein.

- the subdivision name and lot, block, and unit name; and
- a reference to the **plat book** that appears in the county recorder's office.

(ii)   **Metes and bounds description:** This method indicates the area following a course from a specified starting point, usually a natural or artificial focal point such as a monument, and then follows a course so many feet or yards to another point in a given direction. Eventually the course returns to the starting point to create an enclosed area, which is the property in question.

(iii) **Rectangular survey description:** The method of dividing land into rectangular lots was established in 1785 and is used by approximately 30 states. The system is based on lots formed by the intersection of hypothetical lines: the **principal meridians,** which are north-south lines, and **base lines,** which run horizontally east-west. In this fashion the states that use this method have divided up the land into specified rectangular quadrants.

(c) *Title:* The agreement should specify the exact nature of the title the seller possesses. In order for the property to be salable, the seller is expected to provide the buyer with a **marketable title.** A marketable title is one that gives the buyer title to the property free from all **encumbrances.** Encumbrances are any defects in the chain of title that could potentially cause a lawsuit over the right to the property. The most commonly encountered encumbrances are:

(i)   **Liens,** which are creditors' claims on the property to satisfy debts. Liens may take the form of government liens for nonpayment of taxes, **mechanics' liens** for work performed on the property, or a general lien imposed by the court in order to satisfy claims of general creditors of the titleholder.

 EXAMPLE:

A homeowner hires a contractor to construct an addition to her house. The homeowner pays the contractor a portion of the total price when the work begins, but fails to pay the contractor the balance due when the work is completed. The homeowner has no valid complaint with respect to the quality of the work performed by the contractor. Automatically, under the common law, the contractor has a mechanic's lien on the property for the balance of the payment owed to him.

EXAMPLE:

A property owner fails to pay his real estate taxes on some undeveloped property he is holding as an investment. The government imposes a tax lien on the property.

EXAMPLE:

A property owner is found liable, by a competent court, of having severely injured a woman by failing to observe the ordinary standard of care while driving his car. The woman is awarded a large judgment by the court, but the property owner refuses to pay. The injured woman may be able to have a lien imposed on the property to satisfy the judicially imposed debt of the property owner.

Liens are generally recorded on the title to the property at the county recorder's office and represent a claim on the property.

(ii)   Mortgages, which are a special category of security interest held by a person who extends financing for the purchase of realty. Mortgages are discussed in detail later in this chapter.

(iii)   **Clouds on title,** which are any breaks in the chain of title that could give rise to a lawsuit with respect to ownership of the property. Titles and transfers of title should be recorded in the county recorder's office, but occasionally such recording is neglected, or a grantor may attempt to pass title to several persons, all of whom claim ownership. The specifics of recording title are discussed later in this chapter.

Any potential claim or challenge to title renders the title unmarketable. However, the seller is only required to provide a marketable title at the closing (see below), so any encumbrance that is in fact cured by the closing does not render the title unmarketable. Furthermore, a purchaser may be willing, under the contract, to purchase an **insurable title,** one in which the title is not totally clear but which is capable of having insurance issued to cover any potential claim. If a purchaser is willing to accept anything less than a fully marketable title, the contract for sale must specify which encumbrances the buyer is willing to accept.

(d) *Closing.* The *closing,* or **settlement,** is the date on which all parties to the sale and purchase of the land agree to perform all of their contractual obligations. The sales contract should specify the date, place, and time of the closing. If no closing date is indicated in the contract, most courts will impose a closing date "within a reasonable time" from the date of the execution of the contract.

At the closing the seller is typically required to present the following:

(i)   a deed to the property that is in a form that can be recorded at the country recorder's office, specifying the title that is to be acquired by the buyer;

(ii) a **closing statement** that sets forth any adjustments to the costs of the purchase;

(iii) a certified rent roll if the property in question is leased, including a letter sent to the tenants indicating the change in ownership;

(iv) all permits, certificates of occupancy, and licenses issued to the property by government agencies, securing the use and habitability of the property;

(v)   an affidavit that the seller knows of no proceeding or threatened proceeding against the property;

(vi) plans of any improvements designed for the property;

(vii) all keys to the property; and

(viii) all other documents that the seller would reasonably suppose would be necessary for the purchaser as the new titleholder of the property.

The buyer is required to present the following at the closing:

(i)   an **assumption agreement** whereby the buyer assumes all liabilities on the property and agrees to perform all current obligations of the seller with respect to the property;

(ii) a copy of the *closing statement;* and

(iii) the purchase price or the portion of the purchase price that the parties have agreed is to be paid at the closing.

(e) *Transfer of possession.* The sales contract should specify the date on which possession of the property passes from the seller to the buyer. Usually this occurs at the closing, but may be advanced or postponed depending on the wishes of the parties.

EXAMPLE:

The contract for the sale of a house indicates the closing date to be October 1. The buyer would like to take possession on September 15 to settle in, and the seller agrees to vacate the property by midnight on September 14. The agreement with respect to the transfer of possession should appear in the contract.

(f) *Risk of loss.* As discussed above, depending on the jurisdiction, the shifting of the risk of loss or damage to the property may pass from the seller to the buyer at the date of the contract or when possession actually transfers. However, the parties may specify who bears the risk for various types of damage to the property, as well as who will be responsible for maintaining insurance on the property.

(g) *Earnest money.* **Earnest money,** sometimes referred to as the **deposit** or the **down payment,** is the portion of the full purchase price the buyer gives at the time of the signing of the sales contract. Earnest money may be given credit as a partial payment or as a penalty should the buyer default, or back out, of the contract. The sales contract should specify exactly what the earnest money represents, and the funds should be placed in a trust, or **escrow,** account until the sale is consummated. Note that this trust account does not belong to either party until the obligations of the contract have been fulfilled. Furthermore, the contract should indicate who will be entitled to any interest earned on the funds in the account until the funds are finally transferred.

(h) *Rights of the broker.* If the parties utilize the services of a real estate broker, the contract should identify the rights of the broker with respect to a commission, including when the commission is to be paid and by whom. A **commission** is the fee the broker earns for his or her services.

Contracts with real estate brokers with respect to their commissions, known as **listing agreements,** fall into several categories:

(i) **Open listing:** With this type of agreement the property owner engages several brokers to help sell the property, and any commission goes to the one who completes the sale.

(ii) **Exclusive listing:** In this type of agreement the property owner only hires one broker, but retains the right to sell the property himself. If the owner sells the property, the broker receives no commission.

(iii) **Exclusive right to sell:** With this agreement the broker is the only one who may sell the property, and she receives a commission if anyone, including the owner, consummates the sale.

See Exhibit 4.2.

(i) *Assignments.* An **assignment** is the transfer of contractual rights. Generally, most contracts are freely assignable, or transferable, provided that the assignment does not unduly burden the other party to the contract, or the contract was not one that was based on the personal confidence of the transferring party. Such types of confidences in a real estate contract would arise when financing is an issue and one party is lending the other the funds to acquire the property. This type of agreement is based on the personal creditworthiness of the borrower, so the contract is usually nonassignable unless the lending party agrees. Furthermore, the parties to a contract may specify that the contract is or is not assignable, and if it is assignable, what conditions, if any, must be met prior to the transfer.

Exhibit 4.2: Real Estate Listing Agreement

T 486—Real Estate Listing Agreement: Non-exclusive. 11-78   JULIUS BLUMBERG, INC.,
                                                                                                 PUBLISHER, NYC 10013

REAL ESTATE LISTING AGREEMENT

BROKER:	OWNER:	PREMISES:
Address		
	Address	
Telephone No.		
Broker is Licensed in the State of	Telephone No.	Date:
Commission:		

Owner hereby lists the above Premises with Broker for sale in accordance with the information, terms and conditions set forth above and following:

Licensed broker 1. Broker is a licensed real estate broker under the laws of the state set forth above.

When Commissions earned 2. Broker shall not earn the Commission unless:

    a) a contract of sale has been signed by the Owner and a purchaser upon terms acceptable to the Owner in the Owner's sole judgment

    b) the contract was brought about through the Broker's efforts

    c) the deed conveying title is delivered in accordance with the contract and the full purchase price is paid.

Failure to close title 3. If a contract of sale has been signed by Owner and a purchaser and title does not close,

    a) because owner does not have good title conveyable in accordance with the contract, broker is not entitled to the Commission.

    b) Broker is not entitled to the Commission unless Owner intentionally defaulted.

    c) because purchaser defaults, Owner is not required to enforce purchaser's obligations and Broker is not entitled to the Commission.

Price change 4. The purchase price at which the Premises are listed with Broker may be changed by Owner without liability to Broker. Owner is not liable to Broker for any expenses, fees or disbursements paid or incurred by Broker in connection with Broker's efforts to sell the Premises.

Commission Payable 5. If earned, the Commission payable to Broker, shall be paid upon the delivery of the deed.

Termination, withdrawal 6. Owner may terminate this agreement or withdraw the Premises from sale at any time by either oral or written notice to Broker without liability.

Non-exclusive 7. Owner may list Premises with other Brokers

Margin headings 8. The margin headings are for convenience only.

This agreement contains all the terms and conditions of the listing and shall not be changed except by a written agreement signed by both Owner and Broker.

This agreement has been signed by Broker and Owner on the date set forth above.

Broker: ....   Owner:

By ....

                                                      ....

EXAMPLE:

"Purchaser shall have the right to assign this agreement provided that the Seller be given 30 days' prior written notice and agrees to the assignment in writing within 10 days of the transfer. Seller may withhold agreement of the assignment if the Seller, in his sole discretion, believes the assignee to lack sufficient financial resources to conclude the sale."

(j) *Warranties.* A warranty is a statement by a party to a contract in which the party guarantees certain aspects of the agreement. If the party making the warranty fails to fulfill its obligations, the injured party may sue for a breach of the warranty. If the warranty goes to the heart of the contract, a breach of the warranty may be considered a breach of the entire contract.

The typical warranties given by a seller are:
- the seller has title to the property equal to the title being conveyed
- the seller will fulfill all contractual obligations
- the seller has the right to enter into the contract
- there are no claims on the property
- the seller will cause no change in the zoning of the property
- the seller knows of no governmental action against the property
- utilities are available to the property
- the property is accessible by public roads
- the property contains a minimum number of acres or square feet

The typical warranties given by the purchaser are:
- the purchaser has the right to enter into the contract
- the purchaser can finance the purchase
- the purchaser will perform all contractual obligations
- there are no actions pending against the purchaser that will affect the purchaser's ability to perform the contract obligations
- the purchaser will do nothing that diminishes the seller's title prior to the closing

(k) *Time is of the essence clause.* Many contracts specify that **time is of the essence,** meaning that all obligations must be fulfilled on the dates and times specified in the agreement or the contract will be deemed breached, thereby relieving the other party from all further obligations. If such a clause does not appear in the contract, the courts usually infer "reasonable time" for the parties to perform.

(l) *Conditions.* A contractual **condition** is a fact or event, the occurrence or nonoccurrence of which creates or extinguishes an absolute duty to perform. What this means is that the parties are expected to fulfill their contractual obligations *unless* the fact or event specified occurs. Many real estate contracts include a **condition precedent** with respect to financing the sale. A condition precedent is a fact or event that must occur before the party must perform a contractual obligation. In this instance, the condition may specify that the purchaser's obligation to buy is conditioned upon his obtaining financing for the purchase within a specified number of days. If the buyer makes a reasonable effort to secure financing and fails to obtain the necessary funds, the buyer will no longer be obligated to purchase the property.

(m) *Notice.* The contract should specify the manner in which the parties to the agreement wish to receive notice of the various events that are noted in the contract. Typically such notice mandates written notice be posted by certified mail to an address indicated in the contract. All parties to the contract must give all required written notice in the manner specified in the agreement.

(n) *Other provisions.* Real estate contracts, like all contracts, contain certain **boilerplate,** or standard, formalized provisions with respect to the definitions of the terms used in the agreement, for example, which state's law is to apply to its interpretation, arbitration provisions, and so forth. These clauses appear in all contracts and are not specifically related to real property transactions.

(o) *Execution.* The term **execution** refers to the signing of the agreement. The parties should sign according to their position, for example, as an individual, an officer of a corporation, a partner for the partnership, and so forth. The contract does not need to be notarized or witnessed, and the contract itself is generally not recorded with the county recorder's office. After the closing, the deed (see below) is the document that will be used to record the transfer of the title from the seller to the buyer.

After the contract for the sale of the property is executed, the buyer will usually conduct a **title search** to make sure that the seller's title is clear and capable of being transferred subject to the contract. If a cloud on the title appears that the seller does not cure by the closing, the purchaser may avoid the sale or may acquire **title insurance** to protect against a claim by a party asserting title to all or part of the property. The methods for recording titles will be discussed below.

See Exhibits 4.3 and 4.4 at the end of this chapter for examples of a Contract of Sale and a Rider to a Residential Contract of Sale.

Deeds

A **deed** is a document that is used to transfer title to real property. To be valid, the deed must:

1. be in writing;
2. be signed by the grantor;
3. reasonably identify the parties; and
4. describe the land in question in a legally sufficient manner (see above).

If the deed neglects to name the **grantee,** the person who is acquiring the title, the court will assume that the person in possession of the deed is the grantee. However, if the land is not sufficiently described, the deed is considered to be incomplete. The property will be considered sufficiently described, even if not in accordance with its legal description as it appears in the county recorder's office, if it gives sufficient information so that a reasonable person could identify the property. The court will permit oral evidence to complete the description of the land if the description given provides a reasonable lead to the land in question, but cannot accept oral evidence if the overall description is totally inadequate.

EXAMPLE:

A man owns three tracts of land in the same county. In the deed he indicates that he is transferring title to the property he refers to as Honeywell Cottage. The court will permit oral testimony to indicate which of the three parcels the grantor calls "Honeywell Cottage" because the description in the deed is sufficient to provide a lead as to which property is meant.

In order to transfer the title, the deed must be delivered to the grantee. This delivery must indicate a present intention on the part of the grantor to pass the title, even if the right of possession to the property is delayed. This delivery requirement can be satisfied in several ways:

(a) a manual delivery to the grantee or the grantee's agent. Note that a delivery to the grantor's agent with instructions to pass the deed to the grantee does not constitute delivery to the grantee. The delivery must be a direct transfer to the grantee's control.

EXAMPLE:

A woman intends to give some property she owns to her niece. She executes a deed and gives the deed to her lawyer, telling the lawyer to send the deed to the niece. Because the lawyer is the woman's agent, no delivery has yet taken place. When the lawyer gives the deed to the niece, or the niece's lawyer, the delivery is then complete.

(b) a recording of the deed in the county recorder's office; or
(c) a notarized statement by the grantor indicating the intention to transfer the title.

Once a deed has been delivered, the grantor cannot revoke the deed unless the transfer was subject to a condition.

 EXAMPLE:

A man gives the deed to his house to his son, telling the son that the property will be his (the son's) on the man's death. The man's death is a condition to the transfer and so the man may revoke the deed prior to his death.

Finally, to complete the transfer, the grantee must accept the deed; most courts assume acceptance unless the grantee indicates a rejection of the property.

There are three types of deeds used to convey title to property: the general warranty deed, the special warranty deed, and the quitclaim deed. The differences between these types of deed concern the warranties, known as **covenants,** that they contain.

See Exhibit 4.5 at the end of this chapter for an example of a deed.

General Warranty Deed

The general warranty deed usually includes the following covenants, referred to as the **common law covenants:**

1. **Covenant of seizin:** This covenant states that the grantor has the title to the property he or she is purporting to convey and also has possession of the property at the time of the conveyance.
2. **Covenant of right to convey:** This covenant specifies that the grantor has the legal authority to convey the title. In most instances having the title to the property will satisfy this covenant.
3. **Covenant against encumbrances:** In this covenant the grantor warrants against any liens, mortgages, or clouds on title on the property (see above).

These three preceding covenants are breached, if at all, at the time of the closing.

4. **Covenant of quiet enjoyment:** This covenant states that the grantor warrants that the grantee will not have his or her possession of the property disturbed by anyone with a lawful claim to the

property. Note that this does not protect the grantee from specious lawsuits filed by persons who have no lawful claim to the property.

5. **Covenant of warranty:** In this covenant the grantor agrees to defend the grantee against claims to the property made by third persons, and to reimburse the grantee for any loss that the grantee may suffer from claims by persons with a superior title. Note that the covenant for quiet enjoyment concerns possession, whereas this covenant concerns title.

6. **Covenant of further assurances:** In this covenant the grantor agrees to do all things necessary to perfect title in the grantee should any claim against title occur in the future. The distinction between the covenant of warranty and the covenant of further assurances is one of degree; with the former the grantor will protect the grantee from loss, with the latter the grantor will go further and do all things necessary to establish lawful title in the grantee. This last covenant does not form a part of what is called the **usual covenants** and is often deleted, but is always included if the deed calls for the "common law covenants."

Special Warranty Deed

This deed is created by state statute and protects the grantee against two specific acts of the grantor:

1. that the grantor has not conveyed the property to anyone other than the grantee; and
2. that the property is free from any encumbrances created by the grantor.

This type of deed protects the grantee only from these two specific acts, and only if they were caused by the grantor herself. The scope of this type of deed is more limited than the general warranty deed.

Quitclaim Deed

This deed simply conveys to the grantee whatever title the grantor has; no representations are made with respect to the nature of that title or interest. It contains absolutely no covenants whatsoever, and the grantee acquires whatever title that grantor has, which could be none at all.

 EXAMPLE:

A man convinces two foreign tourists in New York City to purchase the Brooklyn Bridge from him. He executes a quitclaim deed in their favor, and they pay him a sum of money. When they discover that he had no title to the bridge at all, the couple has no claim against the man for breach of warranty, because he has conveyed exactly the interest he possessed. (Note that the couple may institute other proceedings against the man not based on property law.)

The rights of the grantee and the grantor are determined by the nature of the covenants in the deed conveying the property. However, if a person conveys a title he or she does not possess, but then subsequently acquires that title, the law, under a doctrine known as **estoppel by deed,** will inure that title to the benefit of the grantee of the deed (not for a quitclaim deed, however). See Exhibit 4.6 at the end of this chapter for an example of a quitclaim deed.

EXAMPLE:

A woman purports, by general warranty deed, to sell some property to a third person. The buyer is unaware that the property in question is owned by the woman's father, and the woman only resides on the land. Several months later the woman's father dies and she inherits the property. Pursuant to the doctrine of estoppel by deed, the title now vests in the purchaser.

Mortgages

A **mortgage** is a security interest given by a debtor to his or her creditor to guarantee the repayment of a loan. Simply put, if the person who is purchasing the property requires financing, he or she will obtain a loan from an individual or institution who then becomes the buyer's creditor. To secure that loan, which is evidenced by a written document referred to as a **bond** or a **note,** the lender will require the borrower to provide another document, the mortgage, that gives the lender the right to attach specified property (the realty) to satisfy the debt should the borrower default on the loan. The borrower/debtor is referred to as the **mortgagor,** the one who gives the security interest, and the lender/creditor is referred to as the **mortgagee.**

EXAMPLE:

A young couple wants to purchase their first home but cannot pay the complete purchase price. To acquire the property, the couple arrange for a loan from their bank. To ensure that the bank will not lose the money loaned, the bank insists that the couple give it a mortgage on the house. Should the couple default on the loan, the bank as the mortgagee will have the right to attach the house to satisfy the outstanding debt.

Because the mortgage represents an interest in land, pursuant to the Statute of Frauds the mortgage must be in writing in order to be enforceable. However, certain transactions that do not meet this requirement may still be enforced under a concept known as an **equitable mortgage.** This doctrine arises whenever a person acquires a deed to property under circumstances in which the apparent intention is to transfer a deed as a security interest rather than as a title. If this situation can be proved, a court may find, under its equitable jurisdiction, that the person in possession of the deed does not have title to the property but merely a security interest in the land.

 EXAMPLE:

A man needs money to pay for his daughter's college education. He is the sole owner of a house he inherited from his father. The man approaches a friend for a loan, and the friend agrees, provided that the man transfers the deed to his house to him until the loan is repaid. The father gives the man the deed, and the friend loans the money. When the loan is repaid, the "friend" claims that the money was intended as a sale of the house, not a loan. Under these circumstances, the court may find that the friend has only an equitable mortgage.

Note that some jurisdictions require some other documentary evidence in addition to the deed to meet the requirements of an equitable mortgage.

A mortgage may be used as a security interest not only for the purchase of realty, but also for improvements on the property and to secure a preexisting obligation.

Any transferable interest in real property may be mortgaged; however, the mortgagor is incapable of mortgaging any interest greater than the one he or she possesses. Consequently if a husband who holds title to property as a tenant by the entirety mortgages his interest, the mortgagee may only attach the property if the wife joins in the mortgage or the wife predeceases the husband, thereby creating a tenancy in severalty in the surviving spouse (see Chapter 1).

A legal axiom holds that the mortgage follows the note. In other words, if the underlying debt obligation is found invalid, so is the mortgage that attaches to it. The validity of the mortgage is controlled by the validity of the underlying note.

 EXAMPLE:

A woman is defrauded into signing a loan agreement and gives a mortgage to secure the debt. If the court deems that the loan agreement is void because of the fraud, the mortgage automatically becomes void as well.

The mortgagor is required to inform and obtain approval from the mortgagee before any changes are made to the subject property because such changes affect the mortgagee's interest. Most mortgages require the mortgagor to obtain **mortgage insurance** to provide funds should the mortgagor be found in default. Also, many mortgage agreements provide for **acceleration payments** if the mortgagor does anything to impinge on the mortgagee's rights, such as changing the nature of the property or defaulting, thereby making the remainder of the unpaid debt immediately due.

 EXAMPLE:

A couple has acquired a house by borrowing money from the bank to which they have executed a mortgage. The mortgage includes an acceleration provision in case the couple default on the note or make substantial changes to the nature of the property without first obtaining the bank's consent. Ten years later the couple decide to demolish the freestanding garage on the property. If they do so without the bank's consent they may be obligated to repay the outstanding debt at once, because the property is now arguably less valuable (see the discussion on waste in Chapter 2).

If the mortgagor transfers the property, the transferee acquires the property either subject to the mortgage or by assuming the mortgage. A transfer **subject to the mortgage** means that the transferor remains principally liable on the debt, and the property can be attached if the transferor defaults. This could mean that the transferee will lose the property if the transferor fails to discharge the debt to the mortgagee.

A transfer in which the transferee **assumes the mortgage** means that the transferee now becomes liable for the underlying debt, and the transferor will only be liable secondarily (if the transferee defaults). To effectuate an assumption of the mortgage:

1. there must be a writing stating that the transferee intends to assume the mortgage; and
2. there must be a document that indicates the assumption of the mortgage.

A transferee who acquires property as an inheritance acquires the property subject to the mortgage, meaning that the estate of the deceased mortgagor is obligated for the debt, not the heir.

 EXAMPLE:

A couple has lived in a small house for three years and are now planning a family and want to purchase a larger home. They sell the house to an elderly woman who wants a small home.

The woman agrees to assume the mortgage so that she can buy the property for a lower purchase price, the difference being made up by the mortgage. One year later the woman dies and the house is willed to her granddaughter. The woman's estate must discharge the mortgage. If the estate assets are insufficient, the mortgagee may be able to attach the house to satisfy the obligation, and the granddaughter will inherit nothing. Furthermore, the original young couple may be liable for any money still outstanding after the house is sold by the mortgagee.

If the mortgagor defaults, the mortgagee is permitted the following remedies:

1. Action in default — the mortgagee can sue the mortgagor in a court of law for the amount of the loan that is outstanding.
2. **Judicial foreclosure** — the mortgagee can request the court to order a **foreclosure** sale of the property in which the property is attached and sold at public auction. If the proceeds of the resulting sale exceed the amount of the debt, the excess is given to the mortgagor; if the proceeds of the sale are insufficient to satisfy the debt, the mortgagee may then proceed against the mortgagor in an action for debt for the difference.
3. **Foreclosure by advertisement** — several jurisdictions, such as New York, permit the mortgagee, provided that such right appears in the mortgage, to foreclose on the property without court order if the mortgagee places a notice of the foreclosure sale for a statutory period of time.

Note that the mortgagee may not proceed in an action in debt and a foreclosure simultaneously. The mortgagee must select which cause of action to pursue first, and if the results of that action are insufficient to satisfy the note, the mortgagee may then seek the alternative remedy.

A mortgagor may be able to stop or redeem a foreclosure under a concept known as **redemption.** Redemption refers to the mortgagor's payment of the debt so as to be able to reclaim title to the property. There are two types of redemption procedures:

1. **Redemption in equity** — at any time prior to the foreclosure sale the mortgagor may redeem the property by satisfying the debt. Virtually every jurisdiction permits this type of redemption.
2. **Statutory redemption** — several jurisdictions also permit a mortgagor to redeem the property within a statutory period of time after the foreclosure sale by satisfying the underlying debt. Note that this form of redemption creates uncertainty for the purchaser of the property in the foreclosure sale, and so is generally not favored.

Mortgages are an important facet of real estate conveyancing because few people are able to purchase property without some form of financing.

The mortgage becomes an important aspect of the closing as well (see Chapter 5).

Mortgages, like deeds, are recorded with the county recorder's office to protect the mortgagee, and mortgages form an encumbrance on the property. In many instances, property owners will refinance their property, thereby creating several mortgages on the same realty. The impact of multiple mortgages on the mortgagee is determined by the nature of the priorities afforded under the particular state law (see below).

See Exhibit 4.7 at the end of this chapter for an example of a Uniform Residential Loan Application.

Sub-prime Mortgages and the Credit Crunch

No discussion of mortgages would be complete without some reference to the current national economic situation.

Recent events have focused attention on what are referred to as sub-prime mortgages and their effect on overall credit. Simply stated, a **sub-prime mortgage** is a loan secured by a mortgage given by a financial institution to a borrower who is considered to be a poor credit risk. Interest rates on mortgage loans are based on the **prime rate**, which is the interest rate that banks charge to their best, i.e., most credit-worthy, customers. When a bank or other financial institution agrees to lend money to a person who is considered to be a credit risk, in order to minimize that risk, the lender loans the funds at a higher interest rate than it would to its credit-worthy borrowers.

In most of the instances in which mortgage loans were given to sub-prime borrowers, in order to entice borrowers, the lender structured the loan with an **adjustable rate mortgage (ARM),** by which the interest payments on the loan were fairly low for the first few years. However, after a short period of time, generally three to five years, the interest rate on the loan ballooned up to a fairly high percentage. Because the borrower was a high risk mortgagor, in most instances he or she could not afford the loan once the interest rate increased. As a consequence, many homes went into the foreclosure proceedings discussed above. However, the economic impact was not limited to the particular lender and borrower.

In order to reduce the potential risk of the default of the sub-prime borrower, many financial institutions used these mortgage-backed loans to create a **structured finance transaction,** also referred to as the **securitization of receivables,** whereby the financial institution would sell shares in the mortgages to investors, thereby transferring the risk of default to the investors. This process created a secondary market in mortgages as investment securities for persons not involved in the actual loan. Because of the potential high rate of return, based on the high interest rate of these mortgages, many corporations and pension funds invested in these securities.

When the borrower defaulted on the mortgage loan, not only did the borrower face losing his or her home, but the lender lost the capital it loaned the borrower as well as the cash flow from the interest payments, and the investors in the structured finance transaction lost their investment and cash flow as well. The result of these defaults has been considered one of the main factors causing the economic decline of the past few years.

Priorities and Recording Statutes

The concept of "priority" refers to the right afforded to persons each of whom has acquired an interest in realty. When multiple persons all assert claims to the same property the law and the courts must devise a system whereby the divergent rights can be satisfied and in which order. To this end, every jurisdiction has enacted **recording acts** that establish a chain of priority with respect to claims against property. The recording acts provide public notice to all persons asserting an interest in realty as to who may have a right to the property.

There are three types of recording acts in effect, and the specifics of each state's statutes must be individually analyzed. The three methods to establish priority are:

1. **Notice:** Under this type of recording statute, a subsequent bona fide purchaser for value of the property will prevail over an earlier grantee who fails to record his or her interest. Because the subsequent purchaser had no actual or constructive notice of any other interest in the property at the time of the creation of the interest, he or she will prevail.

 EXAMPLE:

A man sells some property to Buyer One on August 15, but Buyer One does not record the transaction at the county recorder's office. On August 20 the man sells the same property to Buyer Two, who immediately records the transaction. In a lawsuit to determine title, Buyer Two will prevail in a notice state because he had no notice of the sale to Buyer One at the time of his purchase. Note, however, if Buyer Two did not purchase the property but was given the property as a gift from the man, the title would vest in Buyer One because Buyer Two did not give value to acquire the title.

2. **Race:** In this type of jurisdiction, the first to record prevails regardless of the date of the transaction creating the interest.

EXAMPLE:

Assume that in the prior example Buyer Two knew of the sale to Buyer One but convinced the man to sell the property anyway. Buyer Two records the conveyance before Buyer One. In a pure race jurisdiction Buyer Two would prevail because his actual knowledge of the earlier conveyance is irrelevant since he recorded first. In a notice jurisdiction Buyer One would prevail.

3. **Race-notice:** Under this type of statute, the subsequent purchaser for value must record first *and* have no notice of an earlier conveyance.

EXAMPLE:

Using the parties from the previous examples, assume that Buyer Two has no notice of the sale to Buyer One. After the sale to Buyer Two, Buyer One records. The next day Buyer Two records. Buyer One prevails because Buyer Two did not record first.

In those jurisdictions that require notice to obtain a priority, the transferee must perform a title search to determine whether an earlier claim has been recorded. A title search is merely the process of examining the record books for the subject property at the county recorder's office.

Record offices use one of two methods to record titles. The first method is referred to as a **tract index** or **block and lot index,** in which the searcher looks at the record pages that are indexed by the physical description of the land (see above). The other method utilized by record offices is the **grantor-grantee index** in which the search is conducted by the names of the parties, looking first for the immediate transferor as a grantee, then his or her grantor as grantee, and so on back in the chain of title.

Once a claim is recorded, it protects the claimant from subsequent purchasers or claimants because recording provides notice. Consequently, to protect the rights of the parties, all interests in realty should be recorded in the county recorder's office, which is the official office for recording interests in realty.

Practical Tips

- The legal professional must be accurate and specific in creating a deed.

- Be careful in the description of the property — reference to prior deeds is useful.
- If the seller is the representative of an estate, the representative's name and address must appear on the documents, including his or her authority to act for the estate.
- Check whether the recorder's office requires a cover sheet.
- In many counties, personal checks are not permitted for filing fees — only certified or attorney checks will be allowed.
- Review the lien law of the particular jurisdiction to make sure all requirements for recording liens are met.
- Carefully review all mortgage documents.

Chapter Review

Conveyancing is the process whereby title to realty is transferred from one person to another. The most common method of conveyancing is by means of a sale. To effectuate a sale of realty, two documents are necessary: the contract for the sale of the property and the deed that transfers the title to the property.

All agreements that concern an interest in realty are required to be in writing to be enforceable pursuant to the Statute of Frauds. Furthermore, all contracts for the sale of real estate must meet all of the general contract law requirements to create any valid contract: offer, acceptance, consideration, capacity of the parties, legality of the subject matter, and contractual intent. In addition to these general requirements, certain provisions are specific to real estate transactions, such as the allocation of risk, the date of the closing, financing provisions, and so forth.

At the closing the seller presents to the buyer a deed that transfers the title. The nature of the deed determines the nature of the covenants, or warranties, that the grantor is making to the grantee with respect to the nature of the protection of the title being transferred. There are three types of deeds in common use: the general warranty deed that contains the common law covenants; the special warranty deed that only protects against specific acts committed by the grantor; and the quitclaim deed in which no warranties at all are given.

In order to consummate the sale, most purchasers require a loan. To secure the loan, the lender typically has the borrower give a mortgage — a security interest in the property — to the lender that gives the lender certain rights with respect to the property. The mortgage creates an encumbrance on the title, and affects the rights of all subsequent grantees.

To protect rights with respect to realty, all interests — the deed, all mortgages, and all appropriate liens — should be recorded at the county recorder's office in the county in which the property is located. This recordation puts all subsequent claimants on notice of prior rights to the land.

Ethical Concern

To complete a conveyance of real property much specific information is required. To speed up the process there may be a real temptation to provide information that may not be accurate but seems reasonable to save time and expense. Such conduct is considered to be an ethical violation as a falsification of a legal document. Take the time to check all facts that appear on a contract of sale or a deed.

Key Terms

Acceleration payment
Adjustable rate mortgage (ARM)
Assignment
Assume the mortgage
Assumption agreement
Base line
Block and lot index
Boilerplate
Bond
Condition
Condition precedent
Closing
Closing statement
Cloud on title
Commission
Common law covenants
Consideration
Contractual capacity
Conveyancing
Covenant
Covenant against encumbrances
Covenant of further assurances
Covenant of right to convey
Covenant of seizin
Covenant of quiet enjoyment
Covenant of warranty
Damages
Deed
Deposit
Doctrine of equitable conversion
Donee
Donor
Down payment
Earnest money
Encumbrance

Equitable mortgage
Equitable redemption
Escrow
Estoppel by deed
Exclusive listing
Exclusive right to sell
Execution
Foreclosure
Foreclosure by advertisement
General warranty deed
Grantee
Grantor-grantee index
Installment sale
Insurable title
Judicial foreclosure
Lien
Listing agreement
Marketable title
Mechanic's lien
Metes and bounds description
Mortgage
Mortgagee
Mortgagor
Mortgage insurance
Note
Notice
Offer
Offeree
Offeror
Open listing
Plat book
Plat description
Prime rate
Principal meridian
Quitclaim deed

Race
Race-notice
Recording act
Rectangular survey description
Redemption
Redemption in equity
Securitization of receivables
Settlement
Special warranty deed
Specific performance
Statutory redemption

Structured finance transaction
Subject to the mortgage
Sub-prime mortgage
Survey
Time is of the essence
Title insurance
Title search
Tract index
Usual covenants
Vendor and Purchaser Risk Act
Warranty

Exercises

1. Search the title to your residence at the county recorder's office.
2. Determine which type of recording act is in effect in your state.
3. Analyze the provisions of mortgage agreement to determine the type of information that will be required of the borrower.
4. Obtain a sample land sales contract and analyze its provisions.
5. Discuss the circumstances under which a person might be willing to accept a quitclaim deed. What could be done to protect this person's interest?

Situational Analysis

A real estate agent induces a couple to buy a house by stating that several famous people have owned and stayed in the house. After the sale, the couple learn that no famous person ever resided or visited the house. What, if anything, can the couple do?

Edited Cases

Many legal problems are the result of contractual conflicts. *Danyluk v. Glashow, M.D., P.C.* concerns the breach of a land sales contract, and *Stambovsky v. Ackley* discusses a real estate broker's obligation with respect to the sale of realty.

Danyluk v. Glashow, M.D., P.C.
2004 NY Slip Op 50154U; 2 Misc. 3d 1005A; 784 N.Y.S.2d 919;
2004 N.Y. Misc. LEXIS 217 (N.Y. Civ. Ct. 2004)

On October 8, 1997, Petitioner-Lessor, an individual, entered into a five-year commercial lease for a professional condominium with

Respondent-Lessee, a professional corporation. The lease contained no personal guarantee by the principal of the lessee corporation.

Paragraph 52 of the rider to the lease, the provision giving rise to the present action, states:

> PURCHASE OPTION: In the event Landlord shall elect to sell the Premises during the initial term hereof to a third-party pursuant to an offer by said third-party which offer is accepted by the Landlord, Tenant shall have the first right to match the sales price and terms as offered by said third-party. The right to purchase as granted to Tenant hereunder shall commence upon the date Landlord gives tenant notice and a summary of the material terms of such third-party offer and such right granted to Tenant hereunder shall automatically expire fifteen (15) days thereafter unless Tenant shall give Landlord timely written notice via certified return receipt mail of Tenant's intent to so match said offer in all of its terms which notice once given shall be irrevocable by Tenant.
>
> Upon the giving of such notice by Tenant, Tenant shall become unconditionally liable to Landlord for the full amount of the sales price as contained in such third-party offer and shall have thirty (30) *days after the giving of such notice within which to close the purchase of the Premises. If Tenant shall fail to close the purchase within said thirty (30) day period, Landlord may, in his sole and absolute discretion, sell the Premises to any other party upon such terms and conditions as Landlord may determine without any restriction or obligation to Tenant and Tenant shall nonetheless be liable to Landlord for a sum of money equal to the purchase price of the Premises as contained in the foregoing notice by Tenant to Landlord of Tenant's intent to match the third-party offer.*

Petitioner-Lessor decided to sell the premises and began negotiations with a third-party. On July 31, 2002, Petitioner notified Respondent of the third-party's offer in a note which stated:

> . . . *the current offer is for 540000 [sic]. The current terms are 20% down and the remainder financed at 7.75% rate over a 5-10 year period through me. Please let me know if you wish to match the offer and terms.*

On that same date, Respondent sent Petitioner a letter in response:

> *Re: NOTICE TO EXERCISE*
>
> *FIRST RIGHT TO PURCHASE*
>
> *Please be advised that the undersigned, as Tenant under a lease dated October 8, 1996, for premises at 159 East 74th Street New York, New York, does hereby exercise pursuant to Paragraph 52 of said lease, the option of first right to purchase UNIT 6 in 159 East 74th Street, New York, New York, for the amount of and upon the terms and conditions set forth in Landlord's Notice dated July 31, 2002.*
>
> *Very truly yours,*
>
> */s/*
>
> *Jonathan L. Glashow, M.D., P.C.*
>
> *by JONATHAN L. GLASHOW*

Shortly thereafter Petitioner notified Respondent of another offer that had been made for the premises of $ 545,000, but Petitioner later withdrew his request that Respondent match that purchase price, so the effect of that proposal is not relevant to these proceedings.

On September 9, 2002, Petitioner forwarded to Respondent a draft of the proposed contract of sale. The draft sales agreement provided, in pertinent part, that:

> ...*Purchaser shall execute a mortgage and a mortgage note (and such other instruments as the Seller shall reasonable require in connection therewith) pursuant to which the Purchaser shall agree to pay to the Seller the $432,000 principal borrowed together with interest thereon at the rate of SEVEN AND THREE QUARTERS PERCENT (7.75%) per annum, with amortization based on a 30-year term, with the unpaid principal balance due TEN (10) years following the closing. Such mortgage document shall provide that the purchaser shall not be permitted to repay same prior to its due date without the prior written consent of the Seller.*

The proposed contract also required Respondent's principal to guarantee the agreement personally.

In response to this proposed sales agreement, Respondent requested the name and address of the third-party offeror in order to confirm the terms that had been agreed upon by said offeror and Petitioner.

On September 25, 2002, Petitioner wrote to Respondent inquiring as to its intentions, and indicated that if the proposed sales agreement were not signed by October 7, 2002, Respondent would need to vacate the premises according to the lease provisions.

On October 3, 2002, Petitioner sent Respondent a letter dated October 2, 2002, from the third-party offeror that stated:

> *On July 31, 2002, I as an individual, offered to purchase the office condominium owned by Andrew Danyluk for $ 540,000. The terms of the offer were 20% down payment and the remainder financed through Andrew Danyluk for 10 years at a rate of 7.75% without prepayment.*

Also on October 3, 2002, Petitioner returned Respondent's rent check for that month, saying that Respondent was to vacate the premises on or before October 7, 2002 (the date on which the lease terminated), so that the premises could be re-let.

On October 9, 2002, Petitioner wrote to Respondent the following:

> *On July 31 you exercised your right to match the purchase price of an existing offer for my medical condominium. In doing so you established a contract and consequently a liability to me. As you have failed to close on the purchase of the condominium within the allotted time, your liability to me has not been eliminated.*

When Respondent failed to close on the sale or to vacate, Petitioner commenced the instant holdover proceeding against it without serving Respondent with any predicate notice. Respondent moved for summary judgment, basing its claim on the fact that it was a vendee in possession and therefore must receive a ten-day notice to quit as a predicate to commencing the summary proceeding. The court denied the motion for summary judgment because of the questions of fact and law that we must now address.

Both parties agree that Respondent exercised its right of first refusal based on the July 31, 2002, communications between them. Further, all sides agree that the "summary of the material terms of the third-party's offer" as stated in Petitioner's note of July 31, 2002, consists of:

    a)   the purchase price of $540,000,
    b)   the down payment of 20% of the purchase price,
    c)   the remainder of the purchase price to be financed by Petitioner at an interest rate of 7.75%, and
    d)   the term of a 5–10 year period.

Petitioner contends that the amortization period appearing in the proposed contract for the sale of the premises is neither a material term nor a variance from the summary of material terms appearing in his note of July 31, 2002. Petitioner stated that the third-party offeror was an individual who would be personally liable for the sale. Therefore, the requirement that Respondent's principal agree to guarantee the sale is not a material term nor an alteration of the terms that appeared in his July 31, 2002, communication. Respondent disputes both these assertions.

Respondent argues that this proceeding must be dismissed because, as a vendee in possession, it must be given a ten-day notice to quit as a predicate to commencing a holdover action against it pursuant to *section 713(9) of the Real Property Actions and Proceedings Law*. Petitioner avers that no predicate notice is necessary because when the sales contract did not go through Respondent lost its status as a vendee in possession and remained on the premises as a holdover tenant.

Discussion

The threshold question for this court is the determination of Respondent's status with respect to the subject premises. If it is a vendee in possession, it may be entitled to a predicate notice prior to instituting any summary proceeding against it. Conversely, if it is merely a tenant in possession after the natural termination of its lease no predicate notice may be required. The determining factor in arriving at the answer is the state of the contractual relationship between the parties.

The Right of First Refusal

Paragraph 52 of the lease agreement executed between the parties gave Respondent a right of first refusal to purchase the leased premises if Petitioner decided to sell the premises during the period of the leasehold and received a bona fide offer for the property from a third party.

A right of first refusal or preemptive right as distinguished from an option does not give its holder the power to compel an unwilling owner to sell; it merely requires the owner, when and if he decides to sell, to offer the property first to the party holding the preemptive right so that he may meet a third-party offer. *LIN Broadcasting Corp. v. Metromedia, Inc., 74 N.Y. 2d 54,*

542 N.E.2d 629, 544 N.Y.S. 2d 316 (1989). This right of first refusal binds the owner who wishes to sell his property not to do so without giving the holder of the right the opportunity to purchase such property. *Krieger v. Cornelius, 259 A.D.2d 10, 697 N.Y.S. 2d 766 (3d Dept. 1999)*.

Simply stated, a right of first refusal is a right to receive an offer. *Cipriano v. Glen Cove Lodge #1458, B.P.O.E., 1 N.Y. 3d 53, 801 N.E.2d 388, 769 N.Y.S.2d 168 (2003)*. However, once the holder of the right elects to purchase the property according to the terms of the offer presented by the seller, that right of first refusal is converted into a binding contract. *C & D Food Enterprises, Inc. v. Fudoli, 305 A.D.2d 1093, 759 N.Y.S. 2d 425 (4th Dept. 2003); Yudell Trust I v. API Westchester Associates, 227 A.D.2d 471, 643 N.Y.S. 2d 161 (2d Dept. 1996)*.

Both parties agree that Respondent accepted the offer proffered by Petitioner on July 31, 2002. This is evidenced not only objectively by the documents submitted, but is specifically stated by Petitioner in his letter to Respondent dated October 9, 2002.

Therefore, the primary question for this court is the determination as to whether the terms appearing in the proposed contract for sale represent a material alteration of the terms of the contract formed on July 31, 2002. Petitioner claims that the proposed contract of sale did not alter any material terms of the July 31, 2002, agreement, and Respondent's failure to close on the sale constitutes a breach of that agreement. Respondent argues that Petitioner breached the July 31, 2002, contract by insisting on terms that were not agreed to by the parties.

The Term of the Mortgage

In order to be capable of being accepted, an offer must be certain and definite with respect to all of its material terms. *See* 1 Corbin, Contracts Sec. 95 at 394. This doctrine of definiteness states that if an agreement is not reasonably certain in its material terms, there can be no legally enforceable contract. *Cobble Hill Nursing Home v. Henry & Warren Corp., 74 N.Y. 2d 475, 548 N.E.2d 203, 548 N.Y.S. 2d 920 (1989)*. Further, a mere agreement to agree in which a material term is left for future negotiations is unenforceable. *Martin Delicatessen, Inc. v. Schumacher, 52 N.Y. 2d 105, 417 N.E.2d 541, 436 N.Y.S. 2d 247 (1981)*.

The terms of a mortgage subject to which a purchaser is to take title to real property are generally held to be essential and material elements of a contract. *Marder's Nurseries, Inc. v. Hopping, 171 A.D.2d 63, 573 N.Y.S. 2d 990 (2d Dept. 1991)*. One essential provision of a mortgage is the term of the loan or the method of amortization. *Id*. In *Ashkenazi v. Kelly, 157 A.D.2d 578, 550 N.Y.S. 2d 322 (1st Dept. 1990)*, the court held that an agreement for the sale of real estate that stated that the seller would hold the mortgage for "15 or 20 years" was too indefinite to be enforceable.

As a general proposition, the courts have not applied the doctrine of definiteness enunciated above rigidly. Contracting parties often use fluid language, and imperfect expression does not necessarily indicate that the parties to an agreement do not intend to form a binding contract. As stated in *Cobble Hill Nursing Home v. Henry & Warren Corp., op cit.,* a strict application of the definiteness doctrine could defeat the underlying expectations of the contracting parties.

An offer that might otherwise be deemed unenforceable because of the indefiniteness of one or more of its material terms may be made definite if the agreement invites recourse to an objective extrinsic standard which could make such term or terms explicit. *Martin Delicatessen, Inc. v. Schumacher, op cit.*

In the instant case, the lease provision affording Respondent the right of first refusal refers to an offer to purchase made to Petitioner by a third-party. To exercise that right, Respondent must match the terms proffered by said third-party.

On October 3, 2002, Petitioner forwarded to Respondent a letter from the third-party potential purchaser that stated that the term of the loan in her offer was for ten years. This offer by the third-party which Respondent had to match can be considered an objective standard articulated in the original lease that establishes the essential terms of the contract. Therefore, by the parties referring to the third-party offer as establishing the material terms of the offer, that offer, which might otherwise be considered indefinite, was made certain and enforceable. *Ashkenazi v. Kelly, op cit.* The court also notes that both parties have always agreed that the term of the loan was to be ten years.

"Amortization" is defined as a reduction in a debt by periodic payments covering interest and part of the principal. Amortization involves the operation of paying off an indebtedness by installments, at the expiration of which the entire indebtedness will be extinguished. *Ansonia Residents' Association, Inc. v. New York State Division of Housing and Community Renewal, 141 Misc. 2d 224, 533 N.Y.S. 2d 175 (New York County 1988).*

With a traditional mortgage, the advance of funds is amortized over the life of the loan by regular monthly payments, which continually decrease the outstanding principal balance. *Merrill Lynch Equity Management, Inc. v. Kleinman, 246 A.D.2d 884, 668 N.Y.S.2d 726 (3d Dept. 1998).* Therefore, the term of the mortgage loan is, in effect, the length of the amortization of the loan.

Various methods may be employed by the creditor and debtor to amortize a loan:

> *Fully amortized*: the payment of a constant amount for the duration of the loan, each payment representing a set proportion of interest and principal, *see generally Carver Federal Savings & Loan Ass. v. Glanzer, 186 A.D.2d 706, 588 N.Y.S. 2d 905 (2d Dept. 1992);*
>
> *Straight line amortization*: payments decrease as the loan is repaid, the first amount attributable to principal, the rest to interest;
>
> *Term loan*: payments are attributable to the interest first, then to the principal, *see generally Phoenix Acquisition Corp. v. Campcore, Inc., 81 N.Y. 2d 138, 612 N.E.2d 1219, 596 N.Y.S. 2d 752 (1993);*
>
> *Graduated payment mortgage*: payments are lower in the first few years and increase over the term of the loan, *RPL sec. 279(1);*

Partially amortized: payments are small for the bulk of the term of the loan, representing the payment of interest, and the principal is due at the end in a larger payment known as a balloon payment, *see generally 1300 Avenue P Realty Corp. v. Stratigakis, 186 Misc. 2d 745, 720 N.Y.S. 2d 725 (2d Dept. 2000)*; and

Negative amortization loan: each payment only lowers a portion of the interest, so that the unpaid portion of the interest gets added to the remaining balance, and interest is charged to this amount, *see generally Steinberg v. Williams, 163 A.D.2d 516, 558 N.Y.S. 2d 188 (2d Dept. 1990)*.

However, regardless of the method of amortization employed, there is no difference between the period of the loan and the period of the amortization of the loan; "amortization" merely refers to the amount and attribution between principal and interest of the installment payments over the loan term.

In the instant case Petitioner asserts that the term of the loan was to be ten years, amortized over thirty years. Such a statement is oxymoronic. The duration of the loan and the duration of the amortization period, as indicated by the statutes and cases noted above, are one and the same.

In *Krinsky v. Title Guarantee and Trust Co., 163 Misc. 833, 298 N.Y.S. 31 (1st Dept. 1937)*, (a case involving the rescission of a real estate contract), the court held that a purchaser did not receive what she had bargained for when she was given a mortgage that matured in five years when her agreement of purchase called for a mortgage maturing in not more than three years. The court stated that there is a substantial difference between a mortgage maturing in three years and one that becomes due long thereafter. Such would be the situation in the case at bar.

Petitioner offered, and Respondent accepted, a mortgage that would have a ten year term. The final contract said that the mortgage would amortize over a thirty year period. This amortization period would increase Respondent's repayment time period obligation three-fold, and would increase its actual cost of purchase by approximately $80,000. Therefore, Petitioner's attempt to reconstruct the repayment period to thirty years constitutes a variance of a material term of the accepted offer of sale.

The Guarantee

In his proposed contract of sale Petitioner demanded that Respondent have its principal guarantee the purchase of the premises. Petitioner maintains that because the prospective third-party purchaser was a natural person who would be personally liable under the contract, Respondent, a professional corporation, should also be required to provide for an individual to be personally liable. This argument is specious at best.

The third-party's offer, the terms of which were provided by Petitioner, did not include any provision for an outside person's guarantee of the contract. The third-party, as an individual, was the only person who would be obligated under the agreement.

It is a long established tenet of corporate law that a corporation is a legal entity, separate and distinct from its shareholders, and is legally treated as an individual. *See generally Morris v. New York State Dept. of Taxation & Finance, 82 N.Y. 2d 135, 603 N.Y.S. 2d 807 (1993).* New York's General Obligations law makes no distinction between an individual and a corporate entity. *Fischer v. Panasian Communs., Inc., 87 N.Y. 2d 958, 664 N.E.2d 501, 641 N.Y.S. 2d 590 (1996).* Therefore, Respondent, as a corporate individual, would be obligated under the contract in the same manner as the natural person third-party.

Petitioner provided no additional consideration that would warrant Respondent's agreement to add a guarantee to the contract for the sale of the premises. No such requirement appeared in the July 31, 2002, offer and acceptance. Consequently, Petitioner's insistence on such a clause constitutes a material alteration of the terms of the contract as expressed in the correspondence of July 31, 2002.

Other Clauses

Respondent has also questioned the propriety of Petitioner adding a $600 attorney's fee and refusing to permit a prepayment option. However, both parties at trial have agreed that the $600 fee is *de minimus*, and therefore need not be addressed by the court. Respondent's request for a prepayment clause came into existence when Petitioner attempted to extend the term of the mortgage from ten to thirty years, which the court has determined he cannot do. Therefore, this issue is now moot.

Based on the foregoing, the court concludes that the term of the mortgage and the requirement to add a guarantee to the terms of the contract for the sale of the premises are material alterations in the terms of the binding contract entered into between the parties on July 31, 2002.

The Effect of the Parties' Failure to Close on the Real Estate Sale

Petitioner has argued that because Respondent failed to close on the contract within the time stated in the lease provision providing for the right of first refusal, Respondent has breached the contract entered into between them on July 31, 2002. This argument must fail on three grounds.

First, courts have held that the date of closing of a real estate transaction is not generally considered to be an essential element to establish an enforceable contract. *Safier v. Kassler, 124 A.D.2d 944, 508 N.Y.S. 2d 352 (3d Dept. 1986).*

Second, Petitioner continued to negotiate with Respondent after the presumptive closing date which would estop him from arguing that the closing date is a material term. Also, the court notes that the lease did not contain a time of the essence clause which might have made Respondent's failure to close on that date a material breach.

And third, Petitioner's attempt to insert "creative financing" provisions in the proposed sales contract justifies Respondent in refusing to sign an agreement that materially alters the terms of the parties' contract. *F & S Pharmacy, Inc. v. Dandra Realty Corp., 302 A.D.2d 204, 754 N.Y.S. 2d 256 (1st Dept. 2003).*

The Legal Status of the Parties with Respect to the Premises

Respondent maintains that it is a vendee in possession, whereas Petitioner asserts that Respondent, having failed to close on the contract for sale, is a holdover tenant.

Once Respondent exercised its right of first refusal, a binding contract was formed between the parties. The exercise of a preemptive right to purchase causes the person who exercised the right to became a vendee in possession and the landlord-tenant relationship terminates, *Fulgenzi v. Rink, 253 A.D.2d 846, 678 N.Y.S. 2d 360 (2d Dept. 1998).*

Petitioner commenced this proceeding pursuant to *section 711(1) of RPAPL* which states:

> *Grounds where landlord-tenant relationship exists*
> *1. The tenant continues in possession of any portion of the premises after the expiration of his term, without the permission of the landlord....*
> Pursuant to this section of *RPAPL*, no predicate notice is necessary to commence the holdover proceedings. *Bogatz v. Extra Touch International, Inc., 179 Misc. 2d 1029, 687 N.Y.S. 2d 558 (Kings County 1999).* However, in the instant case Respondent became a vendee in possession on July 31, 2003, and so this section of *RPAPL* does not apply.
> Respondent asserts that, as a vendee in possession, it is entitled to a ten-day notice to quit pursuant to the provisions of *section 713(9) of RPAPL.*
> *Section 713 of the Real Property Actions and Proceedings Law* states, in pertinent part:
> *A special proceeding may be maintained under this article after a 10-day notice to quit has been served upon the respondent ... upon the following grounds ...*
> *9. A vendee under a contract of sale, the performance of which is to be completed within ninety days after its execution, being in possession of all or a part thereof, and having defaulted in the performance of the terms of the contract of sale, remains in possession without permission of the vendor.*

Section 713(9) of RPAPL would only be applicable if Respondent defaulted in its performance of the terms of the contract for sale. Such is not the case in the present situation. No contract of sale was ever executed due to Petitioner's failure to perform according to the terms of the agreement entered into on July 31, 2002.

Every contract has an implied covenant that the party will act in good faith. *Dalton v. Educational Testing Service, 87 N.Y. 2d 384, 663 N.E.2d 289, 639 N.Y.S. 2d 977 (1995).* This implied covenant mandates that neither party shall do anything which will have the effect of destroying or injuring the right of the other party to receive the fruits of the contract. *1-10 Industry Associates, LLC v. Trim Corporation of America, 297 A.D.2d 630, 747 N.Y.S.2d 29 (2d Dept. 2002).* In the present situation, as discussed above, after Respondent accepted the offer proffered by Petitioner, based on the offer made to Petitioner by a third party, a contract between Petitioner and Respondent came into effect. Petitioner's subsequent attempts to change or modify the terms of that agreement in the final contract of sale is the factor that caused the closing to be delayed. Therefore, *Section 713(9) of RPAPL* is inapplicable to the case at bar.

Conclusion

As this court stated in *Montgomery Trading Co. v. Cho, 2003 N.Y. Slip Op. 50665 (U), 2003 N.Y. Misc. LEXIS 316 (2003)*:

> *A summary proceeding is a special proceeding pursuant to the provisions of the New York City Civil Court Act. Section 713 of RPAPL governs situations in which special proceedings may be maintained where no landlord-tenant relationship exists. According to this section of RPAPL, the instant Tenants do*
> *not fall within any of the eleven categories of persons against whom summary proceedings may be maintained:*
> *. . . Under the circumstances that exist in the instant case, Landlord cannot maintain a summary holdover proceeding against Tenants, but may properly maintain an action to eject Tenants from the subject premises. 2955 Shell Associates, L.P. v. Kayani, 234 A.D.2d 287, 651 N.Y.S. 2d 72 (2d Dept. 1996). When a tenancy may be terminated pursuant to a provision of the lease, the landlord must proceed against the former tenant who remains in possession by way of ejectment rather than by summary proceeding. Perrotta v. Western Regional Off-Track Betting Corp., 98 A.D.2d 1, 469 N.Y.S. 2d 504 (4th Dept. 1983), Brause v. 2968 Third Ave., Inc., 41 Misc. 2d 348, 244 N.Y.S. 2d 587, affirmed 43 Misc. 2d 691, 251 N.Y.S. 2d 974 (New York 1963).*
> *Section 203 (j) of the New York City Civil Court Act only grants this court jurisdiction to maintain an action of ejectment where the assessed value of the real property does not exceed $25,000 at the time the action is commenced.*
> *Therefore, this court is without authority to hear this matter.*

The Respondent in the instant matter does not fall within the purview of this court's jurisdiction. It is neither a tenant, because that relationship merged into the vendor-vendee relationship when the parties entered into a contract on July 31, 2002, nor a vendee who breached the contract of sale as is categorized under *section 713(9) of RPAPL*. Therefore, this instant holdover proceeding must be dismissed.

In the court's earlier decision in this matter, dealing with Respondent's motion for summary judgment, the court addressed the problems surrounding a petitioner's failure to serve a respondent with a predicate notice. However, in addressing this matter, the earlier *Danyluk* court inadvertently mischaracterized our earlier decision in *Montgomery Trading Co. v. Cho, supra*. Citing *Rosen v. Wade, 99 Misc. 2d 1114, 418 N.Y.S. 2d 258 (New York County 1979)*, the *Montgomery* court stated that the failure to serve a Notice of Termination *deprives* the court of subject matter jurisdiction [emphasis added]. In analyzing *Montgomery*, the earlier *Danyluk* court confused the concept of immediate deprivation with permanent deprivation. As a predicate to commencing a holdover proceeding, to invoke the court's subject matter jurisdiction, the tenant must be served with the appropriate notice. Failure to do so results in the court's inability to adjudicate the matter, i.e., it lacks the jurisdictional pre-requisite. The court does not lose subject matter jurisdiction, it simply must wait until that jurisdiction is properly initiated. This in no way implies that this jurisdictional defect may not be cured at a later date.

The *Montgomery* decision did not address the amendable aspects of that lack of jurisdictional predicate. As the court correctly noted, the citation to *Rosen v. Wade* was merely introductory dicta and in no way affected the court's ultimate conclusion. The decision in *Montgomery* was based on the fact that the respondent did not come within the category of persons against whom a holdover proceeding may be maintained. Consequently, a predicate notice is irrelevant because the court lacks statutory subject matter jurisdiction.

Another word of clarification is necessary regarding the earlier *Danyluk* decision. That court said "non-amendable defects that do not implicate the court's jurisdiction, however, may be amended in a future proceeding within the court's jurisdiction." What the court apparently meant to say is that certain defects that cause the court to deny (be deprived of) jurisdiction may be amended so as to invoke that jurisdiction at a later date. Something that is "non-amendable" is incapable of being amended.

Based on the foregoing, this action is dismissed.

Case Questions

1. Discuss and explain the different types of amortization enunciated by the court.
2. Why did the court dismiss the action? Do you agree with the court's conclusion? Explain.

Stambovsky v. Ackley
169 A.D.2d 254, 572 N.Y.S.2d 672 (1991)

Plaintiff, to his horror, discovered that the house he had recently contracted to purchase was widely reputed to be possessed by poltergeists, reportedly seen by defendant seller and members of her family on numerous occasions over the last nine years. Plaintiff promptly commenced this action seeking rescission of the contract of sale. Supreme Court reluctantly dismissed the complaint, holding that plaintiff has no remedy at law in this jurisdiction.

The unusual facts of this case, as disclosed by the record, clearly warrant a grant of equitable relief to the buyer who, as a resident of New York City, cannot be expected to have any familiarity with the folklore of the Village of Nyack. Not being a "local," plaintiff could not readily learn that the home he had contracted to purchase is haunted. Whether the source of the spectral apparitions seen by defendant seller are parapsychic or psychogenic, having reported their presence in both a national publication (Readers' Digest) and the local press (in 1977 and 1982, respectively), defendant is estopped to deny their existence and, as a matter of law, the house is haunted. More to the point, however, no divination is required to conclude that it is defendant's promotional efforts in publicizing her close encounters with these spirits which fostered the home's reputation in the community. In 1989, the house was included in a five-home walking tour of Nyack and described in a November 27th newspaper article as "a riverfront Victorian (with ghost)." The impact of the reputation thus created goes to the very essence of the bargain between the parties, greatly impairing both the value of the property and its potential for resale. The extent of this impairment may be presumed for the purpose of reviewing the disposition of this motion to dismiss the cause of action for rescission (*Harris v. City of New York*, 147 A.D.2d 186, 188–189) and represents merely an issue of fact for resolution at trial.

While I agree with Supreme Court that the real estate broker, as agent for the seller, is under no duty to disclose to a potential buyer the phantasmal reputation of the premises and that, in his pursuit of a legal remedy for fraudulent misrepresentation against the seller, plaintiff hasn't a ghost of a chance, I am nevertheless moved by the spirit of equity to allow the buyer to seek rescission of the contract of sale and recovery of his down payment. New York law fails to recognize any remedy for damages incurred as a result of the seller's mere silence, applying instead the strict rule of caveat emptor. Therefore, the theoretical basis for granting relief, even under the extraordinary facts of this case, is elusive if not ephemeral.

"Pity me not but lend thy serious hearing to what I shall unfold" (William Shakespeare, Hamlet, Act I, Scene V [Ghost]).

From the perspective of a person in the position of plaintiff herein, a very practical problem arises with respect to the discovery of a paranormal phenomenon: "Who you gonna' call?" as a title song to the movie "Ghostbusters" asks. Applying the strict rule of caveat emptor to a contract involving a house possessed by poltergeists conjures up visions of a psychic or medium routinely accompanying the structural engineer and Terminix man on an inspection of every home subject to a contract of sale. It portends that the prudent attorney will establish an escrow account lest the subject of the transaction come back to haunt him and his client — or pray that his malpractice insurance coverage extends to supernatural disasters. In the interest of avoiding such untenable consequences, the notion that a haunting is a condition which can and should be ascertained upon reasonable inspection of the premises is a hobgoblin which should be exorcised from the body of legal precedent and laid quietly to rest.

It has been suggested by a leading authority that the ancient rule which holds that mere nondisclosure does not constitute actionable misrepresentation "finds proper application in cases where the fact undisclosed is patent, or the plaintiff has equal opportunities for obtaining information which he may be expected to utilize, or the defendant has no reason to think that he is acting under any misapprehension" (Prosser, Torts Sec. 106, at 696 [4th ed 1971]). However, with respect to transactions in real estate, New York adheres to the doctrine of caveat emptor and imposes no duty upon the vendor to disclose any information concerning the premises (*London v. Courduff*, 141 A.D.2d 803) unless there is a confidential or fiduciary relationship between the parties (*Moser v. Spizzirro*, 31 A.D.2d 537, *aff'd* 25 N.Y.2d 941; *IBM Credit Fin. Corp. v. Mazda Motor Mfg. [USA] Corp.*, 152 A.D.2d 451) or some conduct on the part of the seller which constitutes "active concealment" (see *17 E. 80th Realty Corp. v. 68th Assocs.*, A.D.2d [1st Dept., May 9, 1991] [dummy ventilation system constructed by seller]; *Haberman v. Greenspan*, 82 Misc. 2d 263 [foundation cracks covered by seller]). Normally, some affirmative misrepresentation (e.g., *Tahini Invs. v. Bobrowsky*, 99 A.D.2d 489 [industrial waste on land allegedly used only as farm]; *Jansen v. Kelly*, 11 A.D.2d 587 [land containing valuable minerals allegedly acquired for use as campsite]) or partial disclosure (*Junius Constr. Corp. v. Cohen*, 257 N.Y. 393 [existence of third unopened street concealed]; *Noved Realty Corp. v. A.A.P. Co.*, 250 App. Div. 1 [escrow agreements securing lien concealed]) is required to impose upon the seller a duty to communicate undisclosed conditions affecting the premises (contra, *Young v. Keith*, 112 A.D.2d 625 [defective water and sewer systems concealed]).

Caveat emptor is not so all-encompassing a doctrine of common law as to render every act of nondisclosure immune from redress, whether legal or equitable.

> In regard to the necessity of giving information which has not been asked, the rule differs somewhat at law and in equity, and while the law courts would permit no recovery of damages against a vendor, because of mere concealment of facts under certain circumstances, yet if the vendee refused to complete the contract because of the concealment of a material fact on the part of the other, equity would refuse to compel him so to do, because equity only compels the specific performance of a contract which is fair and open, and in regard to which all material matters known to each have been communicated to the other.

(*Rothmiller v. Stein*, 143 N.Y. 581, 591–592. Even as a principle of law, long before exceptions were embodied in statute law (see, e.g., UCC 2-312, 2-313, 2-314, 2-315; 3-417[2][e]), the doctrine was held inapplicable to contagion among animals, adulteration of food, and insolvency of a maker of a promissory note and of a tenant substituted for another under a lease (see *Rothmiller v. Stein*, supra, at 592-593, and cases cited therein). Common law is not moribund. Ex facto jus oritur (law arises out of facts). Where fairness and common sense dictate that an exception should be created, the evolution of the law should not be stifled by rigid application of a legal maxim.

The doctrine of caveat emptor requires that a buyer act prudently to assess the fitness and value of his purchase and operates to bar the purchaser who fails to exercise due care from seeking the equitable remedy of rescission (see, e.g., *Rodas v. Manitaras*, 159 A.D.2d 341). For the purposes of the instant motion to dismiss the action pursuant to CPLR 3211(a)(7), plaintiff is entitled to every favorable inference which may reasonably be drawn from the pleadings (*Arrington v. New York Times Co.*, 55 N.Y.2d 433, 442; *Rovello v. Orofino Realty Co.*, 40 N.Y.2d 633, 634), specifically, in this

instance, that he met his obligation to conduct an inspection of the premises
and a search of available public records with respect to title. It should be
apparent, however, that the most meticulous inspection and the search
would not reveal the presence of poltergeists at the premises or unearth
the property's ghoulish reputation in the community. Therefore, there is no
sound policy reason to deny plaintiff relief for failing to discover a state of
affairs which the most prudent purchaser would not be expected to even
contemplate (see *Da Silva v. Musso*, 53 N.Y.2d 543, 551).

The case law in this jurisdiction dealing with the duty of a vendor of
real property to disclose information to the buyer is distinguishable from
the matter under review. The most salient distinction is that existing cases
invariably deal with the physical condition of the premises (e.g., *London v.
Courduff*, supra [use as a landfill]; *Perin v. Mardine Realty Co.*, 5 A.D.2d 685,
aff'd 6 N.Y.2d 920 [sewer line crossing adjoining property without owner's
consent]); defects in title (e.g., *Sands v. Kissane*, 282 App. Div. 140 [remain-
derman]); liens against the property (e.g., *Noved Realty Corp. v. A.A.P. Co.*,
supra); expenses or income (e.g., *Rodas v. Manitaras*, supra [gross receipts])
and other factors affecting its operation. No case has been brought to
this court's attention in which the property value was impaired as the result
of the reputation created by information disseminated to the public by the
seller (or, for that matter, as a result of possession by poltergeists).

Where a condition which has been created by the seller materially
impairs the value of the contract and is peculiarly within the knowledge
of the seller or unlikely to be discovered by a prudent purchaser exercising
due care with respect to the subject transaction, nondisclosure constitutes
a basis for rescission as a matter of equity. Any other outcome places
upon the buyer not merely the obligation to exercise care in his purchase
but rather to be omniscient with respect to any fact which may affect the
bargain. No practical purpose is served by imposing such a burden upon a
purchaser. To the contrary, it encourages predatory business practice and
offends the principle that equity will suffer no wrong to be without a
remedy.

Defendant's contention that the contract of sale, particularly the merger or "as is" clause, bars recovery of the buyer's deposit is unavailing.
Even an express disclaimer will not be given effect where the facts are
peculiarly within the knowledge of the party invoking it (*Danann Realty
Corp. v. Harris*, 5 N.Y.2d 317, 322; *Tahini Invs. v. Bobrowsky*, supra). Moreover, a fair reading of the merger clause reveals that it expressly disclaims
only representations made with respect to the physical condition of the
premises and merely makes general reference to representations concerning "any other matter or things affecting or relating to the aforesaid
premises." As broad as this language may be, a reasonable interpretation
is that its effect is limited to tangible or physical matters and does not
extend to paranormal phenomena. Finally, if the language of the contract
is to be construed as broadly as defendant urges to encompass the presence
of poltergeists in the house, it cannot be said that she has delivered the

premises "vacant" in accordance with her obligation under the provisions of the contract rider.

To the extent New York law may be said to require something more than "mere concealment" to apply even the equitable remedy of rescission, the case of *Junius Constr. Corp. v. Cohen* (257 N.Y. 393, supra), while not precisely on point, provides some guidance. In that case, the seller disclosed that an official map indicated two as yet unopened streets which were planned for construction at the edges of the parcel. What was not disclosed was that the same map indicated a third street which, if opened, would divide the plot in half. The court held that, while the seller was under no duty to mention the planned streets at all, having undertaken to disclose two of them, he was obliged to reveal the third (see also *Rosenschein v. McNally*, 17 A.D.2d 834).

In the case at bar, defendant seller deliberately fostered the public belief that her home was possessed. Having undertaken to inform the public-at-large, to whom she has no legal relationship, about the supernatural occurrences on her property, she may be said to owe no less a duty to her contract vendee. It has been remarked that the occasional modern cases which permit a seller to take unfair advantage of a buyer's ignorance so long as he is not actively misled are "singularly unappetizing" (Prosser, Torts Sec. 106, at 696 '4th ed. 1971'). Where, as here, the seller not only takes unfair advantage of the buyer's ignorance but has created and perpetuated a condition about which he is unlikely to even inquire, enforcement of the contract (in whole or in part) is offensive to the court's sense of equity. Application of the remedy of rescission, within the bounds of the narrow exception to the doctrine of caveat emptor set forth herein, is entirely appropriate to relieve the unwitting purchaser from the consequences of a most unnatural bargain.

Accordingly, the judgment of the Supreme Court, New York County (Edward H. Lehner, J.), entered April 9, 1990, which dismissed the complaint pursuant to CPLR 3211(a)(7), should be modified, on the law and the facts, and in the exercise of discretion, and the first cause of action seeking rescission of the contract reinstated, without costs.

Case Questions

1. What does the court conclude are the obligations of the real estate agent?
2. How does the court interpret the vendor's duty to disclose in this case?

Exhibit 4.3: Contract of Sale

REAL ESTATE AGREEMENT 223

Agreement made this   day of

A.D. 19   between

of the first part, and

of the second part.

    The party of the first part hereinafter referred to as the SELLER hereby agrees to sell and the party of the second part hereinafter referred to as the BUYER agrees to purchase a certain estate situated

and bounded and described as follows:

    Included in this sale as a part of said premises are the usual Landlord's fixtures belonging to the SELLER and used in connection therewith including, if any, all furnaces, heaters, stoves, ranges, oil and gas burners and fixtures appurtenant thereto, hot water heaters, electric, gas refrigerators, air conditioning apparatus, mantels, electric and other lighting fixtures, venetian blinds and window shades, screens, screen doors, storm or other detached windows and doors, blinds, awnings, bathroom fixtures, television antennas, fences, gates, garbage disposers, dishwashers, washing machines, driers and hardy shrubs and other fixtures, in so far as the same are or can by agreement of the parties be made a part of the realty.

Exhibit 4.3: *(Continued)*

Said premises are to be conveyed on or before   by a
good and sufficient   deed of the SELLER, conveying a good and
clear title to the same, free from all encumbrances, except:

    (a) Provisions of local zoning laws, if any;

    (b) Existing rights created by instruments of record in party or partition walls (if any);

    (c) Such taxes for the current year as are not due and payable on the date of the delivery of such
        deed, and any liens for municipal betterments assessed after the date of this agreement.

To enable the SELLER to make conveyance as herein provided, the SELLER may, if the SELLER
so desires, at the time of the delivery of the deed, use the purchase money or any portion thereof to clear
the title of any or all encumbrances or interests; all instruments so procured to be recorded simultaneously with the delivery of said deed.

and for such deed and conveyance the BUYER is to pay the sum of

                                                                dollars

of which   dollars

have been paid this day,   dollars

are to be paid in cash upon the delivery of said deed, and the remainder is to be paid by the note of
the BUYER, dated

bearing interest at   per cent per annum, payable

and secured by a power of sale mortgage, in the usual form, upon the said premises, such note to be
payable

Full possession of the said premises, free of all tenants

                                          is to be delivered to the BUYER at the
time of the delivery of the deed, the said premises to be then in the same condition in which they now
are reasonable use and wear of the buildings thereon, and damage by fire or other unavoidable casualty
excepted.

Exhibit 4.3: *(Continued)*

The buildings on said premises shall, until the full performance of this agreement, be kept insured in the sum of
by the SELLER in offices satisfactory to the BUYER, and, in case of any loss, all sums recovered or recoverable on account of said insurance shall be paid over or assigned, on delivery of the deed, to the BUYER, unless the premises shall previously have been restored to their former condition by the SELLER.

Rents, Insurance Premiums, Water Rates, and Taxes, shall be apportioned as of the day of delivery of the deed, and the taxes assessed for the year 19   shall be paid by

The deed is to be delivered and the consideration paid, if the purchaser so requires, at the Registry of Deeds in which the deed should by law be recorded, on   19
at   M. unless some other place and time should be mutually agreed upon.

If the SELLER shall be unable to give title or to make conveyance as above stipulated, any payments made under this agreement shall be refunded, and all other obligations of either party hereunto shall cease, but the acceptance of a deed and possession by the BUYER shall be deemed to be a full performance and discharge hereof.

In consideration of the above,   , wife of the
said   , hereby agrees to join in the said deed
to be made as aforesaid, and to release and convey to the BUYER all statutory and other rights and interests in said premises.

IT IS UNDERSTOOD THAT A BROKER'S COMMISSION OF   per cent
on the said sale is to be paid to   ,
by the said SELLER.

The contracting parties agree that this contract contains all the terms and conditions of this sale. It is mutually agreed that any oral representation made by either party prior to the signing of this agreement is null and void.

In witness whereof.   the said parties hereto, and to another instrument of like tenor, set their hands and seals on the day and year first above written.

Signed and sealed in presence of

....

....

....

Extension

The time for the performance of the foregoing agreement is extended until

Witness our hands and seals this   day of   19

....

....

Exhibit 4.3: *(Continued)*

with

Agreement
[REAL ESTATE]

From the office of

(Please print or type)

RETURN TO ➡

HOBBS & WARREN, INC.
Publishers Standard Legal Forms
Boston - Mass.
FORM 223
Revised 1970

Exhibit 4.4: Rider to a Residential Contract of Sale

RIDER TO CONTRACT OF SALE
between

_____ (the "Seller")

and

_____ (the "Purchaser")

for the Sale of

_____ (the "Premises")

1. CONFLICT: In the event of a conflict between the terms of the printed portion of the Contract and the terms of this Rider, the terms of this Rider shall control, govern and prevail and the contradicted and/or inconsistent provisions of the printed portion of the Contract shall be deemed amended and superseded accordingly.

2. TITLE: Purchaser agrees to order a title report within ten (10) days after the date hereof, and to deliver or make sure that the title insurance company delivers to Seller's attorney, copies of the title insurance company's report, including the exception sheets, tax searches, property description, departmental searches and, if ordered, survey and survey reading, when issued. Since Purchaser is currently an owner of the Premises, Seller shall not be obligated to take any action to clear title and to cure any other violations under this Contract, and shall not be required to bring any action or proceeding or make any expenditure.

3. INSPECTION, CONDITION OF PREMISES: Purchaser acknowledges and represents to Seller that Purchaser has inspected or has had inspected by an inspector of Purchaser's choice, the Premises and all items of personal and real property included in the sale of the Premises, and is fully familiar with and satisfied with the physical nature and condition of same and will accept the Premises and all items of personal and real property included in the sale of the Premises "AS IS." On advance notice to Seller and reasonable appointment within 24 hours prior to closing, Purchaser shall be given the opportunity to reinspect the Premises, only for the purpose of determining whether the Premises are in the condition required by this Contract.

4. REPRESENTATIONS, NON-SURVIVAL: Purchaser expressly acknowledges, agrees and represents that no broker, representative, agent, employee, or attorney of Seller previously did nor does now make, and Purchaser is not relying upon, and has not been induced to enter into this Contract on the basis of, any warranties, representations, information, broker setups, inducements, or other statements (expressed or implied) as to the past, present or future physical condition of the Premises,

Exhibit 4.4: *(Continued)*

the status of any termite infestation, or of any material or chemical, the expenses, taxes, operation, or maintenance, the school district, the quantity, quality or condition of the articles of personal property, fixtures, utilities and equipment agreed to be sold with the Premises, or as to the Premises, except as and only to the extent in this Contract specifically set forth. Acceptance by Purchaser of the deed at closing shall be and be deemed to be full compliance, performance and discharge of every agreement, representation and obligation expressed or implied (other than as required by law) on the part of Seller contained anywhere in this Contract. No representation, warranty or guarantee of Seller shall be deemed to survive the earlier of closing or possession by Purchaser or be the basis of any claim against Seller unless specifically and expressly stated in this Contract to survive.

     5. <u>NOTICE:</u> _____ is the attorney for Purchaser, and _____ are the attorneys for Seller. The aforesaid addresses are the respective addresses for notices to said attorneys pursuant to this Contract. Notices shall be deemed valid and effective when received by the notified party's attorney, at the above address, and mailed to the party to be notified, addressed to the party at the party's address stated at the beginning of this Contract; or to such other address as the party or attorney may hereafter designate by notice as herein provided. Any and all notice, demands or requests required or permitted to be given by any of the provisions of this Contract must be in writing and shall be validly given or made and effective the date when delivered personally against receipt, or actually received, or three (3) days after mailing with postage prepaid by either U.S. certified mail, return receipt requested, or by regular mail receipt of which is acknowledged by the receiving party or attorney. The attorneys are hereby expressly authorized, on behalf of their respective clients, to serve, and/or receive any written notice, whenever such notice is permitted to be given under the terms and conditions of this Contract; and to extend any of the time limitations as provided in this Contract; any such notice and/or extension, if any, shall be in writing and duly signed by said party or said party's attorney.

     6. <u>MISCELLANEOUS:</u>

     a. <u>No Recording:</u> This Contract or any memorandum of notice of same shall not be recorded or tendered for recording by or on behalf of Purchaser and any attempt to record the same by or on behalf of Purchaser shall be deemed a default by Purchaser; and thereupon, at Seller's election, this Contract shall be deemed canceled and Seller shall have any and all remedies for a default by Purchaser provided for herein and by law. If Purchaser files a notice of pendency of action or any other notice or memorandum in any court or land records department and either fails to commence a court action against Seller, or does not obtain judgment against

Exhibit 4.4: *(Continued)*

Seller based on said court action, Purchaser agrees to pay Seller interest at the prime rate plus 1% as published in the New York Times on the unpaid balance of the purchase price commencing on date of filing the notice and ending when the notice is removed, together with reasonable legal, bonding and other costs and expenses, including attorneys fees, incurred by Seller in the defense of said action and as to removal of said notice.

b. No Offer: The transmittal of this document or any written or oral communication by Seller or of any attorney, broker or agent shall not be deemed a binding or continuing offer to sell or a meeting of the minds of the prospective parties on material terms and conditions, nor shall it be deemed a consummation of a contract or an accepted offer. The subject Premises are subject to prior sale, price change and/or withdrawal from sale and there shall be no binding contract unless and until Seller executes and delivers to Purchaser a fully executed Contract.

c. Assessments: Seller represents to Purchaser that Seller is not aware of any assessments affecting the Premises either pending or threatened. If at the time of closing, the Premises are affected by an assessment or assessments which are or may become payable in annual installments, the assessments payable after closing of the title shall be payable by Purchaser and by the owner of the Premises if payable on the date of or prior to closing of title.

d. Fire, Other Major Casualty: If prior to closing there shall be any fire, flood, explosion or other casualty, or condemnation affecting the Premises or any of the property to be conveyed in connection therewith, the New York General Obligations Law, Section 5-1311 shall apply, except that there shall be no abatement of purchase price.

e. Liens at Closing: If there be a mortgage or other lien on the Premises, the Premises shall be conveyed subject to said mortgage or other lien. The existence of said mortgage or other lien shall not constitute an objection to title if Purchaser's title insurance company omits such mortgage or other lien as an exception to title.

7. DOWN PAYMENT, ESCROW: The down payment shall be deemed paid to Seller on account of the purchase price, but shall be paid by check to the Seller's attorney, who shall also act as Escrow Agent. Purchaser's check payable to P.C. ("Escrow Agent"), is to be deposited in escrow by the Escrow Agent subject to clearance and the funds held in escrow in accordance with the provisions of this Contract. The escrow deposit may be delivered to or for Seller, on the stated closing date unless (1) upon Purchaser's default, to Seller, or (2) if Purchaser shall sooner be entitled to a refund thereof pursuant to this Contract, in which case shall be paid to Purchaser, or (3) if Seller shall default or cannot give title as required by this Contract, the escrow deposit shall be repaid to Purchaser. Interest accrued on the down payment will be paid to the party to whom the down payment is paid or refunded.

Exhibit 4.4: *(Continued)*

If the Escrow Agent is notified by a party of an escrow dispute, the Escrow Agent may (i) retain the funds in escrow until receipt by Escrow Agent of a written agreement and authorization from Seller and Purchaser directing the disposition of the funds; or (ii) at any time deposit the escrow funds with the Clerk of the Court, County, or by direction of any Court having jurisdiction over the parties, and thereby be released and discharged by the parties for any and all costs, responsibilities, obligations and liabilities as to the escrow fund; and the Escrow Agent shall be compensated as to any expenses by the losing party. The Escrow Agent shall not be liable for any error, omission or action taken unless resulting from the Escrow Agent's gross negligence or willful breach of the terms of this section. By signing this Rider, who is Seller's agent as to receipt of the funds, agrees to act as the Escrow Agent for the down payment subject to the terms of this Section. In case of a dispute or any threatened or actual litigation, notwithstanding acting as the Escrow Agent, may represent Seller. If Purchaser's down payment check is dishonored for any reason by the bank upon which it is drawn, then Seller, in addition to any other rights and remedies Seller may have, may, at Seller's option, declare this Contract null and void and at an end and thereupon Seller shall be relieved and released from all obligations hereunder.

_____

Seller

_____

Seller

_____

Purchaser

By:_____

Exhibit 4.5: Deed

M 297— Statutory Form F.
Referee's Deed in Foreclosure. 11-98.

DISTRIBUTED BY BlumbergExcelsior Inc.
NYC 10013

This Deed

Made the   day of

Between   Referee

duly appointed in the action hereinafter mentioned, Grantor

And

Grantee:

Witnesseth,   that the Grantor, the Referee appointed in an action between

plaintiff(s),

and

defendant(s),

foreclosing a mortgage recorded on   in the office of the

of the County of   in liber   of mortgages,

at page

in pursuance of a judgment entered at a special term of the

on   and in consideration of

Dollars paid by the Grantee,

being the highest sum bid at the sale under said judgment does hereby grant and convey unto the Grantee, all the

right, title and interest of the defendants

in and to

Exhibit 4.5: *(Continued)*

$\mathfrak{All}$

Exhibit 4.5: *(Continued)*

𝕿𝖔 𝖍𝖆𝖛𝖊 𝖆𝖓𝖉 𝖙𝖔 𝖍𝖔𝖑𝖉 *the premises herein granted unto the Grantee*

and assigns forever.

Whenever the text hereof requires, the singular number as used herein shall include the plural and all genders.

𝕴𝖓 𝖂𝖎𝖙𝖓𝖊𝖘𝖘 𝖂𝖍𝖊𝖗𝖊𝖔𝖋, *the Grantor has hereunto set his hand and seal, the date first above written.*

---{ L. S. }
                                                             Referee

𝕴𝖓 𝕻𝖗𝖊𝖘𝖊𝖓𝖈𝖊 𝖔𝖋:

State of New York
                                          } ss.:   ACKNOWLEDGMENT RPL 309-a (Do not use outside New York State.)
County of

        On   before me, personally appeared

personally known to me or proved to me on the basis of satisfactory evidence to be the individual(s) whose name(s) is (are) subscribed to the within instrument and acknowledged to me that he/she/they executed the same in his/her/their capacity(ies), and that by his/her/their signature(s) on the instrument, the individual(s), or the person upon behalf of which the individual(s) acted, executed the instrument.

                                                        _____
                                                        (signature and office of individual taking acknowledgment)

Exhibit 4.5: *(Continued)*

Deed
REFEREE'S DEED IN FORECLOSURE

TO

Dated,

STATE OF NEW YORK

County of_____ ss.

RECORDED ON THE

............day of.....................................

        at...............o'clock............. M.

in Liber........................of Deeds

at Page........................and examined

....
                                                        CLERK

PLEASE RECORD AND RETURN TO:

Reserve this space for use of Recording Office.

Exhibit 4.6: Quitclam Deed

MASSACHUSETTS QUITCLAIM DEED INDIVIDUAL (LONG FORM) 882

of   County, Massachusetts,

being unmarried, for consideration paid, and in full consideration of

grant to   *

of   with quitclaim covenants

the land in

[Description and encumbrances, if any]

(*Individual — Joint Tenants — Tenants in Common.)

Exhibit 4.6: *(Continued)*

Witness _____hand   and seal   this_____ day of_____ , 19____ .

_____   _____
_____   _____
_____   _____

The Commonwealth of Massachusetts

ss.   19

Then personally appeared the above named

and acknowledged the foregoing instrument to be   free act and deed, before me

_____
Notary Public — Justice of the Peace

My commission expires   19

CHAPTER 183 SEC. 6 AS AMENDED BY CHAPTER 497 of 1969
Every deed presented for record shall contain or have endorsed upon it the full name, residence and post office address of the grantee and a recital of the amount of the full consideration thereof in dollars or the nature of the other consideration therefor, if not delivered for a specific monetary sum. The full consideration shall mean the total price for the conveyance without deduction for any liens or encumbrances assumed by the grantee or remaining thereon. All such endorsements and recitals shall be recorded as part of the deed. Failure to comply with this section shall not affect the validity of any deed. No register of deeds shall accept a deed for recording unless it is in compliance with the requirements of this section.

Exhibit 4.6: *(Continued)*

MASSACHUSETTS

Statute Form of

Quitclaim Deed

(INDIVIDUAL)

TO

_____ 19____

at_____ o'clock and_____ minutes_____ m.

Received and entered with_____

_____ Deeds

Book_____ Page_____ .

Attest:

_____

Register

FROM THE OFFICE OF

(Please print or type)

RETURN TO ➤

FORM 882

REVISED CHAPTER 497-1969 – 727-1980

(H&W) HOBBS & WARREN ™

BOSTON

Exhibit 4.7: Uniform Residential Loan Application

Uniform Residential Loan Application

This application is designed to be completed by the applicant(s) with the Lender's assistance. Applicants should complete this form as "Borrower" or "Co-Borrower," as applicable. Co-Borrower information must also be provided (and the appropriate box checked) when □ the income or assets of a person other than the Borrower (including the Borrower's spouse) will be used as a basis for loan qualification or □ the income or assets of the Borrower's spouse or other person who has community property rights pursuant to state law will not be used as a basis for loan qualification, but his or her liabilities must be considered because the spouse or other person has community property rights pursuant to applicable law and Borrower resides in a community property state, the security property is located in a community property state, or the Borrower is relying on other property located in a community property state as a basis for repayment of the loan.

If this is an application for joint credit, Borrower and Co-Borrower each agree that we intend to apply for joint credit (sign below):

Borrower _____   Co-Borrower _____

I. TYPE OF MORTGAGE AND TERMS OF LOAN					
Mortgage Applied for: □ VA □ FHA	□ Conventional □ USDA/Rural Housing Service	□ Other (explain):	**Agency Case Number**		**Lender Case Number**
Amount $	Interest Rate %	No. of Months	**Amortization Type:**	□ Fixed Rate □ Other (explain): □ GPM □ ARM (type):	

II. PROPERTY INFORMATION AND PURPOSE OF LOAN		
Subject Property Address (street, city, state & ZIP)		No. of Units
Legal Description of Subject Property (attach description if necessary)		Year Built

Purpose of Loan	□ Purchase □ Construction □ Other (explain): □ Refinance □ Construction-Permanent	Property will be: □ Primary Residence □ Secondary Residence □ Investment

Complete this line if construction or construction-permanent loan.

Year Lot Acquired	Original Cost	Amount Existing Liens	(a) Present Value of Lot	(b) Cost of Improvements	Total (a + b)
	$	$	$	$	$

Complete this line if this is a refinance loan.

Year Acquired	Original Cost	Amount Existing Liens	Purpose of Refinance	Describe Improvements □ made □ to be made
	$	$		Cost: $

Title will be held in what Name(s)	Manner in which Title will be held	Estate will be held in: □ Fee Simple □ Leasehold (show expiration date)
Source of Down Payment, Settlement Charges, and/or Subordinate Financing (explain)		

Borrower	III. BORROWER INFORMATION	Co-Borrower
Borrower's Name (include Jr. or Sr. if applicable)		Co-Borrower's Name (include Jr. or Sr. if applicable)

Social Security Number	Home Phone (incl. area code)	DOB (mm/dd/yyyy)	Yrs. School	Social Security Number	Home Phone (incl. area code)	DOB (mm/dd/yyyy)	Yrs. School

□ Married □ Separated	□ Unmarried (include single, divorced, widowed)	Dependents (not listed by Co-Borrower) no. ages	□ Married □ Separated	□ Unmarried (include single, divorced, widowed)	Dependents (not listed by Borrower) no. ages

Present Address (street, city, state, ZIP) □ Own □ Rent ____ No. Yrs.	Present Address (street, city, state, ZIP) □ Own □ Rent ____ No. Yrs.
Mailing Address, if different from Present Address	Mailing Address, if different from Present Address

If residing at present address for less than two years, complete the following:

Former Address (street, city, state, ZIP) □ Own □ Rent ____ No. Yrs.	Former Address (street, city, state, ZIP) □ Own □ Rent ____ No. Yrs.

Borrower	IV. EMPLOYMENT INFORMATION	Co-Borrower
Name & Address of Employer	□ Self Employed	Yrs. on this job	Name & Address of Employer	□ Self Employed	Yrs. on this job
		Yrs. employed in this line of work/profession			Yrs. employed in this line of work/profession
Position/Title/Type of Business	Business Phone (incl. area code)		Position/Title/Type of Business	Business Phone (incl. area code)	

If employed in current position for less than two years or if currently employed in more than one position, complete the following:

Exhibit 4.7: *(Continued)*

Borrower			IV. EMPLOYMENT INFORMATION (cont'd)		Co-Borrower	
Name & Address of Employer	☐ Self Employed	Dates (from – to)	Name & Address of Employer	☐ Self Employed	Dates (from – to)	
		Monthly Income $			Monthly Income $	
Position/Title/Type of Business	Business Phone (incl. area code)		Position/Title/Type of Business	Business Phone (incl. area code)		
Name & Address of Employer	☐ Self Employed	Dates (from – to)	Name & Address of Employer	☐ Self Employed	Dates (from – to)	
		Monthly Income $			Monthly Income $	
Position/Title/Type of Business	Business Phone (incl. area code)		Position/Title/Type of Business	Business Phone (incl. area code)		

V. MONTHLY INCOME AND COMBINED HOUSING EXPENSE INFORMATION

Gross Monthly Income	Borrower	Co-Borrower	Total	Combined Monthly Housing Expense	Present	Proposed
Base Empl. Income*	$	$	$	Rent	$	
Overtime				First Mortgage (P&I)		$
Bonuses				Other Financing (P&I)		
Commissions				Hazard Insurance		
Dividends/Interest				Real Estate Taxes		
Net Rental Income				Mortgage Insurance		
Other (before completing, see the notice in "describe other income," below)				Homeowner Assn. Dues		
				Other:		
Total	$	$	$	Total	$	$

    *   **Self Employed Borrower(s) may be required to provide additional documentation such as tax returns and financial statements.**

Describe Other Income	*Notice:* **Alimony, child support, or separate maintenance income need not be revealed if the Borrower (B) or Co-Borrower (C) does not choose to have it considered for repaying this loan.**	
B/C		Monthly Amount
		$

VI. ASSETS AND LIABILITIES

This Statement and any applicable supporting schedules may be completed jointly by both married and unmarried Co-Borrowers if their assets and liabilities are sufficiently joined so that the Statement can be meaningfully and fairly presented on a combined basis; otherwise, separate Statements and Schedules are required. If the Co-Borrower section was completed about a non-applicant spouse or other person, this Statement and supporting schedules must be completed about that spouse or other person also.

Completed ☐ Jointly ☐ Not Jointly

ASSETS	Cash or Market Value	Liabilities and Pledged Assets. List the creditor's name, address, and account number for all outstanding debts, including automobile loans, revolving charge accounts, real estate loans, alimony, child support, stock pledges, etc. Use continuation sheet, if necessary. Indicate by (*) those liabilities, which will be satisfied upon sale of real estate owned or upon refinancing of the subject property.		
Description				
Cash deposit toward purchase held by:	$			
List checking and savings accounts below		**LIABILITIES**	**Monthly Payment & Months Left to Pay**	**Unpaid Balance**
Name and address of Bank, S&L, or Credit Union		Name and address of Company	$ Payment/Months	$
Acct. no.	$	Acct. no.		
Name and address of Bank, S&L, or Credit Union		Name and address of Company	$ Payment/Months	$
Acct. no.	$	Acct. no.		
Name and address of Bank, S&L, or Credit Union		Name and address of Company	$ Payment/Months	$
Acct. no.	$	Acct. no.		

Exhibit 4.7: *(Continued)*

VI. ASSETS AND LIABILITIES (cont'd)				
Name and address of Bank, S&L, or Credit Union		Name and address of Company	$ Payment/Months	$
Acct. no.	$	Acct. no.		
Stocks & Bonds (Company name/ number & description)	$	Name and address of Company	$ Payment/Months	$
		Acct. no.		
Life insurance net cash value	$	Name and address of Company	$ Payment/Months	$
Face amount: $				
Subtotal Liquid Assets	$			
Real estate owned (enter market value from schedule of real estate owned)	$			
Vested interest in retirement fund	$			
Net worth of business(es) owned (attach financial statement)	$	Acct. no.		
Automobiles owned (make and year)	$	Alimony/Child Support/Separate Maintenance Payments Owed to:	$	
Other Assets (itemize)	$	Job-Related Expense (child care, union dues, etc.)	$	
		Total Monthly Payments	$	
Total Assets a.	$	Net Worth (a minus b) ▶	$	**Total Liabilities b.** $

Schedule of Real Estate Owned (If additional properties are owned, use continuation sheet.)

Property Address (enter S if sold, PS if pending sale or R if rental being held for income) ▼	Type of Property	Present Market Value	Amount of Mortgages & Liens	Gross Rental Income	Mortgage Payments	Insurance, Maintenance, Taxes & Misc.	Net Rental Income
		$	$	$	$	$	$
Totals		$	$	$	$	$	$

List any additional names under which credit has previously been received and indicate appropriate creditor name(s) and account number(s):

Alternate Name	Creditor Name	Account Number

VII. DETAILS OF TRANSACTION		VIII. DECLARATIONS				
a.	Purchase price	$	If you answer "Yes" to any questions a through i, please use continuation sheet for explanation.	**Borrower**		**Co-Borrower**
				Yes No		Yes No
b.	Alterations, improvements, repairs		a. Are there any outstanding judgments against you?	☐ ☐		☐ ☐
c.	Land (if acquired separately)		b. Have you been declared bankrupt within the past 7 years?			☐ ☐
d.	Refinance (incl. debts to be paid off)		c. Have you had property foreclosed upon or given title or deed in lieu thereof in the last 7 years?	☐ ☐		☐ ☐
e.	Estimated prepaid items		d. Are you a party to a lawsuit?	☐ ☐		☐ ☐
f.	Estimated closing costs		e. Have you directly or indirectly been obligated on any loan which resulted in foreclosure, transfer of title in lieu of foreclosure, or judgment?	☐ ☐		☐ ☐
g.	PMI, MIP, Funding Fee		(This would include such loans as home mortgage loans, SBA loans, home improvement loans, educational loans, manufactured (mobile) home loans, any mortgage, financial obligation, bond, or loan guarantee. If "Yes," provide details, including date, name, and address of Lender, FHA or VA case number, if any, and reasons for the action.)			
h.	Discount (if Borrower will pay)					
i.	Total costs (add items a through h)					

Exhibit 4.7: *(Continued)*

VII. DETAILS OF TRANSACTION		VIII. DECLARATIONS				
			Borrower		**Co-Borrower**	
		If you answer "Yes" to any questions a through i, please use continuation sheet for explanation.	Yes	No	Yes	No
j.	Subordinate financing					
k.	Borrower's closing costs paid by Seller	f. Are you presently delinquent or in default on any Federal debt or any other loan, mortgage, financial obligation, bond, or loan guarantee? If "Yes," give details as described in the preceding question.	☐	☐	☐	☐
l.	Other Credits (explain)	g. Are you obligated to pay alimony, child support, or separate maintenance?	☐	☐	☐	☐
		h. Is any part of the down payment borrowed?	☐	☐	☐	☐
m.	Loan amount (exclude PMI, MIP, Funding Fee financed)	i. Are you a co-maker or endorser on a note?	☐	☐	☐	☐
		j. Are you a U.S. citizen?	☐	☐	☐	☐
n.	PMI, MIP, Funding Fee financed	k. Are you a permanent resident alien?	☐	☐	☐	☐
		l. Do you intend to occupy the property as your primary residence? If "Yes," complete question m below.	☐	☐	☐	☐
o.	Loan amount (add m & n)	m. Have you had an ownership interest in a property in the last three years?	☐	☐	☐	☐
p.	Cash from/to Borrower (subtract j, k, l & o from i)	(1) What type of property did you own—principal residence (PR), second home (SH), or investment property (IP)? (2) How did you hold title to the home—solely by yourself (S), jointly with your spouse (SP), or jointly with another person (O)?	———		———	

IX. ACKNOWLEDGEMENT AND AGREEMENT

Each of the undersigned specifically represents to Lender and to Lender's actual or potential agents, brokers, processors, attorneys, insurers, servicers, successors and assigns and agrees and acknowledges that: (1) the information provided in this application is true and correct as of the date set forth opposite my signature and that any intentional or negligent misrepresentation of this information contained in this application may result in civil liability, including monetary damages, to any person who may suffer any loss due to reliance upon any misrepresentation that I have made on this application, and/or in criminal penalties including, but not limited to, fine or imprisonment or both under the provisions of Title 18, United States Code, Sec. 1001, et seq.; (2) the loan requested pursuant to this application (the "Loan") will be secured by a mortgage or deed of trust on the property described in this application; (3) the property will not be used for any illegal or prohibited purpose or use; (4) all statements made in this application are made for the purpose of obtaining a residential mortgage loan; (5) the property will be occupied as indicated in this application; (6) the Lender, its servicers, successors or assigns may retain the original and/or an electronic record of this application, whether or not the Loan is approved; (7) the Lender and its agents, brokers, insurers, servicers, successors, and assigns may continuously rely on the information contained in the application, and I am obligated to amend and/or supplement the information provided in this application if any of the material facts that I have represented herein should change prior to closing of the Loan; (8) in the event that my payments on the Loan become delinquent, the Lender, its servicers, successors or assigns may, in addition to any other rights and remedies that it may have relating to such delinquency, report my name and account information to one or more consumer reporting agencies; (9) ownership of the Loan and/or administration of the Loan account may be transferred with such notice as may be required by law; (10) neither Lender nor its agents, brokers, insurers, servicers, successors or assigns has made any representation or warranty, express or implied, to me regarding the property or the condition or value of the property; and (11) my transmission of this application as an "electronic record" containing my "electronic signature," as those terms are defined in applicable federal and/or state laws (excluding audio and video recordings), or my facsimile transmission of this application containing a facsimile of my signature, shall be as effective, enforceable and valid as if a paper version of this application were delivered containing my original written signature.

Acknowledgement. Each of the undersigned hereby acknowledges that any owner of the Loan, its servicers, successors and assigns, may verify or reverify any information contained in this application or obtain any information or data relating to the Loan, for any legitimate business purpose through any source, including a source named in this application or a consumer reporting agency.

Borrower's Signature	Date	Co-Borrower's Signature	Date
X		X	

X. INFORMATION FOR GOVERNMENT MONITORING PURPOSES

The following information is requested by the Federal Government for certain types of loans related to a dwelling in order to monitor the lender's compliance with equal credit opportunity, fair housing and home mortgage disclosure laws. You are not required to furnish this information, but are encouraged to do so. The law provides that a lender may not discriminate either on the basis of this information, or on whether you choose to furnish it. If you furnish the information, please provide both ethnicity and race. For race, you may check more than one designation. If you do not furnish ethnicity, race, or sex, under Federal regulations, this lender is required to note the information on the basis of visual observation and surname if you have made this application in person. If you do not wish to furnish the information, please check the box below. (Lender must review the above material to assure that the disclosures satisfy all requirements to which the lender is subject under applicable state law for the particular type of loan applied for.)

BORROWER ☐ I do not wish to furnish this information	CO-BORROWER ☐ I do not wish to furnish this information
Ethnicity: ☐ Hispanic or Latino ☐ Not Hispanic or Latino	Ethnicity: ☐ Hispanic or Latino ☐ Not Hispanic or Latino
Race: ☐ American Indian or Alaska Native ☐ Asian ☐ Black or African American ☐ Native Hawaiian or ☐ White Other Pacific Islander	Race: ☐ American Indian or Alaska Native ☐ Asian ☐ Black or African American ☐ Native Hawaiian or ☐ White Other Pacific Islander
Sex: ☐ Female ☐ Male	Sex: ☐ Female ☐ Male

To be Completed by Interviewer This application was taken by: ☐ Face-to-face interview ☐ Mail ☐ Telephone ☐ Internet	Interviewer's Name (print or type)	Name and Address of Interviewer's Employer
	Interviewer's Signature Date	
	Interviewer's Phone Number (incl. area code)	

Exhibit 4.7: *(Continued)*

CONTINUATION SHEET/RESIDENTIAL LOAN APPLICATION		
Use this continuation sheet if you need more space to complete the Residential Loan Application. Mark **B** f or Borrower or **C** for Co-Borrower.	Borrower:	Agency Case Number:
	Co-Borrower:	Lender Case Number:

I/We fully understand that it is a Federal crime punishable by fine or imprisonment, or both, to knowingly make any false statements concerning any of the above facts as applicable under the provisions of Title 18, United States Code, Section 1001, et seq.

Borrower's Signature	Date	Co-Borrower's Signature	Date
X		X	

Exhibit 4.7: *(Continued)*

INTEREST RATE ELECTION AGREEMENT

☐ NEW LOAN	☐ EXISTING LOAN--->>☐ Lock-In ☐ (Product) Change ☐ Relock/Extension
Rate Sheet # ____	Loan #_____ Rate Sheet # _____

BORROWERS MUST MAKE AN INTEREST RATE ELECTION AT TIME OF APPLICATION.
(TO BE COMPLETED BY MORTGAGE CONSULTANT)

BORROWER NAME: _____   SUBJECT PROPERTY:_____

CO-BORROWER NAME:_____   _____

                                              _____

LOAN INFORMATION:

LOAN AMOUNT: _____

PRODUCT (code_____): ☐ Fixed   Variable: ☐ 1YR   ☐ 3/1   ☐ 5/1   ☐ 7/1   ☐ 10/1

TERM: ☐ 15 YR   ☐ 30 YR   ☐ Other_____

PROGRAM :   ☐ Full Doc+   ☐ Hi Q   ☐ Hi Q+   ☐ Agency   ☐ Investor

INITIAL INTEREST RATE: _____   POINTS:_____   MARGIN:_____

INITIAL MONTHLY PRINCIPAL & INTEREST PAYMENT:_____

ESCROW WAIVED: Tax , Homeowner's, & Flood (if applicable) Insurance. ☐ NO   ☐ YES T & I __ I ONLY__

FEES: Application: $_____   Credit Report*: $_____   Appraisal*: $_____
             Lock-In (1% of the loan amount): $_____   Other (specify): $_____
             * Good faith estimate

INTEREST RATE ELECTION

I may elect to lock-in an interest rate and points, in which event these terms will be guaranteed, provided the Loan closes on or before the lock expiration date recited herein. Otherwise, I may elect to have the interest rate and points float with the market until a later date, at which time I may then lock-in an interest rate and points. The locked-in interest rate and points are valid only for the loan product for which I have applied.

☐ **I HAVE ELECTED NOT TO LOCK-IN INTEREST RATE AND DISCOUNT POINTS AT TIME OF APPLICATION**

A. I have elected to allow the interest rate and points to float until such time as I contact Emigrant Mortgage Company, Inc. ("Lender") to lock-in the interest rate and points and execute a Revised Interest Rate Election Agreement in connection herewith. By selecting this option, the Lender does not guarantee a specific interest rate, points or the continued availability of the loan program.

B. I may contact the Lender between the hours of 12:00 P.M. and 5:00 P.M. EST on any business day either to obtain current information on the interest rate and points for the Loan or to lock-in such terms. If locking-in, I must execute a Revised Interest Rate Election Agreement which specifies the interest rate and points applicable to the Loan. I UNDERSTAND I MUST LOCK-IN THE INTEREST RATE AND POINTS AT LEAST THREE (3) BUSINESS DAYS PRIOR TO CLOSING. IF I DO NOT LOCK-IN, MY LOAN WILL AUTOMATICALLY BE LOCKED AS OF THE LATER OF THREE (3) BUSINESS DAYS PRIOR TO CLOSING OR THE DATE ON WHICH THE CLOSING DOCUMENTS ARE DRAWN BY EMIGRANT BASED UPON EMIGRANT'S CURRENT INTEREST RATE ON THAT DATE WITH SIMILAR TERMS.

_____   ____   _____   ____
BORROWER   DATE   CO-BORROWER   DATE

☐ **I HAVE ELECTED TO LOCK-IN INTEREST RATE AND DISCOUNT POINTS.**

A. If the Loan does not close on or before the lock Expiration date stated below, the interest rate and points may change. I will be required to execute a Revised Interest Rate Election Agreement and pay the higher of (i) the interest rate and discount points indicated above, or (ii) the interest rate and discount points prevailing at the time I execute the Revised Interest Rate Election Agreement, as determined by Lender. In any event, the Lender reserves the right to re-qualify me at the new interest rate and discount points. I MUST RE-LOCK THE INTEREST RATE AND POINTS AT LEAST THREE (3) BUSINESS DAYS PRIOR TO CLOSING OR MY LOAN WILL AUTOMATICALLY BE LOCKED AS OF THE LATER OF THREE (3) BUSINESS DAYS PRIOR TO CLOSING OR THE DATE ON WHICH THE CLOSING DOCUMENTS ARE DRAWN BY EMIGRANT BASED UPON EMIGRANT'S CURRENT INTEREST RATE ON THAT DATE WITH SIMILAR TERMS. THE LOCK IN FEE IS DUE UPON RETURN OF THIS SIGNED AGREEMENT TO LENDER.

Lock-in Date: _____   Lock Period: _____   Lock Expiration Date: _____

Exhibit 4.7: *(Continued)*

NEW YORK PROPERTIES:
I must close on this subject property on or before the Lock Expiration Date to be guaranteed the Initial Interest Rate.

A. Monthly escrow payment of 1\12 of the annual real estate taxes and insurance premium may be required.

B. If the Interest Rate is variable, it will be adjusted periodically based on an Index, subject to caps on adjustment. The Index is the weekly average yield on U.S. Treasury Securities adjusted to a constant one year maturity, as published in the Federal Reserve Bulletin by the Federal Reserve Board, and made available each week in Statistical Release 11.15 (519). The new Interest Rate will be calculated by adding _____ Percentage Points to the Index with the result rounded to the nearest one-eighth of a percentage point.

C. The Lock-In Fee, points, deposits or portion thereof paid to the Emigrant Mortgage Company, Inc. ("Lender") upon execution of this Agreement or otherwise prior to issuance of a conditional commitment by the Lender to the Borrower ("Commitment"), shall be refundable only (1) if the Property appraisal report is not favorable for the Loan, (2) if the Borrower has provided complete and correct credit information as required by the Lender's application form for the Loan, and the Lender determines that the Borrower does not qualify as creditworthy for the Loan, or (3) as required by law. If my loan does close, the Lock-In Fee will be applied to any points or closing costs payable at closing.

D. Upon the issuance of the Commitment and my acceptance of such, a Commitment Fee of $ _____ will be required as per the terms of said Commitment. This deposit will be retainable by the Lender, subject to the terms of the Commitment if my loan does not close. If my loan does close, the Commitment Fee plus any Lock-In Fees will be applicable to any closing costs or points payable at closing.

E. This Agreement does not constitute a commitment or agreement by the Lender to make the Loan or any other loan under any terms and conditions to me or to any other person, or an agreement to issue a commitment for the Loan or a commitment for any other loan, or the acceptance of sufficiency or accuracy of any information furnished by me herewith or in or with the Loan application. The Lender expressly reserves the right to decline to issue the Commitment in the event the application form, the Property appraisal, or credit or other information required by the Lender is not furnished to the Lender or is deemed incorrect, incomplete, unverified or otherwise unsatisfactory to the Lender.

F. This Agreement sets forth the terms and conditions for the Lender's agreement to lock in the Initial Interest Rate currently offered by the Lender for the Loan during the Lock-In Term. This Agreement will be otherwise superseded in full by the terms of the Commitment upon issuance of the Commitment. The Commitment will contain additional terms and conditions of the Loan, and requirements for closing of the Loan not set forth in this Agreement. In the event of any discrepancy between the Commitment and this Agreement, the Commitment shall prevail.

G. A loan exceeding 80% loan-to-value (sales price or appraised value, whichever is lower), may require insurance by a private mortgage insurance ("PMI") company of Lender's choice at an additional cost to me. The premium and renewal cost of such insurance is determined by the insurance company. PMI is no longer required when my loan principal balance no longer exceeds 75% of the original appraised value, provided I have not been in default of any payment due on the loan during the preceeding twelve (12) months, or such earlier time as applies under the then current policies and procedures of an investor which has purchased my loan, if applicable.

H. Based on the information I have provided to Lender and should my loan application be accepted, the following property-related documents and conditions are typically required to be satisfied by the borrower in order to close a mortgage loan:

For 1-4 family houses \ condominiums:

(a) title report and insurance;

(b) property survey;

(c) copy of certificate of occupancy for use;

(d) satisfactory final inspection (if new construction);

(e) evidence of appropriate hazard insurance;

(f) evidence of flood insurance as appropriate;

(g) master policy insurance certificate (if applicable in the case of condominiums);

(h) termite inspection report (if required in Commitment);

(i) radon test report;

(j) well water test report;

(k) septic inspection report;

(l) An appraisal of the premises in form and substance satisfactory to Lender. The appraisal must comply in form and substance with Title XI of the Federal Financial Institutions Reform, Recovery, and Enforcement Act of 1989 ("FIRREA") and Part 323 of the Regulations of the Federal Deposit Insurance Corporation. In addition, the Loan is subject to analysis by Lender of the projected future value of the premises as providing adequate security for the loan for the five years following closing. The Loan may be rejected or reduced based upon Lender's review of the appraisal or Lender's analysis of projected future value; and

(m) All prior liens, if any, must be fully satisfied.

For co-operative unit loans:

(a) proprietary lease;

(b) recognition agreement;

(c) pledge of share of stock;

(d) warranty and representation that no outstanding claims against the proprietary lease or stock will exist at closing; and

(e) copy of certificate of occupancy and title policy for the entire building if conversion has occurred within the last six months.

Other conditions which are not foreseeable at this time may be required to be satisfied before the closing of a mortgage loan.

I. In the event the Lock-In Term shall expire prior to the closing of the Loan, the Lender's obligation to lock in the Initial Interest Rate and maintain will

5 Real Estate Closing Procedures

LEARNING OBJECTIVES

After studying this chapter you will be able to:

- Understand what occurs at a real estate closing
- Discuss the responsibilities of the purchaser between the time of entering into the contract for the sale of the property and the closing
- Explain the provisions of the Real Estate Settlement Procedure Act
- Complete the HUD-1 Uniform Settlement Statement
- Discuss the responsibilities of the seller between the time of entering into the contract for the sale of the property and the closing
- Explain the importance of a certificate of occupancy
- Understand the nature of all of the documents that must be prepared for the actual real estate closing
- Explain all of the post-closing procedures
- Apply practical tips to assist you in completing a real estate closing

CHAPTER OUTLINE

Between the Contract and the Closing Date
   Obligations of the purchaser
      Mortgage insurance

Real Estate Settlement Procedure Act
HUD-1 Uniform Settlement Statement
Obligations of the seller
Certificate of occupancy
IRS Form 1099-S
Certificate of non-foreign status
The Closing
Post-closing Procedures
Practical Tips

CHAPTER OVERVIEW

Chapter 4, Conveyancing, provided an introduction to the concept of the real estate closing. The purpose of this chapter is to detail the formalities of the closing procedure, including aspects of the pre- and post-closing process. For the legal professional working in a general and real estate practice, the closing is one of the mainstays of the office.

Prior to the actual closing, the day on which the title to the property passes from the seller to the buyer, certain information must be gathered to assure that the parties are appropriately protected. Many of these items have already been addressed in Chapter 4 in the discussion of the real estate sales contract; however, certain other items must be included as well. Before entering into the sales contract, the buyer must be aware of all the costs that will be involved in the sale. These costs include not only the actual purchase price of the property, but also the financing costs and overall fees associated with purchasing the realty. Generally, the following items are included in the final closing costs:

(a) attorneys' fees, which include the preparation of all legal documents involved in the sale as well as out-of-pocket expenses;

(b) the cost of a title search and the premiums on title insurance if such is deemed advisable with respect to the property (also, many financial institutions require a borrower to acquire title insurance as a condition of granting a mortgage);

(c) surveys;

(d) recording costs — the cost of recording the deed in the county recorder's office;

(e) if the sale involves the purchase of a condominium or cooperative, there may be special assessments that are paid to the homeowners' association, but the specifics vary with each such purchase;

(f) inspection fees for examining the property for safety and code provisions; and

(g) certain costs that are involved in obtaining mortgage loan financing, which may include:
- application fee
- credit check
- financing fee
- loan decision fee
- processing fee
- appraisal fee
- inspection fee
- lender's attorney's fee
- escrow fee
- document preparation fee
- any other fees, including fees for interim loans.

As can be seen, the costs involved in the sale of real estate can far exceed the base purchase price, and many people discover to their chagrin that they can afford the purchase price but not the additional costs involved in the closing. Consequently, all of these financial considerations must be addressed prior to the parties' actually entering into the contract for sale.

This chapter analyzes the procedures involved in three separate time frames: the period between the contract and the closing date, the actual closing, and the period following the closing.

Between the Contract of Sale and the Closing Date

The responsibilities of the parties between the signing of the contract and the transfer of title at the closing vary depending on whether one is the purchaser or the seller.

The Purchaser

After the contract has been entered into, it is the responsibility of the buyer to make sure that any contingencies or conditions in the contract that are her responsibilities are fulfilled. One of the most common of these preliminary steps is to contract for the services of various experts who are responsible for making the many inspection reports that are necessary prior to consummating the sale. Generally, before a financial institution is willing to lend money to the purchaser of realty it wants to make sure that there are no internal problems with the property, and the institution uses these experts' reports to make that decision.

The result of these reports may give rise to a claim that the property contains a defect. A **defect** can be any adverse impact of a physical or structural nature that would cause a significant reduction in the value of the property. If such a condition is discovered as a result of the inspection, the purchaser may be able to seek a reduction in the purchase price or to require the seller to remedy the defect prior to the closing.

If the property passes the inspection satisfactorily, or any discovered defect is cured, the buyer typically submits an application to a financial institution to obtain a mortgage loan. As a rule of thumb, if the purchaser is putting down less than 30 percent of the total purchase price, the lender requires the purchaser to obtain mortgage insurance. **Mortgage insurance** operates to discharge the loan obligation if the insured borrower dies or meets any other condition specified in the contract to trigger the obligation of the insurer. This insurance protects both the lender who is guaranteed repayment of the loan and the borrower who is protected from having the property foreclosed on (see Chapter 4).

Once financing has been arranged, the buyer and the seller agree on the date for the closing, which typically occurs between 30 and 90 days after the signing of the contract or the buyer obtains financing, whichever occurs first.

Many sellers of realty who have covenanted for title will acquire **title insurance** to protect them against claims of ownership to the property. To acquire the insurance, a title search must be conducted to determine the current status of the title, and the cost of the insurance may be borne by either party to the sale, depending on the terms of the sales contract. The title search alerts the purchaser to any encumbrances on the property that might render it unmarketable, and if it is unmarketable, the buyer may avoid the contract (see Chapter 4) if the encumbrance is not removed by the seller by the closing date. As discussed in previous chapters, examples of encumbrances would be existing mortgages, judgments on the property, liens for taxes and other government charges, and mechanics' liens.

During the period between the contract and the closing, the purchaser will conduct a survey of the property to make sure that the property being conveyed corresponds to the terms of the contract for sale. Not only could this have an effect on the sales contract, if the realty turns out to be more or less than described in the contract, but the financial institution providing the funds for the purchase may require the survey prior to approving the loan.

Finally, pursuant to the **Real Estate Settlement Procedure Act,** the federal statute governing all federally guaranteed mortgage loans, a **settlement statement** must be prepared. This form is prepared by the United States Department of Housing and Urban Development, and is usually referred to as the **HUD-1 Uniform Settlement Statement.** This is the standard form used in most real estate transactions, even if no federal mortgage loans are involved. The HUD-1 specifies all items of closing costs, and serves two specific purposes: to reflect the amount to be paid by the seller and to specify the amount to be paid by the purchaser to close the sale. (See Exhibit 5.1. This form can also be accessed online at www.hud.gov.)

Exhibit 5.1: HUD-1 Settlement Statement

A. Settlement Statement

U.S. Department of Housing and Urban Development

OMB Approval No. 2502-0265 (expires 9/30/2006)

B. Type of Loan

| 1. ☐ FHA 2. ☐ FmHA 3. ☐ Conv. Unins. | 6. File Number: | 7. Loan Number: | 8. Mortgage Insurance Case Number: |
| 4. ☐ VA 5. ☐ Conv. Ins. | | | |

C. Note: This form is furnished to give you a statement of actual settlement costs. Amounts paid to and by the settlement agent are shown. Items marked "(p.o.c.)" were paid outside the closing; they are shown here for informational purposes and are not included in the totals.

D. Name & Address of Borrower:	E. Name & Address of Seller:	F. Name & Address of Lender:

G. Property Location:	H. Settlement Agent:	
	Place of Settlement:	I. Settlement Date:

J. Summary of Borrower's Transaction		K. Summary of Seller's Transaction	
100. Gross Amount Due From Borrower		**400. Gross Amount Due To Seller**	
101. Contract sales price		401. Contract sales price	
102. Personal property		402. Personal property	
103. Settlement charges to borrower (line 1400)		403.	
104.		404.	
105.		405.	
Adjustments for items paid by seller in advance		Adjustments for items paid by seller in advance	
106. City/town taxes to		406. City/town taxes to	
107. County taxes to		407. County taxes to	
108. Assessments to		408. Assessments to	
109.		409.	
110.		410.	
111.		411.	
112.		412.	
120. Gross Amount Due From Borrower		**420. Gross Amount Due To Seller**	
200. Amounts Paid By Or In Behalf Of Borrower		**500. Reductions In Amount Due To Seller**	
201. Deposit or earnest money		501. Excess deposit (see instructions)	
202. Principal amount of new loan(s)		502. Settlement charges to seller (line 1400)	
203. Existing loan(s) taken subject to		503. Existing loan(s) taken subject to	
204.		504. Payoff of first mortgage loan	
205.		505. Payoff of second mortgage loan	
206.		506.	
207.		507.	
208.		508.	
209.		509.	
Adjustments for items unpaid by seller		Adjustments for items unpaid by seller	
210. City/town taxes to		510. City/town taxes to	
211. County taxes to		511. County taxes to	
212. Assessments to		512. Assessments to	
213.		513.	
214.		514.	
215.		515.	
216.		516.	
217.		517.	
218.		518.	
219.		519.	
220. Total Paid By/For Borrower		**520. Total Reduction Amount Due Seller**	
300. Cash At Settlement From/To Borrower		**600. Cash At Settlement To/From Seller**	
301. Gross Amount due from borrower (line 120)		601. Gross amount due to seller (line 420)	
302. Less amounts paid by/for borrower (line 220)	( )	602. Less reductions in amt. due seller (line 520)	( )
303. Cash ☐ From ☐ To Borrower		**603. Cash** ☐ To ☐ From Seller	

Section 5 of the Real Estate Settlement Procedures Act (RESPA) requires the following: • HUD must develop a Special Information Booklet to help persons borrowing money to finance the purchase of residential real estate to better understand the nature and costs of real estate settlement services; • Each lender must provide the booklet to all applicants from whom it receives or for whom it prepares a written application to borrow money to finance the purchase of residential real estate; • Lenders must prepare and distribute with the Booklet a Good Faith Estimate of the settlement costs that the borrower is likely to incur in connection with the settlement. These disclosures are manadatory.

Section 4(a) of RESPA mandates that HUD develop and prescribe this standard form to be used at the time of loan settlement to provide full disclosure of all charges imposed upon the borrower and seller. These are third party disclosures that are designed to provide the borrower with pertinent information during the settlement process in order to be a better shopper.

The Public Reporting Burden for this collection of information is estimated to average one hour per response, including the time for reviewing instructions, searching existing data sources, gathering and maintaining the data needed, and completing and reviewing the collection of information.

This agency may not collect this information, and you are not required to complete this form, unless it displays a currently valid OMB control number.

The information requested does not lend itself to confidentiality.

Exhibit 5.1: *(Continued)*

L. Settlement Charges		Paid From Borrowers Funds at Settlement	Paid From Seller's Funds at Settlement
700. Total Sales/Broker's Commission based on price $ @ % =			
Division of Commission (line 700) as follows:			
701. $ to			
702. $ to			
703. Commission paid at Settlement			
704.			
800. Items Payable In Connection With Loan			
801. Loan Origination Fee %			
802. Loan Discount %			
803. Appraisal Fee to			
804. Credit Report to			
805. Lender's Inspection Fee			
806. Mortgage Insurance Application Fee to			
807. Assumption Fee			
808.			
809.			
810.			
811.			
900. Items Required By Lender To Be Paid In Advance			
901. Interest from to @$ /day			
902. Mortgage Insurance Premium for months to			
903. Hazard Insurance Premium for years to			
904. years to			
905.			
1000. Reserves Deposited With Lender			
1001. Hazard insurance months@$ per month			
1002. Mortgage insurance months@$ per month			
1003. City property taxes months@$ per month			
1004. County property taxes months@$ per month			
1005. Annual assessments months@$ per month			
1006. months@$ per month			
1007. months@$ per month			
1008. months@$ per month			
1100. Title Charges			
1101. Settlement or closing fee to			
1102. Abstract or title search to			
1103. Title examination to			
1104. Title insurance binder to			
1105. Document preparation to			
1106. Notary fees to			
1107. Attorney's fees to			
(includes above items numbers:)			
1108. Title insurance to			
(includes above items numbers:)			
1109. Lender's coverage $			
1110. Owner's coverage $			
1111.			
1112.			
1113.			
1200. Government Recording and Transfer Charges			
1201. Recording fees: Deed $; Mortgage $; Releases $			
1202. City/county tax/stamps: Deed S ; Mortgage $			
1203. State tax/stamps: Deed $; Mortgage $			
1204.			
1205.			
1300. Additional Settlement Charges			
1301. Survey to			
1302. Pest inspection to			
1303.			
1304.			
1305.			
1400. Total Settlement Charges (enter on lines 103, Section J and 502, Section K)			

The Seller

Between the contract and the closing, the seller has fewer obligations to perform than the purchaser. Generally, the responsibilities of the seller during this period can be summed up as making sure that he or she can transfer a marketable title on the closing date.

Certain local governments require that a seller produce a **certificate of occupancy** if the property has buildings on it. This certificate is the result of a general inspection of the premises to ascertain that the building is fit to be occupied. If such certificate is required and not provided, the purchaser may avoid the sale.

If the seller utilized the services of a real estate broker to make the sale, the seller must make sure that all commissions owed to the broker are paid prior to the closing, and the seller should obtain a receipt to document the payment. As a general rule, the seller's commission for the seller's broker is simply deducted from the purchase price that is received at the closing.

If any cloud appears on the title to the property, it is the seller's responsibility to see that such cloud is removed pursuant to the provisions of the deed that has been contracted to be conveyed (see Chapter 4).

Finally, during this period the seller must prepare all the documents that he is required to present at the closing. These documents include the following:

- The deed: The deed must conform to the nature of the title that has been agreed to in the sales contract (see Chapter 4).
- Affidavit of title: This is a separate document made by the seller that specifies his title to the property and indicates all improvements made on the property since the seller first acquired the title.
- **Form 1099-S:** This is an IRS form that must be filed for real estate transactions, except for the following:

  Gifts
  Refinancings
  Commercial property

  (See Exhibit 5.2.)
- **Certificate of non-foreign status:** The IRS also requires this form if the parties are U.S. citizens; foreign nationals are required to make certain payments pursuant to section 1445 of the Internal Revenue Code. (See Exhibit 5.3.)
- Survey affidavit, if the seller agrees to provide one to the buyer.
- Settlement statement (discussed above).
- All documents relating to the seller's mortgage.
- **Notice to attorn:** This document applies to property that has been leased to a tenant not a party to the sale. This notice alerts the tenant of the transfer of ownership of the property.
- The seller is usually required to pay a **realty transfer fee** mandated by the government.

- **Payoff amount:** this reflects the amount that is still outstanding on the seller's mortgage and is used by the purchaser to make sure that this encumbrance is discharged by the date of the closing (typically, a portion of the buyer's loan is used to discharge this obligation).
- The seller should have all utility companies provide a final reading of all charges due by the date of the closing so that such charges are allocated between the parties.
- Any other document affecting the right to the property, such as foreclosure papers if the property was acquired by means of a foreclose sale, or estate papers if the property was inherited.

Exhibit 5.2: Form 1099-S

7575 ☐ VOID ☐ CORRECTED

FILER'S name, street address, city, state, ZIP code, and telephone no.	**1** Date of closing	OMB No. 1545-0997	
	2 Gross proceeds $	20**09** Form **1099-S**	**Proceeds From Real Estate Transactions**
FILER'S federal identification number | TRANSFEROR'S identification number	**3** Address or legal description (including city, state, and ZIP code)		**Copy A**
TRANSFEROR'S name			**For Internal Revenue Service Center**
Street address (including apt. no.)			**File with Form 1096.**
City, state, and ZIP code	**4** Check here if the transferor received or will receive property or services as part of the consideration. ▶ ☐		For Privacy Act and Paperwork Reduction Act Notice, see the **2009 General Instructions for Forms 1099, 1098, 3921, 3922,**
Account or escrow number (see instructions)	**5** Buyer's part of real estate tax $		**5498, and W-2G.**

Form **1099-S**   Cat. No. 64292E   Department of the Treasury - Internal Revenue Service

☐ CORRECTED (if checked)

FILER'S name, street address, city, state, ZIP code, and telephone no.	**1** Date of closing	OMB No. 1545-0997	
	2 Gross proceeds $	20**09** Form **1099-S**	**Proceeds From Real Estate Transactions**
FILER'S federal identification number | TRANSFEROR'S identification number	**3** Address or legal description		**Copy B**
TRANSFEROR'S name			**For Transferor**
Street address (including apt. no.)			This is important tax information and is being furnished to the Internal Revenue Service. If you are required to file a return, a negligence penalty or other sanction may be
City, state, and ZIP code	**4** Transferor received or will receive property or services as part of the consideration (if checked). ☐		imposed on you if this item is required to be
Account or escrow number (see instructions)	**5** Buyer's part of real estate tax $		reported and the IRS determines that it has not been reported.

Form **1099-S**   (keep for your records)   Department of the Treasury - Internal Revenue Service

☐ VOID ☐ CORRECTED

FILER'S name, street address, city, state, ZIP code, and telephone no.	**1** Date of closing	OMB No. 1545-0997	
	2 Gross proceeds $	20**09** Form **1099-S**	**Proceeds From Real Estate Transactions**
FILER'S federal identification number | TRANSFEROR'S identification number	**3** Address or legal description (including city, state, and ZIP code)		**Copy C**
TRANSFEROR'S name			**For Filer**
Street address (including apt. no.)			For Privacy Act and Paperwork Reduction Act Notice, see the
City, state, and ZIP code	**4** Check here if the transferor received or will receive property or services as part of the consideration. ▶ ☐		**2009 General Instructions for Forms 1099, 1098, 3921, 3922, 5498,**
Account or escrow number (see instructions)	**5** Buyer's part of real estate tax $		**and W-2G.**

Form **1099-S**   Department of the Treasury - Internal Revenue Service

Exhibit 5.3: F.I.R.P.T.A. Non-Foreign Certification by Individual Transferor

1. Section 1445 of the Internal Revenue Code provides that a transferee of a United States real property interest must withhold tax if the transferor is a foreign person.

2. In order to inform the transferee that withholding of tax is not required upon the disposition by [name of transferor(s)] of the United States real property described as follows:

   the undersigned transferor certifies and declares by means of this certification, the following

   a. I (we) am (are) not non-resident alien(s) for purposes of United States income taxation and,

   b. My United States taxpayer identifying number (Social Security number) is

NAME   SOCIAL SECURITY NUMBER

_____   _____

_____   _____

   c. My home address is _____
                          _____

   d. There are not other persons who have an ownership interest in the above described property other than those persons set forth above in subparagraph b.

3. The undersigned hereby further certified and declares

   a. I (we) understand that the purchaser of the above described property intends to rely on the foregoing representations in connection with the United States Foreign Investment in Real Property Tax Act. (94 Stat 2682 as amended)

   b. I (we) understand this certification may be disclosed to the Internal Revenue Service by transferee and that any false statement contained in this certification may be punished by fine, imprisonment or both.

   Under penalties of perjury I (we) declare I (we) have examined carefully this certification and it is true, correct and complete.

Date: _____

                               _____

Exhibit 5.3: F.I.R.P.T.A. (Foreign Investment in Real Property Tax) Affidavit of Facts Relating to the Withholding of Tax Upon the Disposition of United States Real Property Interests Pursuant to 26 U.S.C. 1445(B)(2)

STATE OF NEW YORK   )

)   SS.:

COUNTY OF   )

The Undersigned, being duly sworn, deposes and says:

1. That the Undersigned are/is the owner(s) of the premises known as _____ being conveyed this date to _____

_____

2. That the Undersigned are/is not a foreign person(s) as defined at 26 U.S.C. 1445 (f)(3).

3. That the Undersigned's United States Taxpayer Identification Number appears following his/her signature below.

_____   _____
_____   _____
_____   _____
_____   _____

Sworn to before me this _____
day of _____ 199_

_____
Notary Public

_____

The Closing

The actual closing usually occurs at the office of the buyer's attorney, but may occur at any mutually agreed-upon location. Generally, the attorneys for the buyer and the seller attend, along with the parties and a representative of the financial institution providing the mortgage loan.

The purchaser usually contacts the title company 24 to 48 hours before the day of the closing to make sure that the title is still free of all clouds and encumbrances. At this point the purchaser will **mark up** the title instrument, meaning that he or she will tick off any item specified in the contract — grantor, grantee, liens, mortgages, judgments, etc. — to indicate that the title is marketable.

When all of the foregoing has taken place, the buyer and the seller transfer all documents and the deed is given to the buyer. In many instances the seller does not appear in person but is represented by an attorney.

The typical closing can be completed in less than two hours.

Post-Closing Procedures

Once the actual closing has taken place, there still remain many items to complete to protect the transferee. The most important of these is to record all the documents necessary to provide a clear chain of title. This includes recording the deed and any mortgage with the county recorder's office.

The financial institution that provides the funds for the purchase will usually create a packet of closing instruments for the borrower, and all the requirements specified in this packet must be completed by the mortgagor. If the purchase includes paying off an existing mortgage, the purchaser must make sure that this encumbrance is discharged and must receive a release from the mortgagee to clear any potential problem with respect to any encumbrance on the property.

Following the purchase of a newly constructed cooperative or condominium, the purchaser can create a **punch list** of items that still require attention, for example, a problem with the flooring. The developer has a specified period of time in which to correct these problems.

Finally, all professionals involved in the transaction must be paid.

Practical Tips

- Be sure to make a complete file of all necessary documents, such as title searches, financing papers, and the parties' information sheets.
- Make a summary of all of the contract information.
- Make sure all contract contingencies have been met.
- Check local rules to determine what searches may be required.
- It is safer to deliver all title documents by hand to minimize the risk of loss or delay.
- Check local statutes to determine what affidavits may be required.
- Check with the local court to determine if there are any special requirements for completing the closing.
- Prepare a log of all important dates and information.
- Prepare the IRS Form 1099-S.

Chapter Review

The process of closing a real estate transaction is a fairly formalized affair that follows set procedures and formats. During the period between the contract and the closing date, most of the burden is on the purchaser to make sure that no problem exists with regard to the property being purchased. No one wants to buy a potential lawsuit.

For the most part, during the pre-closing period the seller is merely required to see that he or she is in a position to provide a marketable title at the closing date.

The closing itself is generally a simple, straightforward, and quick affair in which all documents are signed and transferred, the purchase price is paid, and any existing encumbrances on the property are discharged. After the closing, the purchaser must see that all documents are properly recorded to protect his or her title, and must complete any other documents required by the institution financing the purchase.

Ethical Concern

Once a person is represented by counsel it is unethical for the opposing side to have direct contact with that party. All communication must be made through the attorney. In a real estate closing, because so much information and documents must be gathered, it is tempting to contact the parties directly. Do not do so when the party is represented by counsel.

Key Terms

Certificate of non-foreign status
Certificate of occupancy
Defect
Form 1099-S
HUD-1 Uniform Settlement
  Statement
Mark up
Mortgage insurance

Notice to attorn
Payoff amount
Punch list
Real Estate Settlement Procedure
  Act
Realty transfer fee
Settlement statement
Title insurance

Exercises

1. What are some of the reasons a person would acquire mortgage insurance?
2. What is the benefit of title insurance?

3. Prepare a closing packet based on the documents discussed in this chapter.
4. Indicate the problems that would permit a purchaser to avoid a real estate contract.
5. Analyze the provisions of the HUD-1 statement included in this chapter.

Situational Analysis

Your office represents the buyer of a residential house. The day before the closing you discover that the seller still has not fulfilled all the contract obligations. What are the steps you would take to protect your client's interests?

Edited Cases

The following two cases discuss various problems associated with real estate closings. The first decision, *Rochester Home Equity, Inc.*, concerns recovering fees for a mortgage application that was never consummated, and the second opinion, although fairly lengthy, provides an important discussion of the unauthorized practice of law as it relates to real estate settlements and the details of closing procedures.

Rochester Home Equity, Inc. v. Upton
1 Misc. 3d 412; 767 N.Y.S.2d 201; 2003 N.Y. Misc. LEXIS 1391 (N.Y. Sup. Ct. 2003)

The plaintiff here is suing for application and lock-in fees in a mortgage application that was never consummated. The defendant, in turn, argues that the plaintiff failed to make a federally-mandated disclosure at a time when she could cancel the transaction without penalty. This would appear to be a simple question, and the dispute involves a negligible amount of money—a mere $1,200. Nonetheless, it raises an important point that, to the court's knowledge, has never been resolved by any court in the United States. It requires the court to look at a number of federal and state statutes and regulations that rarely refer to one another and whose combination into a coherent scheme is left to the judiciary. In the end, the court's decision must be based on the evident intent of the legislatures involved, an intent that would be frustrated unless the defendant's position is adopted.

The defendant, who lives in a suburb in the Albany area, was seeking to refinance the house she lived in with her husband. (Although it seems that he was intended to be a party to the mortgage as well, he did not participate in the negotiations and initial document exchanges and thus is not involved in this lawsuit.) She dealt with the plaintiff firm, some 200 miles away, by telephone and fax. The record contains documents signed by the defendant showing receipt of a preapplication disclosure of a $100 application fee and a few other fees, for appraisals and similar charges. She also signed and faxed back a lock-in agreement in full compliance with *3 NYCRR 38.6*. This document secures an offer of a fixed rate mortgage at 5.75% with no points, good for one month, in consideration of a payment of $1,100 (one percent of the loan principal). As the regulations require, this payment would be refunded at the closing of the loan, or if the loan were rejected because of the results of an appraisal, the failure of a third-party lender to cooperate, or the credit worthiness of the applicant. The defendant also signed a credit card authorization for these fees.

After these documents were exchanged the plaintiff took the information needed for a full mortgage application over the telephone. The application was then faxed to the defendant for her signature. At about this time (there is some dispute about the timing of these exchanges) plaintiff also sent defendant a disclosure, in the form required by *12 USC § 2605(a)*, of the number of mortgages routinely assigned or sold on the secondary mortgage by plaintiff.

This was the deal breaker. The document revealed that plaintiff disposed of most of its mortgages — anywhere from 76 to 100%. The defendant, who has maintained that she repeatedly told plaintiff's employees she did not want her mortgage assigned, refused to sign the application once she learned this. She also refused to pay the fees, and this proceeding followed.

The parties have differing views on the timing of the disclosure and its relation to the delivery of the application to the defendant. These arguments may be put to one side. The issue, it seems to the court, is whether the disclosure was made before the transaction was consummated. Because the lock-in agreement secures all relevant terms of the mortgage, the court holds that the disclosure made after defendant signed the lock-in agreement was untimely.

There is nothing in the New York regulations concerning lock-in agreements that sets out what disclosures are required and when they must be made; nor does *3 NYCRR § 38.1 et seq.* provide any guidance on questions regarding the interplay between such agreements and the mortgage application. It is necessary, then, to consult the two federal statutes that control such loans: the Truth in Lending Act (*15 USC § 1601 et seq.*) and the Real Estate Settlement Procedures Act (*12 USC § 2601*), and the regulations under both these statutes.

It is only the Real Estate Settlement Procedures Act (RESPA) which requires disclosure of the number of mortgage loans assigned or sold. To add to the confusion, most other disclosure requirements are found in the Truth in Lending Act. RESPA regulations require that the disclosure be made "[a]t the time an application for a mortgage servicing loan is submitted, or within 3 business days after submission of the application" (*24 CFR 3500.21[b][1]*). They further specify that disclosure must be made at the time of the application when there is a face-to-face interview (*24 CFR 3500.21[c][1]*) and is to be mailed within three days if no such interview takes place (*24 CFR 3500.21[c][2]*).

The parties have also debated whether a telephone application is one made face-to-face. The court finds no merit in any claim that a transaction conducted between two parties in different buildings in different cities is somehow face-to-face because it happens in real time. Surely the letter of these regulations would be met under these circumstances by mailing the disclosure.

But this does not end the discussion. RESPA does not address lock-in agreements, and in the matter of disclosures is basically an appendix to the Truth in Lending Act (TILA). The court has to ask what purpose is to be served by this disclosure, and which party's arguments in the present case best effectuate that purpose.

Fortunately, the announced purpose of TILA is consistent with the timing requirement in that statute. In keeping with the trend toward supplying consumers with more information than market forces alone would provide, TILA is meant to permit a more judicious use of credit by consumers through a "meaningful disclosure of credit terms" (*15 USC § 1601 [a]*). For that reason the disclosures must be made conspicuously and in writing, and they must be made "before consummation of the transaction" (*12 CFR 226.17[b]*).

These two provisions clearly support one another. The purpose of a disclosure is frustrated if one could not act on the information without incurring a penalty. The information required by TILA must be given at a time when the consumer can back out of the transaction. In any other case they would be useless.

This regulation—disclosure before consummation—was promulgated under TILA. What relevance does it have to RESPA? At least one federal court has considered the matter, at least obliquely, holding that RESPA disclosures must be made "within three days of the application,... not at closing when it may be literally or at least practically too late for the borrower to use the information... RESPA (and TILA) require an 'up front' disclosure, at the application stage—not the closing stage—of the loan process." (*Anderson v. Wells Fargo Home Mtge., 259 F. Supp. 2d 1143, 1147 [WD Wash]*.) This language suggests that the three-day requirement was intended to be consistent with the preconsummation standard in TILA.

Applying this principle to the present case is not straightforward. As noted above, the lock-in agreement and the New York regulations governing them are both silent on the applicability of federal law. Although both TILA and RESPA preempt any inconsistent state law, neither of these statutes nor the *Anderson* case deals with lock-in agreements.

The defendant, no doubt aware of the silence of the statute, has argued that the fees are not enforceable because the lock-in agreement is not a binding contract, simply an agreement to agree. The court finds this unpersuasive. The better interpretation, in fact, is that so far from being a mere agreement to agree the lock-in agreement is the functional equivalent of a mortgage commitment. It sets out all the substantive provisions of a mortgage: the property secured, the interest rate, the principal and the duration of payments. It is a lock-in agreement in a double sense. The applicant obtains assurance that she will have the benefit of a particular interest rate; but once she signs the lock-in agreement she is also "locked in" to a particular mortgage lender. All that is left is the information-gathering needed to complete a credit check and to conduct the appraisal.

It would clearly violate the purpose behind TILA and RESPA to allow fees to be levied before all disclosures were made. To do so would be to postpone the disclosure obligation until it was "literally or at least practically too late for the borrower to use the information." Reading these statutes together, it is clear that they aim at providing consumers with all information deemed relevant to a credit decision before the consumer risks any money. A posttransaction disclosure would be pointless at best and a mockery at worst; what good would it do to reveal important details of the transaction when it would cost $1,200 for the borrower to change his mind? For that reason, the court holds that contracts to pay fees such as the lock-in agreement must be preceded by all the disclosures that federal law requires. In a real sense the lock-in agreement is more akin to a consummation of the process than it is to a mere preliminary stage.

This is the only way that the disclosures required by TILA and RESPA would be of any use to the consumer. It would be manifestly improper for the defendant to be penalized for changing her mind on the basis of information supplied pursuant to that federal law. (She also claims that she had not realized until this disclosure that she was dealing with a mortgage broker; this is an error, as plaintiff is a mortgage *banker*—something of a hybrid, but licensed to act as a bank with respect to mortgages.) She did so in a timely fashion, as well. Regardless of the timing of the disclosures vis-à-vis the application, the defendant told the plaintiff that she wished to discontinue the transaction as soon as she received the document. There is no reason not to honor her decision.

The court therefore orders the complaint dismissed, with costs.

Case Questions

1. What factors resulted in the mortgage loan not going through?
2. Discuss the legal purpose of disclosure, and how that affected this case.

In Re Opinion No. 26 of the Committee on the Unauthorized Practice of Law
139 N.J. 323, 654 A.2d 1344 (1995)

We again confront another long-simmering dispute between realtors and attorneys concerning the unauthorized practice of law. See *New Jersey State Bar Ass'n v. New Jersey Ass'n of Realtor Bds.*, 93 N.J. 470,

461 A.2d 1112 (1983). Title companies are also involved. Our resolution of
the dispute turns on the identification of the public interest. Since our
decision today permits sellers and buyers in real estate transactions involving the sale of a home to proceed without counsel, we find it necessary
to state the Court's view of the matter at the outset. The Court strongly
believes that both parties should retain counsel for their own protection
and that the savings in lawyers fees are not worth the risks involved in
proceeding without counsel. All that we decide is that the public interest
does not require that the parties be deprived of the right to choose to proceed without a lawyer.

The question before us is whether brokers and title company officers,
who guide, control and handle all aspects of residential real estate transactions where neither seller nor buyer is represented by counsel, are engaged
in the unauthorized practice of law. That many aspects of such transactions
constitute the practice of law we have no doubt, including some of the
activities of these brokers and title officers. Our power to prohibit those
activities is clear. We have concluded, however, that the public interest
does not require such a prohibition. Sellers and buyers, to the extent
they are informed of the true interests of the broker and title officer, sometimes in conflict with their own interests, and of the risks of not having their
own attorney, should be allowed to proceed without counsel. The South
Jersey practice, for it is in that part of the state where sellers and buyers are
most often unrepresented by counsel in residential real estate transactions,
may continue subject to the conditions set forth in this opinion. By virtue of
this decision, those participating in such transactions shall not be deemed
guilty of the unauthorized practice of law so long as those conditions are
met. Our decision in all respects applies not only to South Jersey, but to the
entire state.

Under our Constitution, this Court's power over the practice of law is
complete. N.J. Const. art. 6, Sec. 2, P 3. We are given the power to permit the
practice of law and to prohibit its unauthorized practice. We have exercised
that latter power in numerous cases. *In re Application of N.J. Soc'y of Certified
Public Accountants*, 102 N.J. 231, 507 A.2d 711 (1986); *New Jersey State Bar
Ass'n v. New Jersey Ass'n of Realtor Bds.*, 93 N.J. 470, 461 A.2d 1112 (1983);
Cape May County Bar Ass'n v. Ludlam, 45 N.J. 121, 211 A.2d 780 (1965); *New
Jersey State Bar Ass'n v. Northern N.J. Mortgage Assocs.*, 22 N.J. 184 (1956);
In re Baker, 8 N.J. 321, 85 A.2d 505 (1951); *Stack v. P.G. Garage*, 7 N.J. 118,
80 A.2d 545 (1951).

The question of what constitutes the unauthorized practice of law
involves more than an academic analysis of the function of lawyers,
more than a determination of what they are uniquely qualified to do. It
also involves a determination of whether non-lawyers should be allowed,
in the public interest, to engage in activities that may constitute the practice
of law. As noted later, the conclusion in these cases that parties need not
retain counsel to perform limited activities that constitute the practice of
law and that others may perform them does not imply that the public
interest is thereby advanced, but rather that the public interest does not

require that those parties be deprived of their right to proceed without counsel. We reach that conclusion today given the unusual history and experience of the South Jersey practice as developed in the record before us.

We determine the ultimate touchstone—the public interest—through the balancing of the factors involved in the case, namely, the risks and benefits to the public of allowing or disallowing such activities. In other words, like all of our powers, this power over the practice of law must be exercised in the public interest; more specifically, it is not a power given to us in order to protect lawyers, but in order to protect the public, in this instance by preserving its right to proceed without counsel. We believe that parties to the sale of a family home, both seller and buyer, would be better served if each were represented by counsel from the beginning to the end of the transaction, from contract signing through closing. We are persuaded, however, that they should continue to have the right to choose not to be represented. They should, of course, be informed of the risks. The record fails to demonstrate that the public interest has been disserved by the South Jersey practice over the many years it has been in existence. While the risks of non-representation are many and serious, the record contains little proof of actual damage to either buyer or seller. Moreover, the record does not contain proof that, in the aggregate, the damage that has occurred in South Jersey exceeds that experienced elsewhere. In this case, the absence of proof is particularly impressive, for the dispute between the realtors and the bar is of long duration, with the parties and their counsel singularly able and highly motivated to supply such proof as may exist. The South Jersey practice also appears to save money. For the record demonstrates what is obvious, that sellers and buyers without counsel save counsel fees. We believe, given this record, that the parties must continue to have the right to decide whether those savings are worth the risks of not having lawyers to advise them in what is almost always the most important transaction they will ever undertake. We realize this conclusion means that throughout the transaction, sellers and buyers may not have the benefit of their own counsel but will look to brokers and title officers, often with conflicting interests, for practical guidance and advice.

I

Proceedings Below

Opinion No. 26 of the Committee on the Unauthorized Practice of Law, 130 N.J.L.J. 882 (March 16, 1992), was issued in response to an inquiry, one of many, from the New Jersey State Bar Association. The inquiry sought a determination of whether the South Jersey practice constituted the unauthorized practice of law. That practice, described in detail later, concerns the sale of a home generally financed by a purchase money mortgage. The essence of the South Jersey practice is that from the beginning of the transaction to the end, neither seller nor buyer is represented by counsel. Every aspect of the transaction is handled by others, every document drafted by others, including the contract of sale, affidavit of title, bond and mortgage. The Committee on the Unauthorized Practice of Law (the Committee), relying largely on our decisions in *New Jersey State Bar Association v. New Jersey Association of Realtor Boards*, 93 N.J. 470, 461 A.2d 1112 (1983); *Cape May County Bar Association v. Ludlam*, 45 N.J. 121, 211 A.2d 780 (1965); *New Jersey State Bar Association v. Northern New Jersey Mortgage Associates*, 32 N.J. 430, 161 A.2d 257 (1960), and its own prior determination in Opinion No. 11 of the Committee on the Unauthorized Practice of Law, 95 N.J.L.J. 1345 (December 28, 1972), ruled that the ordering of a title search by the broker, the preparation of conveyancing and other documents by title officers, their clearing of title questions, and indeed the activities of both broker and title officers at the closing itself, where neither buyer nor seller was represented by counsel, that all of these activities constituted the unauthorized practice of law. The decision was interpreted widely as prohibiting the South Jersey practice, in effect prohibiting a seller and buyer from proceeding with the sale of a home without counsel.

On July 20, 1992, the Committee issued a notice to the bar and the public, clarifying its opinion. 131 N.J.L.J. 910 (July 20, 1992). The Committee explained that it did not intend to prohibit a seller or a buyer from proceeding in these matters without counsel. But at the same time the Committee adhered to its determination concerning what constituted the unauthorized practice of law in these matters, without in any way changing that determination. The result, it appeared to many, was that the right of seller and buyer to proceed without counsel was theoretical, for those whose help they would inevitably require to go through with the transaction seemed, by virtue of the Committee's opinion, to be able to give such help only by engaging in the unauthorized practice of law. Given the concerns of both potential sellers and buyers, as well as those of brokers and title officers, and given the fact that the South Jersey practice had continued for so long, we stayed the effect of Opinion No. 26 pending review by this Court.

Following briefing and oral argument by those interested in the matter — the organized bar, brokers, title officers — we remanded the matter to develop a fuller record, referring it to Judge Edward S. Miller, as Special Master, for that purpose. After sixteen days of hearing, Judge Miller rendered his report to us. While personally strongly favoring a requirement that sellers and buyers be represented by counsel, Judge Miller recommended essentially that we allow the South Jersey practice to continue subject to certain conditions.

The hearing conducted by Judge Miller, leading to his findings and recommendations, is critical to our decision. It was directed not only at determining the extent of the practice of law engaged in by non-lawyers, a circumstance generally known and relatively uncomplicated, but more so at the consequences and implications of the practice. The purpose of the remand was to examine in depth the many factors that would enable this Court to determine whether and to what extent allowing parties to proceed without counsel in such transactions disserved the public interest.

That remand was similar to the action taken by this Court in other unauthorized practice of law cases described later, although the depth and detail of both our inquiry and Judge Miller's hearing and report went beyond most such remands. We asked that the scope of the remand include not only all of the factual aspects of the South Jersey practice, but also its impact on buyers and sellers including both costs and risks; the knowledge of the parties of those risks, and of the conflicting interests of brokers and title officers; the frequency of transactions in which neither party is represented by counsel; comparable advantages and disadvantages to consumers in South Jersey transactions as compared to transactions where both are represented by counsel; the actual incidence of problems in both cases; remedies available to both buyers and sellers for damage caused by brokers or title officers; consumer satisfaction; and other matters. Judge Miller responded to all of our inquiries, and his recommendations covered the issues posed as well as some that arose during the hearings.

Judge Miller found that there had been no proof of actual damage resulting from the South Jersey practice, or more accurately that whatever problems existed did not in the aggregate exceed those in matters where the parties were represented by counsel, that many of the activities undertaken by brokers and title officers, taken in isolation, did not involve the practice of law in any sense, and that, if informed of the risks, and of the interests of those who might otherwise be thought to represent them — including the conflicting interests of the brokers and title officers — sellers and buyers should have the right to decide whether or not to have counsel.

Judge Miller found that when both buyer and seller are represented by counsel, the fees in South Jersey are lower than those in North Jersey. Although he made no explicit finding on the point, implicit in all of his findings is the obvious fact that the unrepresented buyers and sellers in the South Jersey practice save the entire counsel fee they would otherwise have to pay, a fairly substantial sum. He was strongly of the opinion that those savings were not worth the risk that inevitably existed where either seller or buyer went unrepresented. Given this Court's prior decisions on related matters, however, he concluded that the judiciary could not, or would not, mandate representation, but rather that all of the foregoing circumstances called for a determination allowing the continuation of the South Jersey practice subject to various conditions. He recommended that the Court allow brokers to order title reports, contrary to the opinion of the Committee; that only attorneys be allowed to draft the bargain and sale deed, but where that drafting was not accompanied by true representation and advice of counsel, it could be done by others only through the explicit request in writing of the seller; that any other similar conveyancing documents, presumably the bond and mortgage, could be drafted by lawyers representing the title company, again only at the specific written request of either the buyer or mortgagee; that neither the broker nor the title officers present at the closing, or at any other time, could render legal advice; that while the title company could attempt to resolve certain kinds of problems affecting the title, such as arranging to pay off prior mortgages and judgment liens, it could not attempt to resolve others, or presumably give any advice concerning others, such as restrictions on use, easements, and rights of way. Finally, he recommended that the practice, especially the South Jersey practice, of title companies conducting settlements where both buyer and seller are unrepresented be allowed, thereby disagreeing with the Committee's conclusion that such conduct constituted the unauthorized practice of law. He agreed with the Committee's condemnation of conduct that encourages the parties not to retain counsel.

Judge Miller so ruled even though it was his opinion that practically every aspect of a real estate transaction involving the sale of a home constituted the practice of law. As he put it, if he thought he had the power, he would require that both seller and buyer be represented by counsel.

While technically the matter now before us is the review of the opinion of the Committee, R. 1:22-7(b) and R. 1:19-8, we now have the benefit of a full hearing, along with the findings of fact and recommendations that are part of the Special Master's report. The subsequent oral argument and briefing by the parties who participated in that hearing, the New Jersey State Bar Association, the New Jersey Association of Realtors and the New Jersey Land Title Association, focused on both Opinion No. 26 and Judge Miller's report. Our decision today, substantially in accord with Judge Miller's recommendations, affirms portions of Opinion No. 26 and reverses others. Specifically, we rule as follows: a real estate broker may order a title search and abstract; an attorney retained by a title company or a real estate broker may not prepare conveyance documents for a real estate transaction except at the specific written request of the party on whose behalf the document is to be prepared; a title company may not participate in the clearing of certain legal objections to title, see infra at 58; and the practice of conducting closings or settlements without the presence of attorneys shall not constitute the unauthorized practice of law. We hold further, however, that unless the broker conforms to the conditions set forth later in this opinion, all participants at the closing who have reason to believe those conditions have not been complied with will be engaged in the unauthorized practice of law, and any attorney with similar knowledge so participating in such a transaction will have committed unethical conduct.

II

The South Jersey Practice

Although the variations are numerous, the South Jersey practice complained of typically involves residential real estate closings in which neither buyer nor seller is represented by counsel, and contrasts most sharply with the North Jersey practice if one assumes both parties are represented there. Obviously, that is not always the case: the record shows that about sixty percent of the buyers and about sixty-five percent of the sellers in South Jersey are not represented by counsel. In North Jersey, only one half of one percent of buyers, and fourteen percent of sellers, proceed without counsel.

In North Jersey, when both seller and buyer are represented by counsel, they sign nothing, agree to nothing, expend nothing, without the advice of competent counsel. If, initially without counsel, they sign a contract of sale prepared by the broker, they ordinarily then retain counsel who can revoke that contract in accordance with the three-day attorney review clause. They are protected, and they pay for that protection. The seller in North Jersey spends on average $750 in attorney fees, and the buyer in North Jersey spends on average $1,000. The buyer in South Jersey who chooses to proceed without representation spends nothing. The South Jersey seller whose attorney does no more than prepare the deed and affidavit of title, usually without even consulting with the seller, spends about $90. South Jersey buyers and sellers who are represented throughout the process, including closing, pay an average of $650 and $350, respectively. Savings obviously do not determine the outcome of this case; they are but one factor in the mix of competing considerations.

The typical South Jersey transaction starts with the seller engaging a broker who is ordinarily a member of the multiple listing system. The first broker to find an apparently willing buyer gets in touch with the seller and ultimately negotiates a sale price agreeable to both. The potential buyer requires financing arrangements which are often made by the broker. Before the execution of any sales contract the broker puts the buyer in touch with a mortgage company to determine if the buyer qualifies for the needed loan.

At this preliminary stage, no legal obligations of any kind are likely to have been created, except for those that arise from the brokerage relationship itself.

Assuming the preliminary understanding between the seller and buyer remains in effect, the broker will present the seller with the standard form of contract used in that area (usually a New Jersey Association of Realtors Standard Form of Real Estate Contract). That form includes, pursuant to our opinion in *New Jersey State Bar Association v. New Jersey Association of Realtor Boards*, 93 N.J. 470, 461 A.2d 1112 (1983), notice that the attorney for either party can cancel the contract within three business days. If the seller signs the contract, and does not within three days retain counsel, the seller will have become legally bound to perform numerous obligations without the benefit of any legal advice whatsoever, some of which may turn out to be onerous, some costly, some requiring unanticipated expense, and some beyond the power of the seller to perform, with the potential of substantial liability for such nonperformance. Many sellers will not understand just what those obligations are, and just what the risks are. Not only has the seller not retained a lawyer, the only person qualified to explain those risks. Worse yet, the only one the seller has had any contact with in the matter is the broker, whose commission depends entirely on consummation of the transaction, and whose interest is primarily — in some cases it is fair to say exclusively — to get the contract signed and the deal closed.

After the seller signs the contract, the broker delivers it to the buyer for execution. The buyer may not know if the description of the property is precisely that assumed to be the subject of the purchase. The buyer may have no idea if the title described in the contract is that with which he would be satisfied, no sound understanding of what the numerous obligations on the part of the seller mean, and no fair comprehension of whether all of the possible and practical concerns of a buyer have been addressed by the contract. No lawyer is present to advise or inform the buyer; indeed, there is no one who has the buyer's interest at heart, only the broker, whose interests are generally in conflict with the buyer's. Although the record does not dispose of the issue, and although Judge Miller explicitly left it undecided, he noted concern that the broker, through his or her actions, may lead the buyer to believe that the broker is looking out for the buyer's interests. Therefore, without independent advice, the buyer signs the contract. If no attorney is retained within three days, the buyer is bound by all of its terms.

For both seller and buyer, it is that contract that substantially determines all of their rights and duties. Neither one of them can be regarded as adequately informed of the import of what they signed or indeed of its importance. At that point the broker, who represents only the seller and clearly has an interest in conflict with that of the buyer (the broker's interest is in consummation of the sale, the buyer's in making certain that the sale does not close unless the buyer is fully protected) performs a series of acts on behalf of the buyer, and is the only person available as a practical matter to explain their significance to the buyer. The broker orders a binder for title insurance, or a title commitment to make sure that the buyer is going to get good title. The buyer has no idea, and hopefully never will have, whether the broker ordered the right kind of title search, a fairly esoteric question that only an experienced attorney can determine.

The broker also orders numerous inspection and other reports, all primarily of interest to the buyer, to make certain that not only is the title good, but that there are no other problems affecting the premises, the house and their use. Those reports can have substantial legal consequences for both seller and buyer. For example, at what threshold dollar amount of required repairs should the seller (or the buyer) be able to cancel the contract? At what dollar amount should the buyer ignore the repairs? At what dollar amount should the buyer be able to compel the seller to make the repairs, and within what time frame? At this stage of the transaction the help of a lawyer could be invaluable, and the advice of a broker problematic.

The seller in the meantime is happy to hear from no one, for it suggests there are no problems. Eventually, the seller is told that a deed will be arriving drafted by an attorney selected by the broker, the instrument that our decisions clearly require may be drafted only by the seller's attorney. *Cape May County Bar Ass'n v. Ludlam*, 45 N.J. 121, 211 A.2d 780 (1965). Of course, the purpose of that ruling was to assure competent counsel in the drafting of such a uniquely legal document, but "competent" always meant counsel who understood the entire transaction. In South Jersey, the attorney selected by the broker, while theoretically representing the seller, may be primarily interested in the broker, the source of the attorney's "client" and the likely source of future "clients," and consequently primarily interested in completing the sale. That attorney is likely to prepare a deed satisfactory to the title company—in fact that attorney often does not even contact the seller. He or she may have no idea of anything in the contract of sale other than the description of the land and the fact that a certain kind of deed is required. No advice on the substance of the transaction comes from such an attorney even though the seller may get the impression that, since an attorney drafted the deed, the seller's interests are somehow being protected. In fact, the only protection those interests ever received, other than those that happened to appear in the form contract, is in the numbers inserted in that contract, the total purchase price, the down payment, and the closing date, for those are probably the only terms of that contract fully understood by the seller.

The buyer's position is even worse when the closing occurs. The seller will at least know that he or she got paid. Legal training is not required for that fact, even though there is no practical assurance that the seller will not thereafter be sued. The buyer, on the other hand, wants something that is largely incomprehensible to almost all buyers, good and marketable title, one that will not result in problems in the future. What the buyer gets before closing is a "title binder," a piece of paper that may suggest something about the quality of the seller's title, but that is very much in need of explanation for any substantial understanding of its meaning. The title company is required to mail to the unrepresented buyer notice of any exceptions or conditions associated with the title insurance policy. N.J.S.A. 17:46B-9. This notice, which must be sent five days prior to the closing, must also notify the buyer of the right to review the title commitment with an attorney. Ibid. If the buyer chooses not to retain an attorney, there is no one to give the buyer that understanding other than the broker and the title agent. The broker's knowledge will often be inadequate, and the conflicting interest apparent. The title company similarly has a conflicting interest, for it too is interested in completion of the transaction, the sine qua non of its title premium. But the title company is also interested in good title, for it is guaranteeing that to the mortgage company, as well as to the buyer. "Good title," however, may be one on which the title company and the mortgagee are willing to take a risk, but one on which a buyer might or should not be willing to, if the buyer knew what the risk was. Again, there is no one to tell the buyer what those risks are, and in some cases the explicit exceptions found in a title policy, those matters that the title company will not guarantee, are of the greatest importance. The significance of those matters is conceded by all to be something that only attorneys can give advice on, and it is contended by all that they never give such advice. Yet such exceptions exist, and title still closes, and the buyer is totally unrepresented by counsel. One must assume that somewhere, somehow, the buyer is satisfied that there is nothing to worry about, leading to the inescapable conclusion that either the broker or the title officer provides some modicum of assurance or explanation.

The day for closing arrives and everyone meets, usually at the offices of the title company. Seller and buyer are there, each without an attorney; the broker is there, and the title officer is there, representing both the title company and the mortgagee. The funds are there. And the critical legal documents are also on hand: the mortgage and the note, usually prepared by the mortgagee; the deed, along with the affidavit of title, prepared by the attorney selected by the broker or by the title company; the settlement statement, usually prepared by the title company, indicating how much is owed, what deductions should be made for taxes and other costs and what credits are due; and the final marked-up title binder, which evidences the obligation of the title company to issue a title policy to the buyer, and which at that point is probably practically meaningless to the buyer. All are executed and delivered, along with other documents, and the funds are delivered or held in escrow until the title company arranges to pay off prior mortgages and liens.

It would take a volume to describe each and every risk to which the seller and buyer have exposed themselves without adequate knowledge. But it takes a very short sentence to describe what apparently occurs: the deal closes, satisfactory to buyer and seller in practically all cases, satisfactory both at the closing and thereafter.

III

The Unauthorized Practice of Law

As noted above, this transaction in its entirety, the sale of real estate, especially real estate with a home on it, is one that cannot be handled competently except by those trained in the law. The most important parts of it, without which it could not be accomplished, are quintessentially the practice of law. The contract of sale, the obligations of the contract, the ordering of a title search, the analysis of the search, the significance of the title search, the quality of title, the risks that surround both the contract and the title, the extent of those risks, the probability of damage, the obligation to close or not to close, the closing itself, the settlement, the documents there exchanged, each and every one of these, to be properly understood must be explained by an attorney. And the documents themselves to be properly drafted, must be drafted by an attorney. Mixed in with these activities are many others that clearly do not require an attorney's knowledge, such as the ordering of inspection and other reports, and the price negotiation. But after that, even though arguably much can be accomplished by others, practically all else, to be done with full understanding, requires the advice of counsel.

Practically all of the cases in this area are relatively recent. They consistently reflect the conclusion that the determination of whether someone should be permitted to engage in conduct that is arguably the practice of law is governed not by attempting to apply some definition of what constitutes that practice, but rather by asking whether the public interest is disserved by permitting such conduct. The resolution of the question is determined by practical, not theoretical, considerations; the public interest is weighed by analyzing the competing policies and interests that may be involved in the case; the conduct, if permitted, is often conditioned by requirements designed to assure that the public interest is indeed not disserved.

In *Auerbacher v. Wood*, 142 N.J. Eq. 484, 59 A.2d 863 (E. & A. 1948), our then highest court held that someone who performs the usual functions of a labor relations consultant is not guilty of the unauthorized practice of law. The court noted that the issue could not be determined by reference to any satisfactory definition. "What constitutes the practice of law does not lend itself to precise and all inclusive definition. There is no definitive formula which automatically classifies every case." Id. at 485. The court noted that in drawing the line between that which is and is not permitted, "guidance is to be found in the consideration that the licensing of law practitioners is not designed to give rise to a professional monopoly, but rather to serve the public right to protection against unlearned and unskilled advice and service in matters relating to the science of the law." Id. at 486. In *In re Baker*, 8 N.J. 321, 334, 85 A.2d 505 (1951), this Court, holding respondents in contempt for their unauthorized practice of law, similarly observed that "the reason for prohibiting the unauthorized practice of the law by laymen is not to aid the legal profession but to safeguard the public from the disastrous results that are bound to flow from the activities of untrained and incompetent individuals," those not only lacking the many years of preparation, but also the high standards of professional conduct imposed on members of the bar and enforced by the Court.

In a case involving some of the same questions now before us, *New Jersey State Bar Association v. Northern New Jersey Mortgage Associates*, 22 N.J. 184, 123 A.2d 498 (1956), an appeal was taken from the trial court's dismissal of a suit alleging unauthorized practice of law, the trial court concluding that the Supreme Court had exclusive jurisdiction over such matters. The action had been brought by the New Jersey State Bar Association and five individual attorneys. The practice complained of was quite similar to that found in South Jersey, although in fact the business was conducted in North Jersey. The defendants, in the business of searching titles, acting as agents for title companies, and handling the closing of transactions involving sellers, buyers, and mortgagees, admitted that they prepared bonds, mortgages and other instruments connected with titles and mortgage loans, and that the services performed incidental to closing included the giving of legal advice in connection with those transactions. Id. at 190–92.

We ruled that our exclusive power over the practice of law did not divest a court of chancery (the trial court) of its jurisdiction to enjoin the unauthorized practice of law. Id. at 193. We further ruled that the individual plaintiffs could maintain the action only if they could show irreparable damage to their own individual financial interests, and since they could not, the dismissal of the action as to them was affirmed. Id. at 196, 199. The Bar Association, however, was placed on a different footing, for in its attempts to enjoin the unauthorized practice of law it sought to protect the public interest, for the protection of which an injunction could be granted. Id. at 194, 196. In that respect the action was deemed to be "on behalf of the public." Id. at 194.

In analyzing the Bar Association's claim to represent the public interest, we noted that, concerning the nature of the right to practice law, the more recent attitude in New Jersey has been "that admission to our bar is a privilege granted in the interest of the public to those who are morally fit and mentally qualified, solely for the purpose of protecting the unwary and the ignorant from injury at the hands of persons unskilled or unlearned in the law" and that "attorneys enjoy rights peculiar to themselves, not enjoyed by those outside the profession, but only as an incident to the public welfare." Id. at 195. We further noted that the licensing of attorneys " 'is not designed to give rise to a professional monopoly, but rather to serve the public right to protection against unlearned and unskilled advice and service in matters relating to the science of the law.' " Ibid. (quoting Auerbacher v. Wood, supra, 142 N.J. Eq. at 486).

The case was remanded to the Chancery Division to develop a more complete record, similar to the remand in this case to the Special Master. The host of issues set forth by the Court on which further evidence was required before a determination could be made are similar to those in this matter on which we sought further information, at least in the sense that they asked more than questions obviously directed at specific conduct that might constitute the practice of law: the questions sought to know more about the business that was going on, the relationships between the parties, the possibility that independent counsel was being discouraged, the charges made, the exact fee and compensation arrangements, and the percentage of occasions when parties were represented by counsel, id. at 199, all obviously for the purpose of enabling the Court to make a sound decision based on the public interest rather than one premised on some abstract definition of the practice of law.

After remand and plenary hearing, this Court again certified the appeal, on its own motion, from the trial court's dismissal of the charge that defendants were engaged in the unauthorized practice of law. New Jersey State Bar Ass'n v. Northern N.J. Mortgage Assocs., 32 N.J. 430 (1960). In passing on the issues the Court repeated again that the restrictions against the practice of law by non-lawyers "are designed to serve the public interest by protecting 'the unwary and the ignorant from injury at the hands of persons unskilled or unlearned in the law.' " Id. at 436 (citation omitted). Noting that "the line between such activities and permissible business and professional activities by non-lawyers is indistinct," id. at 437, and that some fields may in some areas properly overlap the law, we went on to observe that "each individual set of circumstances must be passed upon 'in a common-sense way which will protect primarily the interest of the public and not hamper or burden that interest with impractical and technical restrictions which have no reasonable justification.' " Ibid. (quoting *Gardner v. Conway*, 234 Minn. 468, 48 N.W.2d 788, 797 (Minn. 1951)).

The message is clear: not only is the public interest the criterion for determining what is the unauthorized practice of law, but in making that determination practical considerations and common sense will prevail, not impractical and technical restrictions that may hamper or burden the public interest with no reasonable justification. That language is from a court that previously had remanded the case to get the full record that would give it all of the facts that would enable it to determine that public interest. The title company, the company that had succeeded to the interests of defendants in the prior case, claimed that on the basis of the entire record its activities did not constitute the unauthorized practice of the law. By then the measuring rod was clear, for the title company's contention was that "the public policy of this State" compelled that conclusion. Id. at 447. The Court disagreed, but not with the standard against which the issue would be determined, for it found that by enjoining the practices involved in the case "the public interest will not be disserved but on the contrary will be significantly advanced." Ibid. There, the public interest consisted of removing "unwarranted charges imposed by the Title Company on purchasers" and encouraging "parties to obtain the important protection of independent counsel." Ibid.

In *State v. Bander*, 56 N.J. 196, 265 A.2d 671 (1970), we sounded the same theme, although in a different context. There we held that the disorderly persons act definition of the unauthorized practice of law did not cover a broker who had prepared a contract for the sale of land even though that conduct, as implied by the decision, clearly constituted the practice of law. We concluded that even if it was the unauthorized practice of law, the broker not being an attorney, the Legislature was free to exclude it (as it did) from its criminal sanctions without offending this Court's exclusive power to determine what constitutes the unauthorized practice of law: in other words, while we may have that exclusive power, it does not prevent the Legislature from criminalizing only certain conduct that constitutes the unauthorized practice of law, leaving others unaffected by the criminal law, although still vulnerable to such prohibitions and remedies as this Court may devise outside of the criminal law. As a result of that conclusion, we noted that we did not have to reach the question "whether defendant's actions constituted an unauthorized practice of law." Id. at 202. The significance of the case, insofar as the present issue is concerned, was in our subsequent discussion of that issue, which "was partially explored at the oral argument" of the case. Ibid.

It developed that the problem has so many ramifications that it could not be intelligently considered on the present record. As to that issue it is suggested that an answer might be obtained in a separate suit for an injunction against the type of acts undertaken by defendant or for a declaratory judgment. In this manner a complete and detailed record could be made disclosing, inter alia, the extent, length of existence, effect and result of the

performance of similar acts by real estate brokers generally and the public
need for such service. This Court could then give a valued and intelligent
reply to such an inquiry. [Id. at 202–203.]

That opinion, commenting on an activity that clearly involved the
practice of law—the drafting of a contract for the sale of land by a
non-lawyer—suggested our approach to the public interest standard
that governed determinations of what constituted the unauthorized practice of law. It was an interest to be determined not by any abstract definition, but by a "complete and detailed record," including "the extent,
length of existence, effect and result of the performance of similar acts
by real estate brokers," and ultimately a record that would show "the
public need for such service." That is, of course, precisely the record developed thereafter in order to determine that specific issue, the public interest
in the right of parties to decline legal representation in the drafting of real
estate sales contracts. *New Jersey Ass'n of Realtor Bds.*, supra.

Although the public interest standard for determination of the issue
of unauthorized practice of law remained intact, Opinion No. 11 of
the Committee on the Unauthorized Practice of Law, 95 N.J.L.J. 1345
(Dec. 28, 1972), reached a conclusion on it different from what we
have determined in this case. The issue there was practically identical
to that now before us. What was involved was the South Jersey practice.
The Committee decided, contrary to our decision today, and based largely on the decision in *Northern New Jersey Mortgage Associates*, supra, 32
N.J. at 430, that title companies are engaged in the unauthorized practice
of law when they issue a title search or policy or abstract at the request
of a broker and that they are similarly guilty when they conduct real
estate settlements on their premises without the presence of an attorney
for any of the parties to the transaction. While the facts in the case were
somewhat different from those here (the Committee finding that the
parties to the transaction were discouraged by brokers from retaining
counsel, that this practice was encouraged when title companies paid
rebates to referring brokers for their business, and that apparently practically all documents were drafted by the title company) their similarity
is remarkable. Indeed, if that opinion were to be followed we would be
obliged to declare the acts challenged before us the unauthorized practice of law. The critical difference, of course, is that there was no showing
in that case before the Committee similar to that found in the record
before us of the impact on the public interest in allowing the South Jersey
practice to continue. Apparently, all that the Committee had before it
was an unadorned description of what occurs prior to and during the
closing, without any evaluation of its benefits and detriments, without
any evaluation of the advantages and disadvantages to the public. For
present purposes, however, Opinion No. 11 is of note in its firm adherence to the standards set by the prior cases. In determining the issue the
Committee said, "the measuring rod is the public interest," 95 N.J.L.J. at
1345, and asked, "Does this practice serve the public interest?" Id.
at 1360. Its conclusion was that it did not. In support of its ultimate

conclusion prohibiting settlements without the presence of attorneys, the Committee said, "Since the practice does constitute the practice of law and such practice by a lay corporation or person is not in the public interest, it constitutes the unauthorized practice of law." Ibid. It is of course remarkable that despite Opinion No. 11 the South Jersey practice flourished, leading ultimately to Opinion No. 26, the matter before us today. The approach we take in this case, the imposition of conditions to assure the public interest is not disserved, as well as that taken in the important cases involving the preparation of real estate contracts by brokers, *New Jersey Association of Realtor Boards*, supra, and inheritance tax returns by accountants, *In re Application of New Jersey Society of Certified Public Accountants*, 102 N.J. 231, 507 A.2d 711 (1986).

In what is undoubtedly the clearest example of the dominating influence of the public interest in this area, we decided in *New Jersey Association of Realtor Boards*, supra, that real estate brokers may draft contracts for the sale of residential property if the contract contains a prominent clause informing the parties of their right, through counsel, to cancel it within three days. While our decision took the form of the approval of a settlement reached between the brokers and the bar, our approval was explicitly based on a finding by Justice Sullivan, sitting as the trial judge, that the settlement was in the public interest, a finding with which we concurred. The initially proposed settlement of the matter had previously been submitted to us and subjected to a public hearing, but after being informed that the settlement had unraveled, we remanded the matter for trial to Justice Sullivan. At that trial a new settlement was arrived at and again subjected to a public hearing before the trial court.

Noting the position of those who objected to the settlement in its entirety, Justice Sullivan concisely summed up the entire law in this area with the observation that "the basic question is how is the public interest best served." *New Jersey State Bar Ass'n v. New Jersey Ass'n of Realtor Bds.*, 186 N.J. Super. 391, 396, 452 A.2d 1323 (Ch. Div. 1982). He concluded that "the settlement is in the public interest" and that the three-day cancellation clause "affords adequate protection to purchasers and sellers of residential real estate or lessors and lessees thereof." Id. at 398. In so concluding, he noted that it had been asserted "without contradiction that 'no State in the Country has prohibited Brokers from completing form contracts in connection with residential property sales.' " Id. at 396. The record in this case also demonstrates that the conduct in question is permitted in many other states. . . .

Our holding today, therefore, accords with the Court's consistent treatment of this issue. Although technically we have overruled the holding of *Northern New Jersey Mortgage Associates*, supra, 32 N.J. 430, that case applied precisely the same standard in passing on the challenged conduct before it — the public interest. As we view it, the real difference is found in the differing records before the Court in the two cases, for in that case the public interest in allowing the challenged practices to continue was apparently nowhere demonstrated, and certainly not with the force of the record before us. Indeed, since the practice challenged apparently related solely to one firm located in North Jersey, and not to the South Jersey practice, it may have seemed that such showing would be irrelevant. More than that, at the time of our decision in that case, we had not yet ruled that brokers could prepare contracts of sale, a change which has affected the entire landscape in this area.

In this case, the record clearly shows that the South Jersey practice has been conducted without any demonstrable harm to sellers or buyers, that it apparently saves money, and that those who participate in it do so of their own free will presumably with some knowledge of the risk; as Judge Miller found, the record fails to demonstrate that brokers are discouraging the parties from retaining counsel, or that the conflict of interest that pervades the practice has caused material damage to the sellers and buyers who participate in it. Given that record, and subject to the conditions mentioned hereafter, we find that the public interest will not be compromised by allowing the practice to continue. We note again that our prior decisions and those of the Committee on this issue did not have the benefit of such a record and were premised on the irrefutable finding that the activities of the non-lawyers in the South Jersey practice constituted the practice of law. That they do, but with the benefit of the record before us it is equally clear that the practice does not disserve the public interest.

Of decisive weight in our determination is the value we place on the right of parties to a transaction to decide whether or not they will retain counsel. We should not force them to do so absent persuasive reasons. Given the importance in our decision of the assumption that the parties have chosen not to retain counsel, and without coercion have made that decision, we have attached a condition to the conclusion that the South Jersey practice does not constitute the unauthorized practice of law. The condition is designed to assure that the decision is an informed one. If that condition is not met, the brokers (and title officers, if aware of the fact) are engaged in the unauthorized practice of law, and attorneys with knowledge of that fact who participate are guilty of ethical misconduct. That ruling is similar to the clear implication in the brokers' and accountants' cases that unless those professions conform to the conditions mentioned in those decisions, they will be guilty of the unauthorized practice of law. *New Jersey Ass'n of Realtor Bds.*, supra, 93 N.J. at 472 ("Licensed real estate brokers and salespersons shall be permitted to prepare certain types of residential sales and lease agreements if these agreements contain specified provisions."); *In re Application of N.J. Soc'y of Certified Public Accountants*, supra, 102 N.J. at 242 (permitting certified public accountants to prepare and file inheritance tax returns "subject to the condition" that client be notified in writing that review by counsel may be desirable).

The public needs protection in these matters. The Legislature has recognized such need and afforded statutory protection for both buyers and sellers at various stages of the real estate transaction. N.J.S.A. 46:3B-1 to -20 (New Home Warranty and Builders' Registration Act); N.J.S.A. 45:15-1 to -42 (Real Estate Broker Regulations); N.J.S.A. 45:22A-1 to -20 (Retirement Community Full Disclosure Act); N.J.S.A. 45:22A-21 to -56 (Planned Real Estate Development Full Disclosure Act); N.J.S.A. 17:46B-1 to -62 (Title Insurance Act); N.J.S.A. 46:10A-6 ("closed shop law" providing that mortgage lenders cannot require borrowers to employ their attorney or to pay lenders' attorney fees and that lenders must also disclose that their attorney works for them and that borrowers should retain their own attorney). In addition, Congress has recognized the need for uniformity in consumer real estate transactions. 12 U.S.C.A. Secs. 2601-2617 (Real Estate Settlement Procedures Act); 15 U.S.C.A. Secs. 1601-1693 (Truth in Lending Act); see Gerald S. Meisel, RESPA: Federal Control of Residential Real Estate, 98 N.J.L.J. 713 (August 21, 1975).

We do not here adopt a "consumerism" that invariably requires that services be made available at the lowest price no matter how great the risk. The record suggests that despite their conflict of interest, brokers' ethical standards have resulted in some diminishment of those risks. Unlike prior cases, there is no finding here, for instance, that brokers are discouraging retention of counsel, no suggestion that title companies are paying rebates to referring brokers. Today's public, furthermore, not only has the benefit of the attorney review clause, but is presumably better educated about the need for counsel, the function of attorneys, and the legal aspects of the sale of the home. The public continues, in South Jersey, to choose not to be represented. We assume that the public has simply concluded that the perceived advantages are worth those risks.

We do not adopt a rule, however, that so long as informed consent from the parties is obtained, any conduct that might otherwise constitute the unauthorized practice of law is permitted. Most of the practices restricted to attorneys can be performed, and may be performed, only by them regardless of the informed consent of the parties and regardless of the lower cost of using non-attorneys. All we decide is that in this case, concerning this practice, the record demonstrates that the public interest will not be compromised by allowing what would otherwise be the unauthorized practice of law if the parties are adequately informed of the conflicting interests of brokers and title officers and of the risks involved in proceeding without counsel.

We emphasize the nature of the public interest standard applied in this case. It is the same as in the cases allowing brokers to prepare real estate sales contracts and certified public accountants to prepare inheritance tax returns. No suggestion was made or implied in those cases that the public was better served if they used brokers and certified public accountants rather than lawyers for the services involved. On the contrary, the conditions imposed by this Court in both—requiring that the parties be informed in advance of their right to retain counsel—reflect our judgment that the parties would be well advised to obtain counsel. We decided only that the protection that lawyers provide and parties need—the basic rationale for prohibiting the unauthorized practice of law—was sufficiently addressed in those cases by assuring that the parties knowingly rejected it; we decided only that the public interest in those cases did not require depriving parties of their right to proceed without counsel, did not require the protection of counsel against their will. That is all we decide here today. We do not conclude that the public is better off without lawyers in the South Jersey practice. As stated several times above, we firmly believe the parties should retain counsel. We decide only that given the history and experience of the South Jersey practice, the public interest will not be disserved by allowing the parties, after advance written notice of their right to retain counsel and the risk of not doing so, to choose to proceed without a lawyer; we decide only that the public interest does not require that the protection of counsel be forced upon the parties against their will. Our required disclosure notice goes beyond that of other cases, reflecting our determination to assure that the parties who decide not to retain lawyers know the conflicting interests of others and know that there are risks of proceeding without one. . . .

IV

Conclusion and Conditions

We premise our holding on the condition that both buyer and seller be made aware of the conflicting interests of brokers and title companies in these matters and of the general risks involved in not being represented by counsel.

We shall ask the Civil Practice Committee to recommend to us practical methods for achieving those aims. Presumably, that Committee will want to form a subcommittee including those who have been involved with this problem for many years. Obviously, the best way to achieve the goal is to have a knowledgeable disinterested attorney sit down with both buyer and seller and carefully explain both the conflict factor and the risk factor, but we doubt if that would be practical. Pending the report of that Committee and our action on it, we have decided to adopt an interim notice requirement that the broker must comply with. If that notice is not given, the broker will be engaged in the unauthorized practice of law. Furthermore, anyone who participates in the transaction, other than buyer and seller, knowing that the notice has not been given when and as required, will also be engaged in the unauthorized practice of law. As for any attorney who, under the same circumstances, continues to participate in the transaction, that attorney will also be subject to discipline for unethical conduct. At the commencement of the closing or settlement, the title officer in charge shall inquire of both buyer and seller whether, how, and when, the notice was given, and shall make and keep a record of the inquiry and the responses at that time.

The interim notice that we require is attached as Appendix A. It is a written notice, and it shall be attached to the proposed contract of sale as its cover page. The notice may be appropriately revised if the broker represents the buyer or is a dual agent, one who represents both seller and buyer.

Whenever a broker presents either buyer or seller with the proposed contract, that cover page shall be so attached, and the broker shall personally advise the buyer or seller at that point that he or she must read it before executing the contract. If the contract is not personally delivered by the broker to the buyer or seller, the broker must make certain, prior to such delivery, that buyer and seller have been so informed, and must do so by speaking to them personally or by phone.

Assuming such notice is given in accordance with the terms and conditions mentioned above, we hold that attendance and participation at the closing or settlement where neither party has been represented by counsel, or where one has not been so represented, does not constitute the unauthorized practice of law; that brokers may order abstracts, title binders, and title policies; that an attorney retained by the broker to draft a deed and/or affidavit of title for the seller may do so but only if the attorney personally consults with the seller; regardless of the prior restriction, any attorney retained by the broker for that purpose, or any attorney acting for the title company, may draft any of the documents involved in the transaction upon written request of the party, be it buyer, seller, lender, mortgagee, bank, or others; that the title company may participate in clearing up those minor objections which Judge Miller refers to as categories one and two: standard exceptions such as marital status and money liens customarily paid at closing, but not those classified as categories three and four: easements, covenants, or other serious legal objections to title.

Other equally important protections for buyer and seller should exist. Any broker participating in a transaction where buyer and seller are not represented should have the experience and knowledge required at least to identify a situation where independent counsel is needed. Under those circumstances the broker has a duty in accordance with the standards of that profession, to inform either seller or buyer of that fact. N.J.A.C.11:5-1.23(a), (f). Presumably, the same duty applies to any title officer, whether or not an attorney, but especially if an attorney, who becomes aware of the need of either party for independent counsel. In addition to whatever potential action might be taken by the bodies that regulate brokers and title officers, as well as by their own associations, their failure to inform exposes them to the risk of civil liability for resulting damages.

Our decision, while allowing continuation of the South Jersey practice, imposes new conditions on that practice and serious consequences for noncompliance. In order that brokers and others may adjust their practices to comply with those conditions, our decision will not become effective until sixty days from the date of this opinion and will apply to all real estate contracts subject to this opinion that are thereafter executed and to the transactions based on those contracts.

The decision of the Committee, Opinion No. 26, is affirmed in part, and reversed in part, and judgment entered declaring the rights of the participants in New Jersey residential real estate transactions in accordance with this opinion.

Case Questions

1. Why do you think the court spent so much time discussing the unauthorized practice of law? Do you believe such practices are commonplace? Explain.

2. What was the "unauthorized practice of law" discussed in this case?

6 Condominiums, Cooperatives, and Commercial Property

LEARNING OBJECTIVES

After studying this chapter you will be able to:

- Define "condominium"
- Understand how a condominium homeowners' association works
- Define "cooperative"
- Understand the considerations that must be addressed when the property in question is commercial property
- Apply some practical tips for guidance in dealing with cooperatives, condominiums, and commercial real estate

CHAPTER OUTLINE

Estoppel letter
Proration
Practical Tips

CHAPTER OVERVIEW

At this point it would be beneficial to examine, briefly, certain hybrid situations that are commonly encountered in a real estate law practice. These special situations include condominiums, cooperatives, and commercial property.

Condominiums and cooperatives first appeared over one hundred years ago, exclusively in urban settings. Land had become increasingly scarce with the growth of cities brought about by the Industrial Revolution. People who wanted to own their own homes had to share their houses with others because of escalating land values on limited space. Landowners began to construct taller buildings to increase the number of units that could be rented, further reducing the availability of land for single-family homes. Eventually, the owners of multi-story buildings decided to sell units rather than renting so that people could, in some way, own their own homes. The result was the condominium and the cooperative. This form of ownership is now popular in suburban and rural areas as well as the cities in which it began.

Although its title tracks the titles of all other property, commercial property involves several additional aspects with regard to its sale, basically because most commercial property involves leases with tenants in possession who have certain rights and obligations that must be taken into consideration when the property is sold.

This chapter briefly examines these three specific situations involving the sale of real property.

Condominiums

A **condominium** is a form of ownership of real property in which the condominium owners hold title outright to a specifically designated unit and, at the same time, hold title as joint tenants with all other condominium unit owners in the development for what are considered to be the "common areas." These common areas include hallways, entryways, roofs, stairways and elevators, and recreational areas such as a common swimming pool, tennis court, and health center. Basically, any area that is used by all of the unit owners may be deemed to be a common area.

EXAMPLE:

A woman wants to retire to the Sun Belt and no longer wants to worry about maintaining her own home. She purchases a two-bedroom unit in a condominium development that has a golf course. The woman holds title to her unit (basically an apartment or a townhouse) as a tenant in severalty, and is a joint tenant with all other unit owners for the golf course and common walkways and areas.

The concept of a condominium did not exist under the common law, and consequently is a creature of statute. Every state has enacted laws that provide for the creation and regulation of condominiums (and cooperatives), and therefore each jurisdiction's statutes must be individually analyzed to determine particular rights and obligations. In addition to statutory regulation, the person who develops the condominium must also prepare a **condominium declaration** that is recorded with the deed to the land in the county recorder's office. This declaration details the specific rights and obligations of the unit owners (see Exhibit 6.1 at the end of this chapter for an example of a Sales Contract for a Condominium).

When creating a condominium, the developer must, usually by statutory mandate, establish rights and regulations for the governance of the condominium, and furthermore must prepare a plat description that shows the physical size and location of each of the units (see Chapter 4). Also, a **homeowners' association** must be formed to oversee the regulation of the condominium and to have authority to maintain the common areas. Before any units in the condominium can be sold, the condominium declaration, plat description, and homeowners' association must be established.

The homeowners' association, sometimes referred to as the **condominium association,** is formed as a non-profit corporation, and therefore, to be legally organized, is required to file **articles of incorporation** with the state secretary of state. These articles act as the association's creating document. The association must also adopt **bylaws** that detail the day-to-day operations of the association. The condominium unit owners elect some of the residents to act as members of the association's **board of directors** who manage the association for a stated period of time, at which point a new board will be elected by the unit owners. To maintain the condominium, the unit owners pay an **assessment** to cover the cost of maintaining and repairing the common areas.

EXAMPLE:

A condominium developer has filed all necessary papers to create a condominium, and has sold almost all the units. The developer has also filed a certificate of incorporation for the homeowners' association with the secretary of state. At this point the developer calls a meeting of the unit owners for the purpose of electing a board of directors. Five people are elected to the board. The board then has the unit owners pay the yearly assessment so that it can maintain the common areas.

With a condominium, each unit owner is liable for the maintenance and repair of his or her own individual unit, and is liable for any injuries that result from the failure to maintain the requisite standard of care associated with property ownership (see Chapter 4). The unit owner is also a joint tenant for the common areas and the owner is jointly liable for any injuries resulting from the failure of the homeowners' association to maintain the common areas in good repair.

Because the condominium represents individual ownership of the unit, the unit owner is free to sell, gift, devise, or rent his or her unit without restriction, *unless* there is some prohibition in the condominium declaration, which is rare. Condominium ownership typically provides for the free transferability of the property.

Cooperatives

A **cooperative** differs from a condominium. Cooperative ownership is considered to be ownership of personal property, not real property, because the owner purchases a share in a cooperative association, and the share entitles the holder to possess a specified unit that is owned by the cooperative. In other words, cooperative ownership is similar to ownership of a corporation. The shareholder owns a share that represents a percentage of corporation, and the share entitles the holder (with the cooperative) to possess, not own, a particular unit. Cooperatives are very popular on the East Coast of the United States.

Because the cooperative owner only holds a share, the shareholder has limited rights with respect to the transferability of that share. The cooperative is managed by a board that is responsible for the financial and physical well-being of the property. As a consequence, the board reviews all prospective purchasers for financial resources and personality, to determine whether the potential owner would be an appropriate tenant in the cooperative. Therefore, if an owner wishes to sell his or her share, the prospective buyer must be approved by the cooperative board. In the case of a stalemate, the cooperative agreement often provides that the cooperative will repurchase the shares from the owner, but the price is usually set at a rate below market value.

 **EXAMPLE:**

The owner of a cooperative wants to move and has found a prospective buyer for his shares, a well-known rock musician. Although financially sound, the board refuses to approve the musician because they do not want "theatrical people" in the building. Therefore the board may block this potential sale.

Because the units are owned by the cooperative, not the shareholders, financing of the property is made by and through the cooperative, and each shareholder pays an assessment to the board to cover the financing. If a shareholder defaults, the other shareholders must make up the shortfall to maintain the property's financing.

Cooperatives, because of their restrictions on transferability, are usually less expensive than condominiums. See Exhibit 6.2 at the end of this chapter for an example of a Sales Contract for a Cooperative.

Commercial Property

The term "commercial property," as used in the context of this book, refers to real estate that has been developed for commercial use, such as office and apartment buildings and shopping centers, and consequently have tenants already in situ. Certain additional considerations must be addressed with any sale of this type of property:

- When the property is described in the contract for sale, items of personal property that are used in the operation of the commercial venture are also usually included, such as landscaping and snow removal equipment. If not included in the description of the property being transferred they must be specifically excluded if the items are not intended to be part of the sale.
- Purchasers of commercial property are entitled to a physical inspection of the property prior to the sale. This inspection can include review of all contracts and financial documents associated with the property, and the buyer typically has the right to withdraw from the contract at this time if there are problems with the property that the seller refuses to remedy.
- In addition to the general covenants discussed in the previous chapter, if the sale involves commercial property, the seller is usually required to provide certain guarantees with respect to any leases that exist on the property, as well as all services and utilities in effect with respect to the property. The seller usually warrants that he or she will not enter into any new lease or contract before the closing date without the buyer's consent.
- If the property is leased to tenants at the time of the sale, the tenants may be required to sign an **estoppel letter,** which is a document that warrants the accuracy of the tenant's lease that is provided for the buyer by the seller. A copy of the purported lease is attached to the estoppel letter for this purpose.

- If the commercial property being sold is subject to a mortgage, and the buyer is taking title subject to the mortgage, the buyer will require the mortgagee to provide an **estoppel certificate** that details all the terms of the note and mortgage, indicating the amount of the outstanding balance and any amount in default as of the date of the signing of the estoppel certificate.
- For commercial property that is leased to tenants, the contract for sale will usually require a **proration** of the rent — a delineation of the amount of rent that will belong to the seller and the amount that will belong to the buyer. Furthermore, the contract must specify the taking over of any **security deposits** made by the tenants to the seller, which represent an amount that must be maintained in a trust account for the benefit of the property owner if the tenant defaults on the rent.
- Usually the buyer will require the seller to include an **indemnification** clause whereby the seller agrees to indemnify, or reimburse, the buyer for any cause of action on the property that was occasioned by events that occurred prior to the closing that are attributable to the seller's breach of a legal obligation.

See Exhibit 6.3 at the end of this chapter for a Land Description of a Commercial Property.

Practical Tips

- Make sure that all requirements of the co-op or condominium board have been met to effectuate a transfer.
- For commercial property, if dealing with an artificial entity, make sure that the entity has been lawfully formed; otherwise the transaction may be invalid.
- For commercial sales, make sure all tenants have received and/or prepared all necessary documents.

Chapter Review

Condominiums, cooperatives, and commercial property present special problems for anyone involved in the purchase and sale of realty.

The condominium represents a dual title to property: individual ownership for a given unit and a joint tenancy for the common areas. Condominiums are easy to transfer, but the unit owner has individual liability for his or her own unit and is jointly liable with the other unit owners for injuries resulting from poor maintenance of the common areas.

Cooperatives represent ownership in personal property of a share certificate that entitles the holder to possess, not own, a given unit. Liability for the cooperative owner is joint with all the other shareholders, and transferability of the share is difficult because alienation is restricted and subject to approval by the cooperative board.

Both condominiums and cooperatives are managed by boards pursuant to their certificates of incorporation.

The sale and purchase of commercial real estate, although following all the other categories of realty, require special attention for certain matters that apply only to property that is occupied by tenants who have rights and obligations with respect to the property. These considerations must be addressed in the contract for the sale of all commercial realty.

Ethical Concern

It is an unethical practice to represent both sides in a legal transaction unless both parties are aware of the representation and agree to it. This means that in a real estate transaction the same law office cannot represent the buyer and the seller, unless they both agree. Even if both sides agree, it still may be wise to decline such representations to avoid the appearance of impropriety.

Key Terms

Articles of incorporation	Cooperative
Assessment	Estoppel certificate
Board of directors	Estoppel letter
Bylaws	Homeowners' association
Condominium	Indemnification
Condominium association	Proration
Condominium declaration	Security deposit

Exercises

1. Review your state's statutes governing cooperatives and condominiums.
2. Briefly discuss the reasons a person might wish to purchase a cooperative rather than a condominium.
3. At the county recorder's office, search for an estoppel letter that appears with a deed to a commercial building.
4. Obtain from a local bank a copy of a mortgage application to purchase a cooperative and analyze its provisions.
5. Briefly discuss the additional factors that must be addressed with the purchase of commercial property.

Situational Analysis

A group of townhouses were constructed as a condominium. After several years the board decides that the exteriors of some of the houses need to be repainted, and it assesses all the unit owners, claiming that this is a common area. Your client is one of the unit owners so assessed whose house is not being painted and she claims this is not a common area. Argue both sides and decide the case.

Edited Cases

The first case underscores the power of a homeowners' association in attempting to bar dogs from the premises. The second case concerns the conversion of rental units to condominiums.

Board of Directors of 175 East Delaware Place Homeowners Association v. Hinojosa
287 Ill. App. 3d 886, 679 N.E.2d 407 (1997)

Plaintiff, board of directors of 175 East Delaware Place Homeowners Association (the Board), filed suit against defendants, Nancy Lee Carlson and Benjamin Tessler, Jorge and Donna Hinojosa, and Independence One Mortgage Corporation, seeking to foreclose on a statutory lien under the Condominium Property Act (the Act) (765 ILCS 605/9(h) (West 1994)). The trial court dismissed plaintiff's complaint. Plaintiff appeals, contending that the trial court erred in finding the Board's no-dog rule unreasonable. For the reasons that follow, we reverse.

Facts

175 East Delaware Place was organized as a condominium in 1973 by the recording of a declaration and bylaws. The property includes floors 45 through 92 of the John Hancock building and contains 705 condominium units. The declaration and bylaws were silent on the issue of pet ownership in the building. In 1976, the Board adopted a rule allowing owners to have pets, including dogs, only with the permission of the Board. On January 21, 1980, during a regular board meeting, the Board adopted a rule barring unit owners from bringing additional dogs onto the premises. In October of 1985, defendants Nancy Lee Carlson and Benjamin Tessler purchased a unit in the building. At this time, they signed a pet agreement acknowledging the no-dog rule. In February of 1993, while leasing out another one of their units, they signed the same agreement again. In March of 1993, the no-dog rule was reincluded in the Board's rules and regulations.

In June of 1993, defendants Carlson and Tessler acquired a dog. This same month, a group of owners brought suit against the Board challenging the no-dog rule. *Rodgers v. Board of Directors of 175 East Delaware Place Homeowners Ass'n*, No. 93 CH 5602. This suit was eventually abandoned and is not part of this appeal. In September of 1993, defendants Carlson and Tessler received notice of a hearing for their violation of the no-dog rule. The hearing was held on November 30, 1993, and the committee recommended to the Board that Carlson and Tessler be ordered to remove the dog within 30 days. If the dog remained on the premises after 30 days, defendants Carlson and Tessler should be assessed a fine of $100 per day for each day the dog remained. The Board adopted the committee's recommendation and on January 23, 1994, began assessing fines on defendants Carlson and Tessler. On April 20, 1994, after Carlson and Tessler failed to pay the fines, the Board recorded a notice and claim of statutory lien.

In August of 1994, defendants Carlson and Tessler sold the unit to defendants Jorge and Donna Hinojosa subject to the lien. In November of 1994, the Board filed the instant action seeking to foreclose on the lien. Defendants moved to dismiss the suit pursuant to section 2-619(a)(9) of the Code of Civil Procedure (735 ILCS 5/2-619(a)(9) (West 1994)), claiming the Board had no authority to adopt the no-dog rule because the rule conflicted with the declaration and bylaws. The trial court ruled that the Board had the power to promulgate the rule but held that the rule was unreasonable.

Analysis

A. Legal Background

Condominiums are creatures of statute and, thus, any action taken on behalf of the condominium must be authorized by statute. "When a controversy regarding the rights of a condominium unit owner in a condominium arises, we must examine any relevant provisions in the Act and the Declaration or bylaws and construe them as a whole." *Carney v. Donley*, 261 Ill. App. 3d 1002, 1008, 199 Ill. Dec. 219, 633 N.E.2d 1015 (1994).

A condominium is an interest in real estate created by statute that gives each owner an interest in an individual unit as well as an undivided interest in common elements. Administration and operation of the condominium are vested in the condominium association, which is comprised of all unit owners. The administration is exercised through the board of directors, which is elected by the owners. In addition to the Act, the operation and administration of the condominium are governed by three principal documents. These are the declaration, bylaws, and board rules and regulations. The declaration and bylaws form the basic framework of the administration, and the day-to-day operations are managed by board rules and regulations.

A condominium comes into being by the recording of a declaration. The declaration is prepared and recorded by either the developer or association. The Act defines the declaration as the "instrument by which the property is submitted to the provisions of [the] Act." 765 ILCS 605/ 2(a) (West 1994). Its primary function is to provide a constitution for the condominium — to guide the condominium development throughout the years. The declaration contains the property's legal description, defines the units and common elements, provides the percentage of ownership interests, establishes the rights and obligations of owners, and contains restrictions on the use of the property. R. Otto, Illinois Act in Condominium Titles, in Illinois Condominium Law Sec. 1.15, at 1-27 (Ill. Inst. for Cont. Legal Educ. 1994). All restrictions contained in the declaration are covenants that run with the land and bind each subsequent owner. They are given a strong presumption of validity. M. Kurtzon, Representing the Condominium Association, in Illinois Condominium Law Sec. 10.19, at 10-17 (Ill. Inst. for Cont. Legal Educ. 1994). Section 4 of the Act details what elements must be contained in the declaration. Paragraph (i) states: "Such other lawful provisions not inconsistent with the provisions of this Act as the owner or owners may deem desirable in order to promote and preserve the cooperative aspect of ownership of the property and to facilitate the proper administration thereof." 765 ILCS 605/4(i) (West 1994).

The second document is the bylaws, which deal with administration and procedural matters concerning the property. Bylaws may be embodied in the declaration or be a separate document. In either case, the bylaws must be recorded with the declaration. 765 ILCS 605/17(a) (West 1994). Should the bylaws conflict with the declaration, the declaration prevails. Section 18 of the Act sets forth certain provisions that shall be included in the bylaws. Relevant to the issue before us is paragraph (k), which states: "Restrictions on and requirements respecting the use and maintenance of the units and the use of the common elements, not set forth in the declaration, as are designed to prevent unreasonable interference with the use of their respective units and of the common elements by the several unit owners." 765 ILCS 605/18(k) (West 1994).

The third item governing condominium conduct is the board rules and regulations. Section 18.4 of the Act deals with powers and duties of the board and provides that the board may: "Adopt and amend rules and regulations covering the details of the operation and use of the property, after a meeting of the unit owners called for the specific purpose of discussing the proposed rules and regulations." 765 ILCS 605/18.4(h) (West 1994).

Under this rule, "a board of managers may not take any action that is beyond the authority granted it under the condominium instruments and the Condominium Property Act." 765 ILCS 605/18.4, Historical & Practice Notes, at 129 (West 1993). The board shall exercise for the association all powers, duties, and authority vested in the association by law or the condominium documents. It generally has broad powers and its rules govern the requirements of day-to-day living in the association. Board rules must be objective, evenhanded, nondiscriminatory, and applied uniformly.

See J. Shifrin, Cooperative, Condominium, and Homeowners' Association Litigation, in Real Estate Litigation Sec. 11.20, at 11-17 (Ill. Inst. for Cont. Legal Educ. 1994).

B. Power of the Board to Promulgate the No-Dog Rule

As noted, pursuant to section 18.4 the Board has the power to adopt rules and regulations. Section 18(k) does discuss restrictions that shall be included in the bylaws. However, this provision merely gives the association the authority to include restrictions in the condominium instruments that will clothe the restrictions with a strong presumption of validity and make them less susceptible to attack. The provision does not state that if a restriction is not contained in the bylaws it will be unenforceable. We thus conclude that the Board's no-dog rule is not in conflict with the Act.

The 175 East Delaware Place declaration and bylaws do not make any reference to pet ownership or dogs, in particular. As to the Board's powers, the declaration provides:

> The Board may adopt such reasonable rules and regulations as it may deem advisable for the maintenance, conservation and beautification of the Property, and for the health, comfort, safety and general welfare of the Owners and Occupants of the Property. Written notice of such rules and regulations shall be given to all Owners and Occupants and the entire Property shall at all times be maintained subject to such rules and regulations.

The declaration clearly gives the Board authority to promulgate rules regarding use of and restrictions on the use of units. Because the Board is authorized to promulgate reasonable rules for the general welfare of the owners and the declaration is silent on the issue of dog ownership, the instant rule does not conflict with either the declaration or the bylaws.

Courts that have addressed the issue have held that dogs may be prohibited or restricted by provisions in the declaration or bylaws. See *Nahrstedt v. Lakeside Village Condominium Ass'n,* 8 Cal. 4th 361, 878 P.2d 1275, 33 Cal. Rptr. 2d 63 (1994) (restriction in recorded declaration barring all pets except fish and birds enforceable unless unreasonable); *Chateau Village North Condominium Ass'n v. Jordan,* 643 P.2d 791 (Colo. App. 1982) (rule barring all pets appended to bylaws and recorded enforceable); *Parkway Gardens Condominium Ass'n v. Kinser,* 536 So. 2d 1076 (Fla. App. 1988) (board rule barring pets unenforceable because declaration allowed them); *Zeskind v. Jockey Club Condominium Apartments, Unit II, Inc.,* 468 So. 2d 1021 (Fla. App. 1985) (no-pet rule in declaration enforceable); *Wilshire Condominium Ass'n v. Kohlbrand,* 368 So. 2d 629 (Fla. App. 1979) (restriction in declaration barring replacement of lap dogs enforceable); *Johnson v. Keith,* 368 Mass. 316, 331 N.E.2d 879 (1975) (board rule barring all pets unenforceable; rule must be included in bylaws); *Noble v. Murphy,* 34 Mass. App. 452, 612 N.E.2d 266 (1993) (restriction barring all pets incorporated in original recorded documents enforceable); but see *Dulaney Towers Maintenance Corp. v. O'Brey,* 46 Md. App. 464, 418 A.2d

1233 (1980) (board rule limiting number of pets enforceable). The issue before us, however, is whether the Board may promulgate a rule restricting dog ownership. This issue has not been addressed in Illinois.

Apple II Condominium Ass'n v. Worth Bank & Trust Co., 277 Ill. App. 3d 345, 213 Ill. Dec. 463, 659 N.E.2d 93 (1995), addresses use restrictions under the Act. In *Apple II*, we set forth standards for evaluating such restrictions and adopted the analysis set forth in *Hidden Harbour Estates, Inc. v. Basso*, 393 So. 2d 637 (Fla. App. 1981). We differentiated use restrictions that are contained in the declaration or bylaws from those promulgated by board rule. The restrictions in the first category "are clothed in a very strong presumption of validity and will not be invalidated absent a showing that they are wholly arbitrary in their application, in violation of public policy, or that they abrogate some fundamental constitutional right. . . . 'Reasonableness' is not the appropriate test for such restrictions." *Apple II*, 277 Ill. App. 3d at 250-51. However, when the board promulgates a rule restricting the use of property, the second category, "the board must affirmatively show the use it wishes to prohibit or restrict is 'antagonistic to the legitimate objectives of the condominium association.'" *Apple II*, 277 Ill. App. 3d at 351, quoting *Basso*, 393 So. 2d at 640. Thus, "when such a rule [use restriction] is adopted by the board alone or requires the board to exercise discretion, we will scrutinize the restriction and uphold it only if it is affirmatively shown to be reasonable in its purpose and application." *Apple II*, 277 Ill. App. 3d at 352.

Based on the above, we conclude that the Board had the power to promulgate a reasonable no-dog rule.

C. Reasonableness of Rule

Because the rule was promulgated by the Board, it is not clothed with a strong presumption of validity. Thus, we must carefully scrutinize the rule to determine if it is reasonable in its purpose and application. Because the facts are not in dispute, the issue is one of law.

In *Dulaney Towers Maintenance Corp. v. O'Brey*, 46 Md. App. 464, 418 A.2d 1233 (1980), the court stated:

"The rationale for allowing the placing of restrictions in, or the barring of pets by way of, house rules is based on potentially offensive odors, noise, possible health hazards, clean-up and maintenance problems, and the fact that pets can and do defile hallways, elevators, and other common areas." *Dulaney Towers Maintenance*, 46 Md. App. at 466, 418 A.2d at 1235.

The above factors, in conjunction with the specific facts of this case, lead us to conclude the Board's no-dog rule is a reasonable exercise of the Board's rule-making power. The John Hancock building is located in a very urban and densely populated area of the city where parks, grass, and other recreational areas for dogs are scarce. The 705 residences are located on the 45th through 92nd floors. In order to take a dog out, one must access elevators and descend anywhere from 45 to 92 floors.

The rule was adopted to prevent possible injury or harm. The original purpose for promulgating the rule was due to an incident in which one dog killed another dog in the building. The Board had tried less restrictive measures to regulate dogs in the past. However, these measures did not cure or alleviate what the Board reasonably perceived to be potential and real problems. It should also be noted that when the no-dog rule was adopted, owners were allowed to retain existing dogs. The rule only prohibited additional and/or replacement dogs.

Because the Board applied the rule to all owners and the purpose for the rule was rational, we conclude that the rule is reasonable under the specific facts of this case.

Conclusion

Based on the foregoing, we reverse the decision of the circuit court of Cook County and remand for further proceedings.

Reversed and remanded.

Case Questions

1. What is the court's conclusion with respect to the board's ability to make a no-dog rule?

2. How does the court determine "reasonableness"?

Fore L Realty Trust v. McManus
71 Mass. App. Ct. 605, 884 N.E.2d 994 (2008)

This is an appeal from a decision of the Appellate Division of the District Court that affirmed a judgment of the District Court in favor of Joseph McManus, the tenant of rental premises being converted to a condominium unit. The sole issue on appeal is whether the statute that abolished rent control, see St. 1994, c. 368 (rent control prohibition act), repealed a previously existing statute that afforded notice and other protections to tenants such as McManus whose rental unit was to be converted to the condominium form of ownership. See St. 1983, c. 527, § 4(a) (condominium conversion act). We affirm the decision and order of the Appellate Division. We conclude that the rent control prohibition act did not repeal the condominium conversion act and abolish the protections afforded to tenants upon conversion of their rental units to condominium units. By its very terms, the rent control prohibition act prohibits only municipal regulation of rents. The protections afforded to all tenants in § 4(a)-(e) of the condominium conversion act are not a municipal regulation of rents, and therefore are not abrogated by the rent control prohibition act.

1. *Background.* The underlying facts are undisputed. Joseph McManus is an elderly resident of an apartment on Cherry Street in Waltham

managed by Fore L Realty Trust (Fore L), which is also his landlord. McManus has lived in his apartment for approximately fifty years. In 2005, Fore L decided to convert the units in the building where McManus maintains his apartment to condominium units. In June of 2005, Fore L sent McManus a notice to terminate his tenancy, but it did not send him a notice informing him of its intent to convert his unit to a condominium unit and of McManus's rights as set forth in the condominium conversion act. When Fore L sought to evict McManus in a summary process action in the District Court, McManus defended against his eviction on the ground that Fore L had failed to provide the required statutory notice of condominium conversion. Judgment entered in favor of McManus, and the Appellate Division affirmed that judgment, concluding that the repeal of rent control laws did not effect a repeal of statutory requirements on conversion.

Fore L concedes that it did not give McManus the notice required under the condominium conversion act, and that if such notice survived the repeal of rent control, then the judgment in favor of McManus is proper. Fore L argues, however, that such notice is not required, the requirement having been repealed along with rent control. We conclude, favorably to McManus, that the rent control prohibition act did not repeal the requirements of the condominium conversion act.

2. *Discussion.* In 1994, Massachusetts voters passed by initiative petition St. 1994, c. 368, inserting into the General Laws as a chapter numbered 40O, the "Massachusetts Rent Control Prohibition Act," prohibiting *any city or town* from enacting, maintaining or enforcing rent control regulations. The voter initiative defines in § 3 of the act the "rent control" that § 4 of the act prohibits a city or town from enacting, maintaining, or enforcing. See G. L. c. 40O, §§ 3, 4; St. 1994, c. 368, §§ 3, 4. *Section 3* declares that "[f]or the purposes of this chapter, the term 'rent control' shall mean: (a) any regulation that in any way requires below-market rents for residential properties; and (b) any regulation that is part of a regulatory scheme of rent control as defined in subsection (a), including the regulation of occupancy, services, evictions, condominium conversion and the removal of properties from such rent control scheme...." G. L. c. 40O, § 3.

Concerned with the consequences of an immediate cessation of rent control,[4] the Legislature enacted transition legislation, St. 1994, c. 282, to establish a uniform Statewide policy for ending rent control. By its express terms, the transition legislation was to "apply notwithstanding the provisions of chapter forty O of the General Laws, or any general or special law to the contrary." St. 1994, c. 282, § 1. Among its other transition provisions, St. 1994, c. 282 excluded the condominium conversion act from the definition of rent control and from the scope of the rent control prohibition act.

---

4. The rent control prohibition act took effect on January 1, 1995. St. 1994, c. 368, § 2.

See St. 1994, c. 282, § 3(*e*).[5] While St. 1994, c. 282 included a "sunset provision" that caused certain of its transitional provisions to expire within one year (on December 31, 1996), the sunset provision did not extend to the provision that excluded the condominium conversion act from the definition of rent control. See St. 1994, c. 282, §§ 3(*e*), 9. In consequence, the provision excluding the condominium conversion act from the definition of rent control did not expire with the sunset provisions of St. 1994, c. 282.

It soon became apparent that the voter initiative that provided for the codification of the rent control prohibition act in *c. 40O of the General Laws* unwittingly created a numerical anomaly. There already existed a *c. 40O of the General Laws* that dealt with an unrelated subject. To eliminate the confusion arising from the duplicate numbering, the Legislature enacted corrective legislation that renumbered *c. 40O* as *c. 40P*, retroactive to January 1, 1995. See St. 1997, c. 19, § 10. However, the corrective legislation made no reference to the transition legislation's exclusion of the condominium conversion act from the definition of rent control. Rather, the corrective legislation retained the provision of the original rent control prohibition act and stated "this chapter shall preempt, supersede or nullify any inconsistent, contrary or conflicting state or local law." *G. L. c. 40P, § 5*, as inserted by St. 1997, c. 19, § 10. See also St. 1994, c. 368, § 5.

The crux of Fore L's contention arises from this legislative correction of the numerical anomaly created by the voter initiative. Fore L argues that the definition of rent control in *G. L. c. 40P, § 3*, and the omission in *c. 40P* of any reference to St. 1994, c. 282 (and its exclusion of the condominium conversion act from the definition of rent control), establish that in enacting *c. 40P*, the Legislature intended to abolish not only rent control but also the protections of the condominium conversion act. We disagree. Such an argument misconstrues the scope and purpose of both the rent control prohibition act and the condominium conversion act. Moreover, such an argument attempts, by definitional legerdemain, to transform a purely corrective change in the numbering of a general law prohibiting a city or town from imposing rent control into a repeal by implication of the protections that the condominium conversion act affords to tenants. See *Greater Boston Real Estate Bd. v. Boston, 428 Mass. 797, 799, 705 N.E.2d 256 & n.2 (1999); Gross v. Prudential Ins. Co. of Am., 48 Mass. App. Ct. 115, 117 n.2, 718 N.E.2d 383 (1999)* (redesignation a purely technical amendment in recognition of fact that different *c. 40O* already existed).

---

5. Statute 1994, c. 282, § 3(*e*) provides:

"(e) 'Rent Control' means any controls, restrictions or other regulations imposed *by any city or town* with respect to the rents which may be charged for any residential housing accommodations, the conversion of such housing accommodations to the condominium or [***6] cooperative form of ownership, or the removal of such housing accommodations from the rental market, including without limitation those regulatory schemes currently in effect in ... [Boston, Brookline, and Cambridge] pursuant to ... [various acts], *but excluding Chapter 527 of the Acts of 1983* [the condominium conversion statute]" (emphasis supplied).

We view the condominium conversion act as a protection of Statewide application, afforded to all tenants, that differs materially from a municipal regulation or ordinance that regulates or requires below-market rents for residential properties. Prior to the abolition of rent control, the condominium conversion act afforded *all* tenants — those paying market rents and those paying controlled rents alike — certain rights and protections upon conversion of the tenant's unit to a condominium unit. We discern nothing in the rent control prohibition act that would provide tenants of units formerly subject to rent control fewer protections upon conversion than those who were not.

Fore L's central argument rests on the flawed premise that the rent control prohibition act, which prohibits a "city or town" from enacting, enforcing, or maintaining rent control of any kind (with certain immaterial exceptions) is in conflict with the protections that the condominium conversion act affords to all tenants. There is no such conflict. The condominium conversion act and the rent control prohibition act are part of a delicately balanced legislative approach to addressing the shortage of affordable housing for the citizens of the Commonwealth.[6] The requirements and purposes of the condominium conversion act are related to, but distinct from, the limitation that the rent control prohibition act imposes on a city or town controlling rent at the municipal level. The condominium conversion act is a legislative grant of protections to all tenants of rental units being converted to condominiums. The rent control prohibition act is a legislative restriction on the ability of municipalities to regulate rents at the local level, a factor that may discourage new rental housing production. The condominium conversion act affords tenants notice rights, pre-eviction lease extensions, first rights of refusal, purchasing rights at market price, and relocation assistance. None of these provisions regulates rents. To the extent that § 4(*e*) of the condominium conversion act works a limitation on the rental increases that a landlord may lawfully impose upon a tenant in possession at the time of conversion, such a limitation is a legislative

---

6. As noted in the Declaration of Emergency to the condominium conversion act:

"[A] serious public emergency exists...with respect to the housing of a substantial number of the citizens of the commonwealth. This rental housing emergency has been created by [inter alia]...the effect of conversion of rental housing into condominiums.... [A]bsent sufficient new rental housing production, such conversion necessarily reduces the stock of rental housing otherwise available. A substantial and increasing shortage of rental housing accommodations, especially for the elderly, the handicapped, and persons and families of low and moderate income, has been and will continue to be the result of this emergency.... It is therefore necessary that such emergency be dealt with immediately." St. 1983, c. 527, § 1.

Similarly, the rent control prohibition act declares:

"The purpose of this chapter is to establish a uniform statewide policy that broadly prohibits any regulatory scheme based upon or implementing rent control.... This policy is based on the belief that the public is best served by free-market rental rates for residential properties and by unrestricted home ownership." St. 1994, c. 368, § 2.

determination of Statewide application and not a prohibited municipal regulation of rent within the ambit of the rent control prohibition act.[7] While §§ 3 and 4 of the rent control prohibition act preclude a *municipality* from regulating rent (including during a period of condominium conversion), no similar prohibition prevents the Legislature itself doing so, either in that act or elsewhere. See *Greater Boston Real Estate Bd. v. Boston, 428 Mass. at 798-802* (invalidating *city* ordinance enacted under condominium conversion act as beyond that statute's enabling act and violative of rent control prohibition act).

We also find unpersuasive Fore L's argument that the definition of rent control in *G. L. c. 40P*, and the absence of any reference in that corrective statute to the transition legislation and its exclusion of the condominium conversion act from the definition of rent control, signified the Legislature's intention to repeal the requirements of the condominium conversion act along with the prohibition against municipal control of rents. There was no need to make reference to the condominium conversion act in the corrective statute. As previously discussed, there is simply no conflict between the condominium conversion act and the rent control prohibition act where the challenged rights are those granted by the Legislature itself and not by cities or towns under the enabling provisions of the condominium conversion act. Contrast *Greater Boston Real Estate Bd. v. Boston, supra.* The failure of the Legislature to make specific reference to the transitional legislation in *c. 40P* does not speak to a repeal of the condominium conversion act by implication. See *Salem & Beverly Water Supply Bd. v. Commissioner of Rev., 26 Mass. App. Ct. 74, 78, 523 N.E.2d 473 (1988)* ("Repeals by implication are disfavored by the appellate courts of the Commonwealth, particularly where general statutes are said to supersede earlier special acts"). Rather, such omission only fortifies the conclusion that the rights in question under the condominium conversion act are not a form of municipal rent control and remain unaffected by the rent control prohibition act and its codification in *c. 40P*.

Decision and order of the Appellate
Division affirmed.

Case Questions

1. The case concerns a jurisdiction with rent control regulations. Does your community have rent control? How would this decision affect your location?

2. What is meant by a "serious public emergency"?

---

7. Statute 1983, c. 527, § 4(*e*), permits a landlord to impose reasonable cost of living rent increases during the applicable notice period, but limits such increases to increases in the consumer price index. Absent such limitation, a landlord might well impose rent increases in an amount designed to displace tenants during the conversion period and thwart the purposes of the condominium conversion act.

Exhibit 6.1: Sales Contract for a Condominium

⬚ Blumbergs® M 146—Contract of sale, condominium unit, 5-98
Law Products   Prepared by the Committee on Real Property Law of the Association of the Bar of the City of New York.   DISTRIBUTED BY **Blumberg**Excelsior Inc.
NYC 10013

Note: This form is intended to deal with matters common to most transactions involving the sale of a condominium unit. Provisions should be added, altered or deleted to suit the circumstances of a particular transaction. No representation is made that this form of contract complies with Section 5-702 of the General Obligations Law ("Plain Language Law").

CONSULT YOUR LAWYER BEFORE SIGNING THIS AGREEMENT

Contract of Sale – Condominium Unit

Agreement made as of   between

residing at

and   ("Seller")

residing at

                                                                                    ("Purchaser")

1. Unit: Seller agrees to sell and convey, and Purchaser agrees to purchase, Unit No.   ("Unit") in the building ("Building") known as   Condominium·("Condominium") and located at   , New York, together with a   percent undivided interest in the Common Elements (as defined in para. 6) appurtenant thereto, all upon and subject to the terms and conditions set forth herein. The Unit shall be as designated in the Declaration of Condominium Ownership (as the same may be amended from time to time, the "Declaration") of the Condominium, recorded in   County, New York or the By-Laws (as the same may be amended from time to time, the "By-Laws") of the Condominium.

2. Personal Property: (a) The sale includes all of Seller's right, title and interest, if any, in and to:

(i) the refrigerators, freezers, ranges, ovens, dishwashers, washing machines, clothes dryers, cabinets and counters, lighting and plumbing fixtures, air conditioning equipment, venetian blinds, shades, screens, storm windows and other window treatments, wall-to-wall carpeting, bookshelves, switchplates, door hardware, built-ins and articles of property and fixtures attached to or appurtenant to the Unit, except those listed in subpara. 2(b), all of which included property and fixtures are represented to be owned by Seller, free and clear of all liens and encumbrances other than those encumbrances ("Permitted Exceptions") set forth on Schedule A annexed hereto and made a part hereof *(strike out inapplicable items)*; and

(ii)

(b) Excluded from this sale are:
(i) furniture and furnishings (other than as specifically provided in this Contract); and
(ii)

(c) The property referred to in subpara. 2(a)(i) and (ii) may not be purchased if title to the Unit is not conveyed hereunder.

3. Purchase Price: (a) The purchase price ("Purchase Price") is $, payable as follows:
(i) $ ("Downpayment") on the signing of this Contract by check subject to collection, the receipt of which is hereby acknowledged, to be held in escrow pursuant to para. 16; and
(ii) $ constituting the balance of the Purchase Price, by certified check of Purchaser or official bank check (except as otherwise provided in this Contract) on the delivery of the deed as hereinafter provided.

(b) All checks in payment of the Purchase Price shall represent United States currency and be drawn on or issued by a bank or trust company authorized to accept deposits in New York State. All checks in payment of the Downpayment shall be payable to the order of Escrowee (as hereinafter defined). All checks in payment of the balance of the Purchase Price shall be payable to the order of Seller (or as Seller otherwise directs pursuant to subparas. 6(a)(ix) or 19(b)).

(c) Except for the Downpayment and checks aggregating not more than one-half of one percent of the Purchase Price, including payment for closing adjustments, all checks delivered by Purchaser shall be certified or official bank checks as hereinabove provided.

4. Closing of Title: The closing documents referred to in para. 6 shall be delivered, and payment of the balance of the Purchase Price shall be made, at the closing of title ("Closing"), to be held on   at   M., at the offices of

or at the office of Purchaser's lending institution or its counsel; provided, however, that such office is located in either the City or County in which either (a) Seller's attorney maintains an office or (b) the Unit is located.

5. Representations, Warranties and Covenants: Seller represents, warrants and covenants that:
(a) Seller is the sole owner of the Unit and the property referred to in subpara. 2(a), and Seller has the full right, power and authority to sell, covey and transfer the same;

(b) The common charges (excluding separately billed utility charges) for the Unit on the date hereof are $ per month;

(c) Seller has not received any written notice of any intended assessment or increase in common charges not reflected in subpara. 5(b). Purchaser acknowledges that it will not have the right to cancel this Contract in the event of the imposition of any assessment or increase in common charges after the date hereof of which Seller has not heretofore received written notice;

(d) The real estate taxes for the Unit for the fiscal year of   through   are $

(e) Seller is not a "sponsor" or a nominee of a "sponsor" under any plan of condominium organization affecting the Unit;

(f) All refrigerators, freezers, ranges, dishwashers, washing machines, clothes dryers and air conditioning equipment included in this sale will be in working order at the time of Closing;

(g) If a copy is attached to this Contract, the copy of the Certificate of Occupancy covering the Unit is a true and correct copy; and

(h) Seller is not a "foreign person" as defined in para. 18. *(If inapplicable, delete and provide for compliance with Code Withholding Section, as defined in para. 18.)*

6. Closing Documents: (a) At the Closing, Seller shall deliver to Purchaser the following:

(i) Bargain and sale deed with   covenant against grantor's acts ("Deed"), complying with RPL §339-0 and containing the covenant required by LL § 13(5), conveying to Purchaser title to the Unit, together with its undivided interest in the Common Elements (as such term is defined in the Declaration and which term shall be deemed to include Seller's right, title and interest in any limited common elements attributable to or used in connection with the Unit) appurtenant thereto, free and clear of all liens and encumbrances other than Permitted Exceptions. The Deed shall be executed and acknowledged by Seller and, if requested by the Condominium, executed and acknowledged by Purchaser, in proper statutory form for recording;

(ii) If a corporation and if required pursuant to BCL § 909, Seller shall deliver to Purchaser (1) a resolution of its board of directors authorizing the delivery of the Deed and (2) a certificate executed by an officer of such corporation certifying as to the adoption of such resolution and setting forth facts demonstrating that the delivery of the Deed is in conformity with the requirements of BCL § 909. The Deed shall also contain a recital sufficient to establish compliance with such law;

(iii) A waiver of right of first refusal of the board of managers of the Condominium ("Board") if required in accordance with para. 8;

(iv) A statement by the Condominium or its managing agent that the common charges and any assessments then due and a payable the Condominium have been paid to the date of the Closing;

(v) All keys to the doors of, and mailbox for, the Unit;

(vi) Such affidavits and/or other evidence as the title company ("Title Company") from which Purchaser has ordered a title insurance report and which is authorized to do business in New York State shall reasonably require in order to omit from its title insurance policy all exceptions for judgments, bankruptcies or other returns against Seller and persons or entities whose names are the same as or are similar to Seller's name;

(vii) Official New York State Real Property Transfer Gains Tax Tentative Assessment and Return (or, if applicable, Official Statement of No Tax Due) duly completed by the New York State Department of Taxation and Finance (or, if applicable, a duly executed and acknowledged affidavit of Seller in form required pursuant to the Gains Tax Law (as hereinafter defined) claiming exemption therefrom;

(viii) New York City Real Property Transfer Tax Return, if applicable, and combined Real Property Transfer Gains Tax Affidavits, prepared, executed and acknowledged by Seller in proper form for submission;

Exhibit 6.1: *(Continued)*

(ix) Checks in payment of all applicable real property transfer taxes except a transfer tax which by law is primarily imposed on the purchaser ("Purchaser Transfer Tax") and any New York State Real Property Transfer Gains Tax ("Gains Tax") due in connection with the sale. In lieu of delivery of such checks, Seller shall have the right, upon not less than 3 business days notice to Purchaser, to cause Purchaser to deliver said checks at the Closing and to credit the amount thereof against the balance of the Purchase Price. Seller shall pay the additional transfer taxes and Gains Taxes, if any, payable after the Closing by reason of the conveyance of the Unit, which obligation shall survive the Closing;

(x) Certification that Seller is not a foreign person pursuant to para. 18. *(If inapplicable, delete and provide for compliance with Code Section, as defined in para. 18.)*; and

(xi) Affidavit that a single station smoke detecting alarm device is installed pursuant to New York Executive Law §378(5).

(b) At the Closing, Purchaser shall deliver to Seller the following:

(i) Checks in payment of (y) the balance of the Purchase Price in accordance with subpara. 3(b) and (z) any Purchaser Transfer Tax;

(ii) If required by the Declaration or By-Laws, power of attorney to the Board, prepared by Seller, in the form required by the Condominium. The power of attorney shall be executed and acknowledged by Purchaser and, after being recorded, shall be sent to the Condominium;

(iii) New York City Real Property Transfer Tax Return executed and acknowledged by Purchaser and an Affidavit in Lieu of Registration pursuant to New York Multiple Dwelling Law, each in proper form for submission, if applicable, and combined Real Property Transfer Gains Tax Affidavits; and

(iv) If required, New York State Equalization Return executed and acknowledged by Purchaser in proper form for submission.

(c) It is a condition of Purchaser's obligation to close title hereunder that:

(i) All notes or notices of violations of law or governmental orders, ordinances or requirements affecting the Unit and noted or issued by any governmental department, agency or bureau having jurisdiction which were noted or issued on or prior to the date hereof shall have been cured by Seller;

(ii) Any written notice to Seller from the Condominium (or its duly authorized representative) that the Unit is in violation of the Declaration, By-Laws or rules and regulations of the Condominium shall have been cured; and

(iii) The Condominium is a valid condominium created pursuant to RPL Art. 9-B and the Title Company will so insure.

7. Closing Adjustments: (a) The following adjustments shall be made as of 11:59 P.M. of the day before the Closing:

(i) Real estate taxes and water charges and sewer rents, if separately assessed, on the basis of the fiscal period for which assessed, except that if there is a water meter with respect to the Unit, apportionment shall be based on the last available reading, subject to adjustment after the Closing, promptly after the next reading is available; provided, however, that in the event real estate taxes have not, as of the date of Closing, been separately assessed to the Unit, real estate taxes shall be apportioned on the same basis as provided in the Declaration or By-Laws or, in the absence of such provision, based upon the Unit's percentage interest in the Common Elements;

(ii) Common charges of the Condominium; and

(iii) If fuel is separately stored with respect to the Unit only, the value of fuel stored with respect to the Unit at the price then charged by Seller's supplier (as determined by a letter or certificate to be obtained by Seller from such supplier), including any sales taxes.

(b) If at the time of Closing the Unit is affected by an assessment which is or may become payable in installments, then, for the purposes of this Contract, only the unpaid installments which are then due shall be considered due and are to be paid by Seller at the Closing. All subsequent installments at the time of Closing shall be the obligation of Purchaser.

(c) Any errors or omissions in computing closing adjustments shall be corrected. This subpara. 7(c) shall survive the Closing.

(d) If the Unit is located in the City of New York, the "customs in respect to title closings" recommended by The Real Estate Board of New York, Inc., as amended and in effect on the date of Closing, shall apply to the adjustments and other matters therein mentioned, except as otherwise provided herein.

8. Right of First Refusal: If so provided in the Declaration or By-Laws, this sale is subject to and conditioned upon the waiver of a right of first refusal to purchase the Unit held by the Condominium and exercisable by the Board. Seller agrees to give notice promptly to the Board of the contemplated sale of the Unit to Purchaser, which notice shall be given in accordance with the terms of the Declaration and By-Laws, and Purchaser agrees to provide promptly all applications, information and references reasonably requested by the Board. If the Board shall exercise such right of first refusal, Seller shall promptly refund to Purchaser the Downpayment (which term, for all purposes of this Contract, shall be deemed to include interest, if any, earned thereon) and upon the making of such refund this Contract shall be deemed cancelled and of no further force or effect and neither party shall have any further rights against, or obligations or liabilities to, the other by reason of this Contract. If the Board shall fail to exercise such right of first refusal within the time and in the manner provided for in the Declaration or By-Laws or shall declare in writing its intention not to exercise such right of first refusal (a copy of which writing shall be delivered to Purchaser promptly following receipt thereof), the parties hereto shall proceed with this sale in accordance with the provisions of this Contract.

9. Processing Fee: Seller shall, at the Closing, pay all fees and charges payable to the Condominium (and/or its managing agent) in connection with this sale, including, without limitation, any processing fee, the legal fees, if any, of the Condominium's attorney in connection with this sale and, unless otherwise agreed to by Seller and Purchaser in writing, all "flip taxes," transfer or entrance fees or similar charges, if any, payable to or for the Condominium or otherwise for the benefit of the Condominium unit owners, which arise by reason of this sale.

10. No Other Representations: Purchaser has examined and is satisfied with the Declaration, By-Laws and rules and regulations of the Condominium, or has waived the examination thereof. Purchaser has inspected the Unit, its fixtures, appliances and equipment and the personal property, if any, included in this sale, as well as the Common Elements of the Condominium, and knows the condition thereof and, subject to subpara. 5(f), agrees to accept the same "as is," i.e., in the condition they are in on the date hereof, subject to normal use, wear and tear between the date hereof and the Closing. Purchaser has examined or waived examination of the last audited financial statements of the Condominium, and has considered or waived consideration of all other matters pertaining to this Contract and to the purchase to be made hereunder, and does not rely on any representations made by any broker or by Seller or anyone acting or purporting to act on behalf of Seller as to any matters which might influence or affect the decision to execute this Contract or to buy the Unit, or said personal property, except those representations and warranties which are specifically set forth in this Contract.

11. Possession: Seller shall, prior to the Closing, remove from the Unit all furniture, furnishings and other personal property not included in this sale, shall repair any damage caused by such removal, and shall deliver exclusive possession of the Unit at the Closing, vacant, broom-clean and free of tenancies or other rights of use or possession.

12. Access: Seller shall permit Purchaser and its architect, decorator or other authorized persons to have the right of access to the Unit between the date hereof and the Closing for the purpose of inspecting the same and taking measurements, at reasonable times and upon reasonable prior notice to Seller (by telephone or otherwise). Further, Purchaser shall have the right to inspect the Unit at a reasonable time during the 24-hour period immediately preceding the Closing.

13. Defaults and Remedies: (a) If Purchaser defaults hereunder, Seller's sole remedy shall be to retain the Downpayment as liquidated damages, it being agreed that Seller's damages in case of Purchaser's default might be impossible to ascertain and that the Downpayment constitutes a fair and reasonable amount of damages under the circumstances and is not a penalty.

(b) If Seller defaults hereunder, Purchaser shall have such remedies as Purchaser shall be entitled to at law or in equity, including, but not limited to, specific performance.

14. Notices: Any notice, request or other communication ("Notice") given or made hereunder (except for the notice required by para. 12), shall be in writing and either (a) sent by any of the parties hereto or their respective attorneys, by registered or certified mail, return receipt requested, postage prepaid, or (b) delivered in person or by overnight courier, with receipt acknowledged, to the address given at the beginning of this Contract for the party to whom the Notice is to be given, or to such other address for such party as said party shall hereafter designate by Notice given to the other party pursuant to this para. 14. Each Notice mailed shall be deemed given on the third business day following the date of mailing the same and each Notice delivered in person or by overnight courier shall be deemed given when delivered.

15. Purchaser's Lien: The Downpayment and all other sums paid on account of this Contract and the reasonable expenses of the examination of title to, and departmental violation searches in respect of, the Unit are hereby made a lien upon the Unit, but such lien shall not continue after default by Purchaser hereunder.

16. Downpayment in Escrow: (a) Seller's attorney ("Escrowee") shall hold the Downpayment for Seller's account in escrow in a segregated bank account at the depository identified at the end of this Contract until Closing or sooner termination of this Contract and shall pay over or apply the Downpayment in accordance with the terms of this para. 16. Escrowee shall *(not) (Delete if inapplicable)* hold the Downpayment in an interest-bearing account for the benefit of the parties. If interest is held for the benefit of the parties, it shall be paid to the party entitled to the Down-payment and the party receiving the interest shall pay any income taxes thereon. If interest is not held for the benefit of the parties, the Down-payment shall be placed in an IOLA account or as otherwise permitted or required by law. The Social Security or Federal Identification numbers of the parties shall be furnished to Escrowee upon request. At closing, the Downpayment shall be paid by Escrowee to Seller. If for any reason Closing does not occur and either party gives Notice (as defined in paragraph 14) to Escrowee demanding payment of the Downpayment, Escrowee shall give prompt Notice to the other party of such demand. If Escrowee does not receive Notice of objection from such other party to the proposed payment within 10 business days after the giving of such Notice, Escrowee is hereby authorized and directed to make such payment. If Escrowee does receive such Notice of objection within such 10 day period or if for any other reason Escrowee in good faith shall elect not to make such payment, Escrowee shall continue to hold such amount until otherwise directed by Notice from the parties to this Contract or a final, nonappealable judgment, order or decree of a court. However, Escrowee shall have the right at any time to deposit the Downpayment with the clerk of a court in the county in which the Unit is located and shall give Notice of such deposit to Seller and Purchaser. Upon such deposit or other disbursement in accordance with the terms of this para. 16, Escrowee shall be relieved and discharged of all further obligations and responsibilities hereunder.

(b) The parties acknowledge that, although Escrowee is holding the Downpayment for Seller's account, for all other purposes Escrowee is

Exhibit 6.1: *(Continued)*

22. Broker: Seller and Purchaser represent and warrant to each other that the only real estate broker with whom they have dealt in connection with this Contract and the transaction set forth herein is

and that they know of no other real estate broker who has claimed or may have the right to claim a commission in connection with this transaction. The commission of such real estate broker shall be paid by Seller pursuant to separate agreement. If no real estate broker is specified above, the parties acknowledge that this Contract was brought about by direct negotiation between Seller and Purchaser and each represents to the other that it knows of no real estate broker entitled to a commission in connection with this transaction. Seller and Purchaser shall indemnify and defend each other against any costs, claims or expenses (including reasonable attorneys' fees) arising out of the breach on their respective parts of any representation, warranty or agreement contained in this para. 22. The provisions of this para. 22 shall survive the Closing or, if the Closing does not occur, the termination of this Contract.

23. Mortgage Contingency: *(Delete if inapplicable)* (a) The obligations of Purchaser hereunder are conditioned upon issuance on or before   (the "Commitment Date") of a written commitment from any Institutional Lender pursuant to which such Institutional Lender agrees to make a loan, other than a VA, FHA or other governmentally insured loan to Purchaser, at Purchaser's sole cost and expense, of $ or such lesser sum as Purchaser shall be willing to accept, at the prevailing fixed rate of interest not to exceed   or initial adjustment rate of interest not to exceed   for a term of at least   years and on other customary commitment terms, whether or not conditioned upon any factors other than an appraisal satisfactory to the Institutional Lender, secured by a first mortgage on the Unit together with its undivided interest in the Common Elements. Purchaser shall (i) make prompt application to an Institutional Lender for such mortgage loan, (ii) furnish accurate and complete information on Purchaser and members of Purchaser's family, as required, (iii) pay all fees, points and charges required in connection with such application and loan, (iv) pursue such application with diligence, (v) cooperate in good faith with such Institutional Lender to the end of securing such first mortgage loan and (vi) promptly give Notice to Seller of the name and address of each Institutional Lender to which Purchaser has made such application. Purchaser shall comply with all requirements of such commitment (or of any commitment accepted by Purchaser) and shall furnish Seller with a copy thereof promptly after receipt thereof. If such commitment is not issued on or before the Commitment Date, then, unless Purchaser has accepted a commitment that does not comply with the requirements set forth above, Purchaser may cancel this Contract by giving Notice to Seller within 5 business days after the Commitment Date, in which case this Contract shall be deemed cancelled and thereafter neither party shall have any further rights against, or obligations or liabilities to, the other by reason of this Contract except that the Downpayment shall be promptly refunded to Purchaser and except as set forth in para. 22. If Purchaser fails to give Notice of cancellation or if Purchaser shall accept a commitment that does not comply with the terms set forth above, then Purchaser shall be deemed to have waived Purchaser's right to cancel this Contract and to

receive a refund of the Downpayment by reason of the contingency contained in this para. 23.

(b) For purposes of this Contract, an "Institutional Lender" is any bank, savings bank, private banker, trust company, savings and loan association and credit union or similar banking institution whether organized under the laws of this state, the United States or any other state; foreign banking corporation licensed by the Superintendent of Banks of New York or the Comptroller of the Currency to transact business in New York State; insurance company duly organized or licensed to do business in New York State; mortgage banker licensed pursuant to Article 12-D of the Banking Law; and any instrumentality created by the United States or any state with the power to make mortgage loans.

(Delete if inapplicable) (c) Purchaser and Seller agree that the submission of an application to a mortgage broker registered pursuant to Article 12-D of the New York Banking Law ("Mortgage Broker") shall constitute full compliance with the terms and conditions set forth in para. 23(a)(i) of this Contract, and that Purchaser's cooperation in good faith with such Mortgage Broker to obtain a commitment from an Institutional Lender (together with Purchaser's cooperation in good faith with any Institutional Lender to which Purchaser's application has been submitted by such Mortgage Broker), and the prompt giving of Notice by Purchaser to Seller of the name and address of each Mortgage Broker to which Purchaser has submitted such application shall constitute full compliance with the terms and conditions set forth in para. 23(a)(v) and (vi) of this Contract.

24. Gender, Etc.: As used in this Contract, the neuter includes the masculine and feminine, the singular includes the plural and the plural includes the singular, as the context may require.

25. Entire Contract: All prior understandings and agreements between Seller and Purchaser are merged in this Contract and this Contract supersedes any and all understandings and agreements between the parties and constitutes the entire agreement between them with respect to the subject matter hereof.

26. Captions: The captions in this Contract are for convenience and reference only and in no way define, limit or describe the scope of this Contract and shall not be considered in the interpretation of this Contract or any provision hereof.

27. No Assignment by Purchaser: Purchaser may not assign this Contract or any of Purchaser's rights hereunder.

28. Successors and Assigns: Subject to the provisions of para. 27, the provisions of this Contract shall bind and inure to the benefit of both Purchaser and Seller and their respective distributees, executors, administrators, heirs, legal representatives, successors and permitted assigns.

29. No Oral Changes: This Contract cannot be changed or terminated orally. Any changes or additional provisions must be set forth in a rider attached hereto or in a separate written agreement signed by both parties to this Contract.

30. Contract Not Binding Until Signed: This Contract shall not be binding or effective until properly executed and delivered by Seller and Purchaser.·

In Witness Whereof, the parties hereto have duly executed this Contract on the day and year first above written.

Seller	(Soc. Sec. No.)	Purchaser	(Soc. Sec. No.)
Seller	(Soc. Sec. No.)	Purchaser	(Soc. Sec. No.)

Agreed to as to para. 16: _____   Escrow Depository: _____
                                                    Escrowee

SCHEDULE A - Permitted Exceptions

1. Zoning laws and regulations and landmark, historic or wetlands designation which are not violated by the Unit and which are not violated by the Common Elements to the extent that access to or use of the Unit would be materially and adversely affected.

2. Consents for the erection of any structure or structures on, under or above any street or streets on which the Building may abut.

3. The terms, burdens, covenants, restrictions, conditions, easements and rules and regulations set forth in the Declaration, By-Laws and rules and regulations of the Condominium, the Power of Attorney from Purchaser to the board of managers of the Condominium and the floor plans of the Condominium, all as may be amended from time to time.

4. Rights of utility companies to lay, maintain, install and repair pipes, lines, poles, conduits, cable boxes and related equipment on, over and under the Building and Common Elements, provided that none of such rights imposes any monetary obligation on the owner of the Unit or materially interferes with the use of or access to the Unit.

5. Encroachments of stoops, areas, cellar steps, trim, cornices, lintels, window sills, awnings, canopies, ledges, fences, hedges, coping and retaining walls projecting from the Building over any street or highway or over any adjoining property and encroachments of similar elements projecting from adjoining property over the Common Elements.

6. Any state of facts which an accurate survey or personal inspection of the Building, Common Elements or Unit would disclose, provided that

The survey referred to in No. 6 above was prepared by
dated   and last revised

such facts do not prevent the use of the Unit for dwelling purposes. For the purposes of this Contract, none of the facts shown on the survey, if any, identified below, shall be deemed to prevent the use of the Unit for dwelling purposes, and Purchaser shall accept title subject thereto.

7. The lien of any unpaid common charge, real estate tax, water charge, sewer rent or vault charge, provided the same are paid or apportioned at the Closing as herein provided.

8. The lien of any unpaid assessments to the extent of installments thereof payable after the Closing.

9. Liens, encumbrances and title conditions affecting the Common Elements which do not materially and adversely affect the right of the Unit owner to use and enjoy the Common Elements,

10. Notes or notices of violations of law or governmental orders, ordinances or requirements (a) affecting the Unit and noted or issued subsequent to the date of this Contract by any governmental department, agency or bureau having jurisdiction and (b) any such notes or notices affecting only the Common Elements which were noted or issued prior to or on the date of this Contract or at any time hereafter.

11. Any other matters or encumbrances subject to which Purchaser is required to accept title to the Unit pursuant to this Contract.

Exhibit 6.1: *(Continued)*

acting solely as a stakeholder at their request and for their convenience and that Escrowee shall not be liable to either party for any act or omission on its part unless taken or suffered in bad faith or in willful disregard of this Contract or involving gross negligence on the part of Escrowee. Seller and Purchaser jointly and severally agree to defend, indemnify and hold Escrowee harmless from and against all costs, claims and expenses (including reasonable attorneys' fees) incurred in connection with the performance of Escrowee's duties hereunder, except with respect to actions or omissions taken or suffered by Escrowee in bad faith or in willful disregard of this Contract or involving gross negligence on the part of Escrowee.

(c) Escrowee may act or refrain from acting in respect of any matter referred to herein in full reliance upon and with the advice of counsel which may be selected by it (including any member of its firm) and shall be fully protected in so acting or refraining from action upon the advice of such counsel.

(d) Escrowee acknowledges receipt of the Downpayment by check subject to collection and Escrowee's agreement to the provisions of this para. 16 by signing in the place indicated in this Contract.

(e) Escrowee or any member of its firm shall be permitted to act as counsel for Seller in any dispute as to the disbursement of the Downpayment or any other dispute between the parties whether or not Escrowee is in possession of the Downpayment and continues to act as Escrowee.

17. New York State Gains Tax: (a) Seller and Purchaser agree to comply in a timely manner with the requirements of article 31-B of the Tax Law and the regulations applicable thereto, as the same from time to time may be amended (collectively, the "Gains Tax Law"). Purchaser agrees to deliver to Seller a duly executed and acknowledged Transferee Questionnaire simultaneously with the execution of this Contract or within 5 business days after subsequent written request from Seller or Seller's attorney. At the Closing, Seller shall deliver (i) an Official Statement of No Tax Due or (ii) an Official Tentative Assessment and Return accompanied by a certified or official bank check drawn on any banking institution described in subpara. 3(b), payable to the order of the State Tax Commission, in the amount of the tax shown to be due thereon, or (iii) if applicable, a duly executed and acknowledged affidavit in form permitted under the Gains Tax Law claiming exemption therefrom.

(b) Seller agrees (i) to pay promptly any tax due under the Gains Tax Law and any interest and penalties thereon which may be assessed or due after the Closing, (ii) to indemnify and save Purchaser harmless from and against any of the foregoing and any cost, claim and expense (including reasonable attorneys' fees) incurred by Purchaser by reason of the non-payment thereof, and (iii) to make any other payments and execute, acknowledge and deliver such further documents as may be necessary to comply with the Gains Tax Law.

(c) The obligations under this para. 17 shall survive the Closing.

18. FIRPTA: Seller represents and warrants to Purchaser that Seller is not a "foreign person" as defined in IRC § 1445, as amended, and the regulations issued thereunder ("Code Withholding Section"). At the Closing Seller shall deliver to Purchaser a certification stating that Seller is not a foreign person in the form then required by the Code Withholding Section. In the event Seller fails to deliver the aforesaid certification or in the event that Purchaser is not entitled under the Code Withholding Section to rely on such certification, Purchaser shall deduct and withhold from the Purchase Price a sum equal to 10% thereof and shall at Closing remit the withheld amount with the required forms to the Internal Revenue Service.

19. Title Report; Acceptable Title: (a) Purchaser shall,promptly after the date hereof, or after receipt of the mortgage commitment letter, if applicable, order a title insurance report from the Title Company. Promptly after receipt of the title report and thereafter of any continuations thereof and supplements thereto, Purchaser shall forward a copy of each such report, continuation or supplement to the attorney for Seller. Purchaser shall further notify Seller's attorney of any other objections to title not reflected in such title report of which Purchaser becomes aware following the delivery of such report, reasonably promptly after becoming aware of such objections.

(b) Any unpaid taxes, assessments, water charges and sewer rents, together with the interest and penalties thereon to a date not less than two days following the date of Closing, and any other liens and encumbrances which Seller is obligated to pay and discharge or which are against corporations, estates or other persons in the chain of title, together with the cost of recording or filing any instruments necessary to discharge such liens and encumbrances of record, may be paid out of the proceeds of the monies payable at the Closing if Seller delivers to Purchaser at the Closing official bills for such taxes, assessments, water charges, sewer rents, interest and penalties and instruments in recordable form sufficient to discharge any other liens and encumbrances of record. Upon request made not less that 3 business days before the Closing, Purchaser shall provide at the Closing separate checks for the foregoing payable to the order of the holder of any such lien, charge or encumbrance and otherwise complying with subpara. 3(b). If the Title Company is willing to insure Purchaser that such charges, liens and encumbrances will not be collected out of or enforced against the Unit and is willing to insure the lien of Purchaser's Institutional Lender (as hereinafter defined) free and clear of any such charges, liens and encumbrances, then Seller shall have the right in lieu of payment and discharge to deposit with the Title Company such funds or to give such assurances or to pay such special or additional premiums as the Title Company may require in order to so insure. In such case the charges, liens and encumbrances with respect to which the Title Company has agreed so to insure shall not be considered objections to title.

(c) Seller shall convey and Purchaser shall accept fee simple title to the Unit in accordance with the terms of this Contract, subject only to: (a) the Permitted Exceptions and (b) such other matters as (i) the Title Company or any other title insurer licensed to do business by the State of New York shall be willing, without special or additional premium, to omit as exceptions to coverage or to except with insurance against collection out of or enforcement against the Unit and (ii) shall be accepted by any lender which has committed in writing to provide mortgage financing to Purchaser for the purchase of the Unit ("Purchaser's Institutional Lender"), except that if such acceptance by Purchaser's Institutional Lender is unreasonably withheld or delayed, such acceptance shall be deemed to have been given.

(d) Notwithstanding any contrary provisions in this Contract, express or implied, or any contrary rule of law or custom, if Seller shall be unable to convey the Unit in accordance with this Contract (provided that Seller shall release, discharge or otherwise cure at or prior to Closing any matter created by Seller after the date hereof and any existing mortgage, unless this sale is subject to it) and if Purchaser elects not to complete this transaction without abatement of the Purchase Price, the sole obligation and liability of Seller shall be to refund the Downpayment to Purchaser, together with the reasonable cost of the examination of title to, and departmental violation searches in respect of, the Unit, and upon the making of such refund and payment, this Contract shall be deemed cancelled and of no further force or effect and neither party shall have any further rights against, or obligations or liabilities to, the other by reason of this Contract. However, nothing contained in this subpara. 19(d) shall be construed to relieve Seller from liability due to a willful default.

20. Risk of Loss; Casualty: (a) The risk of loss or damage to the Unit or the personal property included in this sale, by fire or other casualty, until the earlier of the Closing or possession of the Unit by Purchaser, is assumed by Seller, but without any obligation of Seller to repair or replace any such loss or damage unless Seller elects to do so as hereinafter provided. Seller shall notify Purchaser of the occurrence of any such loss or damage to the Unit or the personal property included in this sale within 10 days after such occurrence or by the date of Closing, whichever first occurs, and by such notice shall state whether or not Seller elects to repair or restore the Unit and/or the personal property, as the case may be. If Seller elects to make such repairs and restorations, Seller's notice shall set forth an adjourned date for the Closing, which shall be not more than 60 days after the date of the giving of Seller's notice. If Seller either does not elect to do so or, having elected to make such repairs and restorations, fails to complete the same on or before said adjourned date for the Closing, Purchaser shall have the following options:

(i) To declare this Contract cancelled and of no further force or effect and receive a refund of the Downpayment in which event neither party shall thereafter have any further rights against, or obligations or liabilities to, the other by reason of this Contract; or

(ii) To complete the purchase in accordance with this Contract without reduction in the Purchase Price, except as provided in the next sentence. If Seller carries hazard insurance covering such loss or damage, Seller shall turn over to Purchaser at the Closing the net proceeds actually collected by Seller under the provisions of such hazard insurance policies to the extent that they are attributable to loss of or damage to any property included in this sale, less any sums theretofore expended by Seller in repairing or replacing such loss or damage or in collecting such proceeds; and Seller shall assign (without recourse to Seller) Seller's right to receive any additional insurance proceeds which are attributable to the loss of or damage to any property included in this sale.

(b) If Seller does not elect to make such repairs and restorations, Purchaser may exercise the resulting option under (i) or (ii) of (a) above only by notice given to Seller within 10 days after receipt of Seller's notice. If Seller elects to make such repairs and restorations and fails to complete the same on or before the adjourned closing date, Purchaser may exercise either of the resulting options within 10 days after the adjourned closing date.

(c) In the event of any loss of or damage to the Common Elements which materially and adversely affects access to or use of the Unit, arising after the date of this Contract but prior to the Closing, Seller shall notify Purchaser of the occurrence thereof within 10 days after such occurrence or by the date of Closing, whichever occurs first, in which event Purchaser shall have the following options:

(i) To complete the purchase in accordance with this Contract without reduction in the Purchase Price; or

(ii) To adjourn the Closing until the first to occur of (1) completion of the repair and restoration of the loss or damage to the point that there is no longer a materially adverse effect on the access to or use of the Unit or (2) the 60th day after the date of the giving of Seller's aforesaid notice. In the event Purchaser elects to adjourn the Closing as aforesaid and such loss or damage is not so repaired and restored within 60 days after the date of the giving of Seller's aforesaid notice, then Purchaser shall have the right either to (x) complete the purchase in accordance with this Contract without reduction in the Purchase Price or (y) declare this Contract cancelled and of no further force or effect and receive a refund of the Downpayment, in which latter event neither party shall thereafter have any further rights against, or obligations or liabilities to, the other by reason of this Contract.

(d) In the event of any loss of or damage to the Common Elements which does not materially and adversely affect access to or use of the Unit, Purchaser shall accept title to the Unit in accordance with this Contract without abatement of the Purchase Price.

21. Internal Revenue Service Reporting Requirement: Each party shall execute, acknowledge and deliver to the other party such instruments, and take such other actions, as such other party may reasonably request in order to comply with IRC § 6045(e), as amended, or any successor provision or any regulations promulgated pursuant thereto, insofar as the same requires reporting of information in respect of real estate transactions. The provisions of this para. 21 shall survive the Closing. The parties designate

as the attorney responsible for reporting this information as required by law.

Exhibit 6.2: Sales Contract for a Cooperative

Blumbergs Law Products   **123**-Contract of sale cooperative apartment, 7-01
Prepared by The Committee on Condominiums and Cooperatives of the Real Property Section of the New York State Bar Association

BlumbergExcelsior Inc., Publisher NYC 10013
www.blumberg.com

CONSULT YOUR LAWYER BEFORE SIGNING THIS AGREEMENT
Contract of Sale – Cooperative Apartment

This Contract is made as of   between the **"Seller"** and the **"Purchaser"** identified below.

1 Certain Definitions and Information
1.1 The "Parties" are:
1.1.1 "Seller":

Prior names used by Seller:
Address:

S.S. No.:
1.1.2 "Purchaser":

Address:

S.S. No.:
1.2 The "Attorneys" are *(name, address and telephone, fax):*
    1.2.1 "Seller's Attorney"

    1.2.2 "Purchaser's Attorney"

1.3 The "Escrowee" is the *[Seller's]* *[Purchaser's]* Attorney.

1.4 The Managing Agent is *(name, address and telephone, fax):*

1.5 The real estate "Broker(s)" (see ¶12) is/are:

Company Name:

1.6 The name of the cooperative housing corporation
("Corporation") is:

1.7 The "Unit" number is:

1.8 The Unit is located in "Premises" known as:

1.9 The "Shares" are the   shares of the
Corporation allocated to the Unit.

1.10 The "Lease" is the Corporation's proprietary lease or occupancy agreement for the Unit, given by the Corporation which expires on   .

1.11 "Personalty" is the following personal property, to the extent existing in the Unit on the date hereof: the refrigerators, freezers, ranges, ovens, built-in microwave ovens, dishwashers, garbage disposal units, cabinets and counters, lighting fixtures, chandeliers, wall-to-wall carpeting, plumbing and heating fixtures, central air-conditioning and/or window or sleeve units, washing machines, dryers, screens and storm windows, window treatments, switch plates, door hardware, mirrors, built-ins not excluded in ¶ 1.12 and

1.12 Specifically excluded from this sale is all personal property not included in ¶ 1.11 and:

1.13 The sale *[does] [does not]* include Seller's interest in *[Storage]/[Servant's Rm]/[Parking Space]* ("Included Interests")

1.14 The "Closing" is the transfer of ownership of the Shares and Lease.

1.15 The date scheduled for Closing is
("Scheduled Closing Date") at   .M (See ¶¶ 9 and 10)

1.16 The "Purchase Price" is: $
    1.16.1 The "Contract Deposit" is: $
    1.16.2 The "Balance" of the Purchase Price due at Closing is:
$ (See ¶ 2.2.2)

1.17 The monthly "Maintenance" charge is
$ (See ¶ 4)

1.18 The "Assessment", if any, payable to the Corporation, at the date of this Contract is $, payable as follows:

1.19 *[Seller] [Purchaser]* shall pay the Corporation's flip tax, transfer fee (apart from the transfer agent fee) and/or waiver of option fee ("Flip Tax"), if any.

1.20 Financing Options *(Delete two of the following ¶¶ 1.20.1, 1.20.2 or 1.20.3)*

    1.20.1 Purchaser may apply for financing in connection with this sale and Purchaser's obligation to purchase under this Contract is contingent upon issuance of a Loan Commitment Letter by the Loan Commitment Date (¶ 18.1.2).

    1.20.2 Purchaser may apply for financing in connection with this sale but Purchaser's obligation to purchase under this Contract is not contingent upon issuance of a Loan Commitment Letter.

    1.20.3 Purchaser shall not apply for financing in connection with this sale.

1.21 If ¶ 1.20.1 or 1.20.2 applies, the "Financing Terms" for ¶ 18 are:
a loan of $ for a term of   years or
such lesser amount or shorter term as applied for or acceptable to

Exhibit 6.2   211

Exhibit 6.2: *(Continued)*

Purchaser; and the "Loan Commitment Date" for ¶ 18 is   calendar days after the Delivery Date.

1.22 The "Delivery Date" of this Contract is the date on which a fully executed counterpart of this Contract is deemed given to and received by Purchaser or Purchaser's Attorney as provided in ¶ 17.3.

1.23 All "Proposed Occupants" of the Unit are:

    1.23.1 persons and relationship to Purchaser:

    1.23.2 pets:

1.24 The Contract Deposit shall be held in [*a non-*] [*an*] IOLA escrow account. If the account is a non-IOLA account then interest shall be paid to the Party entitled to the Contract Deposit. The Party receiving the interest shall pay any income taxes thereon. The escrow account shall be a segregated bank account at

Depository:

Address:

                               (See ¶ 27)

1.25 This Contract is [*not*] continued on attached rider(s).

2 Agreement to Sell and Purchase; Purchase Price; Escrow

2.1 Seller agrees to sell to Purchaser, and Purchaser agrees to purchase from Seller, the Seller's Shares, Lease, Personalty and any Included Interests and all other items included in this sale, for the Purchase Price and upon the terms and conditions set forth in this Contract.

2.2 The Purchase Price is payable to Seller by Purchaser as follows:

    2.2.1 the Contract Deposit at the time of signing this Contract, by Purchaser's good check to the order of Escrowee; and

2.2.2 the Balance at Closing, only by cashier's or official bank check or certified check of Purchaser payable to the direct order of Seller. The check(s) shall be drawn on and payable by a branch of a commercial or savings bank, savings and loan association or trust company located in the same City or County as the Unit. Seller may direct, on reasonable Notice (defined in ¶ 17) prior to Closing, that all or a portion of the Balance shall be made payable to persons other than Seller (see ¶ 17.7).

3 Personalty

3.1 Subject to any rights of the Corporation or any holder of a mortgage to which the Lease is subordinate, this sale includes all of the Seller's interest, if any, in the Personalty and the Included Interests.

3.2 No consideration is being paid for the Personalty or for the Included Interests; nothing shall be sold to Purchaser if the Closing does not occur.

3.3 Prior to Closing, Seller shall remove from the Unit all the furniture, furnishings and other property not included in this sale, and repair any damage caused by such removal.

4 Representations and Covenants

4.1 Subject to any matter affecting title to the Premises (as to which Seller makes no representations or covenants), Seller represents and covenants that:

    4.1.1 Seller is, and shall at Closing be, the sole owner of the Shares, Lease, Personalty and Included Interests, with the full right, power and authority to sell and assign them. Seller shall make timely provision to satisfy existing security interest(s) in the Shares and Lease and have the same delivered at Closing (See ¶ 10.1);

    4.1.2 the Shares were duly issued, fully paid for and are non-assessable;

    4.1.3 the Lease is, and will at Closing be, in full force and effect and no notice of default under the Lease is now or will at Closing be in effect;

    4.1.4 the Maintenance and Assessments payable as of the date hereof are as specified in ¶ 1.17 and 1.18;

    4.1.5 as of this date, Seller neither has actual knowledge nor has received any written notice of any increase in Maintenance or any Assessment which has been adopted by the Board of Directors of the Corporation and is not reflected in the amounts set forth in ¶¶ 1.17 and 1.18;

    4.1.6 Seller has not made any material alterations or additions to the Unit without any required consent of the Corporation or, to Seller's actual knowledge, without compliance with all applicable law. This provision shall not survive Closing.

    4.1.7 Seller has not entered into, shall not enter into, and has no actual knowledge of any agreement (other than the Lease) affecting title to the Unit or its use and/or occupancy after Closing, or which would be binding on or adversely affect Purchaser after Closing (e.g. a sublease or alteration agreement);

    4.1.8 Seller has been known by no other name for the past 10 years except as set forth in ¶ 1.1.1.

    4.1.9 at Closing in accordance with ¶ 15.2:

        4.1.9.1 there shall be no judgments outstanding against Seller which have not been bonded against collection out of the Unit ("Judgments");

        4.1.9.2 the Shares, Lease, Personalty and any Included Interests shall be free and clear of liens (other than the Corporation's general lien on the Shares for which no monies shall be owed), encumbrances and adverse interests ("Liens");

        4.1.9.3 all sums due to the Corporation shall be fully paid by Seller to the end of the payment period immediately preceding the date of Closing;

        4.1.9.4 Seller shall not be indebted for labor or material which might give rise to the filing of a notice of mechanic's lien against the Unit or the Premises; and

        4.1.9.5 no violations shall be of record which the owner of the Shares and Lease would be obligated to remedy under the Lease.

4.2 Purchaser represents and covenants that:

    4.2.1 Purchaser is acquiring the Shares and Lease for residential occupancy of the Unit solely by the Proposed Occupants identified in ¶ 1.23

    4.2.2 Purchaser is not, and within the past 7 years has not been, the subject of a bankruptcy proceeding;

    4.2.3 if ¶ 1.20.3 applies, Purchaser shall not apply for financing in connection with this purchase.

    4.2.4 Each individual comprising Purchaser is over the age of 18 and is purchasing for Purchaser's own account (beneficial and of record);

    4.2.5 Purchaser shall not make any representations to the Corporation contrary to the foregoing and shall provide all documents in support thereof required by the Corporation in connection with Purchaser's application for approval of this transaction; and

    4.2.6 there are not now and shall not be at Closing any unpaid tax liens or monetary judgments against Purchaser.

4.3 Each Party covenants that its representations and covenants contained in ¶ 4 shall be true and complete at Closing and, except for ¶ 4.1.6, shall survive Closing but any action based thereon must be instituted within one year after Closing.

5 Corporate Documents

Purchaser has examined and is satisfied with, or (except as to any matter represented in this Contract by Seller) accepts and assumes the risk of not having examined, the Lease, the Corporation's Certificate of Incorporation, By-laws, House Rules, minutes of shareholders' and directors' meetings, most recent audited financial statement and most recent statement of tax deductions available to the Corporation's shareholders under Internal Revenue Code ("IRC") §216 (or any successor statute).

6 Required Approval and References

6.1 This sale is subject to the unconditional consent of the Corporation.

6.2 Purchaser shall in good faith:

    6.2.1 submit to the Corporation or the Managing Agent an application with respect to this sale on the form required by the Corporation, containing such data and together with such documents as the Corporation requires, and pay the applicable fees and charges that the Corporation imposes upon Purchaser. All of the foregoing shall be submitted within 10 business days after the Delivery Date, or, if ¶ 1.20.1 or 1.20.2 applies and the Loan Commitment Letter is required by the Corporation, within 3 business days after the earlier of (i) the Loan Commitment Date (defined in ¶ 1.21) or (ii) the date of receipt of the Loan Commitment Letter (defined in ¶ 18.1.2);

    6.2.2 attend (and cause any Proposed Occupant to attend) one or more personal interviews, as requested by the Corporation; and

    6.2.3 promptly submit to the Corporation such further references, data and documents reasonably requested by the Corporation.

Exhibit 6.2: *(Continued)*

6.3 Either Party, after learning of the Corporation's decision, shall promptly advise the other Party thereof. If the Corporation has not made a decision on or before the Scheduled Closing Date, the Closing shall be adjourned for 30 business days for the purpose of obtaining such consent. If such consent is not given by such adjourned date, either Party may cancel this Contract by Notice, provided that the Corporation's consent is not issued before such Notice of cancellation is given. If such consent is refused at any time, either Party may cancel this Contract by Notice. In the event of cancellation pursuant to this ¶ 6.3, the Escrowee shall refund the Contract Deposit to Purchaser.

6.4 If such consent is refused, or not given, due to Purchaser's bad faith conduct, Purchaser shall be in default and ¶ 13.1 shall govern.

7 Condition of Unit and Personalty; Possession

7.1 Seller makes no representation as to the physical condition or state of repair of the Unit, the Personalty, the Included Interests or the Premises. Purchaser has inspected or waived inspection of the Unit, the Personalty and the Included Interests and shall take the same "as is", as of the date of this Contract, except for reasonable wear and tear. However, at the time of Closing, the appliances shall be in working order and required smoke detector(s) shall be installed and operable.

7.2 At Closing, Seller shall deliver possession of the Unit, Personalty and Included Interests in the condition required by ¶ 7.1, broom-clean, vacant and free of all occupants and rights of possession.

8 Risk of Loss

8.1 The provisions of General Obligations Law Section 5-1311, as modified herein, shall apply to this transaction as if it were a sale of realty. For purposes of this paragraph, the term "Unit" includes built-in Personalty.

8.2 Destruction shall be deemed "material" under GOL 5-1311, if the reasonably estimated cost to restore the Unit shall exceed 5% of the Purchase Price.

8.3 In the event of any destruction of the Unit or the Premises, when neither legal title nor the possession of the Unit has been transferred to Purchaser, Seller shall give Notice of the loss to Purchaser ("Loss Notice") by the earlier of the date of Closing or 7 business days after the date of loss.

8.4 If there is material destruction of the Unit without fault of Purchaser, this Contract shall be deemed canceled in accordance with ¶ 16.3, unless Purchaser elects by Notice to Seller to complete the purchase with an abatement of the Purchase Price; or

8.5 Whether or not there is any destruction of the Unit, if, without fault of Purchaser, more than 10% of the units in the Premises are rendered uninhabitable, or reasonable access to the Unit is not available, then Purchaser shall have the right to cancel this Contract in accordance with ¶ 16.3 by Notice to Seller.

8.6 Purchaser's Notice pursuant to ¶ 8.4 or ¶ 8.5 shall be given within 7 business days following the giving of the Loss Notice except that if Seller does not give a Loss Notice, Purchaser's Notice may be given at any time at or prior to Closing

8.7 In the event of any destruction of the Unit, Purchaser shall not be entitled to an abatement of the Purchase Price (i) that exceeds the reasonably estimated cost of repair and restoration or (ii) for any loss that the Corporation is obliged to repair or restore; but Seller shall assign to Purchaser, without recourse, Seller's claim, if any, against the Corporation with respect to such loss.

9 Closing Location

The Closing shall be held at the location designated by the Corporation or, if no such designation is made, at the office of Seller's Attorney.

10 Closing

10.1 At Closing, Seller shall deliver or cause to be delivered:

10.1.1 Seller's certificate for the Shares duly endorsed for transfer to Purchaser or accompanied by a separate duly executed stock power to Purchaser, and in either case, with any guarantee of Seller's signature required by the Corporation;

10.1.2 Seller's counterpart original of the Lease, all assignments and assumptions in the chain of title and a duly executed assignment thereof to Purchaser in the form required by the Corporation;

10.1.3 FIRPTA documents required by ¶ 25;

10.1.4 keys to the Unit, building entrance(s), and, if applicable, garage, mailbox, storage unit and any locks in the Unit;

10.1.5 if requested, an assignment to Purchaser of Seller's interest in the Personalty and Included Interests;

10.1.6 any documents and payments to comply with ¶ 15.2

10.1.7 If Seller is unable to deliver the documents required in ¶ 10.1.1 or 10.1.2 then Seller shall deliver or cause to be delivered all documents and payments required by the Corporation for the issuance of a new certificate for the Shares or a new Lease.

10.2 At Closing, Purchaser shall:

10.2.1 pay the Balance in accordance with ¶ 2.2.2;

10.2.2 execute and deliver to Seller and the Corporation an agreement assuming the Lease, in the form required by the Corporation; and

10.2.3 if requested by the Corporation, execute and deliver counterparts of a new lease substantially the same as the Lease, for the balance of the Lease term, in which case the Lease shall be canceled and surrendered to the Corporation together with Seller's assignment thereof to Purchaser.

10.3 At Closing, the Parties shall complete and execute all documents necessary:

10.3.1 for Internal Revenue Service ("IRS") form 1099-S or other similar requirements;

10.3.2 to comply with smoke detector requirements and any applicable transfer tax filings; and

10.3.3 to transfer Seller's interest, if any, in and to the Personalty and Included Interests.

10.4 Purchaser shall not be obligated to close unless, at Closing, the Corporation delivers:

10.4.1 to Purchaser a new certificate for the Shares in the name, of Purchaser; and

10.4.2 a written statement by an officer or authorized agent of the Corporation consenting to the transfer of the Shares and Lease to Purchaser and setting forth the amounts of and payment status of all sums owed by Seller to the Corporation, including Maintenance and any Assessments, and the dates to which each has been paid.

11 Closing Fees, Taxes and Apportionments

11.1 At or prior to Closing,

11.1.1 Seller shall pay, if applicable:

11.1.1.1 the cost of stock transfer stamps; and

11.1.1.2 transfer taxes, except as set forth in ¶ 11.1.2.2

11.1.2 Purchaser shall pay, if applicable:

11.1.2.1 any fee imposed by the Corporation relating to Purchaser's financing; and

11.1.2.2 transfer taxes imposed by statute primarily on Purchaser (e.g., the "mansion tax").

11.2 The Flip Tax, if any, shall be paid by the Party specified in ¶ 1.19.

11.3 Any fee imposed by the Corporation and not specified in this Contract shall be paid by the Party upon whom such fee is expressly imposed by the Corporation, and if no Party is specified by the Corporation, then such fee shall be paid by Seller.

11.4 The Parties shall apportion as of 11:59 P.M. of the day preceding the Closing, the Maintenance, and any other periodic charges due the Corporation (other than Assessments) and STAR Tax Exemption (if the Unit is the beneficiary of same), based on the number of the days in the month of Closing.

11.5 Assessments, whether payable in a lump sum or installments, shall not be apportioned, but shall be paid by the Party who is the owner of the Shares on the date specified by the Corporation for payment. Purchaser shall pay any installments payable after Closing provided Seller had the right and elected to pay the Assessment in installments.

11.6 Each Party shall timely pay any transfer taxes for which it is primarily liable pursuant to law by cashier's, official bank, certified, or attorney's escrow check. This ¶ 11.6 shall survive Closing.

11.7 Any computational errors or omissions shall be corrected within 6 months after Closing. This ¶ 11.7 shall survive Closing.

12 Broker

12.1 Each Party represents that such Party has not dealt with any person acting as a broker, whether licensed or unlicensed, in connection with this transaction other than the Broker(s) named in ¶ 1.5.

12.2 Seller shall pay the Broker's commission pursuant to a separate

Exhibit 6.2   213

Exhibit 6.2: *(Continued)*

agreement. The Broker(s) shall not be deemed to be a third-party beneficiary of this Contract.

12.3 This ¶ 12 shall survive Closing, cancellation or termination of this Contract.

13 Defaults, Remedies and Indemnities

13.1 In the event of a default or misrepresentation by Purchaser, Seller's sole and exclusive remedies shall be to cancel this Contract, retain the Contract Deposit as liquidated damages and, if applicable, Seller may enforce the indemnity in ¶ 13.3 as to brokerage commission or sue under ¶ 13.4. Purchaser prefers to limit Purchaser's exposure for actual damages to the amount of the Contract Deposit, which Purchaser agrees constitutes a fair and reasonable amount of compensation for Seller's damages under the circumstances and is not a penalty. The principles of real property law shall apply to this liquidated damages provision.

13.2 In the event of a default or misrepresentation by Seller, Purchaser shall have such remedies as Purchaser is entitled to at law or in equity, including specific performance, because the Unit and possession thereof cannot be duplicated.

13.3 Subject to the provisions of ¶ 4.3, each Party indemnifies and holds harmless the other against and from any claim, judgment, loss, liability, cost or expense resulting from the indemnitor's breach of any of its representations or covenants stated to survive Closing, cancellation or termination of this Contract. Purchaser indemnifies and holds harmless Seller against and from any claim, judgment, loss, liability, cost or expense resulting from the Lease obligations accruing from and after the Closing. Each indemnity includes, without limitation, reasonable attorneys' fees and disbursements, court costs and litigation expenses arising from the defense of any claim and enforcement or collection of a judgment under this indemnity, provided the indemnitee is given Notice and opportunity to defend the claim. This ¶ 13.3 shall survive Closing, cancellation or termination of this Contract.

13.4 In the event any instrument for the payment of the Contract Deposit fails of collection, Seller shall have the right to sue on the uncollected instrument. In addition, such failure of collection shall be a default under this Contract, provided Seller gives Purchaser Notice of such failure of collection and, within 3 business days after Notice is given, Escrowee does not receive from Purchaser an unendorsed good certified check, bank check or immediately available funds in the amount of the uncollected funds. Failure to cure such default shall entitle Seller to the remedies set forth in ¶ 13.1 and to retain all sums as may be collected and/or recovered.

14 Entire Agreement; Modification

14.1 All prior oral or written representations, understandings and agreements had between the Parties with respect to the subject matter of this Contract, and with the Escrowee as to ¶ 27, are merged in this Contract, which alone fully and completely expresses the Parties' and Escrowee's agreement.

14.2 The Attorneys may extend in writing any of the time limitations stated in this Contract. Any other provision of this Contract may be changed or waived only in writing signed by the Party or Escrowee to be charged.

15 Removal of Liens and Judgments

15.1 Purchaser shall deliver or cause to be delivered to Seller or Seller's Attorney, not less than 10 calendar days prior to the Scheduled Closing Date a Lien and Judgment search, except that Liens or Judgments first disclosed in a continuation search shall be reported to Seller within 2 business days after receipt thereof, but not later than the Closing. Seller shall have the right to adjourn the Closing pursuant to ¶ 16 to remove any such Liens and Judgments. Failure by Purchaser to timely deliver such search or continuation search shall not constitute a waiver of Seller's covenants in ¶ 4 as to Liens and Judgments. However, if the Closing is adjourned solely by reason of untimely delivery of the Lien and Judgment search, the apportionments under ¶ 11.3 shall be made as of 11:59 P.M. of the day preceding the Scheduled Closing Date in ¶ 1.15.

15.2 Seller, at Seller's expense, shall obtain and deliver to the Purchaser the documents and payments necessary to secure the release, satisfaction, termination and discharge or removal of record of any Liens and Judgments. Seller may use any portion of the Purchase Price for such purposes.

15.3 This ¶ 15 shall survive Closing.

16 Seller's Inability

16.1 If Seller shall be unable to transfer the items set forth in ¶ 2.1 in accordance with this Contract for any reason other than Seller's failure to make a required payment or other willful act or omission, then Seller shall have the right to adjourn the Closing for periods not exceeding 60 calendar days in the aggregate, but not extending beyond the expiration of Purchaser's Loan Commitment Letter, if ¶ 1.20.1 or 1.20.2 applies.

16.2 If Seller does not elect to adjourn the Closing or (if adjourned) on the adjourned date of Closing Seller is still unable to perform, then unless Purchaser elects to proceed with the Closing without abatement of the Purchase Price, either Party may cancel this Contract on Notice to the other Party given at any time thereafter.

16.3 In the event of such cancellation, the sole liability of Seller shall be to cause the Contract Deposit to be refunded to Purchaser and to reimburse Purchaser for the actual costs incurred for Purchase's lien and title search, if any.

17 Notices and Contract Delivery

17.1 Any notice or demand ("Notice") shall be in writing and delivered either by hand, overnight delivery or certified or registered mail, return receipt requested, to the Party and simultaneously, in like manner, to such Party's Attorney, if any, and to Escrowee at their respective addresses or to such other address as shall hereafter be designated by Notice given pursuant to this ¶ 17.

17.2 The Contract may be delivered as provided in ¶ 17.1 or by ordinary mail.

17.3 The Contract or each Notice shall be deemed given and received:

   17.3.1 on the day delivered by hand;

   17.3.2 on the business day following the date sent by overnight delivery;

   17.3.3 on the 5th business day following the date sent by certified or registered mail; or

   17.3.4 as to the Contract only, 3 business days following the date of ordinary mailing.

17.4 A Notice to Escrowee shall be deemed given only upon actual receipt by Escrowee.

17.5 The Attorneys are authorized to give and receive any Notice on behalf of their respective clients.

17.6 Failure or refusal to accept a Notice shall not invalidate the Notice.

17.7 Notice pursuant to ¶¶ 2.2.2 and 13.4 may be delivered by confirmed facsimile to the Party's Attorney and shall be deemed given when transmission is confirmed by sender's facsimile machine.

18 Financing Provisions

18.1 The provisions of ¶¶ 18.1 and 18.2 are applicable only if ¶ 1.20.1 or 1.20.2 applies.

   18.1.1 An "Institutional Lender" is any of the following that is authorized under Federal or New York State law to issue a loan secured by the Shares and Lease and is currently extending similarly secured loan commitments in the county in which the Unit is located: a bank, savings bank, savings and loan association, trust company, credit union of which Purchaser is a member, mortgage banker, insurance company or governmental entity.

   18.1.2 A "Loan Commitment Letter" is a written offer from an Institutional Lender to make a loan on the Financing Terms (see ¶ 1.21) at prevailing fixed or adjustable interest rates and on other customary terms generally being offered by Institutional Lenders making cooperative share loans. An offer to make a loan conditional upon obtaining an appraisal satisfactory to the Institutional Lender shall not become a Loan Commitment Letter unless and until such condition is met. An offer conditional upon any factor concerning Purchaser (e.g. sale of current home, payment of outstanding debt, no material adverse change in Purchaser's financial condition, etc.) is a Loan Commitment Letter whether or not such condition is met. Purchaser accepts the risk that, and cannot cancel this Contract if, any condition concerning Purchaser is not met.

18.2 Purchaser, directly or through a mortgage broker registered pursuant to Article 12-D of the Banking Law, shall diligently and in good faith:

   18.2.1 apply only to an Institutional Lender for a loan on

Exhibit 6.2: *(Continued)*

the Financing Terms (see ¶ 1.21) on the form required by the Institutional Lender containing truthful and complete information, and submit such application together with such documents as the Institutional Lender requires, and pay the applicable fees and charges of the Institutional Lender, all of which shall be performed within 5 business days after the Delivery Date;

18.2.2 promptly submit to the Institutional Lender such further references, data and documents requested by the Institutional Lender;

18.2.3 accept a Loan Commitment Letter meeting the Financing Terms and comply with all requirements of such Loan Commitment Letter (or any other loan commitment letter accepted by Purchaser) and of the Institutional Lender in order to close the loan; and

18.2.4 furnish Seller with a copy of the Loan Commitment Letter promptly after Purchaser's receipt thereof.

18.2.5 Purchaser is not required to apply to more than one Institutional Lender.

18.3 If ¶ 1.20.1 applies, then

18.3.1 provided Purchaser has complied with all applicable provisions of ¶ 18.2 and this ¶ 18.3, Purchaser may cancel this Contract as set forth below, if:

18.3.1.1 any Institutional Lender denies Purchaser's application in writing prior to the Loan Commitment Date (see ¶ 1.21); or

18.3.1.2 a Loan Commitment Letter is not issued by the Institutional Lender on or before the Loan Commitment Date; or

18.3.1.3 any requirement of the Loan Commitment Letter other than one concerning Purchaser is not met (e.g. failure of the Corporation to execute and deliver the Institutional Lender's recognition agreement or other document, financial condition of the Corporation, owner occupancy quota, etc.); or

18.3.1.4 (i) the Closing is adjourned by Seller or the Corporation for more than 30 business days from the Scheduled Closing Date and (ii) the Loan Commitment Letter expires on a date more than 30 business days after the Scheduled Closing Date and before the new date set for Closing pursuant to this paragraph and (iii) Purchaser is unable in good faith to obtain from the Institutional Lender an extension of the Loan Commitment Letter or a new Loan Commitment Letter on the Financing Terms without paying additional fees to the Institutional Lender, unless Seller agrees, by Notice to Purchaser within 5 business days after receipt of Purchaser's Notice of cancellation on such ground, that Seller will pay such additional fees and Seller pays such fees when due. Purchaser may not object to an adjournment by Seller for up to 30 business days solely because the Loan Commitment Letter would expire before such adjourned Closing date.

18.3.2 Purchaser shall deliver Notice of cancellation to Seller within 5 business days after the Loan Commitment Date if cancellation is pursuant to ¶ 18.3.1.1 or 18.3.1.2 and on or prior to the Scheduled Closing Date if cancellation is pursuant to ¶ 18.3.1.3 or 18.3.1.4.

18.3.3 If cancellation is pursuant to ¶ 18.3.1.1, then Purchaser shall deliver to Seller, together with Purchaser's Notice, a copy of the Institutional Lender's written denial of Purchaser's loan application. If cancellation is pursuant to ¶ 18.3.1.3, then Purchaser shall deliver to Seller together with Purchaser's Notice evidence that a requirement of the Institutional Lender was not met.

18.3.4 Seller may cancel this Contract by Notice to Purchaser, sent within 5 days after the Loan Commitment Date, if Purchaser shall not have sent by then either (i) Purchaser's Notice of cancellation or (ii) a copy of the Loan Commitment Letter to Seller, which cancellation shall become effective if Purchaser does not deliver a copy of such Loan Commitment Letter to Seller within 10 business days after the Loan Commitment Date.

18.3.5 Failure by either Purchaser or Seller to deliver Notice of cancellation as required by this ¶ 18.3 shall constitute a waiver of the right to cancel under this ¶ 18.3.

18.3.6 If this Contract is canceled by Purchaser pursuant to this ¶ 18.3, then thereafter neither Party shall have any further rights against, or obligations or liabilities to, the other by reason of this Contract, except that the Contract Deposit shall be promptly refunded to Purchaser and except as set forth in ¶ 12. If this Contract is canceled by Purchaser pursuant to ¶ 18.3.1.4, then Seller shall reim-

burse Purchaser for any non-refundable financing and inspection expenses and other sums reimbursable pursuant to ¶ 16.

18.3.7 Purchaser cannot cancel this Contract pursuant to ¶ 18.3.1.4 and cannot obtain a refund of the Contract Deposit if the Institutional Lender fails to fund the loan:

18.3.7.1 because a requirement of the Loan Commitment Letter concerning Purchaser is not met (e.g., Purchaser's financial condition or employment status suffers an adverse change; Purchaser fails to satisfy a condition relating to the sale of an existing residence, etc.) or

18.3.7.2 due to the expiration of a Loan Commitment Letter issued with an expiration date that is not more than 30 business days after the Scheduled Closing Date.

19 Singular/Plural and Joint/Several
The use of the singular shall be deemed to include the plural and vice versa, whenever the context so requires. If more than one person constitutes Seller or Purchaser, their obligations as such Party shall be joint and several.

20 No Survival
No representation and/or covenant contained herein shall survive Closing except as expressly provided. Payment of the Balance shall constitute a discharge and release by Purchaser of all of Seller's obligations hereunder except those expressly stated to survive Closing.

21 Inspections
Purchaser and Purchaser's representatives shall have the right to inspect the Unit within 48 hours prior to Closing, and at other reasonable times upon reasonable request to Seller.

22 Governing Law and Venue
This Contract shall be governed by the laws of the State of New York without regard to principles of conflict of laws. Any action or proceeding arising out of this Contract shall be brought in the county or Federal district where the Unit is located and the Parties hereby consent to said venue.

23 No Assignment by Purchaser; Death of Purchaser
23.1 Purchaser may not assign this Contract or any of Purchaser's rights hereunder. Any such purported assignment shall be null and void.

23.2 This Contract shall terminate upon the death of all persons comprising Purchaser and the Contract Deposit shall be refunded to the Purchaser. Upon making such refund and reimbursement, neither Party shall have any further liability or claim against the other hereunder, except as set forth in Par. 12.

24 Cooperation of Parties
24.1 The Parties shall each cooperate with the other, the Corporation and Purchaser's Institutional Lender and title company, if any, and obtain, execute and deliver such documents as are reasonably necessary to consummate this sale.

24.2 The Parties shall timely file all required documents in connection with all governmental filings that are required by law. Each Party represents to the other that its statements in such filings shall be true and complete. This ¶ 24.2 shall survive Closing.

25 FIRPTA
The parties shall comply with IRC §§ 897, 1445 and the regulations thereunder as same may be amended ("FIRPTA"). If applicable, Seller shall execute and deliver to purchaser at Closing a Certification of Non-Foreign Status ("CNS") or deliver a Withholding Certificate from the IRS. If Seller fails to deliver a CNS or a Withholding Certificate, Purchaser shall withhold from the Balance, and remit to the IRS, such sum as may be required by law. Seller hereby waives any right of action against Purchaser on account of such withholding and remittance. This ¶ 25 shall survive Closing.

26 Additional Requirements
26.1 Purchaser shall not be obligated to close unless all of the following requirements are satisfied at the time of the Closing:

26.1.1 the Corporation is in good standing;

26.1.2 the Corporation has fee or leasehold title to the Premises, whether or not marketable or insurable; and

26.1.3 there is no pending *in rem* action, tax certificate/lien sale or foreclosure action of any underlying mortgage affecting the Premises.

26.2 If any requirement in ¶ 26.1 is not satisfied at the time of the Closing, Purchaser shall give Seller Notice and if the same is not satisfied within a reasonable period of time thereafter, then either Party may cancel this Contract (pursuant to ¶ 16.3) by Notice.

Exhibit 6.2   215

Exhibit 6.2: *(Continued)*

27 Escrow Terms

27.1 The Contract Deposit shall be deposited by Escrowee in an escrow account as set forth in ¶ 1.24 and the proceeds held and disbursed in accordance with the terms of this Contract. At Closing, the Contract Deposit shall be paid by Escrowee to Seller. If the Closing does not occur and either Party gives Notice to Escrowee demanding payment of the Contract Deposit, Escrowee shall give prompt Notice to the other Party of such demand. If Escrowee does not receive a Notice of objection to the proposed payment from such other Party within 10 business days after the giving of Escrowee's Notice, Escrowee is hereby authorized and directed to make such payment to the demanding party. If Escrowee does receive such a Notice of objection within said period, or if for any reason Escrowee in good faith elects not to make such payment, Escrowee may continue to hold the Contract Deposit until otherwise directed by a joint Notice by the Parties or a final, non-appealable judgment, order or decree of a court of competent jurisdiction. However, Escrowee shall have the right at any time to deposit the Contract Deposit and the interest thereon, if any, with the clerk of a court in the county as set forth in ¶ 22 and shall give Notice of such deposit to each Party. Upon disposition of the Contract Deposit and interest thereon, if any, in accordance with this ¶ 27, Escrowee shall be released and discharged of all escrow obligations and liabilities.

27.2 The Party whose Attorney is Escrowee shall be liable for loss of the Contract Deposit. If the Escrowee is Seller's attorney, then Purchaser shall be credited with the amount of the contract Deposit at Closing.

27.3 Escrowee will serve without compensation. Escrowee is acting solely as a stakeholder at the Parties' request and for their convenience. Escrowee shall not be liable to either Party for any act or omission unless it involves bad faith, willful disregard of this Contract or gross negligence. In the event of any dispute, Seller and Purchaser shall jointly and severally (with right of contribution) defend (by attorneys selected by Escrowee), indemnify and hold harmless Escrowee from and against any claim, judgment, loss, liability, cost and expenses incurred in connection with the performance of Escrowee's acts or omissions not involving bad faith, willful disregard of this Contract or gross negligence. This indemnity includes, without limitation, reasonable attorneys' fees either paid to retain attorneys or representing the fair value of legal services rendered by Escrowee to itself and disbursements, court costs and litigation expenses.

27.4 Escrowee acknowledges receipt of the Contract Deposit, by check subject to collection.

27.5 Escrowee agrees to the provisions of this ¶ 27.

27.6 If Escrowee is the Attorney for a Party, Escrowee shall be permitted to represent such Party in any dispute or lawsuit.

27.7 This ¶ 27 shall survive Closing, cancellation or termination of this Contract.

28 Margin Headings

The margin headings do not constitute part of the text of this Contract.

29 Miscellaneous

This Contract shall not be binding unless and until Seller delivers a fully executed counterpart of this Contract to Purchaser (or Purchaser's Attorney) pursuant to ¶17.2 and 17.3. This Contract shall bind and inure to the benefit of the Parties hereto and their respective heirs, personal and legal representatives and successors in interest.

30 Lead Paint

If applicable, the complete and fully executed Disclosure of Information on Lead Based Paint and or Lead-Based Paint Hazards is attached hereto and made a part hereof.

In Witness Whereof, the Parties hereto have duly executed this Contract as of the date first above written.

ESCROW TERMS AGREED TO: SELLER: PURCHASER:

_____

ESCROWEE

                                 _____   _____

                                 _____   _____

Rider to, and Part of, Contract of Sale Between   **as Seller**
and   **as Purchaser for Unit**   **at**

Suggested Purchaser's representations for use when applicable.

31 Purchaser's Additional Representations and Covenants

31.1 Supplementing ¶ 4.2 of the Contract. Purchaser also represents and covenants that:

    31.1.1 Purchaser has, and will at Closing have, available unencumbered cash and cash equivalents (including publicly traded securities) in a sum at least equal to (and having a then current value of) the Balance; and

    31.1.2 Purchaser has, and will at and immediately following the Closing have, a positive net worth.

31.2 the Maintenance and the monthly amount of the Assessment (if any) do not aggregate more than 25% of the current total gross monthly income of the individuals comprising the Purchaser;

31.3 (if ¶ 1.20.1 or ¶ 1.20.2 applies) the monthly debt service (interest and amortization of principal, if any) of the proposed financing, together with the Maintenance and the monthly Assessment amount (if any), do not aggregate more than 35% of said current total gross monthly income.

32 Supplementing paragraph 4.1. Seller has no actual knowledge of a material default or condition which the Lessee is required to cure under the Lease and which remains uncured. If, prior to Closing, Seller acquires knowledge of a such default or condition which the Lessee would be required to cure, then Seller shall cure same at or prior to Closing. This provision shall not survive closing.

The Parties have duly executed this Rider as of the same date as the Contract.

                                 SELLER: PURCHASER:

                                 _____   _____

                                 _____   _____

Exhibit 6.3: Land Description of a Commercial Property

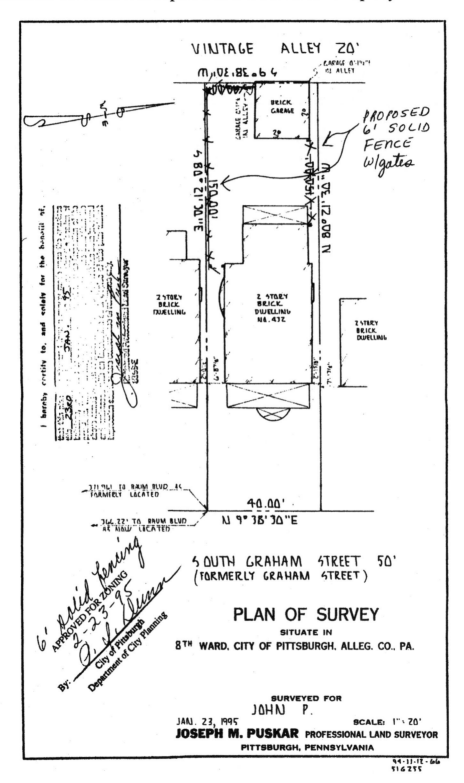

7
Landlord-Tenant Law

LEARNING OBJECTIVES

After studying this chapter you will be able to:

- Explain the concept of a leasehold
- Define "lessor" and "lessee"
- Explain a tenancy for years
- Understand the landlord's right of reentry
- Explain a periodic tenancy
- Discuss a tenancy at will
- Define a tenancy at sufferance
- Discuss implications of the holdover doctrine
- List the different types of rent arrangements that may exist
- Explain what is meant by a "radius clause" in a lease
- Discuss a tenant's duties with respect to a leasehold
- Define "mitigation of damages"
- Discuss a landlord's duties with respect to a leasehold
- List the different types of evictions to which a tenant may be subject
- Explain the concept of a warranty of habitability
- Differentiate an assignment from a sublease
- Apply some practical tips to assist you in a landlord-tenant practice

CHAPTER OUTLINE

The Lease
     Tenancy for years
     Periodic tenancy
     Tenancy at will
     Tenancy at sufferance
     Holdover doctrine
     Gross lease
     Net rent lease
Tenant's Duties
     Mitigation of damages
Landlord's Duties
     Eviction
          Actual
          Partial
          Constructive
     Warranty of habitability
Assignments and Subleases
Practical Tips

CHAPTER OVERVIEW

As explained in Chapter 1, property is divided into two broad categories: freeholds and leaseholds. The preceding chapters concentrated on various aspects of freehold estates; this chapter focuses on the second group of estates — the leasehold.

A **leasehold** is a possessory interest in property, either real or personal, that is created and governed by the terms of a lease. A **lease** is the contract that establishes the possessory rights and obligations and, for the most part, is governed by general contract law. Various aspects of contract law have been discussed in earlier chapters and a detailed examination of the law of contracts is beyond the scope of this text. However, the legal professional must always be cognizant of the fact that the rights and obligations of the lessor and the lessee are determined by the provisions of the lease.

This chapter highlights the various types of leasehold arrangements that may exist, as well as the rights (and responsibilities) of both the landlord and the tenant. Note that personal property as well as real property can be subject to lease arrangements.

The Lease

A *lease* is a contract that establishes the relationship between the lessor and the lessee. The **lessor** is the person who has rights in the subject property sufficient to permit him or her to transfer a right of possession. The **lessee** is the person who contracts for the right of possession of the leased property. It must be borne in mind that the lessee, as such, only acquires a possessory right in the property.

EXAMPLE:

A widow decides to take a one-year trip around the world and to let her house for that period. The widow owns the house as a tenant in severalty, which gives her the right to transfer any estate up to the one she has to another person. She rents her house for the one-year period to a middle-aged couple who, pursuant to the terms of the lease, have the right to use and enjoy the house for the year, but they do not "own" the house, and the lease has prohibitions against the couple transferring their interests (see below).

If the property that is subject to the lease is realty, it is referred to as a *leasehold;* leases of personalty are referred to simply as leases.

Generally, there are four types of leaseholds that may be created:

1. **Tenancy for years:** These tenancies are created for a fixed period of time. If the leasehold period is intended to exist for more than one year, the Statute of Frauds requires that the lease be in writing to be enforceable, and the lease automatically terminates at the date specified in the lease. Furthermore, most jurisdictions permit the landlord to retain a **right of entry** to gain access to the premises in the event the tenant breaches any of the lease covenants. **Landlord** is the term generally employed to refer to the lessor of realty.

EXAMPLE:

A student has enrolled in a law school in a city several hundred miles from her home. She enters into a lease for an apartment near the school for a term of three years. At the end of three years the lease will automatically terminate.

A tenancy for years may be terminated by the landlord earlier than the termination date if the tenant fails to pay the specified rent (see below), or the tenant may surrender the property to the landlord prior to the expiration of the lease, which will excuse further obligations *if* the landlord accepts such early termination. The rights of early termination depend on the specific jurisdiction in which the property is located.

2. **Periodic tenancy:** This type of lease continues for successive periods specified in the lease until terminated by notice of either party. Periodic tenancies may be created by:
   (a) an express agreement;
   (b) implication, if the lease specifies a monthly or weekly rental and no specific termination; and
   (c) operation of law if a tenant remains in possession after the termination of a tenancy for years.

Periodic tenancies typically remain in effect until one party informs the other of its termination.

EXAMPLE:

A student rents an apartment for a one-year lease for a yearly rental of $6000, payable in monthly installments of $500. At the termination of the lease the student does not leave, and the landlord continues to accept the student's rent check of $500 for each of the next three months. After the third month the landlord sends the student a notice of termination to be effective at the end of the current month. The tenancy for years turned into a periodic tenancy but was terminated by the landlord's notice.

3. **Tenancy at will:** This tenancy is created by the will and intent of either the lessor or the lessee, and must be created by an express agreement (not necessarily a writing). This type of tenancy may be terminated at any time without notice, or automatically by operation of law if one of the parties dies or the tenant acquires title to the property.

EXAMPLE:

A writer who lives in the city wants to go into seclusion to complete his novel. His friend has a mountain cabin that he uses infrequently, and the friend agrees to let the writer live in the cabin to finish the novel. In consideration of this use, the writer agrees to pay all utilities and taxes due on the property while he is in possession. After six months the novel is complete and the writer quits the cabin. The writer is obligated for utilities and taxes attributable to these six months, and the tenancy is terminated.

4. **Tenancy at sufferance:** A tenancy at sufferance is created when a tenant unlawfully remains in possession of the property after the termination of a lawful tenancy. This tenancy only remains in effect until the lessor takes steps to evict the tenant, and no notice of the termination is required.

EXAMPLE:

A tenancy for years has ended, but the tenant refuses to leave. The landlord commences eviction proceedings. Until the tenant is evicted, the tenant is a tenant at sufferance.

If a tenant remains in possession after the termination of the lease, the lessor has two options:

(a) the lessor may commence proceedings in a court of competent jurisdiction to **evict** the tenant, meaning that the court will order the tenant to quit the premises and have the order enforced by a marshal; or

(b) the lessor may bind the lessee to a new periodic tenancy, under the terms of the expired lease or at an increased rent *if* the lessor has notified the lessee of an increased rental prior to the expiration of the valid lease.

Be alert to the fact that this right, known as the **holdover doctrine,** does not apply if the lessee only remains in possession for a few hours after the lease expired or is delayed in quitting because of reasons not the tenant's fault, such as a severe illness.

The typical lease for realty will include the names of the parties; a description of the property to be rented, referred to as the **premises;** the use to which the property may be put; and the termination of the lease. Because the lease is a contract, the tenant's right of possession or use is granted in consideration of the tenant's obligation to compensate the landlord. The most common form of such obligation is the payment of money, referred to as **rent.**

Rent clauses fall into one of two categories: gross lease or a net rent lease. A **gross lease** requires the tenant to pay rent, and all operating costs on the premises — taxes, water, utilities, and so forth — are the obligation of the landlord. In a **net rent lease** the tenant pays the rent to the landlord and further is responsible for the operating costs, which the tenant pays directly to the provider of such services.

In many instances, residential rent may be regulated by the government, in which case rent renewals of the lease may be guaranteed to the tenant, and rent increases for the new lease are established under the provisions of the particular statute. In other locations and with commercial leases, the lessor may indicate a **rent escalation clause** in which the parties agree to periodic rent increases based on either costs or inflation.

Many commercial leases contain a **percentage rent** that requires the tenant to pay the landlord a set percentage of the tenant's gross sales. With this type of lease rent is usually due on a quarterly or annual basis to correspond to the tenant's payment of taxes. A variation on this type of lease is a **percentage breakpoint** clause in which a set rent is established, but if the tenant's gross receipts exceed a stated dollar amount, called the breakpoint, the landlord is entitled to additional rent based on a percentage of the gross sales above the breakpoint amount. In certain instances, this type of lease may also contain a **radius clause** that prohibits the tenant from operating a similar enterprise within a specific geographic distance from the rented premises, which could limit the tenant's gross sales at the leased location.

EXAMPLE:

A man rents an apartment under a net rent lease. According to the lease, he must pay the landlord a monthly rental of $750 and is responsible for his own utilities—gas, electricity, and water. The landlord remains responsible for taxes and insurance.

EXAMPLE:

A man rents a location to open a bookstore. Under the terms of the lease, the tenant must pay the landlord a monthly net rent based on a yearly rental of $200 per square foot of leased space. Furthermore, if the bookstore's gross sales exceed $500,000, the tenant must pay the landlord an additional 1% of all sales in excess of $500,000. This lease also restricts the tenant from opening another bookstore within ten blocks of this location. This is an example of a percentage breakpoint lease with a radius clause.

In addition, a lease will usually indicate which party is responsible for the maintenance and repair of the premises and, for commercial leases, may specify that one of the parties must maintain minimum insurance on the property. See Exhibit 7.1 at the end of this chapter for a sample lease.

Tenants' Duties

Under a typical lease agreement, the tenant warrants to maintain the property in good repair. In this context the tenant is precluded from committing waste on the property (see Chapter 2). If the tenant, under the lease contract, has specifically covenanted to make repairs, the tenant's duty will be higher than that imposed under the law of contract, and she may even be obligated to reconstruct the property if the property is destroyed, even if the property is destroyed without the fault of the tenant or the landlord. Furthermore, even absent such a contract, if the premises are destroyed without fault, in most jurisdictions the tenant, absent an agreement to the contrary, is still obligated to continue paying rent for the duration of the lease.

EXAMPLE:

> A man enters into a lease to rent a house for a two-year period. Three months later the house is destroyed by a tornado. In most jurisdictions the tenant may still be liable to pay rent on the now nonexistent house for the next 21 months. If the tenant had specifically contracted to make repairs, he might be obligated to rebuild the house. In this type of contract the tenant is usually further obligated to maintain insurance on the property, for obvious reasons.

A tenant is precluded from using the leased premises for an unlawful purpose. Such unlawful use gives the landlord the right to terminate the lease, sue for damages, and/or seek injunctive relief.

EXAMPLE:

> A woman rents a large apartment. She then uses that apartment as a brothel. When the landlord finds out he may either terminate the lease and evict the tenant or seek an injunction, a court order requiring the woman to stop using the premises for an unlawful purpose.

The primary obligation of a tenant is to pay the agreed-upon rent at the time and manner specified in the lease. A landlord may also require the tenant to give a **security deposit** to cover a portion of the rent in the case of a default. At the termination of the lease the tenant's rent obligation terminates and the tenant is entitled to the return of the security deposit, less any amount deducted for damage to the premises caused by the tenant. Also, the tenant is entitled to receive interest accruing on the security deposit during the tenancy.

If the tenant fails to pay the rent when due, the landlord, in most states, is entitled to one of two options:

1. the landlord may sue the tenant for money damages for the amount of rent that was due and unpaid; or
2. the landlord may sue to have the tenant evicted.

If the tenant abandons the premises without justification, most states require the landlord to attempt to re-rent the property to lessen the amount of rent the tenant owes under the lease. This obligation is known as the duty of **mitigation of damages.** If the new tenant pays less rent than the abandoning tenant, the abandoning tenant is obligated to the landlord for the difference. Conversely, if the new tenant pays a higher rent, the abandoning tenant is discharged. Note, though, that if the landlord accepts the surrender of the premises the tenant will not be obligated for rent under the lease.

EXAMPLE:

The owner of a two-family house rents one of the units to a family. However, the man and the family have constant arguments over matters not concerned with the property. The family decides to move with nine months left on the lease. If the man accepts their departure, they are not obligated under the lease. If the man does not accept their departure, he must attempt to re-rent the property, and the family will only be obligated for the difference between their rent and the new rent if it is less. If the man refuses to attempt to find a new tenant for the property he may be denied relief from the court for failure to mitigate damages.

Landlord's Duties

Absent a statutory or contractual obligation, under the general law a landlord is under no duty to repair or maintain leased premises. Basically, a landlord's obligations fall into three categories:

1. The landlord has a duty to deliver actual possession to the tenant on the date agreed upon. If there are holdover tenants or squatters on the premises, it is the landlord's duty to see that they are evicted so that the tenant may take possession.
2. The landlord, under all lease agreements, has imposed a covenant of quiet enjoyment (see Chapter 5), meaning that the landlord guarantees that no one, including the landlord, will interfere with the tenant's use and possession of the property. This covenant may be breached in one of the following ways:
   (a) actual eviction, which occurs when the tenant is evicted from the entire property, at which time the tenant's rent obligation is considered terminated;
   (b) **partial eviction,** which occurs when the tenant is precluded from possession of a portion of the property. If the partial eviction is caused by the landlord, as opposed to a third person, the tenant's obligation to pay rent on the entire property is terminated.

EXAMPLE:

A man rents a house with a garage. There is a mechanic's lien on the garage and the contractor who holds the lien attaches the garage. This is an example of a partial eviction. Because the partial eviction was caused by the landlord's failure to pay the contractor, the tenant is relieved from paying rent on the property.

(c) **constructive eviction,** which occurs if the landlord does anything that renders the property uninhabitable, such as failing to provide essential services. The tenant may terminate the lease and seek damages from the landlord. However, to terminate the lease and seek damages, the tenant must vacate the property and the condition that caused the problem must be the fault of the landlord, not a third party.

EXAMPLE:

A man rents a house under a gross rent lease. The landlord refuses to pay any utility bills although it is his obligation, and all utilities are turned off in the house, rendering it uninhabitable. The tenant may terminate the lease by vacating the house and then suing the landlord for damages, or he may pay the utilities himself and sue the landlord for reimbursement.

3. Most jurisdictions impose an implied **warranty of habitability** on residential leases, which is deemed to be non-waivable (exclusively) by the tenant. What is considered "habitable" is determined by local housing codes. If this warranty is breached, the tenant may:

   (a) terminate the lease;
   (b) make the necessary repairs and offset the cost against the rent;
   (c) seek an **abatement** whereby the rent is proportionately reduced for the lack of use; or
   (d) remain in possession but sue for damages.

If a tenant attempts to assert his or her legal rights, the landlord is prohibited, in most states, from terminating the lease or otherwise penalizing the tenant in retribution. Any attempt to do so is considered **retaliatory eviction,** which, depending on the jurisdiction, may entitle the tenant to certain legal remedies against the landlord. Each state's statutes must be individually analyzed.

If the entire property is condemned by the government, or taken over under a right of eminent domain (see Chapter 3), the lease is deemed terminated. However, a partial or temporary taking does not relieve the tenant of his or her obligation under the lease.

Assignments and Subleases

Unless the parties have agreed to the contrary, tenants are typically permitted to assign or sublease their rights. An **assignment** is a transfer of all rights the tenant has under the lease. A **sublease** is a transfer of a portion of the tenant's rights under the lease. If the tenant retains the right to return to the property any time prior to the termination of the lease, including the right to renew the lease, the transfer is deemed to be a sublease.

EXAMPLE:

> Three young women share an apartment, but do not get along. One of them finds a fourth young woman to take over her portion of the lease. When the dissatisfied tenant transfers all of her rights to the fourth woman, she has effectuated an assignment; however, if she retained the right to renew the lease in her own name this is considered a sublease.

The effect of an assignment is to make the **assignee** (the transferee) primarily obligated to the landlord for the rent. The **assignor** (the transferor) remains secondarily liable, meaning that if the assignee defaults the assignor will be liable for the rent to the landlord.

With a sublease, the original tenant remains obligated to the landlord, and he or she is the only one who can enforce the lease's covenants against the landlord. The tenant and the sublessee are contractually obligated to each other, and the sublessee's only remedies are against the tenant/sublessor.

A lease may contain a provision prohibiting assignments and subleases, but such provisions are generally construed against the landlord. In jurisdictions that provide for regulated residential leases, such provisions may be prohibited, but each state's statutes must be independently analyzed. If a transfer is made in violation of the lease, and the landlord knows about it but does not object, the lease provision prohibiting the transfer is deemed waived. If the landlord does object, the landlord may be able to terminate the lease.

EXAMPLE:

> A lease contains a non-assignment provision. Six months after the lease starts the tenant must move to a new city, and assigns her lease to a friend. The landlord accepts the friend's rent check. Under these circumstances, the law will assume that the landlord has waived his right to object to the assignment.

The landlord may assign any and all of his or her rights without the tenant's consent. The tenant's obligation will be to the landlord's assignee, and the tenant must be given a notice to attorn (see Chapter 5).

Practical Tips

- Leases for rentals exceeding one year must be in writing, and long-term leases may be recorded to protect the parties.

- If a lease is going to be recorded, only record a memorandum of the lease provisions. It is not necessary to record all the terms of the lease itself.
- Review all leases in the same manner in which a contract would be reviewed — it must meet all the requirements of a valid contract to be enforceable.
- Only use a form lease as a guide; make sure to personalize each lease to protect the client.

Chapter Review

Landlord-tenant law is a subset of general real property law that is governed by contract. This contract, known as a lease, determines the rights and obligations of the parties.

There are four types of lease agreements generally in effect: a tenancy for years, in which property is leased for a fixed period of time; a periodic tenancy, created for successive periods; a tenancy at will, which is formed by agreement and which may be terminated at any time without notice; and a tenancy at sufferance, which comes about when a tenant remains in unlawful possession of a formerly leased premise.

The consideration given to the landlord to support the contract is known as rent, and the tenant may be obligated for utilities, or they may be the landlord's responsibility. For commercial tenants, the landlord may also contract for a portion of the tenant's gross sales or profit.

The tenant is required to maintain the premises in good repair, absent an agreement or statute to the contrary, and may even have to rebuild a premise that is destroyed.

Leases, as a general rule, are freely assignable, which means all the tenant's rights are transferred, and capable of being sublet, which means the tenant retains some interest in the lease, even if just the ability to renew the contract.

Ethical Concern

Leases are fairly common legal documents, and most law offices maintain a form lease on file. It is unethical to charge every client the cost of creating the same lease. This is known as double billing. However, it is permissible to charge each client for the particular work that was performed to personalize that form lease for the client.

Key Terms

Abatement	Assignor
Assignee	Constructive eviction
Assignment	Evict

Gross lease
Holdover doctrine
Landlord
Lease
Leasehold
Lessee
Lessor
Mitigation of damages
Net rent lease
Partial eviction
Percentage breakpoint
Percentage rent
Periodic tenancy

Premises
Radius clause
Rent
Rent escalation clause
Retaliatory eviction
Right of entry
Security deposit
Sublease
Tenancy at sufferance
Tenancy at will
Tenancy for years
Warranty of habitability

Exercises

1. Using the library or the Internet, determine whether your locality provides for residential rent regulation. If so, analyze its provisions.
2. Obtain a form lease for your jurisdiction and analyze its provisions.
3. Determine what constitutes "habitability" in your locality.
4. Many states have a landlord-tenant court for housing disputes. Find out whether such a court exists for your county, and if so, list its jurisdictional requirements.
5. Briefly discuss how the parties could determine "gross sales" under a percentage lease.

Situational Analysis

A tenant leases a two-bedroom apartment in a major city. She is the only tenant on the lease. To meet expenses, she lets one of the bedrooms to another woman by an oral agreement. The other woman is not listed on the lease. Each woman pays one-half the rent by check, and the landlord accepts these checks. After one year they begin to have problems living with each other, and the woman named on the lease asks the other woman to leave, but she refuses. What are the rights of the parties? How would you advise each woman?

Edited Cases

Ballesteros v. Rosello is a New York case dealing with a holdover tenant, and the *Tsitsires* decision concerns the eviction of a mentally ill tenant.

Ballesteros v. Rosello
183 Misc. 2d 448, 703 N.Y.S.2d 686 (1999)

Petitioner commenced these two summary holdover proceedings, L&T index No. 91705/99, against respondent Calexi Rosello, and L&T index No. 91706/99 against respondent Rose Cardona, to recover possession of the subject premises, 199 Jackson Street, apartment No. 1 and apartment No. 2, respectively, in Brooklyn, New York. Both proceedings were initiated by service of separate 30-day notices of termination, dated July 15, 1999, on the identical basis that respondents had no current lease, were neither rent stabilized nor rent controlled, and were month-to-month tenants whose respective tenancies would be terminated as of August 31, 1999. Petitioner subsequently served these two instant petitions alleging each respondent was a tenant who entered into possession of their respective apartments under a rental agreement between herself and petitioner's predecessor. The proceedings are consolidated for decision.

On October 15, 1999, the Honorable Delores Thomas consolidated both the instant proceedings; dismissed respondents' cross motions seeking dismissal of the petitions based on the argument that there was no existing landlord tenant relationship, and that the proceedings were not brought under the appropriate section of the Real Property Actions and Proceedings Law with leave to renew at trial; and granted petitioner's motions solely to the extent of striking respondents' defenses of a lack of personal and subject matter jurisdiction. Both matters were adjourned to November 3, 1999 for trial.

On November 3, 1999, counsel for both parties agreed that in lieu of a trial they would submit papers on the sole legal issue for both proceedings, namely, whether or not respondents in this particular instance have a landlord-tenant relationship with petitioner, and are month-to-month tenants; or have no landlord-tenant relationship with petitioner and are licensees. It is undisputed that respondents are neither rent stabilized nor rent controlled, and have never tendered rent nor use and occupancy to, or executed a lease with, the current petitioner. It is also undisputed that respondents and the petitioner's predecessor in interest entered into rental agreements for respondents' respective apartments, and had a landlord-tenant relationship.

Respondents submitted a supplemental affirmation dated November 9, 1999, requesting the instant proceedings be dismissed as no landlord-tenant relationship exists between petitioner and respondents. Respondents assert that as they have never executed a lease with, or paid any rent or use and occupancy to petitioner, they are licensees, not month-to-month tenants. Respondents further assert that as licensees, petitioner should have proceeded with licensee proceedings against them by first serving upon them 10-day notices to quit pursuant to RPAPL 713 (7), rather than the 30-day notices to vacate they received pursuant to Real Property Law Sec. 232-a. Respondents rely in part on an April 26, 1999 unreported Kings County Housing Part case—*Francis v. Coral* (L&T index

No. 64963/99), in which the Honorable Jose Rodriquez dismissed a holdover petition after trial as no landlord-tenant relationship was established.

Petitioner subsequently submitted a memorandum of law dated
November 15, 1999, in opposition to respondents' posttrial motion to dismiss, requesting respondents' motions be denied in their entirety and judgment entered in favor of petitioner forthwith. Petitioner asserts that as
respondents enjoyed a landlord-tenant relationship with petitioner's predecessor in interest, respondents did not lose their possessory interest and
therefore cannot be reduced to licensee status merely because the prior
landlord sold the building. Petitioner asserts that *Francis v. Coral* (supra)
has no binding stare decisis effect on this court's decision, and also distinguishes it from the facts in the instant proceedings because respondents'
counsel herein has stipulated to evidence of a preexisting landlord-tenant
relationship. Petitioner further asserts no other support in case law can be
found. Petitioner submits that the respondents received the additional protection of 30-day notices as opposed to the 10-day notices they would have
received as licensees.

The common-law principle of attornment, which is the "act or agreement of a tenant accepting one person in the place of another as his landlord," has been abolished by Real Property Law Sec. 248. (Rasch, New York
Landlord and Tenant—Summary Proceedings Sec. 2:3, at 106 [3d ed.].)
Pursuant to Real Property Law Sec. 248, "[a]n attornment to a grantee is
not requisite to the validity of a conveyance of real property occupied by a
tenant, or of the rents or profits thereof, or any other interest therein."

Additionally, Real Property Law Sec. 223 states, "The grantee of
leased real property, or of a reversion thereof, or of any rent, the devisee
or assignee of the lessor of such a lease, or the heir or personal representative of either of them, has the same remedies, by entry, action or otherwise, for the nonperformance of any agreement contained in the assigned
lease for the recovery of rent . . . or for other cause of forfeiture as his
grantor or lessor had, or would have had, if the reversion had remained
in him." Thus, as petitioner's predecessor in interest had a landlord-tenant
relationship with respondents, and would have been entitled to institute
holdover summary proceedings against them as month-to-month tenants,
the petitioner has the same remedies available to it against respondents,
and is correct in treating respondents as month-to-month tenants as it has
in the instant matters. The petitioner, as purchaser, succeeds "to all the title
and rights of the original landlord, becomes the landlord by operation of
law, with all the rights and remedies of the original landlord," creating a
conventional relation of landlord and tenant. (*Commonwealth Mtge. Co. v.
De Waltoff*, 135 App. Div. 33, 35 [1st Dept. 1909]; see also, *Costagliola v. Home
Owners' Loan Corp.*, 35 F. Supp. 930 [S.D.N.Y. 1940].) Therefore, petitioner is
entitled to the same rights and obligations of the landlord-tenant relationship with respondents as they had with petitioner's predecessor in
interest.

Based upon the foregoing, the court denies respondents' motions
to dismiss both proceedings, and pursuant to the parties' stipulated

agreement to accept the court's decision on this legal question in lieu of a trial, the petitioner is awarded a final judgment of possession against each of the respondents for their respective apartments. Issuance of the warrants of eviction against each of the respondents is forthwith, and the execution of the warrants is stayed for 10 days.

Case Questions

1. What is a holdover tenant?
2. How does the court apply the concept of attornment to this case?

TOA Construction Co., Inc. v. Tsitsires
54 A.D.3d 109, 861 N.Y.S.2d 335 (1st Dept 2008)

The laws of rent stabilization do not allow for the indefinite retention of the right to rent-stabilized premises by a tenant who does not actually reside in the premises and has no intent to return to reside there at any point in the future. This is no less true where, as here, the tenant's inability to ever reside there is caused by his mental illness. An apartment used by the tenant solely as a mail drop and storage space and occupied, when it is occupied at all, only by the tenant's companion, should not be treated as the tenant's residence. Unless there is evidence at trial supporting a conclusion that the tenant will at some point be able to actually reside in the apartment, his absence should not be deemed excusable, and his abandonment of the premises as his residence should be acknowledged as such.

The facts of this case were fully presented to the trial court, and that court's findings were not disputed, challenged, or altered by Appellate Term. Indeed, Appellate Term explicitly declined to second-guess either the trial court's assessment of credibility or its conclusion that respondent's mental illness prevented him from actively using the apartment. Although it reversed the trial court's holding, the reversal was based only upon the application of the law to the facts found by the trial court. Yet, our dissenting colleagues would make an entirely new set of findings, based upon their own assessment of the evidence, after rejecting consideration of certain materials upon which they say the trial court improperly relied. Further, the dissent would rely upon materials entirely outside the record, including assertions contained in recent newspaper articles. We reject the implicit suggestion that we adopt the dissent's alternative assessment of the evidence instead of the trial court's assessment. Rather, we rely upon the previously undisturbed findings of the trial court, especially its rejection of respondent's testimony that he resided in the unit for extended periods of time during the *Golub* period (*see Golub v. Frank, 65 NY2d 900, 483 N.E.2d 126, 493 N.Y.S.2d 451 [1985]*).

The sad facts of this case, as found by the trial court, naturally incline one's sympathies toward respondent tenant, who suffers from debilitating mental illness that has propelled him into the life of a homeless person, despite his rights as a tenant in petitioner's deteriorating single-room occupancy (SRO) building. However, the tone employed by the dissent, accusing this Court of "facilitating a notorious slumlord's 20-year effort to empty its building of all tenants by evicting respondent tenant from his rent stabilized apartment," is misguided. It is the responsibility of this Court to dispassionately apply the law to the facts as found, notwithstanding the well-intentioned impulse to protect the interests of a mentally ill individual or the desire to rule against the interests of a party characterized by newspapers as a "slumlord." It is incumbent upon us to correctly frame the rules of law that apply in this primary residence litigation. When the law is accurately stated, and applied neutrally to the facts as found by the trial court, it becomes clear that the findings of fact and conclusions of law of the trial court should have been upheld. We therefore reverse the order of Appellate Term, which, contrary to the ruling of the trial court, held that the tenant's extended absence from the subject premises was excusable and that he had not abandoned the tenancy.

This holdover proceeding to terminate respondent's tenancy, on the ground that the apartment was not his primary residence, was commenced on December 7, 2000, following the landlord's service on July 14, 2000 of a *Golub* notice of expiration of respondent's tenancy as of November 30, 2000.

Respondent has been a rent-stabilized tenant in the SRO since 1970. Over the years, the building fell into a state of chronic disrepair, and the trial court found the apartment to be uninhabitable when it inspected the premises on April 27, 2005. [***5] But, this litigation does not turn on the habitability of the apartment, or even on the nefariousness of the landlord; it simply concerns whether petitioner established that respondent did not maintain his primary residence there during the *Golub* period, December 1, 1998 through November 30, 2000.

Although his exact diagnosis was disputed, it is established that respondent suffers from a mental illness, which includes a panic disorder, that has resulted in his feeling compelled to spend virtually all his time away from the subject apartment. The credible evidence established that respondent lived the lifestyle of a homeless person in a psychologically "safe" area within a 20-block radius of the building. He kept his personal possessions in the apartment, and his mail was delivered there, but notwithstanding his testimony to the contrary, which the trial court rejected as incredible, he rarely went there. He did not even maintain possession of the key, having given it into the custody of his girlfriend of 35 years, who used the apartment somewhat more frequently, as a place to shower and for storage of her personal possessions. The testimony that the trial court found to be credible, which Appellate Term left undisturbed, reflected that during the relevant period respondent stopped in at the apartment a handful of times but cannot be said to have resided there.

To begin the necessary analysis, we must first consider the landlord's initial burden in this unusual situation. The Rent Stabilization Code permits a landlord to recover possession of a rent-stabilized apartment that "is not occupied by the tenant ... as his or her primary residence" (*9 NYCRR 2524.4[c]*). Respondent suggests that to do so the landlord has the legal obligation to establish not only that the tenant does not reside in the subject apartment but also that the tenant has an alternative primary residence. In this regard, respondent relies upon this Court's holding that "[i]n a nonprimary residence case, the burden is on the landlord to establish that the tenant maintains a primary residence in a place other than the subject premises" (*Sharp v. Melendez, 139 A.D.2d 262, 264, 531 N.Y.S.2d 554 [1988]*).

Respondent also emphasizes the word "primary" in the phrase "primary residence," arguing that the concept implicitly requires the existence of a second residence, rendering one residence primary and the other secondary, and that the concept of primary residence is therefore, by definition, inapplicable when the tenant concededly has no other residence. Where there is only one residence, respondent contends, that residence is *necessarily* the tenant's primary residence.

We conclude, however, that the dissenting justice at Appellate Term in this case is correct: The statement made in *Sharp v. Melendez* imposing on the landlord the burden of establishing that the tenant maintains a primary residence in a place other than the subject premises is simply inapplicable to circumstances such as these. Importantly, *Sharp v. Melendez* and similar cases involved situations in which the basis of the landlord's claim was that the tenant resided in different premises than the one at issue. But, as the trial court here explained, establishing that the tenant has an alternative primary residence is merely one way for the landlord to meet its evidentiary burden; it is not the only way.

The essence of the nonprimary residence claim is that the tenant lacks an "ongoing, substantial, physical nexus with the controlled premises for actual living purposes" (*Emay Props. Corp. v. Norton, 136 Misc 2d 127, 129, 519 N.Y.S.2d 90 [App Term, 1st Dept 1987]*). The terms of the Rent Stabilization Code do not require proof that the tenant maintain an alternative primary residence (*see 9 NYCRR 2524.4[c], supra*). A prima facie showing of nonprimary residence could be successfully made simply by proof that a rent-paying tenant was absent from the apartment and kept no belongings there during the relevant period, without the introduction of any information about where the tenant had gone.

The majority at Appellate Term, without rejecting the finding that respondent did not actually live in the apartment, held that his absence must be deemed excusable for purposes of nonprimary residence analysis because the record showed that "there was no abandonment of the premises or establishing of any new residence" (quoting *Katz v. Gelman, 177 Misc 2d 83, 84, 676 N.Y.S.2d 774 [App Term, 1st Dept 1998]*). But, the facts here are not comparable to those in *Katz v. Gelman* or other cases in which tenants established that their extended absences from their apartments were excusable (*see e.g. Coronet Props. Co. v. Brychova, 122 Misc 2d 212, 469 N.Y.S.2d 911 [1983], affd 126 Misc 2d 946, 488 N.Y.S.2d 1020 [App Term, 1st Dept 1984]*).

In *Brychova* the tenant demonstrated that she had to be away from home due to the exigencies of her profession. In *Katz*, the tenant was absent because of his health. Importantly, in each instance it was established that the tenant fully intended to return to and reside in the apartment as soon as practicable. In *Brychova*, the tenant was an itinerant professional soprano and voice teacher who spent all but a handful of days each year away from home at professional engagements. In *Katz* the tenant was absent from his leased premises while he was institutionalized in various transitional residential facilities for treatment of depression and substance abuse, with the intent of preparing to return to independent living.

While, as in *Katz* (*177 Misc 2d at 84*), it is clearly a mental health problem that causes respondent to be absent from the subject premises, unlike the situation in *Katz*, there is no credible evidence indicating that respondent will ever return to and reside in the subject premises, or even that he has any intent to do so. Indeed, there is no reason to conclude, based upon the credible evidence in the record, that respondent can be cured of his need or compulsion to stay out of the subject premises. Regardless of how understandable is his decision to decline any offered medication or treatment, nothing in the record supports a conclusion that respondent had any true intent or ability to achieve a cure for his illness that would allow him to take up real residence in the apartment. Since there is no credible basis in the record to conclude that respondent might in the future be willing or able to resume actual residence in the apartment, the logic of *Katz v. Gelman* has no application to this case.

The dissent, while agreeing with the conclusion of Appellate Term that respondent's absence is excusable and that he did not abandon the premises, also emphasizes testimony rejected by the trial court to the effect that respondent actually resided in the apartment during the period in question. While paying lip service to the rule that the trial court's findings of fact should not be disturbed unless they could not be reached under any fair interpretation of the evidence, the dissent essentially relies on the testimony of respondent and his companion to find, contrary to the trial court's finding, that respondent intends to reside in the premises in the future, and, indeed, that he has resided there since at least 2001. The dissent even cites the testimony that the trial court squarely rejected, in which both respondent and his companion stated that during the *Golub* period respondent was present in the apartment every day.

However, we decline to make new findings of fact upon our own review of the record, despite our authority to do so. There are important reasons for the deference with which we generally approach the findings of a trial court, particularly regarding credibility. A decision by a trial court adds up to more than the sum of its parts; it takes into account the judge's firsthand impressions, as well as the judge's experience with similar cases, particularly in specialized courts such as the Housing Court.

The trial court's finding regarding respondent's credibility should stand; by the same token, we should defer to the court's rejection of respondent's and his companion's testimony as to their continued presence in the apartment during the *Golub* period. Reliance on respondent's telephone bills to buttress the conclusion that respondent did not abandon the apartment is misplaced. It is already established that respondent's companion frequently uses the apartment and that respondent keeps personal possessions there and uses it as a mail drop. None of these facts establish his intent to return to live there, and neither do his telephone bills. The manner in which respondent uses the subject premises, as a storage facility and mail drop, should be recognized, and treated, as tantamount to an abandonment of the premises for residential purposes.

The dissent's citation to recent newspaper articles to support its assertion of facts regarding respondent's recent residence at the premises should not be countenanced. When we review an order on appeal, we do so on the evidence presented in the record on appeal, not on purported facts gleaned from newspaper articles. Indeed, in this matter the relevant time period of residency was December 1, 1998 through November 30, 2000. To the extent the respondent's future intent to reside in the premises was relevant, such intent had to be established before the trial court, not in assertions extraneous to the record and not even introduced by the parties. Furthermore, judicial notice of facts is reserved for "matter[s] of common and general knowledge, well-established and authoritatively settled" (*Prince, Richardson on Evidence § 2-201* [Farrell 11th ed] [internal quotations marks and citation omitted]). Judicial notice of a fact such as a tenant's residency in a building may not properly be based upon a factual assertion simply because the assertion is contained in a newspaper article.

The evidence contained in the record that was accepted as credible by the trial court shows that respondent did not reside in the apartment during the *Golub* period, that he did not intend to return to reside there, and that there is no reason to believe he will be able to reside there in the future. However sympathetic respondent's plight, the concept of rent-stabilized tenancy is warped beyond recognition if a tenant who is permanently absent from the apartment, using it only as showering facilities for his companion and as storage space and mail drop for himself, without any indication that he will ever be able to reside there again, may nevertheless be entitled to be treated as a rent-stabilized tenant who has not abandoned the apartment.

It should be noted that when we conclude that a tenant who does not reside in his apartment may not properly be said to be using it as his primary residence, we are not "finding" that the tenant's primary residence is a park bench. I think we all agree that a person *cannot* maintain a primary residence on a park bench. But, the question for the court is solely whether the tenant has maintained an "ongoing, substantial, physical nexus with the controlled premises for actual living purposes" (*see Emay Props. Corp. v. Norton, 136 Misc 2d 127, 129, 519 N.Y.S.2d 90 [1987], supra*), or whether, instead, he has abandoned the premises that served at some earlier time as his residence. The answer is, during the relevant period respondent did not maintain the required substantial physical nexus with the premises for actual living purposes, and he had no expectation of doing so.

Having determined that respondent failed to counter petitioner's showing with his own credible evidence demonstrating either that during the *Golub* period he used the premises as his primary residence or that his absence is excusable, we may not allow respondent to claim the rights of primary residency based solely upon the use of the apartment by his long-time companion. This is not because we find that she is some sort of "transient girlfriend," as the dissent implies, but because the record does not establish tenancy rights on her part, despite her longtime relationship with respondent. As the dissent acknowledges, this proceeding did not raise or address any claim to succession rights or any other rights invested directly in respondent's companion.

I recognize that part of the impetus for the dissent's view is that the landlord here allowed the premises to become uninhabitable with the intent of emptying the SRO building of all tenants. Yet, the landlord's conduct and intentions, whatever we think of them, had no impact on respondent's virtual abandonment of the apartment as his residence. Had respondent successfully demonstrated that his absence from the apartment was due to its uninhabitable condition, and that he would return and reside there if it were made habitable, the landlord's conduct would have been relevant to the question whether respondent's absence from the premises should be considered "excusable" for purposes of primary residence analysis. But, the evidence established that respondent's absence from the premises was due to his mental illness, not the condition of the apartment.

Additionally, the fact that respondent applied for public housing that would accommodate his disability, stating on the application that he was homeless, but failed to take the necessary action to accept the ultimate offer of an apartment within his "safe area" of the city lends further credence to the conclusion that his mental illness was the substantial impediment to his maintaining his residence in the subject apartment, or any apartment. Had he been motivated by the need for a clean and habitable apartment, rather than impelled by his mental illness, he would have done what was necessary to take the offered apartment.

The dissent correctly observes that the goal of the rent stabilization framework, "to alleviate the shortage of housing in New York City by returning underutilized apartments to the market place" (*Matter of Herzog v. Joy*, 74 A.D.2d 372, 374, 428 N.Y.S.2d 1 [1980], affd 53 N.Y.2d 821, 422 N.E.2d 582, 439 N.Y.S.2d 922 [1981]), is not served by permitting the ouster of this tenant, since the landlord's interest is in emptying the building of all tenants, rather than in replacing this tenant with a tenant who will actually reside there. Nevertheless, application of the primary residence rules is not limited to those landlords who can establish that they are acting in good faith to return underutilized housing to the market. Whether the tenant maintains an "ongoing, substantial, physical nexus with the controlled premises for actual living purposes" (*Emay Props. v. Norton, 136 Misc 2d at 129*), depends upon the tenant's conduct in relation to the property, not the landlord's intended future use of the building.

The questions the Court must answer are: (1) did the petitioner establish that the tenant lacked an "ongoing, substantial, physical nexus with the premises for actual living purposes," and (2) if so, did the tenant establish an intent to resume living in the premises when it became possible? Here, petitioner made the requisite showing, and respondent failed to establish an intent to return so as to overcome the prima facie showing. On the evidence before it, the trial court correctly determined that the apartment was not being used as respondent's primary residence and would not be so used in the future.

We conclude that petitioner's claim is established, based upon the facts as found by the trial court, that respondent does not, and will not in the future, use the subject premises "for actual living purposes," and that therefore it is not his residence.

Accordingly, the order of the Appellate Term of the Supreme Court of the State of New York, First Department, entered December 21, 2006, which reversed a final judgment of the Civil Court, New York County (Gerald Lebovits, J.), entered July 7, 2005, awarding possession after nonjury trial to petitioner landlord in a nonprimary residence proceeding, and awarded final judgment to respondent tenant dismissing the petition, should be reversed, on the law, without costs, and the judgment of possession awarded in favor of petitioner landlord reinstated.

Case Questions

1. What is your opinion of the court's ultimate decision to displace a mentally ill tenant?

2. Should the court have provided a guardian for the respondent? Discuss.

Exhibit 7.1: Sample Commercial or Residential Lease

This lease made in _____ [*city*], state of _____ [*date*] between _____ of _____ as lessor, and _____ of _____ as lessee, witnesses:

Lessor, for and in consideration of the agreements of lessee mentioned below, hereby leases to lessee, and lessee hereby leases from lessor, the premises [or as the case may be] located at _____ [*city*], state of _____ described as follows: _____ excepting and reserving to lessor _____ including the right to _____.

This lease is for the terms of _____ years [or as the case may be], beginning _____ [*date*], and ending _____ [*date*], unless sooner terminated as provided below.

A. Agreements of Lessee

Lessee, in consideration of the leasing, agrees:

1. To pay as rent for premises the sum of $_____ per month [or as the case may be], payable on the day of _____ each month [or as the case may be] during the term of this lease, at _____.

2. To pay all charges for light, heat, fuel, power and water furnished or supplied to or on any part of premises.

3. To pay all taxes and assessments, ordinary and extraordinary, general and specific, including the same for _____ [*year*], which may be levied or assessed on premises.

4. To pay all reasonable costs, attorneys' fees and expenses that shall be made and incurred by lessor in enforcing the agreements of this lease.

5. To use and occupy the premises for _____ purposes only, and for no other object or purpose without written consent of lessor, and to not use premises for any unlawful purpose or purpose deemed extra hazardous.

6. To keep the premises in as good repair as the same shall be at the commencement of the term, wear and tear arising from the reasonable use of the same and damages by the elements excepted.

7. To keep the buildings and improvements on the premises insured in a responsible insurance company or companies for not less than $_____ payable, in case of loss, to lessor as lessor's interest may appear.

8. To permit lessor and lessor's agents to enter on the premises or any part thereof, at all reasonable hours, for purpose of examining or exhibiting same or making such repairs or alterations as may be necessary for safety or preservation thereof; also to permit lessor to place on premises notice of "For Sale" and "To Rent" and not interfere with same.

9. To deliver to lessor within _____ days from execution of this lease a surety bond in amount of $____ from a reputable bonding company, guaranteeing faithful performance by lessee of all terms and conditions of this lease.

10. Not to assign this lease nor sublet the premises or any portion thereof without written consent of _____.

Exhibit 7.1   239

Exhibit 7.1: *(Continued)*

11. Not to make any contract for construction, repair, or improvements on, in, of, or to premises, or any part thereof, or for any work to be done or materials to be furnished on or to premises, or any part thereof, without providing in such contract or agreement that no lien of mechanics or materialmen shall be created or shall arise against above-described land and/or the building or improvements at any time located thereon. All persons furnishing any work, labor or materials, as well as all other persons whatever, shall be bound by this provision and by the notice of it from and after date of this lease, and notice is hereby given that no mechanic's lien, materialmen's lien, or any other incumbrance made by or obtained against lessee, or lessee's interest in demised land and/or the building or improvements thereon, shall in any manner or degree affect the title or interest of lessor in land and/or the building or improvements thereon. To that end, lessee agrees not to make any contract or agreement, either oral or written, for any labor, services, fixtures, material or supplies in connection with altering, repairing or improving any building or improvement on premises without providing in such contract or agreement that contractor or contractors waive all right to a mechanic's lien, and waive all right of any subcontractor or subcontractors to mechanics' liens, by reason of furnishing any labor, services and/or material under such contract or contracts, whether written or oral, and that such contract or contracts shall, upon execution, be immediately filed in office of recorder _____ of deeds of _____ county, _____ and a copy thereof lodged with lessor.

12. Lessee has examined and knows condition of premises, and has received same in good order and repair, except as otherwise specified in this lease, and no representations as to condition or repair thereof have been made by lessor or lessor's agent, prior to, or at execution of, this lease.

13. Lessor shall have a lien on all of property of lessee used or situated on premises, to secure payment of rent (and other indebtedness owing from lessee to lessor at any time during existence of this lease) to become due under this lease, and in default of payment may take possession of and sell such of the property as may be sufficient to pay deliquent rent [or indebtedness].

14. Lessor shall have the right to sell premises, provided, however, that notice of such contemplated sale shall be given in writing to lessee at last prior to time fixed for vacation of premises by lessee, and provided, further, that during such period lessee shall have option to buy premises at price and on terms of such contemplated sale. In event of a sale of premises by lessor, after such notice and failure of lessee to exercise the option to purchase, lessee agrees to vacate and give possession of premises within _____ days after written notice of sale, given by lessor to lessee, and after payment by lessor to lessee of $_____ on or before the expiration of _____ days' notice.

15. If lessee shall abandon or vacate the premises, they may be relet by lessor for such rent and on such terms as lessor may see fit; and, if a sufficient sum shall not be thus realized, after paying all expenses of such reletting and collecting to satisfy the rent hereby reserved, lessee agrees to satisfy and pay all deficiency.

Exhibit 7.1: *(Continued)*

16. At expiration of this lease, to give peaceable possession of premises to lessor, in as good condition as they now are, the usual wear, inevitable accidents, and loss by fire excepted.

17. The lease may be terminated by lessor in the event of the breach of any of the agreements of lessee contained herein, in which case lessor may reenter on the premises, and this lease shall immediately terminate.

18. This lease, at option of lessor, shall terminate in case lessee shall by any court be adjudged as bankrupt or insolvent, or in case lessee shall make an assignment for benefit of creditors.

19. To observe and comply with all rules, regulations and laws now in effect or which may be enacted during the continuance of this lease by any municipal, county, state or federal authorities having jurisdiction over the premises, and to indemnify lessor for any damage caused by violation thereof.

20. In case lessor, by reason of the failure of lessee to perform any of the agreements or conditions contained herein, shall be compelled to pay or shall pay any sum of money, or shall be compelled to do or shall do any act which requires payment of money, the sum or sums so paid or required to be paid, together with all interest, costs, and damages, shall be added to instalment of rent, next becoming due or to any subsequent instalment of rent, and shall be collectable as additional rent in same manner and with same remedies as if it had been originally reserved. On failure of lessee to make repairs, as provided for herein, lessor may make necessary repairs, and add the amount of cost of such repairs to the rent due on the first month following date of repairs, and such cost of repairs shall be and constitute such rent together with the rent above provided for.

21. Failure of lessor to insist on the strict performance of the terms, agreements and conditions contained herein, or any of them, shall not constitute or be construed as a waiver or relinquishment of lessor's right to enforce any such term, agreement or condition, but the same shall continue in full force and effect.

22. Lessor shall not be liable for any damage to persons or property occurring or arising on premises from any cause whatever.

23. [*add any other affirmative or negative provisions which lessor and lessee have agreed on*].

B. Agreements of Lessor

Lessor, in consideration of the agreements of lessee set forth above, agrees as follows:

1. To keep leased building [or as the case may be] in good repair.

2. Lessee may make such alterations, additions, or improvements in such parts of building as lessee deems necessary, provided, however, written consent of lessor is first obtained.

3. Lessee shall have the right to assign this lease or sublet the premises or any part thereof, subject to the following limitations, viz.:

4. To extend the term of this lease for a further term of _____ years, at the same rental, payable in like manner, and subject to same agreements as are contained in this lease, provided lessee gives written notice to lessor

Exhibit 7.1   241

Exhibit 7.1: *(Continued)*

of a desire to renew lease, at least _____ days [or "months"] before expiration of terms of this lease, and provided lessee is not in default in performance of terms and conditions of this lease, and provided this lease is not terminated before expiration of term thereof as provided for herein.

5. In event that at any time during the term of this lease, _____ [*state occurrence*], lessee shall have the right to terminate this lease on the giving of at least _____ days' written notice to lessor.

6. All fixtures erected in or attached to premises by lessee may be removed by lessee at the termination of this lease, provided (a) lessee shall not then be in default in the performance of any of the agreements herein, (b) that such removal shall not permanently injure the building, and (c) that removal shall be made before the expiration of this lease or any extension thereof.

7. Lessee shall have the right, at the end of the term of this lease, or at any time during the term thereof, to purchase property from lessor, or lessor's heirs, executors, administrators and assigns, for $_____ and, on tendering of such amount in lawful money of United States by lessee as above provided, lessor agrees immediately to deliver to lessee a sufficient warranty deed of premises.

8. Should any more favorable condition be included in any other leases on space in this building, during the life of the instrument, pertaining to termination of lease or rate of rental per square foot, in particular or other conditions in general, these same conditions are made a part of the contract.

9. Not to engage, during the life of this lease, in the city of _____ directly or indirectly, whether as owner, partner, stockholder, or otherwise, in the _____ [*rival*] business.

10. Not to rent, during the term of this lease, the adjoining premises [or as the case may be], owned by lessor, for a business in competition with that of the lessee which is _____.

C. Mutual Agreements of Lessor and Lessee

1. Lessee agrees to deposit with lessor, on signing of this lease, $____ in cash as security for payment of rent herein received and faithful performance by lessee of all terms, conditions and agreements of lease, as well as to indemnify lessor for any costs or expense to which lessor may be put by reason of any default by lessee. Lessor agrees to pay interest to lessee on before-mentioned security deposit of $____ at rate of $____ per annum and to repay lessee the $____ so deposited as security, by crediting same on account of payment of rent for last _____ months of demised term, provided that all of terms, conditions and agreements of lease shall have then been fully complied with by lessee.

2. If during the term of this lease the premises shall be destroyed by fire, the elements, or any other cause, this lease shall cease and become null and void from date of such damage or destruction and lessee shall immediately surrender premises to lessor and shall pay rent only to time of such surrender. If premises shall be damaged by fire or other cause so as to be capable of being repaired within a reasonable time, lessor shall

Exhibit 7.1: *(Continued)*

have to option to repair the same and during time that repairs are being made lessor shall remit to lessee a just and fair portion of rent according to nature of damage sustained and according to extent that lessee is deprived of use of premises.

3. This lease shall be deemed renewed and extended for the further term of _____ from expiration of term hereby granted, unless either lessor or lessee, at least _____ months prior to termination thereof, shall give written notice to the other of an intention to take possession of, or to surrender, as the case may be, the premises on date fixed herein for the expiration of term. The rent during such extended term shall be at same rate as rate provided for herein, and extension shall be on the terms, conditions and agreements contained in this lease, including this clause.

4. If default be made in the payment of the rent above reserved, or any part thereof or in any of the agreements herein contained, to be kept by lessee, it shall be lawful for, and lessee hereby requests lessor without notice, to declare said term ended, and to reenter premises or any part thereof, either with or without process of law, and lessee or any other person or persons occupying the same, to expel, remove and put out, using such force as may be deemed necessary in so doing, and premises again to repossess and enjoy as in lessor's first estate; and in order to enforce a forfeiture of this lease for default in any of its conditions it shall not be necessary to make demand or to serve notice on lessee, and lessee waives all right to any demand or notice from lessor of lessor's election to declare this lease at an end or of declaring it so to be; but the fact of nonperformance of any of the agreements of this lease, shall in itself at election of lessor, without notice or demand, constitute a forfeiture of lease, and at any and all times after such default, lessee shall be deemed guilty of a forcible detainer of the premises and all notices required by any statute of the state of or otherwise are hereby waived.

5. If lessee shall hold over, after expiration of the term hereby created, with consent of lessor, if shall be deemed a renewal of this lease, and of all the conditions and agreements therein contained for term of _____ and so on from year to year until lease is terminated by either party giving to the other not less than _____ days' notice of termination prior to end of any term.

6. Notices and demands by either lessor or lessee may be given by registered mail with prepaid postage addressed to lessor at _____ or to lessee at _____ subject to the right of either the lessor or lessee to designate by notice in writing a new address to which such notices or demands must be sent. The agreements, conditions and undertakings herein contained shall extend to and be binding on the representatives, heirs, executors, administrators, successors and assigns, of respective parties hereto as if they were in all cases named.

7. Wherever the worlds "lessor" and "lessee" are used herein they shall be read as "lessors" and "lessees" in all cases where there is more than one lessor or lessee and with necessary grammatical changes as if duly made herein. In witness whereof, the parties have set their hands [and seals] the day and year first above written.

Exhibit 7.2 243

Exhibit 7.2: Lease for Rent Stabilized Apartment
[To view additional forms, go to www.blumberglegalforms.com/forms]

M 56—Apartment lease, Rent Stabilized, 3-08   Blumberg Excelsior, Inc., Publisher, NYC 10013
www.blumberg.com

Prepared by Adam Leitman Bailey and Dov Treiman, © 2008 by Adam Leitman Bailey, P.C.

LEASE FOR A RENT STABILIZED APARTMENT

ATTACHED RIDER SETS FORTH RIGHTS AND OBLIGATIONS OF THE TENANTS AND THE LANDLORDS UNDER THE RENT STABILIZATION LAW.

LOS DERECHOS Y RESPONSABILIDADES DE INQUILINOS Y CASEROS ESTÁN DISPONIBLE EN ESPAÑOL.

Lease dated: 20
The Landlord is:

(the "Landlord")
Address:

The Apartment (¶ 1) no.   in the building at

(the "Apartment")
Term (¶ 3) Lease starts: 20
(the "Start Date"), and ends: 20
(the "End Date") Years   Months   Days
The Occupants are: (Name, Date of Birth and Relation to The Tenant)

The Tenant is:

(the "Tenant")
SSN: Driver's Lic. No.:
Present address: Apartment No.

The starting Rent and Surcharges (¶ 1,6) are:

The Security (¶ 12 & 13) $ ("the Security")
is deposited at:

("the Bank")
Other Riders (¶ 2)

Insurance required (¶ 43) $
The Additional Utilities (¶ 4)

1. The Apartment Rental Agreement
By this Lease, the Landlord rents to the Tenant the Apartment above for the Term and for the Rent stated above. **Whether or not either side reads this Lease, both sides are bound by it.**

2. Riders
Attached are riders and notices that set forth additional rights and obligations of the Tenant and the Landlord, including those under the Rent Stabilization Law. The riders and notices include:

☐ Window Guard Notice
☐ New York City And Federal Lead Paint Notices
☐ Pending Applications For Rent Increases (Schedule A)
☐ Tax Benefits Rider For J51
☐ Tax Benefits Rider For 421-A For All Tenants
☐ Tax Benefits Rider For 421-A For Low Income Tenants

☐ Preferential Rent Rider
☐ Guarantee Of Payment
☐ Rent Stabilization Lease Rider
☐ Additional Rules Under Section 20 Of This Lease Rider
☐ Additional Sections Of This Lease Rider
☐ Pest Control Rider
☐ Other Riders stated above.

3. The Term of the Lease
This Lease runs from the Start Date to the End Date. If the Tenant violates the Tenant's responsibilities under this Lease, the Landlord has the right to end this Lease before the end of the Term. If The Landlord does not obey all the Landlord's responsibilities under this Lease, under certain circumstances, the Tenant may have the right to end this Lease before the end of the Term.

4. Services and Utilities
The Landlord will provide hot and cold water, heat, and repairs as required by law. The Additional Utilities stated above are included in the Rent. The Tenant must make separate arrangements with the providers of the following utilities not included in the rent: Telephone, Cable Television, Internet, Electricity.
It is expressly understood and agreed that the Landlord shall not supply electrical utilities or service to the Apartment. The Tenant shall make the Tenant's own arrangements with the public utility company servicing the Apartment for the furnishing of and payment of all charges for electricity. Interruption or curtailment of any such service shall not constitute a constructive or partial eviction, or entitle the Tenant to any compensation or abatement of rent.

5. Military Status
The provisions of this Section are intended for information for the Landlord to be used only for the purpose of protecting The Tenants who are, may enter into, or may become dependent upon persons who enter into military status. STRIKE OUT ONE OF THE TWO FOLLOWING PROVISIONS.

–The Tenant states that the Tenant is neither in the U.S. military service nor is dependent on a member of the U.S. military service.

–The Tenant shall inform the Landlord within ten (10) days after enlisting in the U.S. military service or becoming dependent on a member of the U.S. military service.

6. The Rent
a. The starting Rent and Surcharges for the Apartment are as stated above.

b. However, this Rent may be adjusted up or down according to the law, as is described in Section 11 of this Lease. The Rent is due for the entire month, in advance on the first day of the month. It must be paid at the office of the Landlord at the address that is stated at the top of this Lease as being the Landlord's address. However, the Landlord may give the Tenant notice in writing of a different address to which rent must be sent and the Tenant must obey that notice.

c. At the time of the signing of this Lease, if the term of this Lease starts on any day other than the first day of the month, then the Tenant must pay in advance both the rent due for the partial month of the term from the Start Date through the last day of that calendar month and the full rent for the following calendar month. If the Tenant makes a pattern of paying the rent late, the Landlord will terminate this Lease according to the Landlord's rights under the law.

d. If the Tenant pays the rent on any day of the month after the first day of the month, there are serious legal consequences to the Tenant. The Landlord intends to hold the Tenant to them.

e. Both the Landlord and the Tenant agree that paying rent on time is an essential responsibility of the Tenant under this Lease and the tenancy. Therefore, the Landlord and the Tenant agree that if the Tenant pays the rent late enough to cause the Landlord to serve a rent demand [as defined in New York State Real Property Actions and Proceedings Law §711(2)] three (3) or more times in the course of one (1) period of 365 consecutive days or five (5) or more times in the course of twenty-four (24) consecutive months, the Landlord will be entitled to terminate this Lease before the end of the Term by following those legal procedures that allow the Landlord to terminate a lease under the law. For purposes of this paragraph, it shall make no difference that the occasions of the late payment of rent may or may not fall during the Term of this Lease or during different terms of the renewal of this Lease. The only thing that will matter as to frequency of late payment is how far apart those late payments are on the calendar.

f. Every payment of rent the Landlord receives may be credited by the Landlord to the oldest rent owed to the Landlord regardless of any marking on or accompanying the payment contradicting the Landlord's right under this sentence of this Lease. This provision shall bind the parties no matter what is said anywhere on the payment or any documentation accompanying the payment.

g. The Tenant may establish direct payment (ACH Debit) where the amounts due under this Lease are automatically debited to the Tenant's bank account if the Landlord offers such service.

7. Services and Utilities
The Landlord will provide hot and cold water, heat, and repairs as required by law. The following utilities are included in the rent: hot water, cold water, and heat, as required by law. The Tenant must make separate arrangements with the providers of the following utilities not included in the rent: electricity, telephone, cable television and internet. It is agreed that the Landlord shall not supply electrical utilities or service to the Apartment. The Tenant shall make the Tenant's own arrangements with the public utility company servicing the Apartment for the furnishing of and payment of all charges for electricity. Interruption or curtailment of any such service shall not constitute a constructive or partial eviction, or entitle the Tenant to any compensation or abatement of rent.

Exhibit 7.2: *(Continued)*

8. Complete Agreement

This Lease contains all the agreements between the Landlord and the Tenant. There are no oral agreements between the Landlord and the Tenant that are not set forth in this Lease. Any claimed agreements between the Landlord and the Tenant not set forth in this Lease are void. The Tenant is not relying on anything that was said by the Landlord, the Landlord's agent, or the Building's superintendent about the condition of the Apartment or the Building. The Tenant is not relying on any promises made by anyone unless set forth in writing and signed by the Landlord. The Tenant is not relying on any floor plans or brochure. The Tenant has inspected the Apartment. The Tenant is accepting the Apartment "as is," except for those things that the Tenant could not reasonably see by inspecting the Apartment. The Landlord has not made any promises to do any work on or in the Apartment unless set forth in a writing signed by the Landlord. No changes to this Lease are enforceable unless they are in writing signed by both the Landlord and the Tenant. However, both the Landlord and the Tenant have other rights and responsibilities provided by New York State and City Law in addition to the rights and responsibilities set forth in this Lease. This Lease is not meant to violate any of those rights and responsibilities provided by New York State and New York City Law.

9. Titles

At various places in this Lease, there are titles given to certain sections. These titles are meant only to make it easier to find provisions in this Lease and these titles have no legal effect.

10. The Apartment: Purpose

a. The Apartment is rented to the Tenant for residential living purposes only. The Apartment may only be occupied by the Tenant, the immediate family of the Tenant, and other occupants defined by §235-f of the Real Property Law of the State of New York. Occupancy of the Apartment by persons other than or in addition to those allowed by this paragraph is a violation of the Tenant's responsibilities under this Lease and a valid ground for the Landlord to follow those legal procedures that allow a landlord to terminate a lease under the law.

b. The Tenant acknowledges that the Apartment is located in a residential building. The Tenant represents that it shall not use the apartment for commercial or office use of any nature whatsoever. The provisions of this Article shall be deemed a material inducement to the Landlord for the execution of this Lease and any default by the Tenant under this Article shall be deemed a material default entitling the Landlord to exercise any or all of the remedies provided in this Lease. The apartment may not at any time during the term of this Lease be used for occupancy by any person on a transient basis, including, but not limited to, use as a hotel, motel, dormitory, fraternity house, sorority house, rooming house, hospital, nursing home, sanitarium, or rest home. This does not prohibit the Tenant from providing transient accommodations to the Tenant's guests during their occasional visits to the Tenant in the manner common and expected in one's own home and consistent with a residential apartment.

11. Adjustments to the Rent Under Rent Stabilization

a. Because the Apartment is subject to Rent Stabilization, the Rent may be adjusted up or down during the Term, including retroactively, to conform to the Rent Guidelines set forth under the Rent Stabilization Law and Code and set out by the New York City Rent Guidelines Board.

b. The Landlord and the Tenant agree that they will be bound by any lawful adjustment made to the Rent, including retroactive adjustments, by the New York State Division of Housing and Community Renewal, ("The DHCR") subject to both sides' rights to challenge such adjustments in the DHCR itself and in the courts of the State of New York. The Tenant agrees that the Tenant will pay all rent increases issued by the DHCR as set forth in the DHCR order, subject to the DHCR rules.

c. If there are any pending applications before the DHCR to adjust the rents in the Building, they are described in a document called "Schedule A – Pending Applications for Rent Adjustments," which is attached to this Lease. The Tenant agrees to pay all increases the DHCR may order with regard to those applications, including retroactive increases in the rent.

12. Security Deposit: The Landlord's Rights

a. The Tenant is required to keep on deposit with the Landlord at all times a Security Deposit equal to one (1) month's rent, as such rent is adjusted under Section 11 of this Lease. If during the Term of this Lease or any renewal of it, the rent increases, the Tenant shall deposit enough additional money with the Landlord to bring the amount of the Security Deposit up to the level of one (1) full month's rent at that time. If the Tenant fails to deposit the additional sums for a Security Deposit required by this Section, then the Landlord shall have the option to follow those legal procedures that allow a Landlord to terminate a lease under the law. If the Tenant fails to deposit the additional sums for a Security Deposit required by this Section of this Lease, then the Landlord shall also have the option to declare such additional sums to be "Additional Rent" and to bring a summary proceeding under §711(2) of the New York State Real Property Actions and Proceedings Law to recover those additional sums. In addition to the Landlord's rights under this Section, the Landlord may bring any summary proceeding under §711(2) of the New York State Real Property Actions and Proceedings Law to recover any rent or Additional Rent.

b. The Tenant is not allowed to use the Security Deposit to pay the rent. If, in spite of that prohibition, the Tenant uses the Security Deposit to pay the Rent, the Tenant will be required to pay a special handling fee in the amount of fifty (50) dollars that shall be considered to be Additional Rent due to the Landlord on the last day of the last month of the Term.

c. The Landlord may at any time apply all or part of the Security Deposit to the payment of all or part of any rent that is owed to the Landlord.

13. Security Deposit: The Tenant's Rights

The bank account where the Security Deposit is located will pay the Landlord interest. From that interest, the Landlord is entitled to keep the first

1% of the Security Deposit annually as an administrative fee. The Landlord will either pay to the Tenant, or issue a credit for, any additional interest earned on the security deposit each year. So long as the Tenant is not in default of any of the Tenant's obligations under this Lease and the Tenant returns the Apartment to the Landlord broom clean, in good order, and in the same condition as at the Start Date of this Lease, except for ordinary wear and tear and damage caused by things outside of the Tenant's control or cause, then the Landlord will return to the Tenant the full amount of the Security Deposit plus any interest still owed to the Tenant. Such return of the Security Deposit shall be within sixty (60) days after the Tenant surrenders possession of the Apartment to the Landlord. The Landlord has the right to retain all or part of the Security Deposit and any interest not previously paid to the Tenant to pay the Landlord for any of the Landlord's losses, including, but not limited to, damage to the Apartment, rent, Additional Rent, and the Landlord's attorneys' fees.

If the Landlord sells or leases the entire Building, the Landlord will turn over the security deposit and the interest then payable on it to the purchaser or renter of the entire Building within five (5) days after selling or renting it to that person. The Landlord will then notify the Tenant of the Apartment by mail addressed to the Apartment of the name and address of the new owner or renter of the entire Building. Once the Landlord has sent the Tenant that notification, the Landlord will have no further responsibility with respect to the Security Deposit. The new owner or renter of the entire Building will then bear the sole responsibility, if any, to the Tenant for the Security Deposit.

14. Delays in the Apartment Being Ready For Move In

If for any reason, the Apartment is not ready for the Tenant to move in on the Start Date, the Landlord is not responsible to the Tenant for damages or expenses, and this Lease will remain in effect. Under those circumstances, the Landlord will notify the Tenant in writing of a new Start Date. This Lease shall be considered to be amended to reflect that. The "End date" in this Lease will be considered to be changed to the same number of days later as the new Start Date created under this Section is later than the original Start Date. No rent shall be owed by the Tenant from the original Start Date set forth in this Lease to the new Start Date created under this Section. If the new Start Date is more than ninety (90) days after the original Start Date, then the Tenant has the option of notifying the Landlord by certified mail or overnight mail that the new Start Date must be fifteen (15) days after the notification. If the Tenant sends such a notification, and the Landlord does not make the Apartment available for the Tenant to move into within those fifteen (15) days, then, at the Tenant's option, this Lease shall be considered canceled, and all monies paid by the Tenant to the Landlord will be refunded by the Landlord to the Tenant.

15. Surrender of the Apartment at the End of The Term

a. If the Tenant does not renew this Lease, the Tenant shall move out of the Apartment at the end of the Term. If the Tenant does renew this Lease, the Tenant shall move out of the Apartment at the end of the last Term for which the Tenant has renewed this Lease. If this Lease is terminated by the Landlord, the Tenant shall move out of the Apartment on or before the termination date the Landlord sets. The Tenant shall leave the Apartment broom clean, in good order, and in the same condition as at the Start Date of this Lease except for ordinary wear and tear and damage caused by things outside of the Tenant's control or cause. The Tenant shall leave the Apartment empty of all movable property and empty of all persons. All walls and floors are to be left in the same condition in which they were received, reasonable wear and tear, and events outside Tenant's control or cause, excepted. Prior to the termination of this Lease, the Tenant shall, at the Tenant's own cost and expense, remove any wall coverings, bookcases, bookshelves, cabinets, mirrors, painted murals, or any other wall attachments the Tenant, or a previous tenant may have installed, make any necessary repairs, including prime paint, and leave the walls in the condition they would have been in without such attachments. The Tenant shall also, at the Tenant's own cost and expense, remove tile, linoleum, carpeting or any other floor covering that the Tenant, or a previous tenant, may have installed, including all nails, tacks or stripping by or to which the same may have been attached, and have that floor, and the entire adjacent area repaired and left in the condition it would have been absent such floor covering. The Landlord may choose to hold the Tenant liable to the Landlord for rent for any period of time after the Tenant has moved out and the Tenant has not yet removed all movable property and persons from the Apartment. After the Tenant moves out, the Landlord may treat all property remaining in the Apartment as belonging to the Landlord and may either discard or store such property at the Tenant's expense. The Tenant's liability under this Section shall continue in effect after the termination of this Lease and after the issuance of any warrant to evict the Tenant from the Apartment.

b. In the event the Tenant fails to renew this Lease, but continues in possession of the Apartment after the expiration of the Term, the Landlord shall in addition to all other rights at law, have the right to consider this Lease to be renewed for one (1) year at the rate set forth in the Lease renewal offer for a one (1) year lease renewal. The Landlord shall exercise that right by sending a notice to that effect to the Tenant. The Tenant shall thereupon be under all obligations the Tenant would have been under had the Tenant properly exercised the Tenant's option to renew the lease for one (1) year.

16. Care of the Apartment and Appliances

The Tenant will take good care of the Apartment and the appliances furnished by the Landlord and will neither permit nor cause damage to them, except through ordinary wear and tear. The Tenant shall not permit conditions to exist in the Apartment that are unhealthy or unsanitary. The Tenant will neither permit the Tenant's health or safety nor the health nor that of any other persons living or working in the Building to be endangered by any conditions in the Apartment, regardless of whether such conditions in the Apartment require repair or are a matter of cleaning and maintenance. If the appliances furnished by the Landlord are damaged by misuse or abuse by the Tenant, the cost of the replacement or repair of those items by the Landlord may be charged to the Tenant and collected as Additional Rent.

Exhibit 7.2: *(Continued)*

17. Alterations to the Apartment, Appliances, and Fixtures

a. The Tenant will not build on, build in, add to, subtract from, change, or alter the Apartment in any way. The Tenant will neither wallpaper, paint, or repaint the Apartment, nor affix anything to the walls, floors, ceilings, windows, or doors of the Apartment without the Landlord's prior written consent.

b. The Tenant will neither install nor use in the Apartment any water filled furniture, dishwashing machines, clothes washing or drying machines, electric stoves, garbage disposal units, heating, ventilating equipment or air conditioning units without the Landlord's prior written consent. This paragraph shall not prohibit the Tenant from using any appliance installed by the Landlord.

c. The Tenant will not overload the existing wiring installation in the Apartment or in the Building, or interfere with the use of such electrical wiring facilities by other tenants of the Building.

d. The Tenant will neither overload the plumbing systems of the Building, nor use such plumbing systems to dispose of other than normal waste water from cooking, bathing and washing of humans and human waste products.

e. The Tenant shall only dispose of human waste products through the use of the toilet in the bathrooms of the Apartment.

f. If natural gas is supplied to the Apartment, the Tenant will only use the gas for cooking.

g. The Tenant will not waste or consume unreasonable amounts of water, electricity, or natural gas.

h. If enclosed air-conditioning units have been installed in the Apartment by the Landlord, these units will be individually operated and connected to the Tenant's electric meter. If these units are not connected to the Tenant's electric meter, the Tenant will be responsible for the electric charges as Additional Rent. The Landlord will be responsible for the maintenance of these units unless they are damaged by the fault or negligence of the Tenant, guests, servants or invitees. The Tenant will not be permitted to install any other air-conditioning equipment in the Apartment nor shall Landlord be responsible for any damages nor shall the Tenant be entitled to an abatement of Rent, Surcharge and Additional Rent due to the removal of or breakdown of these units.

18. The Tenant's Compliance With the Law and Insurance Requirements

a. The Tenant will obey and comply with all present and future city, state and federal laws, rules and regulations, including the Rent Stabilization Code and Law, which affect the Building or the Apartment. The Tenant will comply with all orders and regulations of Insurance Rating Organizations which affect the Apartment and the Building.

b. The Tenant will obey all laws with respect to the installation of Window Guards and shall not interfere with their installation or maintenance. Attached to this Lease is a rider with respect to window guards.

c. The Tenant shall not allow the Apartment or any part of it to be used or occupied for any unlawful purpose, any dangerous trade or business or any use in violation of any certificate of occupancy affecting the Apartment or in violation of the Building or zoning laws of the City of New York.

d. The Tenant shall not allow the Apartment to be occupied by more persons than are permitted by the New York City Administrative Code with respect to an apartment of the description of the Apartment, it being the intent of this sentence to give the Landlord the right to evict the Tenant for violating this Lease by overcrowding the Apartment.

e. The Tenant shall not paint, alter, hang anything from, or in any way tamper with sprinkler heads, if any, in the Apartment. Since covering or painting will render the sprinkler inoperative and irreparable, the Tenant shall be liable for the full cost of their replacement plus any loss or damage that may occur due to fire, which sum shall be collectible as Additional Rent. Should flooding occur due to tampering with or bringing hot objects too close to the sprinkler heads, causing them to activate, the Tenant will be responsible for any damages caused by the same. The Tenant knows that it is a crime to tamper with the fire sprinkler system.

f. The Tenant agrees, at the Tenant's sole cost and expense, to comply with all present and future laws, orders and regulations of all state, federal, municipal and local governments, departments, commissions, and boards regarding the collection, sorting, separation, and recycling of waste products, garbage, refuse, and trash. The Tenant shall sort and separate such waste products, garbage, refuse and trash into such categories as provided by law, and in accordance with the rules and regulations adopted by the Landlord for the sorting and separating of such designated recyclable materials. The Tenant shall comply with the requirement to rinse recyclable bottles and containers before placing them in the designated receptacles, in accordance with the law and local regulations. The Landlord reserves the right, where permitted by law, to refuse to collect or accept from the Tenant any waste products, garbage, refuse or trash which is not separated and sorted as required by law. Where permitted by law, the Landlord reserves the right to require the Tenant to arrange for such collection, at the Tenant's sole cost and expense, utilizing a contractor satisfactory to the Landlord. The Tenant shall pay all costs, expenses, fines, penalties, or damages which may be imposed on the Landlord or the Tenant by reason of the Tenant's failure to comply with the provisions of this Section. At the Tenant's sole cost and expense, the Tenant shall indemnify, defend and hold the Landlord harmless (including legal fees and expenses) from and against any actions, claims, and suits arising from the Tenant's such noncompliance, utilizing counsel reasonably satisfactory to the Landlord, if the Landlord so elects. The Tenant's failure to comply with this Section shall constitute a violation of a substantial obligation of the tenancy and the Landlord's rules and regulations. The Tenant shall be liable to the Landlord for any costs, expenses, or disbursements, including attorney's fees, of any action or proceeding by the Landlord against the Tenant, predicated upon the Tenant's breach of this Section. The Tenant understands that local regulations governing recycling make residents liable for non-compliance. Any and all of the Tenant's financial obligations and liabilities under this paragraph shall be deemed to be Additional Rent.

19. Windows

a. The Tenant will not allow any cleaning of the windows of the Apartment to take place without compliance to the laws regarding the use of equipment and safety devices regarding the cleaning of windows.

b. Tenant hereby acknowledges that Tenant has rented the Apartment without any obligation on the part of the Landlord to furnish Tenant with window screens or to maintain window screens or any other personal property left in the Apartment by a previous Tenant.

c. The Tenant is hereby placed on notice that the windows located on perimeter walls of the Building that abut the lot line of the property are subject to covering or removal due to possible construction which may occur on adjacent lots. The Tenant hereby grants the Landlord access to the Apartment for purposes of closing, removal or covering said lot line windows at any time and acknowledges that the Tenant is aware that such windows may be removed, closed or covered at any time, without any change in the rent payable hereunder and without any liability of any person, including the Landlord or the owner of any adjacent lot, to the Tenant. Neighboring buildings may be the subject of construction, renovation or demolition. The Landlord will not be liable to the Tenant, nor shall the Tenant seek to hold the Landlord liable for interference with views, light, air flow, ventilation, whether such interference is temporary or permanent, if such interference results from activities conducted adjoining owners' properties.

d. In no event shall sheets or blankets or similar items be hung in the windows or be visible from outside of the Apartment. Tenant shall not hang or otherwise install lighting systems in the windows or on the window sills so as to be visible from the street side of the window for a period in excess of six consecutive weeks.

20. House Rules

The Tenant shall obey all of the following House Rules, it being understood that each and every one of these rules is a substantial obligation of the Tenant under this Lease.

a. **Plumbing.** The Tenant shall not use any plumbing fixture for any purpose other than that for which it was designed or built. The Tenant shall not put sweepings, rubbish, the contents of vacuum cleaners, or acids in toilets or drains in the Apartment or in toilets or drains anywhere else in the Building.

b. **Blockage.** The Tenant shall not place, leave, allow to be placed or allow to be left anything in or on fire escapes, sidewalks, entrances, driveways, elevators, stairways, or halls. The Tenant shall not place, leave, allow to be placed or allow to be left property of any kind, interfering with ingress to the Building, egress from the Building or free passage along the halls and through the public areas, lobbies, courts, courtyards, garages, and driveways of the Building.

c. **Disposal of Waste – Generally.** The Tenant shall not place or allow to be placed dirt, garbage, or refuse in the halls, elevators, and public areas of the Building, except that the Tenant may carry such dirt, garbage, or refuse to places designated by the Landlord for the disposal of such matter.

d. **Disposal of Waste – Obedience to Law.** The Tenant shall not place anything or dispose of anything outside of the Apartment or outside of the Building except in safe containers and only at places designated by the Landlord and in compliance with all applicable rules and regulations of all departments, units, and agencies of the City of New York.

e. **Windows.** The Tenant shall not hang, shake, or throw any articles, dirt, or debris out of the windows of the Apartment. The Tenant shall not display any sign, advertisement, notice or any other lettering inscribed, painted, or affixed by the Tenant on any part of the outside or the inside of the Apartment or the Building. Such rule is not intended to interfere with any rights the Tenant might possess under the First Amendment to the Constitution of the United States of America or law of this state. The Tenant shall not allow anything whatsoever to fall from the windows, terraces or balconies of the Apartment. The Tenant agrees that no object shall be placed on the window sills outside of the Apartment.

f. **Terraces – Restrictions on Use.**

i. Anywhere in this Lease the word "terrace" is used, it is understood to include terraces, balconies, and patios.

ii. The Tenant shall permit the Landlord full access to the terrace to make any alterations, repairs, or improvements to the Building or the terrace whenever the Landlord in the Landlord's sole discretion shall deem it necessary or desirable to do so. The Landlord has this right whether or not the alterations, repairs, or improvements are being done to comply with any law. The Landlord has this right even if the use of the terrace is to store materials in preparation for making alterations, repairs, or improvements. The Tenant shall make no claim for actual partial eviction on account of the Landlord's use of the terrace in any manner permitted to the Landlord by this paragraph.

iii. The Tenant shall not use the terrace as a bedroom.

iv. The Tenant shall not use the terrace for storage.

v. The Tenant shall not erect a fence or other enclosure on the terrace.

vi. The Tenant shall not place furniture or furnishings on the terrace other than furniture and furnishing which are designed for outdoor use.

vii. The Tenant shall not use the terrace for cooking, barbecuing, or charcoaling of food.

viii. The Tenant shall not allow to be present on the terrace any highly inflammable materials, including but not limited to, gasoline, turpentine, benzene, mineral spirits, charcoal starter fluid, kerosene, diesel, fuel oil, black powder, explosives, and fireworks.

ix. The Tenant shall not affix to the terrace any awnings or projections of any kind.

Exhibit 7.2: *(Continued)*

x. The Tenant shall not place any objects on the railings of the terrace and shall not hang clothing or other articles on or from the terrace.

xi. The Tenant shall not shake out clothing or rugs on the terrace.

xii. The Tenant shall not allow anything to fall from the terrace.

xiii. The Tenant shall not paint the Terrace.

xiv. The Tenant shall not interfere with any gate and shall not make any claim or defend any claim by the Landlord on account of any gate that the Landlord installs allowing access to and from the terrace to other parts of the Building. The Landlord may use such access gate at will without any notice to or permission from the Tenant. The Tenant is responsible for controlling access to the Apartment from the terrace.

xv. Whatever property the Tenant places on the terrace, the Tenant places there at the Tenant's own risk.

xvi. The Tenant shall remove from the terrace all accumulations of leaves, debris, water, ice, and snow, regardless of whether other persons have access to the terrace.

xvii. The Tenant shall not install any dish or other antenna on the terrace without the Landlord's prior consent in writing.

xviii. The Tenant shall not install on the terrace any swimming pool, wading pool, Jacuzzi, fountain, or plant watering system.

xix. The Tenant shall not permit on the terrace any child of ten years of age or younger without the supervision of a person fifteen years of age or older.

xx. The Tenant shall not permit on the terrace any unrestrained pet, regardless of whether such pet belongs to the Tenant or to some other person. This paragraph shall not be understood to mean that the Tenant may have pets.

xxi. The Tenant shall not permit there to be on the terrace any plantings exceeding the load bearing capacity of the terrace. The Tenant shall not permit any plantings on the terrace to cause water, snow, or ice to accumulate on, damage, or infiltrate the terrace. The tenant shall not possess any plants that attach themselves to the walls, floors, or other surfaces of the Building.

g. **Terraces, Floors and Flat Surfaces – Weight and Water Restrictions.** The Tenant shall not place anything on the terraces, floors, and other flat surfaces of the Apartment or of the Building that will place more weight on such terrace, floor or flat surface than that terrace, floor, or flat surface is designed to bear. The Tenant shall not tamper with any of the structural elements of the Building, including but not limited to walls, terraces, floors, balconies, and roofs of the Building, so as to make them less resistant to the intrusion of water.

h. **Laundry.** The Tenant shall not use the roof or string laundry lines for drying or airing laundry. The Tenant shall not use any clothes washing or drying machines in the Building except those, if any, placed by the Landlord in the Apartment and such as may be in a laundry room designated by the Landlord as operated by a party contracting with the Landlord to operate a laundry room in the Building. The laundry equipment located in the laundry room, if any, is being operated and maintained by a separate vendor as an accommodation to the tenants of the Building. The Landlord is not responsible for the maintenance of the laundry equipment in the laundry room, if any, any damage to Tenant's personal property caused by such equipment, or the operations of the laundry service itself.

i. **Antennas.** The Tenant may not attach any dish or other antenna to the roof, outside walls, or windows of the Building without the written consent of the Landlord. This shall not be construed to limit the rights granted by any federal or state law to any cable communications company.

j. **Freight.** The Tenant shall only use for freight those elevators designated by the Landlord to be used for freight and only on designated days and hours after making reservations in accordance with then-existing procedures. Proof of reasonable and appropriate insurance protecting the Landlord and other tenants is required from any person moving furniture or possessions into or out of the building before access is permitted. A reasonable cash security deposit may also be required. The Tenant shall obey the Landlord's rules as to which days and hours elevators may be used for moving furniture and freight. The Landlord shall not be liable to the Tenant for any delays caused by or the result of such rules.

k. **Operation of Elevators.** The Tenant shall not operate any elevators in the Building except those elevators for which the Landlord has not hired operators.

l. **Use of Elevators.** The Landlord may designate which elevators are to be used for servants, messengers, and trades people and the Tenant shall obey such designations and be responsible for such obedience by the servants, messengers, and trades people, coming to and from the Apartment.

m. **Use of Entrances.** The Landlord may designate which entrances are to be used for servants, messengers, and trades people and the Tenant shall obey such designations and be responsible for such obedience by the servants, messengers, and trades people, coming to and from the Apartment.

n. **Keys.** The Landlord shall provide the Tenant with keys to the locks to the entrance to the Apartment. The Tenant may install an additional lock to the entrance to the Apartment, provided such lock is of no more than three (3) inches in circumference and has been submitted to and approved by the Landlord to conform in general appearance to the locks installed by other tenants in the Building. The Tenant must provide the Landlord with a key to that additional lock. Every time the Tenant changes the locks to the Apartment, the Tenant shall furnish to the Landlord a key to the new lock within three (3) business days after the installation of the new lock. The Landlord retains the right to enter the Apartment by breakage or otherwise for purposes of responding to emergencies. At the end of the Term, the Tenant must surrender to the Landlord all keys to the Apartment, regardless of how the Tenant came into possession of them. In the event the Tenant fails to conform to the Tenant's obligations under this paragraph, the Landlord shall

have the right to replace the door to the Apartment when the Tenant moves out of the Apartment and the Landlord shall have the option of treating the expenses associated with such door replacement, including both labor and materials, as Additional Rent and as damages due to the Landlord that may be charged against the Tenant's Security Deposit. If the Landlord elects to treat such door replacement as Additional Rent, it shall become due and payable to the Landlord fifteen (15) days after the Landlord replaces the door.

o. **Noise.** The Tenant shall not make or permit any disturbing noises in the Building by the Tenant, the Tenant's family, friends, guests, employees or servants, nor do or permit anything by such persons that will interfere with the rights, comforts or convenience of other tenants. The Tenant shall not play or permit the playing of any musical instrument in the premises between the hours of 8:00 p.m. and the following 9:30 a.m. on weekdays that are not legal holidays and 11:00 a.m. on weekends and legal holidays. The Tenant shall not practice or allow to be practiced either vocal or instrumental music in a way that disturbs or annoys other occupants of the Building. The Tenant shall not practice or allow to be practiced either vocal or instrumental music for more than two (2) hours in any day or at all between the hours of 8:00 p.m. and 9:30 a.m. on weekdays that are not legal holidays and 11:00 a.m. on weekends and legal holidays. The Tenant shall not at any time operate, play or permit the operation or playing of any audio, video, television, radio, computer, music instruments or other equipment in a manner that shall disturb or annoy other occupants of the Building.

p. **Carpeting.** The floors in the Apartment shall be covered with sufficient insulated floor coverings so as to insulate against the transmission of sound from the Apartment to another apartment in the Building. The Tenant shall carpet the Apartment with at least 80% of the floor space of each room of the Apartment covered, except in the kitchen, pantry, and bathrooms. In the event the Tenant uses wall to wall carpeting, the tacking strip shall be glued and not nailed to the floor. Wall to wall carpeting shall only be installed with water soluble adhesive or no adhesive or with other products that shall not damage the underlying flooring in any way. Tenant shall be responsible for any damage to the flooring caused by any carpet installation.

q. **Mold and Mildew.**

i. The Tenant acknowledges that it is necessary for the Tenant to provide appropriate climate control in the Apartment and take other measures to retard and prevent mold and mildew from accumulating in the Apartment. The Tenant shall:

1. Maintain the Apartment in clean condition, dust the Apartment on a regular basis and remove any visible moisture accumulation in or on the Apartment, including on windows, walls, floors, ceilings, bathroom fixtures, and other surfaces; mop up spills and thoroughly dry affected area as soon as possible after occurrence; and

2. Not block or cover any of the heating, ventilation or air-conditioning ducts in the Apartment and keep climate and moisture in the Apartment at reasonable levels. In addition, and in furtherance of the foregoing, Tenant agrees to insure that the apartment shall be sufficiently ventilated during periods of prolonged absence. For purposes of this paragraph, a prolonged absence is a period lasting more than seven (7) days.

ii. The Tenant shall promptly notify management in writing of the presence of the following conditions:

1. Any evidence of a water leak or excessive moisture or standing water inside the Apartment or in any Common Area or the garage at the Building;

2. Any evidence of mold or mildew-like growth in the Apartment that persists after Tenant has tried several times to remove it with a common household cleaner containing disinfectants and/or bleach;

3. Any failure or malfunction in the heating, ventilation and air conditioning systems; the dishwasher or the laundry equipment, if any, in the Apartment, it being understood that nothing in this paragraph shall be deemed the Landlord's consent to the presence of any equipment listed in this paragraph; and

4. Any inoperable doors or windows.

iii. If the Tenant fails to comply with the provisions of this Article, then, in addition to the Tenant's obligation to indemnify Owner in accordance with the terms of this Lease for all damage, loss, cost and expense, including attorneys fees and disbursements, suffered or incurred by Owner in connection with said failure to comply, the Tenant shall also be responsible for all damage or loss to and all costs and/or expenses suffered or incurred by the Tenant, the Tenant's personal property and other occupants of the Building and their respective personal property.

iv. In addition to whatever other remedies the Landlord has under this Lease, the parties recognize that there is no adequate remedy at law for the Landlord if the Tenant violates this Section entitled "Mold and Mildew" and the Landlord shall also be entitled to an injunction to enforce this Section entitled "Mold and Mildew."

r. **Animals – Generally.** No pets of any kind shall be kept or harbored in the Apartment except by the written consent of the Landlord. Consent given by the Landlord with respect to any number or type of animals for any particular tenant in the Building shall not mean that the Landlord will consent to the same number or type of animals for another tenant in the Building. Such consent shall be given with respect to all animals kept by the Tenant for purposes of engaging in basic life functions as understood by the Fair Housing Act and may be given with respect to other animals as well. The Tenant must, however, restrain and control all animals the Tenant possesses or harbors so as not to interfere with the health, comfort or safety of others in the Building. Barking of unreasonable duration, timing, or volume shall be considered to be such an interference with the health, comfort and safety of other tenants. Defecation and urination on terraces, as well as common or public areas of the Building, by animals harbored by the Tenant shall be considered to be such an interference with the health, comfort and safety of other tenants. The Tenant shall not permit dogs or other animals to be in any grass area or garden on the Landlord's property around the Building. No

Exhibit 7.2: *(Continued)*

animals shall be allowed in the public areas of the Building unless carried or restrained by a leash. The Tenant shall not feed birds on the Landlord's property around the Building.

s. **Animals – Identification.** Independent of the Tenant's obligation not to have any pets without the Landlord's written consent, the Tenant also has the obligation to furnish the Landlord with two (2) photographs of all animals in the Tenant's possession. The photographs shall be taken within seven (7) days after the Tenant's acquisition of an animal or within seven (7) days after the Tenant moves into the Apartment, whichever is later. One such photograph shall be of the animal's face and the other photograph shall be of the animal's full body as seen from the side. Together with the photographs, the Tenant shall give to the Landlord a statement setting forth the animal's species, age, weight, breed, if any, and colors. The Tenant's full compliance with this paragraph marked "Animals – Identification" shall be considered to be a substantial obligation of the Tenant under this Lease independent of all other obligations of this Lease. Nothing in this paragraph marked "Animals – Identification" shall be understood to waive any other right of the Landlord under this Lease.

t. **Appliances and Fixtures.** No cabinets, fixtures, sinks, wires or appliances of any sort shall be attached to or connected with the gas or electric fixtures within the Apartment, except such as are approved by the Landlord, and no pipes or radiators shall be moved or tampered with in any manner at all. No doors shall be removed from their hinges.

u. **Landscaping.** The Tenant shall not disturb, plant, or use in any manner the gardens, landscaping, or lawns on the Landlord's property around the Building.

v. **Emergency Services.** The Landlord is not required to have any program providing for the safety of the Tenant from fire or crime. The Tenant shall cooperate with any program the Landlord may propose for providing safety for the Tenants from crime and fire. The Tenant shall not use the Apartment intercom system to allow persons to enter the Building unless the person desiring entrance has identified himself or herself and is known to the Tenant. The Tenant has inspected all smoke detectors and all carbon monoxide detectors in the Apartment and has determined that they are in good working order. The Tenant shall at all times maintain at least one (1) smoke detector in the Apartment, and one (1) carbon monoxide detector in each bedroom, in good operating condition and maintain additional smoke detectors and carbon monoxide detectors as the Landlord may reasonably require. The Tenant shall cooperate with the reasonable requests of police and fire department officers and officials.

w. **Courtyard.** If the Building contains a courtyard, its use is strictly prohibited except for the purpose of entry to the residents' apartments. The Tenant may not use the courtyard for any other purpose, including, but not limited to, storage, drying of clothes, plantings, access to other apartments, or any recreational use whatsoever.

x. **Building Personnel.** The Tenant shall not send any employee of the Landlord out of the Building on any private business of the Tenant.

y. **Apartment Tours and Other Group Uses**

i. No group tour or exhibition of the Apartment or its contents shall be conducted without the prior written consent of the Landlord or its managing agent. Consent for any such tour or exhibition shall not imply that consent will be given for another such tour or exhibition.

ii. The Tenants may not use, or permit others to use, the Apartment (including, without limitation, any terrace, balcony or roof), public hallway or any other part of the Building, for film shoots, video or sound recordings, photography shoots, screenings, auctions, classes, fund raisers, social or other gatherings or events that require the payment of any tuition, admission charge, fee or other compensation to the Tenant of any kind, or any similar activities, without the prior written consent of the Landlord or its managing agent in each instance.

z. **Social Areas.** If a roof deck, terrace, club, meeting room, children's play room or similar area (a "Social Area") is provided for the use of residents: no pets, food, beverages, smoking or unauthorized parties shall be permitted in a Social Area without the prior permission of the Landlord or in accordance with the Landlord's posted rules; the Tenant must remove all personal effects and debris after using a Social Area; the Landlord may close any Social Area if undue noise or disturbance exists; No one under age eighteen (18) shall be permitted in a Social Area unless accompanied and supervised by an adult; the use of each Social Area shall be during posted dates and hours only and shall be subject to the rules and regulations of the Building (all of which may be changed by the Landlord from time to time, in the Landlord's sole discretion); entry to a Social Area may be by a hand recognition system, a keyed or coded access system or other access system; the number of guests per tenant that may use a Social Area is limited at the Landlord's discretion; and the Landlord may make any of the Social Areas available for private parties, at such times and dates as the Landlord, in the Landlord's discretion, may determine. If the Landlord makes a Social Area available for private parties, such use shall be limited to tenants and permitted occupants who shall be required to sign a separate agreement and comply with its terms (including, but not limited to, the payment of fees).

aa. **Bicycle Storage.** If the Landlord designates a room or place for the storage of bicycles, the following rules shall apply to such bicycle storage room:

i. Spaces are not guaranteed; they are allocated on a "first come first served" basis. Space may not be available for every bicycle.

ii. All bicycles must be placed on the bicycle racks if they are provided and must be locked and chained. The Landlord may remove bicycles that are not locked without notice, at the Tenant's expense.

iii. All bicycles must be properly identified in accordance with any system the Landlord may have in place for identifying bicycles. Such system shall call for the annual re-identification of bicycles. Any bicycle which has not been identified to the Landlord under the Landlord's identification system for more than one year shall be deemed abandoned by the Tenant and to have become the sole property of the Landlord for the Landlord to dispose of as the Landlord sees fit.

iv. Only bicycles may be stored in the bicycle room; no baby strollers or other furnishings and equipment are permitted.

v. The Tenant must use care for the property of others when securing and removing bicycles. The Tenant will be responsible for any damage the Tenant causes to the bicycles of other tenants.

vi. Bicycle storage is at the Tenant's own risk. The Landlord, the managing agent, and all of the Landlord's employees and agents shall be absolved of responsibility for any loss or damage due to theft, accidents, mishandling or other cause, except to the extent such loss or damage is due to gross negligence or willful misconduct.

bb. **Smoking.** The Tenant shall not permit smoking in the Apartment so as to interfere with the health, comfort, or safety of other occupants of the Building.

21. Enforcement of the Tenant's Obligations

a. The Tenant shall hold the Landlord harmless for any alleged failure by the Landlord to enforce the obligations of another tenant in the Building.

b. The Tenant shall be considered to be in violation of substantial obligations of this Lease if the Tenant, any member of the Tenant's family residing in the Apartment, any other person residing in the Apartment, any servant of the Tenant, any employee of the Tenant or anyone visiting the Tenant violates any of the Tenant's obligations under this Lease.

c. All expenses, including but not limited to, fines, court expenses, and attorneys' fees incurred by the Landlord in enforcing the Tenant's obligations under this Lease or by reason of the Tenant failing to abide by the Tenant's obligations under this Lease shall be, at the Landlord's option, considered to be Additional Rent.

d. Such Additional Rent may be collected by the Landlord in any summary proceeding under the New York State Real Property Actions and Proceedings Law.

22. The Tenant's Obligation Not To Be Objectionable

In addition to all the Tenant's other obligations under this Lease, the Tenant may not engage in objectionable conduct towards or against the Landlord or any other occupants of the Building. Objectionable conduct includes violating of any of the Tenant's obligations of this Lease, but also includes engaging in any conduct which interferes with the right of others to properly and peacefully enjoy their Apartments. It also includes creating or tolerating any conditions which are dangerous, hazardous, unsanitary or detrimental to other occupants in the Building. If the Tenant engages in objectionable conduct, the Landlord will be entitled to terminate this Lease before the end of the Term by following those legal procedures that allow a landlord to terminate a lease under the law.

23. Assignment and Subletting

a. The Landlord may refuse permission for the Tenant to assign this Lease for any reason or for no reason at all.

b. This Lease may not be sublet except in accordance with the procedures set forth in §226-b of the New York State Real Property Law with respect to the subletting of leases and in accordance with the Rent Stabilization Law and Code. If the Tenant sublets the Apartment without following the procedures set forth in §226-b of the New York State Real Property Law, the Landlord will be entitled to terminate this Lease before the end of the Term by following those legal procedures that allow a Landlord to terminate a lease under the law.

c. If the Landlord consents to any assignment or subletting, the Landlord will not be obligated to consent to any other assignment or subletting.

d. Each and every time the Tenant applies for permission to assign or sublet, the Landlord may impose a reasonable processing fee. If the Apartment is sublet, the Landlord may choose to collect the rent directly from the sublessee without releasing the Tenant from this Lease, but such sums collected shall be applied to the Tenant's account. No funds paid to the Landlord by a sublessee or by any other person shall be understood to mean that the Landlord accepts anyone other than the Tenant named on this Lease as being the Landlord's tenant.

24. Abandonment

If the Tenant moves out or is evicted before the end of the Term, except by a surrender of possession to the Landlord duly accepted by the Landlord, the Tenant shall remain liable for every monthly payment of rent as it comes due until the end of the Term. If this Lease has been renewed, then such liability shall continue until the end of the renewal term.

25. Reduction of Services Which Are Not The Landlord's Fault

If due to strike, labor, trouble, war, national emergency, act of terrorism, repairs, the fault of any utility company, governmental action, or any other cause beyond the Landlord's reasonable control, the Landlord may not be able to provide or may be delayed in providing or making any repairs to the Building, the Tenant shall have no rights against the Landlord except such as are required by law.

26. Right of Entry

The Landlord may enter the Apartment in any manner and at any time in the event of an emergency.

The rent shall not be reduced by reason of the Landlord's exercise of any right given the Landlord by this Section.

Where there is no emergency, the Landlord may enter and the Tenant must give access during reasonable hours and upon reasonable notice, for the purposes of:

a. Erecting, using, or maintaining pipes and conduits through the walls, floors, and ceilings of the Apartment.

b. Inspecting the Apartment to ascertain what repairs or changes to the Apartment the Landlord might deem necessary.

c. Showing the Apartment to persons to whom the Landlord may wish to sell or lease the entire Building and persons from whom the Landlord may wish to borrow money.

Exhibit 7.2: *(Continued)*

d. Showing the Apartment to persons acting on behalf of an insurance carrier from whom the Landlord may wish to purchase insurance.

e. Showing the Apartment during the period that is five (5) months before the end of the Term, to persons who might wish to rent the Apartment.

f. Making changes, repairs, or redecorations during the last month of the Term, if the Tenant has substantially or completely moved out.

27. The Tenant's Defaults

a. If the Tenant defaults under this Lease as defined in this Section, except for defaulting on the Tenant's obligation to pay rent, then the Landlord may serve on the Tenant a "notice to cure" that sets forth the following:

i. What the Tenant's defaults are; and

ii. Notification that if the Tenant does not cure the default within ten (10) days, then the Landlord may serve a "termination notice" on the Tenant.

b. If the Tenant does not cure the default within ten (10) days after the service of the notice to cure, and if the Tenant does not begin the cure ten (10) days after the service of the notice to cure and continue the cure every day thereafter until it is completed, then the Landlord may serve a "termination notice" on the Tenant setting forth that the Lease shall terminate seven (7) days after the service of the termination notice.

c. Seven (7) days after the service of the termination notice, the lease shall terminate and the Tenant must surrender the Apartment to the Landlord. The Tenant, however, shall remain responsible for the unpaid rent up to the termination of this Lease in addition to use and occupancy after this Lease ends and through the date the Tenant actually moves out.

d. If the Tenant defaults in paying rent or Additional Rent, this Lease shall not restrict the Landlord's rights in summary proceedings or mandate additional procedures for the Landlord to follow beyond those set forth in the summary proceeding statute.

e. The Tenant shall be considered to be in default of this Lease if the Tenant:

i. Fails to meet any of the Tenant's responsibilities under this Lease, regardless of whether such responsibility is noted as one for which the Landlord can terminate this Lease.

ii. Behaves in an objectionable manner.

iii. Fails to take possession of the Apartment within thirty (30) days after the Start Date of this Lease as defined in Sections 3 and 14 of this Lease.

iv. Moves out of the Apartment permanently before the end of the Term.

v. Makes a material misrepresentation in the Application for the Apartment.

28. Rights Under the Tenant's Defaults

If the Tenant is in default of the Tenant's obligations under this Lease then the Landlord shall be entitled to the following rights in addition to other rights the Landlord may have:

a. The Tenant shall continue being responsible for rent until the end of the Term, even though the lease is terminated earlier by the Landlord.

b. The Tenant must pay the Landlord "use and occupancy" for all the time that the Tenant or persons claiming rights of occupancy through the Tenant, are occupying the Apartment.

c. Once the Tenant and all persons claiming rights of occupancy through the Tenant have left the Apartment, the Landlord may rent the Apartment for a period that is longer than, the same as, or shorter than the time remaining on the Term. The Landlord may rent the Apartment at the same amount of rent, a lower rent, or a higher rent than the most recent Rent due under this Lease. If the rental rate is lower than the most recent Rent due under this Lease or for a shorter term, then the Tenant shall be liable to the Landlord for the difference between what the Tenant should have paid to the Landlord and what the Landlord actually collected. No part of this Lease shall be interpreted to mean that the Landlord is under any obligation to rent the Apartment during the time remaining on the Term that the Tenant is not in occupancy.

d. The Tenant shall be liable to the Landlord for all advertising expenses, fees, real estate fees, attorneys' fees, and other costs of putting the Apartment in good condition for re-rental.

e. The Tenant shall be liable for all of the Landlord's attorneys' fees in enforcing any of the Landlord's rights in the event of the Tenant's default of any kind or nature.

f. In the event the Tenant moves out of the Building, the Landlord has the right to declare all of the rent due from the time the Tenant moves out until the end of the term immediately due and owing to the Landlord and to sue for the entire accelerated sum immediately.

g. The Landlord has no duty to mitigate the Landlord's damages for nonpayment of rent for any reason whatsoever.

29. Additional Rent

For the purposes of this Lease, "Additional Rent" shall mean all sums, charges, or amounts of any nature other than "Rent" that are to be paid or deposited by the Tenant to the Landlord in accordance with the provisions of this Lease, whether or not such things are referred to as "Additional Rent" in this Lease. The Landlord shall have the same remedies for the Tenant's default in the payment of "Additional Rent" as for Rent. If no date is otherwise given in this Lease for the date on which a particular item of Additional Rent is due, then such item shall be due to the Landlord ten (10) days after the Landlord sends to the Tenant an invoice for that item.

The Tenant shall reimburse the Landlord for the following items and the Landlord shall be entitled to consider the following items to be Additional Rent regardless of whether they are caused by the Tenant or they are caused by persons who live with the Tenant, visit the Tenant, or work for the Tenant, and regardless of whether they are caused by the malice, neglect, or negligence of any such persons:

a. Repairs to the Apartment, to the Building, or to any appliances in the Apartment or in the Building.

b. Correction of violations of city, state, or federal laws or orders and regulations of insurance rating organizations with respect to the Apartment or to the Building.

c. Preparing the Apartment for the next Tenant if the Tenant moves out before the end of the Term defined in Sections 3 and 14 of this Lease.

d. Any attorneys' fees and disbursements for legal actions or proceedings brought by the Landlord against the Tenant because of a Default by the Tenant of any of the Tenant's obligations under this Lease.

e. Any attorneys' fees and disbursements for legal actions or proceedings brought against the Landlord by persons not party to this Lease because of any Default by the Tenant of any of the Tenant's obligations under this Lease.

f. Removing the Tenant's movable property after this Lease is ended.

g. Any other expenses the Landlord bears because of the Tenant's defaults in the Tenant's obligations under this Lease.

The Tenant shall pay all these items set forth in this Section to the Landlord as Additional Rent within ten (10) days after the Landlord sends a bill or statement for these items. Whether or not this Lease has ended by its original terms or has been terminated by the Landlord, the Tenant shall still be liable for payment of all these items set forth in this Section.

30. Miscellaneous Fees and Charges

a. The Tenant agrees to pay a late charge of fifty (50) dollars every time rent is received by the Landlord after the fifth day of the month in which that rent is due, to cover the Landlord's extra expense involved in handling a delinquent rent payment. That late charge shall be considered to be Additional Rent and shall be due and payable with the late rent payment. If the rent is deposited to a lock box system, then the date the bank shows as the date the rent was received shall be conclusive evidence that the rent was received on that date.

b. The Tenant agrees to reimburse the Landlord for all charges the bank levies against the Landlord for any check that the Tenant remits to the Landlord that is returned to the Landlord as dishonored. In addition to such bank charges, the Tenant agrees to pay a dishonored check fee of fifty (50) dollars for every such dishonored check to cover the extra expense involved in handling a dishonored check. Such reimbursement and fees shall be considered to be Additional Rent and shall be due to the Landlord with the next payment of rent to be due under this Lease after the check is dishonored, or if there is no such next rent due, then immediately.

31. The Landlord's Nonliability

Unless caused by the negligence or other misconduct of the Landlord or the Landlord's agents or employees, the Landlord and the Landlord's agents and employees are not liable to the Tenant and none of the following matters shall cause a suspension or reduction of the rent or allow the Tenant to cancel the Lease:

a. Damage or inconvenience caused to the Tenant by the actions, negligence, or lease violations of another tenant or person in the Building, unless required by law.

b. Poor reception of a television, radio, cellular telephone, or internet signal.

c. Temporary or permanent interference with light, air, or ventilation in the Apartment, or view from the Apartment by reason of construction, whether done by the Landlord or by another person.

d. Permanent interference with light, air, or ventilation in the Apartment, or view from the Apartment caused by blockage of the windows required by law.

e. Curtailment or elimination of any amenities, conveniences, services, or businesses provided by persons other than the Landlord in space leased, rented, or licensed to such persons by the Landlord. Any fees, charges or conditions for such amenities, conveniences, services, or businesses are to be separately negotiated between the Tenant and the provider of such amenities, conveniences, services, or businesses.

32. Fire and Casualty

If the Apartment becomes totally or partially unusable because of fire, accident, or other casualty:

a. This Lease will not be cancelled unless the Landlord or the Tenant terminates it by using the procedures set forth in this Section.

b. The rent will be reduced based on how much of the Apartment is made unusable by such fire, accident, or casualty.

c. Unless the Landlord terminates the Lease by using the procedures set forth in this Section, the Landlord will repair and restore the Apartment.

d. The Landlord may decide to tear down or substantially rebuild the Building. If so,

i. The Landlord need not restore the Apartment and may terminate this Lease,

ii. The Landlord may terminate this Lease even if the Apartment has not been damaged by giving the Tenant sixty (60) days notice of termination within thirty (30) days after the fire, accident, or casualty. However, termination may be immediate if the fire, accident, or casualty made the Apartment unusable.

e. If the Apartment is made completely unusable because of the fire, accident, or other casualty and is not repaired in thirty (30) days, then the Tenant may give the Landlord notice that the Tenant is terminating this Lease. Such termination shall be effective the date of the fire, accident, or casualty and the Landlord shall refund the rent paid attributable to the days after the fire, accident, or casualty plus the security deposit, but shall be offset by any monetary claims of the Landlord prior to the fire.

Exhibit 7.2   249

Exhibit 7.2: *(Continued)*

f. Unless forbidden by any applicable insurance policies, the Landlord and the Tenant waive all rights of subrogation against each other or any other claimant, through or under either of them.

33. Condemnation for Public Use
If the Building, any part of it, or the land on which it is located is condemned by any governmental agency for public use or purpose, then this Lease shall automatically terminate on the day the government takes title, and the Tenant shall have no claim against the Landlord for any resulting damage. In that event, the Tenant assigns to the Landlord any claim against the government for compensation for the value of the unexpired portion of this Lease.

34. Subordination
This Lease is subordinate to any present and future leases and mortgages on the Building, including, but not limited to, any renewals, consolidations, modifications or replacements of these leases or mortgages. If, pursuant to their rights under such leases and mortgages, the lessees and mortgagees terminate this Lease, the Tenant shall not hold the Landlord, lessee, or mortgagee liable for any damages the Tenant may suffer from that termination. Upon request by the Landlord, the Tenant will promptly sign an acknowledgement of the subordination, in any form the Landlord requires.

Any time the Landlord requests, the Tenant shall sign a written acknowledgement, if true, to any third party designated by the Landlord that:

a. This Lease is in effect;

b. The Landlord is performing the Landlord's obligations under this Lease; and

c. The Tenant has no present claim against the Landlord.

35. Mechanics' Liens
The Tenant shall not suffer or permit any mechanic's lien to be filed against the Apartment, the Building, or any leasehold interest in the Building, by reason of work, labor, services, or materials supplied to, or claimed to have been supplied to, the Tenant or anyone holding any interest in the Apartment or any part thereof through or under the Tenant. If any such mechanic's lien shall at any time be filed, the Tenant shall, within fifteen (15) days after the mechanic's lien is filed, cause the mechanic's lien to be discharged of record by payment, deposit, bond, court order, or otherwise.

36. Quiet Enjoyment
So long as the Tenant is not in default of any of the Tenant's obligations under this Lease, the Landlord will not terminate the Lease or interfere with the Tenant's occupancy prior to the end of the Term.

37. Bills and Notices to the Tenant
The Landlord, the Landlord's agent or the Landlord's attorney, regardless of whether the Tenant has had previous dealings with such agent or attorney, may give any notice to the Tenant called for by this Lease, and the notice shall be considered to be proper if it is:

a. In writing;

b. Signed by, or in the name of, the Landlord;

c. Is hand delivered to the Tenant personally or is sent by certified mail or overnight courier and additionally by first class mail to the Tenant addressed to the Tenant at the Apartment.

The date the notice is sent shall be considered the date it has been served, regardless of when it is actually delivered, unless otherwise required by law.

38. Notices to The Landlord
The Tenant may give any notice to the Landlord called for by this Lease, and the notice shall be considered to be proper if it is:

a. In writing;

b. Signed by, or in the name of, the Tenant;

c. Is sent by certified mail or overnight courier and additionally by first class mail to the Landlord at the address for the Landlord stated at the top of this Lease, unless the Landlord shall have previously given the Tenant written notice of some other address.

The date the notice is sent shall be considered the date it has been served, regardless of when it is actually delivered, unless otherwise required by law.

No communication to the Landlord by electronic means shall be considered proper notice under this Lease for any purpose.

39. Waiver of Rights in Legal Proceedings
a. The Landlord and the Tenant both waive the right to a trial by jury in a court action, proceeding or counterclaim on any matters concerning this Lease, including, but not limited to, the relationship as the Landlord and the Tenant or any court action, proceeding or counterclaim regarding the Tenant's use or occupancy of the Apartment.

b. Neither the Landlord nor the Tenant gives up the right to trial by jury of any claim for personal injury or property damage.

c. In any proceeding brought by the Landlord under Article 7 of the New York State Real Property Actions and Proceedings Law, the Tenant agrees not to counterclaim against the Landlord.

d. The Tenant states that the Tenant is not subject to foreign subject or diplomatic immunity. The Tenant waives all rights to foreign sovereign immunity and waives all rights to diplomatic immunity. The Tenant consents to the jurisdiction of the Housing Part of the Civil Court of the City of New York and all other courts.

e. The Tenant agrees that in the event a judgment is entered against the Tenant, the Landlord may enforce the judgment against any property or assets of the Tenant, regardless of where they are located.

40. No Waiver of Rights Under This Lease
a. The acceptance by the Landlord of rent from the Tenant at a time when the Tenant is in default of any of the Tenant's obligations under this Lease shall not be considered to waive any of the Landlord's rights under this Lease.

b. If the Landlord has a right to bring an action or proceeding by reason of the Tenant's breach of an obligation under this Lease, and the Landlord delays in bringing that action by a period shorter than six (6) years, then the Landlord shall not be considered to waive any of the Landlord's rights under this Lease.

c. The waiver by the Landlord of a default by the Tenant in any of the Tenant's obligations under this Lease shall not be considered a waiver by the Landlord of the Landlord's right to enforce its rights regarding the Tenant's further defaults of the same nature.

d. The Landlord will only be considered to have waived any of its rights under this Lease, if such waiver is set forth in a writing signed by the Landlord.

e. The acceptance by the Landlord of rent which is less than the complete rent the Landlord is owed shall not be considered a waiver by the Landlord of its entitlement to the full rent.

f. No surrender of this Lease is effective to release the Tenant from the Tenant's obligations under this Lease unless recorded in a writing signed by the Landlord.

41. The Landlord's Assets
The Landlord's liability to the Tenant is limited to the Landlord's then interest in the Building, and, except for that interest, the Tenant waives whatever rights the Tenant may have to levy against any other assets of the Landlord.

42. Property Loss and Damage; Personal Injury; Personal Security
a. **The Landlord Not Liable for Damage.** The Landlord and the Landlord's agents and employees will not be responsible to the Tenant for any loss of or damage to the Tenant or the Tenant's property in the Apartment (even when the Landlord or the Landlord's agents or employees are permitted to enter the Apartment) or the Building (including, without limitation, any of the Common Facilities) due to any accidental or intentional cause, including, but not limited to, a theft or other crime committed in the Apartment or elsewhere in the Building; any loss of or damage to the Tenant's property delivered to any of the Landlord's agents or employees (such as the superintendent, doorman, concierge, maintenance personnel, etc.); any damage or inconvenience caused to the Tenant by any other tenant, occupant, or person in the Building; any loss or damage (including, without limitation, any consequential losses) caused by or due to the installation, removal, operation, maintenance, malfunction, interference with or discontinuance of any television, radio, cellular telephone, or internet signal; and any loss or damage caused by or due to any leaks in any air-conditioning unit or window.

b. **Deliveries.** Notwithstanding anything to the contrary set forth in this Lease or otherwise: the Tenant acknowledges that the Landlord's agents and employees are prohibited from receiving any mail or packages of any kind exceeding a value of $500.00 and from receiving any keys for or from family, friends, guests, employees or servants. The Tenant must personally receive deliveries of property exceeding $500 in value directly from the shipper. Property left with any of the Landlord's agents or employees shall be conclusively deemed to have a value of $500 or less (notwithstanding its actual value). Any Building employee to whom any of the Tenant's property shall be entrusted shall be considered to be acting on the Tenant's behalf, as the Tenant's agent, with respect to such property. The Tenant acknowledges that the Landlord has set the level of security for deliveries in reliance on the Tenant's agreements and representations as set forth in this subparagraph. The Tenant shall maintain renter's insurance as provided elsewhere in this Lease insuring the contents of all mail and packages delivered to the Building, including, without limitation, any packages left with the Landlord's agents and employees or in any package or mail room in the Building. Keys may not be left with the doormen or other employees of the Landlord or the Landlord's agents (except when requested for repairs in the Apartment) for any person, including, without limitation, family, friends, guests, employees or servants. If entry to the Building or any of the Common Areas requires the use of a key or access card, in no event shall the Tenant give any such key or access card to anyone who is not a Tenant or legal occupant of the Apartment, unless the Tenant first obtains the Landlord's prior written consent and the Tenant signs a separate agreement pertaining to such key or access card (if required by the Landlord).

c. **Loss by Building Employees.** The Landlord shall not be responsible for any fault or misconduct of the Landlord's agents and employees unless they were grossly negligent or engaged in willful misconduct while performing work that is part of their duties for the Landlord. If any agent or employee of the Landlord renders assistance in the parking or delivery of an automobile, handling or delivery of any furniture, household goods, keys or other articles, or in providing any other service that is beyond the scope of their employment, whether at the Tenant's request, the request of any lawful occupant, or at the request of any of the Tenant's employees or guests, then said employee shall be deemed an agent of the person making such request, and the Landlord is expressly relieved from any and all loss or liability in connection therewith.

d. **Prohibited Areas.** The Tenant is strictly prohibited from opening, or attempting to open, entering, or attempting to enter, accessing or attempting to access, or tampering with, any areas of the Building or the Apartment whether locked or unlocked, that are limited to Building employees or service personnel, or otherwise off-limits to the Tenants. This includes, without being limited to, locked or closed access doors, panels, shafts, bus ducts, mechanical and telecommunications rooms and closets. These areas may contain high voltage or other dangerous equipment or conditions. The Tenant (and not the Landlord or the Landlord's agents or employees) will be held responsible for any loss or injury to the Tenant or anyone else caused by the Tenant's violation of the foregoing prohibition (except if, and to the extent, caused by the Landlord's gross negligence or willful misconduct). Empty spaces above closets and alcoves in the Apartment are off-limits to the Tenant.

Exhibit 7.2: *(Continued)*

e. **The Landlord's Security System.** The Landlord makes no representation and assumes no responsibility whatsoever with respect to the functioning or operation of any human or automated security systems that the Landlord does or may provide, including, but not limited to, desk-persons, lobby attendants, hand recognition system or TV monitoring. The Landlord shall not be responsible or liable for any bodily harm or property loss or damage of any kind or nature that the Tenant or any members of the Tenant's family, employees or guests may suffer or incur by reason of any claim that the Landlord, the Landlord's agents or employees, or any such system in the Building has been negligent or has not functioned properly or that some other or additional security measure or system could have prevented the bodily harm or property loss or damage.

f. **The Tenant's Security System.** If the Tenant installs a security system, the Landlord shall not be responsible for its maintenance. Neither the superintendent nor the Landlord nor any of the Landlord's employees shall be responsible for responding to any alarm or security alert.

43. Insurance

a. **Insurance Required, Generally.** Within ten (10) days after signing this Lease, the Tenant must obtain and keep in full force and effect during the term of this Lease, Homeowners-Tenants (HO-4) insurance or its equivalent with minimum limits stated above for Personal Liability covering Bodily Injury and Property Damage and Contents coverage at 100% replacement cost and waiver of subrogation clause in favor of the Landlord, and the Landlord's agents and employees. Such policy shall cover, among other things, loss of or damage to all property in the Apartment; loss of any property left in the care, custody or control of the Landlord or any of the Landlord's agents or employees, loss of use of the Apartment and all other perils commonly insured against by prudent residential tenants. The Tenant must provide the Landlord with:

i. A copy of such policy, upon request; and

ii. An original certificate signed by an authorized representative of the Tenant's insurer, evidencing in a form that expressly states that the Landlord may rely upon it, the Tenant's compliance with the insurance requirements set forth in this Lease.

b. Flood Insurance Required. The Tenant must obtain and keep in full force and effect during the term of this Lease, flood insurance that shall cover flood caused loss of or damage to all property in the Apartment; loss of any property left in the care, custody or control of the Landlord or any of the Landlord's agents or employees; loss of use of the Apartment; and all other perils commonly insured against by prudent residential tenants insuring against floods.

c. **Contractor's Insurance Required.** If the Tenant has anyone perform any work in the Apartment or the Building, the Tenant must provide to the Landlord, prior to the start of any work, evidence satisfactory to the Landlord of the Tenant's contractor's having policies of general liability insurance with builders risk coverage and compensation insurance with limits as reasonably required by the landlord at the time. Such policies must name the Landlord and the Landlord's agents as additional insureds. Nothing in this paragraph shall mean that the Landlord consents to any such work.

44. Common Facilities

a. **In General.** The terms "Common Facility" (when referring to one) and "Common Facilities" (when referring to all) shall mean any fitness center, roof deck, terrace, laundry room, conference center, club room, storage room, bicycle room or other amenity or facility that is for the use of occupants of the Building. The Tenant understands that the use of any of the Common Facilities will be at the Tenant's own risk and expense. The Tenant may not store any material in any of the Common Facilities or any other area of the Building without the prior written consent of the Landlord and in accordance with all applicable laws, rules and regulations. The Landlord shall not be responsible for any loss or damage to property left in any Common Facilities or other Building space.

b. **Changes In Facilities.** The Tenant understands that unless the Landlord charges a separate designated fee, the Common Facilities are made available to the Tenants for free and that no rent is attributable to the Common Facilities. The Landlord, so far as the law allows, may, in the Landlord's discretion, limit, curtail, change or remove any or all of the Common Facilities or impose charges for the use of the same, at any time, for any or no reason, without the same constituting a reduction in services to the Tenant and without the Tenant being entitled to any rent reduction, abatement, off-set or credit.

c. **Specific Common Facilities.** The Landlord reserves the right to limit the use of any Common Facility to the tenants and permitted occupants (who, in the case of any fitness center must be eighteen (18) years of age or older), who shall be required to sign a separate agreement and/or Lease rider for each of these Common Facilities and comply with its terms (including, without limitation, the payment of fees, if any). If the Tenant signs any separate Lease Rider, the Tenant's failure to comply with any of its terms and conditions will be considered a default under this Lease. But if the agreement with respect to the Common Facilities is separate from this Lease, then default under the terms of that separate agreement shall not be considered a default under this Lease.

d. **Elimination or Reduction of Building Facilities.** If the Landlord changes, eliminates or reduces the hours of operation or changes, eliminates or reduces any of the components of any of the Common Facilities or other facilities, such action by the Landlord shall not be deemed a breach of this Lease or a reduction of services for which the Tenant may claim any abatement or reduction of rent. The Tenant shall not have any right to restoration of any such Common Facility.

45. Credit Reports

The Tenant authorizes the Landlord to use the Social Security Number of the Tenant to obtain any and all credit reports for all purposes concerning this Lease, all renewals of this Lease, and this right will remain in effect through any period the Tenant owes the Landlord money. The Tenant consents to the use by the Landlord of these reports for all purposes regarding the occupancy and continuing occupancy of the Tenant of the Apartment.

46. Guarantor

The Tenant agrees that if there is a guarantor of this Lease, the Landlord shall be entitled to have, as a condition to the renewal of this Lease and all renewals of those renewals, guarantors of equal or greater credit worthiness to that of the guarantor of this Lease.

47. Parties Bound

This Lease binds the Landlord, the Tenant, and all persons who legally succeed to their interests.

This Lease is the agreement of the Landlord and of the Tenant.

The Landlord: The Tenant:

_____   _____
Signature   Signature

Witness's Signature:

_____   _____
Print name   Signature

GUARANTEE

1. The undersigned Guarantor guarantees to the Landlord the performance of and observance by the Tenant of all obligations, agreements, provisions and Rules in the attached Lease and the rules and regulations of the Landlord.

2. Guarantor agrees to waive all notices when the Tenant is not paying rent or not observing any and all of the provisions of the attached Lease.

3. Guarantor agrees to be equally liable with the Tenant, so that the Landlord may sue Guarantor directly without first suing the Tenant.

4. The Guarantor further agrees that this guaranty shall remain in full effect even if the Lease is renewed, changed or extended in any way, and even in the event that the Landlord has to make a claim against Guarantor.

5. The Landlord and Guarantor agree to waive trial by jury in any action, proceeding or counterclaim.

6. Guarantor agrees to pay the Landlord's attorneys' fees in any action or proceeding by the Landlord against the Guarantor.

7. Guarantor agrees that this Guarantee shall be governed by the laws of the State of New York.

8. Guarantor consents to the jurisdiction of the courts of the State of New York.

Guarantor's Name:_____
                                                 Signature

Guarantor's
Address:_____

8

Personal Property

LEARNING OBJECTIVES

After studying this chapter you will be able to:

- Distinguish between the different categories of personal property
- Define "tangible," "intangible," and "chose in action"
- Categorize general intangibles
- Explain the difference between stocks and bonds
- Define "promissory note"
- Discuss the concept of intellectual property
- Explain patents, marks, and copyrights
- List the different types of gift transfers
- Understand the concept of a bailment
- Distinguish a bailment from a pledge
- Explain the legal rights and obligations of common carriers and innkeepers
- Discuss the property rights incident to accession
- Discuss the property rights incident to confusion
- Apply some practical tips regarding transferring personal property

251

CHAPTER OUTLINE

Categories of Personal Property
    Tangible
    Intangible
    Chose in action
General Tangibles
Intangibles
    General
        Stocks
        Bonds
        Debentures
        Promissory notes
    Intellectual property
        Copyrights
        Patents
        Marks
Methods of Transferring Property
    Gifts
        Inter vivos
        Testamentary
        Causa mortis
        Donative intent
    Bailments
        Pledge
Common Carriers and Innkeepers
Other Issues
    Accession
        Confusion
Practical Tips

CHAPTER OVERVIEW

As stated in the first chapter, the titles that apply to real estate apply equally to personalty. However, there are certain legal rules and doctrines that are applicable only to personal property. This chapter examines the two different categories of personalty — tangible and intangible property — and then addresses the unique rules with respect to the transfer of these items. Bear in mind that the rules and procedures outlined earlier, excluding those that are exclusive to real estate transactions, apply to personalty as well.

Categories of Personal Property

Generally, all non-real property is considered to be personal property, which is divided into tangible and intangible property. **Tangible property** is anything that can be touched and moved, and its value is intrinsic to the item itself. **Intangible property** is that personal property that may have little monetary value, but is representative of something of value. This type of personal property is often referred to as a **chose in action.**

EXAMPLE:

> A man buys a gold watch from Tiffany's. The watch has intrinsic value, and therefore is tangible personal property.

EXAMPLE:

> A woman opens a bank account with $5000 and receives a bank-book. The bankbook has little intrinsic value, but it represents her right to possess the $5000. The bankbook is intangible property.

General Tangibles

Most people are only superficially aware of their personal property. Because they see and use the property every day they tend not to identify it. But if a person wishes to transfer an item of personalty, the item must be identified in such a way that there will be no confusion in determining which item was meant should the transferor own similar types of property. Unlike real estate, there is no deed at a county recorder's office to provide a legally sufficient description.

EXAMPLE:

> A man owns two 14K gold chains and wants to sell one. The bill of sale should make specific reference to the chain in question to iden-tify it, such as "the 14K gold rope chain, 18 inches long, manufac-tured in Italy."

Intangibles

General Intangibles

General intangibles include such items as certificates of deposit, cor-porate stocks, corporate and government bonds, and so forth. Savings and time accounts are typical of the intangible property many people possess.

**EXAMPLE:**

A man inherits 1,000 shares of IBM stock. These shares are an example of a general intangible.

Corporate **stocks** are documents that represent the owner's percentage interest in the company that issued the stock. Either these **shares** are traded in the open market (the New York Stock Exchange, the American Stock Exchange, NASDAQ, and so forth) or are **closely held,** meaning that the shares are only owned by a few people. In either event, these shares are known as securities whose value represents the value of the company that issued the shares. Shares that are publicly traded on the open market have values that fluctuate each day; the value, or selling price, is reported in the newspaper. Closely held stock, on the other hand, is not publicly traded, so its value is determined each time the shareholder wishes to transfer his shares. Additionally, most closely held companies restrict the transferability of their shares, meaning that the shareholder may not have the right to sell, give, or leave by will the share to whomever he or she wants.

EXAMPLE:

Three friends decide to start a business that they establish as a corporation. To limit the number of owners, they do not sell shares to the public. Furthermore, to maintain control of the business, they sign an agreement whereby none of them can sell his shares to an outsider. These shares thereby become non-transferable.

Bonds can be issued either by companies or by the government, and are evidences of indebtedness. Bonds operate by having the bondholder lend money to the issuer for a set number of years, and during the period of the loan the bondholder receives interest on the loan. At the end of the period, the bondholder gets her money back. Bonds are usually publicly traded like stock. Bonds are **secured investments,** meaning that the debtor must set aside some property that the bondholder can attach in the case of default. If a bond is issued that does not have some secured property attached to it, it is called a **debenture.**

EXAMPLE:

To raise money, a corporation issues a bond for $300,000. It agrees to pay the holder 4% interest on the bond for 30 years. The corporation puts $30,000 into a trust account as security for the bondholder in case it defaults on the bond.

Another form of debt intangibles are **promissory notes** that are loans evidenced by a document stating interest payments and a payback date. They are similar to bonds and debentures except that they are issued for a shorter period of time. They are considered items of value because they represent the promissee's right to receive the money indicated in the note.

EXAMPLE:

A man lends his friend $250 and has the friend sign a promissory note, due in three months. The note represents the man's right to the return of the money, and he may sue the friend on the note if the friend does not repay the loan.

Another example of intangible property is a mortgage, discussed in previous chapters. The mortgage and underlying note represent a debt, an intangible, secured by realty.

Intellectual Property

Intellectual property is any property that was created by a person to which he or she has exclusive use. Intellectual property falls into three categories: copyrights, patents, and marks.

Copyrights are government grants to the author of a writing or the creator of a work of art. Anyone who creates a book, a poem, or any work of art automatically has a common law right to the exclusive use of the work. However, in order to document and protect this right, the work can be statutorily copyrighted with the federal government in Washington, D.C. Once copyrighted, the author or creator has an exclusive right to use the copyrighted property for his life plus 75 years, meaning that it is an asset that can be inherited.

EXAMPLE:

A lawyer decides to write a text on property law. Once the work is finished, she has the exclusive right to the material for her life, plus 75 years.

The monetary value of a copyright comes from the owner's licensing of that right. A **license** allows the licensee to use the copyrighted work, paying the copyright owner a fee for the use. As a typical example, a book is copyrighted by the author, and the publisher is licensed to print and sell that book, paying the author a fee known as a **royalty.**

A **patent** is a government grant of exclusive use of an invention, given to the inventor. The patent must be registered with the U.S. Patent Office, and the exclusive right is good only for a period of 20 years, at which point it passes into the public domain. Like a copyright, a patent can be licensed to produce an income to the patent holder.

A **trademark** is the exclusive right to use a name, symbol, or group of words that signify a particular product or service, distinguishing it from similar products and services. If the item is a product, the mark is called a trademark; if the item is a service, the mark is called a **service mark.** Examples would be "Calvin Klein" for a trademark because it identifies a clothing product, or "Schleppers Movers" for a service mark because it represents a moving company.

Marks are registered with the federal government, and the government grants the owner the exclusive right to use the mark for ten years. The mark may be renewed for unlimited ten-year periods, but if not renewed, the owner loses his rights. Additionally, if the owner permits someone to use the mark without his authorization, the owner will lose this exclusive right to the mark.

Methods of Transferring Personal Property

Gifts

A **gift** is a transfer of property from one person to another without a mutual exchange of consideration. If each party receives consideration, the transfer would be a contract of sale (see Chapter 4). With a gift, the title-holder, known as the **donor,** transfers her title to another, the **donee.** Gifts are characterized by the time and method of their transfer:

1. **Inter vivos gift:** This transfer occurs during the life of both the donor and the donee. Typical examples of inter vivos gifts are birthday and wedding presents.
2. **Testamentary gifts:** These are transfers of property that occur upon the death of the donor. The donor's intent to make the gift is evidenced by a legal document called a will that operates to transfer title to a person's property upon the person's death according to his or her expressed intention.
3. **Gifts causa mortis:** These transfers are gifts made in contemplation of the donor's imminent death. Unlike the other types of gifts, a gift causa mortis may be revoked by the donor any time prior to death, and, if the donor does not succumb to the imminent death, the gift is revoked by operation of law. Furthermore, should the donee predecease the donor, the gift is likewise deemed revoked.

To effectuate a gift, three elements must exist:

1. The donor must evidence a **donative intent,** the present intent to make a gift.
2. There must be a delivery of the gifted object to the donee or the donee's agent in the same fashion as the transfer of a deed discussed in Chapter 5.

3. There must be an acceptance of the gift by the donee; the law presumes acceptance absent an indication to the contrary.

Gifts and sales form the two primary methods of transferring property. Although personal property may be transferred without documentation, to transfer realty by gift the donor must still execute a deed as previously described.

EXAMPLE:

To celebrate her graduation from law school, a woman's friends get together and buy her a pearl necklace. They present it to her at the graduation ceremony. All three elements to perfect a gift of personal property have been met — intent, delivery, and acceptance.

Bailments

A **bailment** is the transfer of possession of personal property from one person, the **bailor,** to another person, the **bailee.** A bailment does not transfer title to the object, simply the right of the bailee to possess, and sometimes use, the object until the item is returned. A bailment may be created by an express agreement. The agreement may be either oral or written.

No bailment exists until the object is physically transferred. Several jurisdictions indicate that possession alone may not be sufficient to create a bailment. To create the bailment, an essential feature is the ability of the bailee to exercise control over the object.

Some states will imply a bailment if mere possession exists, but in those jurisdictions the possession, while creating a bailment, does not impose duties on the bailee. Duties do attach once control is demonstrated (see below). Also, a person may become a bailee even if he or she does not know the precise value of the object but has in fact demonstrated the intent to exercise control over the item. This situation is referred to as a constructive bailment.

EXAMPLE:

A woman brings a cloth coat to a dry cleaner. The owner of the store accepts the coat. Unbeknownst to the owner, the coat is a designer original valued at $8000, and the woman has left a diamond brooch in the coat's pocket. The dry cleaner is a bailee for the coat, even though he was not aware of its value, but not for the diamond brooch because he did not know of its presence in the pocket, would not expect such an item in the pocket, and cannot have a bailment thrust upon him.

Several specific situations with respect to bailments have given rise over the years to particular rules of law:

- *Pledges.* A **pledge** is a bailment in which the possession of personal property is transferred to secure a debt, somewhat like the collateral for a loan. The bailee, in this instance the creditor, has possession of the object until the debt is repaid. If the debtor defaults, the bailee acquires title to the property. A pawnbroker typifies this type of relationship. In the normal bailment situation, the transfer of title is not an element.
- *Safe deposit boxes.* Because both the bank and the bank customer have keys to the box, the law has determined that a bailor-bailee relationship exists, holding the bank liable as a bailee.
- *Cloakrooms.* A customer leaving a coat with a cloakroom attendant creates a bailment; however, the liability of the owner of the cloakroom may be limited by specific state statute.
- *Parking lots.* Leaving a car in a parking lot does not in and of itself create a bailment, because no actual transfer of possession has occurred. However, if the car owner leaves the keys to the car with the parking lot attendant, a bailment is been created because the attendant now has control of the car.
- *Health clubs and retail stores.* The owner of a health club is a bailee for the customer's clothing left in a locker while the facility is being used, even if the customer keeps the key to the locker. A retailer is a bailee for items set aside while the customer shops, such as putting down packages while trying on clothes.

A bailment only transfers the right of possession, and sometimes use, of the property. It does not transfer title, as would be the case with a sale or a gift.

Typically, a bailee is entitled to absolute possession of the object during the period of the bailment, and may maintain legal actions against anyone who attempts to interfere with this possessory right. Also, a bailee may have certain rights with respect to the use of the property:

- *Express use.* The parties to the bailment may contract, or agree, that the bailee may use the property during the term of the bailment.
- *Implied use.* Certain types of personal property by their nature indicate that the bailee may use the property.

 EXAMPLE:

A man puts his dog in a kennel while he is away on a business trip. As part of her responsibility to care for the dog the kennel owner can take the dog for long walks.

- *Incidental use.* Certain necessary use by the bailee may be expected in order to complete the bailment.

**EXAMPLE:**

A woman lends her friend a diamond necklace. As an incidental use, the friend can clean and polish the gems.

If a bailee uses a bailed item for purpose that is not expressly agreed upon, implied, or incidental to the bailment, the bailee will be held liable to the bailor for any damage that results from such unauthorized use of the item.

EXAMPLE:

A couple lends their boat to a neighbor so that the neighbor can row across the lake to the town center rather than drive. While it is in his possession, the neighbor decides to rent the boat to some tourists, who damage the boat. The neighbor is held liable because of this unauthorized use of the item.

The modern trend of the law is to hold the bailee liable for ordinary negligence that causes damage to the bailed items. However, the bailee may be held to a standard of absolute liability if the bailee departs from the terms of the bailment or misdelivers the bailed item to someone other than the bailor.

The parties may agree to a limitation of liability clause in their contract, but a blanket waiver of liability is usually disfavored. The bailor may maintain an action against the bailee for breach of contract, or for any injury or destruction of the item.

Common Carriers and Innkeepers

A **common carrier** is a commercial enterprise that transports goods and people for consideration. The definition does not include public agencies that perform the same services. A common carrier is held to the responsibility of an insurer for all goods it transports, meaning that the common carrier is liable for the value of goods if they are damaged or destroyed, even if the injury or destruction is caused by an act of God. However, unless there is an agreement to the contrary, the carrier will not be liable if goods are not delivered according to its printed timetable or its estimated time of delivery. Note that the common carrier is only held to a standard of ordinary care for any injury to the passengers.

An **innkeeper** is a commercial enterprise that rents temporary accommodation to members of the public. As such, the innkeeper is considered an insurer of the guests' property, similar to the common carrier. However, the innkeeper is not liable if the damage to or destruction of the property is caused by the guests' own negligence or fault, an act of God, or a fire not caused by the innkeeper's lack of care. Moreover, the innkeeper is liable for any loss due to burglary, theft, or negligence. The burden is on the innkeeper to evidence that she was not negligent. The innkeeper may limit her liability for loss if she conspicuously posts a notice of such limitation of liability.

Both common carriers and innkeepers have insurer liability with respect to goods left in their possession. Both types of businesses are entitled to a lien on the property in their possession. A **lien** is a right (intangible personal property) of a person who has improved property to retain possession of that property until the cost of the improvement has been paid. To create a lien, there must be a debt created by the lienor having performed a service on the item. Title to the property remains in the debtor, but possession of the property is in the lienor.

A common carrier is given a common law lien on all items it has agreed to transport. No lien attaches if the property is received from people other than the owner. Innkeepers have liens on all property a guest brings into the inn, even if the property does not belong to the guest. The lienor has the right to retain possession of the items until the debt is discharged, and if it is not discharged, title will vest in the lienor.

 EXAMPLE:

A man travels on the Metroliner from Boston to New York. At the train station in New York someone steals his suitcase. The thief checks into a motel with the suitcase. The thief stays one night and then departs without paying his motel bill. Amtrak is liable to the man for the value of his suitcase unless it has limited its liability, and the motel can keep the suitcase left by the thief, even though the suitcase did not belong to the thief.

Other Issues

In addition to the above-discussed methods of transfer, property may be transferred from one person to another without a specific interest or relationship having been created. These methods of acquiring property—accession and confusion—may operate to transfer both personal and real property.

Accession

Accession occurs when one person's labor or materials are added to another person's property so as to increase the value of that property. If this additional value can be severed (removed) from the original item, the court will order such removal. If removal is impossible, the original party may sue for damages. If the change in the nature of the property is deemed so significant that the object is completely altered and its value is greatly increased, the title to the property will pass to the person whose labor or property caused the change.

 EXAMPLE:

A person takes lumber from a hardware store and builds a cabinet with the wood. The hardware store owner is entitled to the value of the lumber taken, but the person who made the cabinet may retain the cabinet because the nature of the lumber has now been completely changed. This result is true if the person took the lumber unintentionally, believing that he had purchased it. If the person intentionally took the lumber knowing that he had no right to it, the cabinet will belong to the hardware store owner.

Confusion

Confusion occurs when the personal property of two individuals is mixed together. If the goods are of the same kind and quality and the mixture occurred by inadvertence, the mixture is deemed owned by both parties as tenants in common. If the confusion was caused by the willful act of one of the parties, the wrongdoer is required to identify his or her portion. If identification is impossible, the entire mixture belongs to the innocent party. If the mixed property can be separated, the court will order such separation.

 EXAMPLE:

Two farmers send their grain to the same mill to have it ground into flour. The mill owner fails to realize that two different farmers have brought the grain because they both use the same carrier. He innocently mills all the grain together, and it cannot be determined how much each farmer owns. In this situation, both farmers as tenants in common will own all the flour.

Practical Tips

- Document transfers of personal property in writing to avoid problems with respect to ownership later on.
- Remember that titles to personal property are the same as those for real property, with all the same rights and obligations.
- Transfers of property may be subject to gift taxation—always check the tax implications of the transfer of valuable property.

Chapter Review

No discussion of the law of property is complete without an examination of the law concerning personal property. Personal property is divided into two broad categories: tangible property, moveable property that has intrinsic value, and intangible property, items whose value is representative.

Tangible property is exemplified by clothing, jewelry, art, antiques, electronic equipment, cars, and so forth. It is the type of property that most people own or possess. Intangible property is exemplified by stocks and bonds, bank savings and checking accounts, loans, and the various types of intellectual property such as copyrights, patents and marks. The intangible aspect of intellectual property is the grant of exclusive use of the item given by the government to the item's creator, inventor, or owner.

Personal property is transferred using procedures that differ from the general methods of conveyancing used to transfer realty. The most common methods of transfer are by gift, in which title passes from the titleholder to another without consideration; by bailment, in which possession, not title, is transferred to a person not the title holder; and by accession and confusion. Furthermore, specific rules apply to common carriers and innkeepers when they acquire possession of another person's personal property.

Ethical Concern

The legal professional often acts as the agent of the client, and is called upon to keep the client's property. The legal professional may not place the client's property with his or her own, which is known as commingling. Such a practice violates the ethical standards of the legal profession. All client property must be kept separate and distinct from that of the legal professional.

Key Terms

Accession	Intangible property
Bailee	Inter vivos gift
Bailment	License
Bailor	Lien
Bonds	Patent
Chose in action	Pledge
Closely held	Promissory note
Common carrier	Royalty
Confusion	Secured investments
Copyright	Service mark
Debenture	Share
Donative intent	Stock
Donee	Tangible property
Donor	Testamentary gift
Gift	Trademark
Gift causa mortis	Will
Innkeeper	

Exercises

1. Determine the type of duty that is owed by innkeepers in your jurisdiction.
2. Differentiate between tangible and intangible property.
3. Indicate how one might demonstrate donative intent.
4. Give three examples of your own experience with bailments.
5. Briefly discuss the concept of intellectual property.

Situational Analysis

A famous artist finishes a painting just before he leaves for a vacation. He gives the painting to a friend to keep it safe while he is away. The artist says that if anything happens to him the friend can keep the painting. On the flight home the plane on which the artist is traveling crashes and the artist is killed. Both the friend and the estate claim the painting. Argue for both sides and decide the matter.

Edited Cases

The two cases that follow highlight some concepts discussed in this chapter. *Pitchford v. Commonwealth of Virginia* underscores the obligations incident to bailments, and *In the Matter of the Estate of McGeath* provides insight into gifts causa mortis.

Pitchford v. Commonwealth of Virginia
50 Va. Cir. 266 (1999)

"In this [case] involving a bailment, [the court] must decide what standard of care is imposed upon the bailee by the relationship." *Morris v. Hamilton*, 225 Va. 372, 302 S.E.2d 51 (1983).

The case was tried to the court on September 8, 1999. The court took the decision under advisement after all the evidence. The term bailment is used advisedly because the defendant argues that no bailment is involved for lack of proof that it ever came into possession of the plaintiff's property. A summary of the salient facts are as follows.

Plaintiff, a nurse employed at the Medical College of Virginia, arrived for work around 8:00 to 8:30 on the evening of May 8, 1999. After parking her vehicle in a parking deck adjacent to the hospital, she was accosted there by two men who attacked and beat her. The two ran away after plaintiff said she thought she heard one of them say others were approaching. Plaintiff testified that the next thing she remembered was looking up at the face of a medical resident who found her lying face up on the parking deck floor.

After being attended to by ambulance personnel and fitted with a neck collar at the scene, the plaintiff was transported to the MCV emergency room. While in the receiving room, nurses in attendance removed her jewelry consisting of earrings and a necklace. This was necessary to take x-rays of her upper extremities. Plaintiff testified that she was told to keep still and close her eyes. She was bloodied and beaten about the face, and blood was present over one eye due to a head wound.

At issue is a diamond pendant which was attached to the necklace plaintiff was wearing. Plaintiff has alleged in four counts that the pendant, though taken, was not returned with her other personal effects. Plaintiff testified that she felt the pendant in the back and around the side of her neck during the process of removal by the nurse. The two nurses who were present, one of whom actually removed the necklace while the other observed, both testified that, when the necklace came off, no pendant was present. During the hearing, the court examined the necklace. There was no visible sign of damage to it.

After remaining in the emergency room for about six to eight hours, plaintiff was released without being admitted to the hospital. As mentioned, after removal of the necklace and after personal items were placed in a bag, the bag was put on the table beside plaintiff's bed. The bag was eventually turned over to plaintiff's supervisor who in turn gave it to plaintiff or plaintiff's daughter after plaintiff's release. Later at home, she discovered that, while the necklace was present, the pendant was not. The parties have stipulated that the diamond pendant has a value of $6,000.

The court will assume that for purposes of a ruling that the diamond pendant was attached to the necklace at the time of removal. Thus, contrary to the position of the hospital, the court assumes a bailment arose. Again, the question is what standard of care is applicable. As I mentioned during the proceedings, it depends on how the bailment is classified. Applicable here, the circumstances suggest either a bailment for mutual benefit or a gratuitous one.

In a bailment "for the mutual benefit of the bailor and bailee, the bailee must use ordinary care for the protection, preservation, and return of the bailed property. If the bailee fails to use ordinary care, he is liable to the bailor for any loss or damage to the property resulting from the bailee's failure." *Volvo White Truck Corp. v. Vineyard*, 239 Va. 87, 91, 387 S.E.2d 763 (1990) (citation omitted). A gratuitous bailment, on the other hand, is one where the possession is given the bailee solely for the benefit of the bailor. "A bailee who acts gratuitously is not held to the same standard of care as one who enters upon the same undertaking for pay. The latter owes a duty of reasonable or ordinary care, while a gratuitous bailee owes only a duty of slight care. Thus, in order for a bailor to recover from a gratuitous bailee, he must prove the bailee was guilty of gross negligence." *Morris v. Hamilton* at 375 (citation omitted).

As noted, plaintiff was asked to remove her personal effects including the necklace, to facilitate the taking of x-rays of her upper extremities, where she had sustained injury. There was testimony that this was needed to exclude skull and bone fracture, among other things. Under these circumstances the hospital came by possession of the necklace for the benefit of plaintiff in the rendition of medical care.

As has also been noted, plaintiff was not admitted to the hospital, but was rather treated in the emergency room and released. Contrary to plaintiff's contention, the evidence does not establish a contract of bailment. Were this the case "[a] different set of principles would apply." *Volvo White Truck Corp. v. Vineyard*, 239 Va. 87, 92, 387 S.E.2d 763 (1990). In such an instance the bailee, here the hospital, would have the burden of persuasion of showing the exercise of "due care to prevent the damage." Id. at 92.

Here, the proof falls short of demonstrating the applicable standard, gross negligence in the instance of a gratuitous bailment; given this finding, plaintiff cannot recover on this basis.

This outcome applies to three of the counts plaintiff has raised: detinue, contract of bailment, and tort of bailment. To the extent that the plaintiff relies on bailment as a basis for detinue, her action fails.

As to the remaining count, conversion, the court will not rely on the assumption that the property was given over. This count alleges essentially a theft of the pendant to the extent that there was an unauthorized exercise of dominion and control with intent to permanently deprive the plaintiff thereof, either by taking or embezzlement. Here the testimony is equally believable as to a taking and a non taking, plaintiff's testimony that she felt the pendant around her neck when the nurses were removing it and the nurses' who both testified they did not observe it when the necklace was pulled away. There is no evidence of who may have deprived the plaintiff of the pendant after it came in rightful possession to constitute an embezzlement. Accordingly, the conversion count also fails.

For the foregoing reasons, the court has entered judgment for the defendant.

Case Questions

1. What factors did the court look to to determine that a bailment existed?

2. How does the court define a "conversion"?

In the Matter of the Estate of McGeath
2001 Ohio App. LEXIS 2470

Suzanne C. Munger appeals from a judgment of the Montgomery County Court of Common Pleas, Probate Division, which sustained exceptions to the final account she had filed as executrix of Joyce A. McGeath's estate.

The record reveals that on August 9, 1996, McGeath died as a result of a brain tumor. Her will was admitted to the probate court and it appointed

Munger to be the executrix of the estate. At the time of McGeath's death, she had had $17,652.34 in a Universal 1 Credit Union Account. The disagreement in this case concerns that money.

Munger testified as follows. On the day before McGeath's death, Munger was in Michigan. During a phone conversation with McGeath, she told Munger that she was having a second brain tumor surgery the next day and that she knew that she would "likely be a vegetable" after the surgery "or that she would pass away[.]" She told Munger that there was approximately $17,000 in her checking account. McGeath said that she would leave a check with her mother, Dorothy Yacchari, and that Yacchari would give that amount of money to Munger. McGeath told Munger that if she became a vegetable, Munger should use the money to take care of her and to make sure that she was placed in a nice nursing home. McGeath told Munger that if she died, she wanted Munger to pay her funeral expenses from the money and then to use the remaining funds to go to Italy, a place the two of them had previously planned to go together. McGeath wrote the check and gave it to Yacchari.

Munger returned to Ohio on the day of McGeath's death. When she arrived, Yacchari told Munger that she had the check. Munger told Yacchari to "just hold on to" the check so that the funeral expenses could be paid from that amount.

Yacchari deposited the check into her own account. Yacchari later wrote a check to the funeral home in the amount of $5,825.84. Yacchari also wrote a check to Munger for the remaining amount of $11,826.50. Debra Shaw, McGeath's daughter, testified as follows. McGeath had two brain surgeries "within a matter of days." While McGeath was in the hospital, Shaw and other family members visited her. During one of those visits, McGeath told Shaw that she wanted the $17,652.34 to be used to take care of her if she survived. McGeath stated that if she died, the money should be used to pay her funeral expenses and any outstanding bills and that the remainder of the money was to go to her estate.

McGeath told her that a check was being written to Yacchari and that Yacchari was to give the check to Munger so that Munger could pay the funeral expenses and outstanding bills from that amount and such expenses and bills would not be charged to the estate. McGeath also stated that she was writing the check "because she did not want money tied up in probate."

Munger filed the final fiduciary's account with the probate court on October 25, 2000. The account did not list the $17,652.34. The court appointed a guardian ad litem for the minor beneficiaries of the estate. On December 4, 2000, the guardian ad litem filed exceptions to the account. On that same day, some of McGeath's family members, acting as "guardians for the benefit of minors," also filed exceptions to the account. One of the exceptions filed by both asked the court to determine whether the $17,652.34 was a gift causa mortis or an asset of the estate.

A hearing was held on December 13, 2000. On January 3, 2001, the court filed its decision, finding that Munger had not proven that McGeath had made the gift causa mortis and thus that the amount of $17,652.34

should have been included as an asset in McGeath's estate. The court decided that the payment of the $5,825.84 funeral bill had been "correct" however and decided not to disturb such amount. The court sustained the exception as to the remaining $11,826.50 and ordered that such money belonged to the estate.

On January 17, 2001, Munger filed a notice of appeal of the probate court's decision. She now raises a single assignment of error.

THE TRIAL COURT ERRED IN SUSTAINING THE EXCEPTIONS OF THE GUARDIAN AD LITEM AND THE PRO SE FAMILY AS TO THE AMOUNT OF $11,826.50.

Munger argues that the trial court erred in concluding that the $11,826.50 belonged to the estate. She claims that she proved that the money was a gift causa mortis and thus such money should not have been part of McGeath's estate.

The essential elements of a gift causa mortis are as follows:

1. It must be of personal property.
2. The gift must be made in the last illness of the donor, while under the apprehension of death as imminent, and subject to the implied condition that if the donor recovers of the illness, or if the donee dies first, the gift shall be void; and
3. Possession of the property given must be delivered at the time of the gift to the donee, or to some one for [her], and the gift must be accepted by the donee.

In re Estate of Newland (1946), 34 Ohio Op. 235, 236, 70 N.E.2d 234, *affirmed* (1946), 47 Ohio L. Abs. 252, 70 N.E.2d 238. Although courts do not favor gifts causa mortis, they will be given effect when the elements are proven by clear and convincing evidence. Id. at 237–238; *Adams v. Fleck* (1961), 171 Ohio St. 451, 455–456, 172 N.E.2d 126, 129–130, paragraph 3(b) of syllabus.

Munger argues that she presented evidence to meet all of the essential elements of a gift causa mortis. While her testimony might have presented evidence to support that conclusion, Munger's testimony was disputed. Shaw's testimony contradicted Munger's testimony. Thus, the question of whether McGeath made a gift causa mortis was a question of credibility. See *Citizens Natl. Bank v. DeLuca*, 2000 Ohio App. LEXIS 4413 (Sept. 27, 2000), Crawford App. No. 3-2000-12, unreported. Credibility issues are within the discretion of the trial court. Id. Thus, in this case we will not interfere with the trial court's determination that Munger failed to prove that McGeath made a gift causa mortis where there was competent, credible evidence that McGreath had not done so.

The assignment of error is overruled.

The judgment of the trial court will be affirmed.

Case Questions

1. How did the decedent attempt to transfer her funds?
2. Why was this not a gift causa mortis?

Glossary

Abatement: Reduction of rent due to lack of habitability.

Absolute ownership doctrine: Allows an owner the unrestricted use of ground water.

Abstract of title: Summary of title transfers of realty maintained by the county recorder's office.

Acceleration payment: Mortgage clause that requires immediate repayment of the outstanding balance if certain occurrences take place.

Accession of the loan: Increase in value of property caused by an act of someone not the property's owner.

Adjustable rate mortgage (ARM): Mortgage with low interest rate the first few years that increases over time.

Adverse possession: Obtaining title to property by possessing the property in an open and notorious manner that is adverse to the interests of the true owner.

Alienate: Transfer property.

Ameliorative waste: Action of a life tenant or possessor that changes the character of the property in a way that increases its value.

Appropriation rights doctrine: Allows water use based on historical use; used in several western states.

Articles of incorporation: Document filed with the secretary of state to create a cooperative or condominium board.

Assessment: Financial obligation of condominium and cooperative unit owners to maintain common areas.

Assignee: Transferee of contractual rights.

Assignment: Transfer of contract rights.

Assignor: Transferor of contractual rights.

Assume the mortgage: The mortgagor's transferee becomes primarily liable on the mortgage.

Assumption agreement: Contract by which a mortgage is assumed.

Attractive nuisance: A natural or artificial situation on land that would entice children onto the realty.

Bailee: Person who acquires possession of personalty.

Bailment: Transfer of possession of personalty.

Bailor: Transferor of the possession of personalty.

Base line: Artificial line used to create rectangular indexing of land; runs east-west.

Block and lot index: Method of recording title to land by the land's description.

Board of directors: Manager of the condominium and cooperative.

Boilerplate: Standard clauses not specifically related to real estate.

Bond: Underlying loan for a mortgage. When issued by the government or a company it is evidence of indebtedness.

Building code: Government rules regarding construction of buildings.

Bylaws: Document establishing day-to-day operations of an enterprise.

Certificate of non-foreign status: IRS document filed by U.S. citizens involved in a real estate transfer.

Certificate of occupancy: Document prepared by the government indicating that a building is safe to be occupied.

Chattel: Tangible personal property.

Chose in action: Another name for intangibles.

Closely held: Corporation whose shares are not publicly traded.

Closing: The formality of completing the transfer of realty and transferring title; can also refer to the date on which title to property is transferred.

Closing statement: Document determining all costs of a closing.

Cloud on title: Any break in the chain of title that could give rise to a lawsuit with respect to ownership of the property.

Co-tenant: A person who shares title to property.

Commission: Broker's fee.

Common carrier: Transporter of goods and people.

Common enemy: Concept of draining and removing surface water by any method the landowner chooses.

Common law covenants: Covenants of seizin, right to convey, against encumbrances, quiet enjoyment, warranty, and further assurances.

Community property: Form of title in nine jurisdictions in the United States for legally married couples in which each spouse is deemed to own one-half of the property outright.

Concurrent ownership: Title to property shared by two or more persons collectively.

Condemn: To destroy property for public welfare and safety.

Condition: Fact or event that creates or extinguishes a contractual duty.

Condition precedent: Condition that must occur to create a contractual duty.

Condominium: Form of ownership in which a person owns a portion of the property outright and is a tenant in common with others for common areas.

Condominium association: Group that oversees regulation of the condominium and has authority to maintain common areas.

Condominium declaration: Document used to create a condominium.

Confusion: Mixture of personal property that cannot be separated after the mixing.

Consideration: Benefit conferred or a detriment incurred at the request of the other party.

Constructive eviction: Action by the landlord that interferes with tenant's possession.

Contingent remainder: Future interest that takes effect only if a condition is met.

Contractual capacity: Legal ability to contract.

Conveyancing: The process of transferring title to land.

Cooperative: Ownership of shares in an association that permits the holder to possess a unit of the association's property.

Copyright: Exclusive right to a work of art.

Correlative rights doctrine: California doctrine permitting landowner reasonable use of ground water.

Covenant: Permanent restriction on land use.

Covenant against encumbrances: Warranty that there are no liens, mortgages, or clouds on the title on the property.

Covenant of further assurances: Warranty that the grantor will protect the grantee from claims on the title in the future.

Covenant of quiet enjoyment: Warranty that no one else has a lawful claim on the property.

Covenant of right to convey: Warranty that the grantor has the legal ability to transfer the title.

Covenant of seizin: Warranty that the grantor has title to and possession of the property.

Covenant of warranty: Warranty that a good title will be passed.

Damages: Monetary remedy.

Debenture: Unsecured corporate loan.

Deed: Document that transfers title to realty.

Defeasible fee: Interest that can be totally lost upon the occurrence of a specified event.

Defect: Condition that causes a significant reduction in the value of property.

Deposit: Money paid to secure a sales contract; a portion of the purchase price.

Doctrine of equitable conversion: Risk of loss passes to the buyer on the signing of the contract.

Dominant tenement: Property that holds an easement.

Donative intent: Desire to make a gift.

Donee: Recipient of a gift.

Donor: Giver of a gift.

Down payment: Portion of the purchase price given to the seller to secure the sale.

Earnest money: Another name for the deposit given when the sales contract is signed.

Easement: The right of access over or use of another's property.

Easement appurtenant: Easement created by adjoining properties.

Easement by necessity: Easement that arises in landlocked situations to give property owner access to public roads.

Easement by prescription: Easement that is created over time in a manner similar to adverse possession.

Easement in gross: Easement that is created for non-adjoining properties.

Emblements: Profits from land use, such as crops, minerals, and timber.

Eminent domain: Power of the government to take private property for the welfare and safety of the public.

Encumber: Place a cloud on title; give a third person some right to the property.

Encumbrance: Anything that puts a cloud on title.

Equitable mortgage: Mortgage is assumed if deed is transferred to secure a loan.

Equitable redemption: A right of a defaulting mortgagor to reacquire the property by paying the loan prior to the foreclosure sale.

Equitable servitude: Restriction on land use enforceable by an injunction.

Equitable waste: Waste arising from the failure to exercise good husbandry.

Escrow: Trust account where funds are held until contract is completed.

Estate: Title to real or personal property.

Estoppel by deed: Doctrine whereby a purchaser of property not owned by the seller will acquire title if the seller subsequently acquires ownership.

Estoppel certificate: Document provided to the buyer by the seller's mortgagee in a sale of commercial realty.

Estoppel letter: Letter provided by tenants in a commercial building indicating the accuracy of their leases.

Eviction: Process of having a tenant removed from a leased premise.

Exclusive listing: Only broker or owner may sell the property.

Exclusive right to sell: Broker receives commission regardless of who sells the property.

Execution: Signing of an agreement.

Executory interest: Future interest that takes effect after a gap in an earlier interest.

Express grant: Easement created by agreement.

Fee: Type of freehold estate.

Fee simple absolute: Complete, unfettered ownership of property.

Fee simple determinable: Fee interest that is lost if a specified use of the property changes.

Fee simple subject to a condition subsequent: Fee interest that can be lost if a specified condition occurs.

Fee simple subject to an executory interest: Fee interest that takes place after a gap.

Fee tail: Fee interest that can only pass to lineal descendants.

Fixture: Chattel that is permanently affixed to the land.

Foreclosure: Right of the mortgagee to sell the land to satisfy the debt.

Foreclosure by advertisement: Foreclosure permitted without court order.

Form 1099-S: IRS tax form filed for real estate sales.

Four unities: The elements a conveyance must contain to create a joint tenancy: time, title, interest, and possession.

Freehold: Estate in land held for an indefinite period of time.

Fructus industriales: Emblements arising from a possessor's efforts.

Fructus naturales: Emblements naturally growing on the land.

General warranty deed: Deed with the common law covenants.

Gift: Transfer of personalty without consideration.

Gift causa mortis: Gift made in contemplation of donor's imminent death.

Grantee: Transferee.

Grantor: Transferor.

Grantor-grantee index: Method of recording titles to realty by transferor and transferee names.

Gross lease: Lease in which the tenant is liable for rent plus utilities.

Ground water: Underground or percolating water.

Hold-over doctrine: Right of landlord against tenant who remains in unlawful possession after the termination of a lawful lease.

Homeowners' association: Another name for the condominium association.

Horizontal privity: Original parties to a covenant must share a common interest.

HUD-1 Uniform Settlement Statement: Government form generally used for all real estate settlements and mandated for those backed by government loans.

Implied easement: Easement that arises by actual use of adjacent property without consent.

Indefeasibly vested remainder: Future interest that cannot be lost.

Indemnification: Agreement to be financially responsible if another is held legally liable.

Innkeeper: One who offers public accommodation.

Installment sale: Sale in which the purchase price is paid over a number of years.

Insurable title: Less clear than marketable title but one that can be insured against claims.

Intangible property: Personal property that represents something of value.

Inter vivos gift: Gift that is transferred during the life of both donor and donee.

Invitee: Person who lawfully enters land for his or her own benefit.

Joint tenancy: Multiple ownership of property with an undivided interest and a right of survivorship.

Judicial foreclosure: Foreclosure sale authorized by a court.

Landlord: Person who grants the use of property through a lease.

Landlord-tenant law: Law concerned with leaseholds.

Land use: Right of access to land permitted to persons who are not owners/possessors of the land.

Lease: Contract for the right to possess property, creating a leasehold.

Leasehold: Possessory estate in property.

Lessee: Tenant.

Lessor: Landlord.

License: Permission to enter property for a specific act or series of acts. Allows use of a copyrighted work.

Licensee: Person who can enter land subject to a license.

Lien: Claim on property to satisfy a debt.

Life estate: Freehold held for the term of a person's life.

Life estate pur autre vie: Life estate held for the life of a person other than the titleholder.

Life tenant: Person who holds title to a life estate.

Listing agreement: Real estate broker's contract.

Marketable title: Title without any encumbrances.

Measuring life: Person whose life determines duration of the life estate.

Mechanic's lien: Lien automatically given to anyone who performs work on property.

Merger: Where dominant and servient tenement titles are owned by the same person.

Metes and bounds description: Method of describing land by following a course around the boundaries.

Mitigation of damages: Duty of non-breaching party to lessen the money owed by the breaching party.

Mortgage: Security interest to guarantee repayment of a loan.

Mortgage insurance: Insurance to protect against a default on a mortgage loan.

Mortagee: Creditor who receives a mortgage.

Mortgagor: Debtor who gives a mortgage.

Natural flow theory: Owner may use water from watercourses in a manner that does not affect quality or quantity of the water.

Net rent lease: Landlord remains responsible for utilities.

Note: Underlying debt used to create a mortgage.

Notice: Recording statute giving priority to bona fide purchaser with no notice of other claim.

Notice to attorn: Notice to tenants of a change in ownership of the property.

Nuisance: Interference with the use and enjoyment of real property.

Offer: Proposal to enter into a contract.

Offeree: Person to whom an offer is made.

Offeror: Person who makes an offer.

Open listing: Owner engages several brokers to sell the property, and the commission only goes to the one who consummates the sale.

Ouster: Court-ordered termination of a co-tenant's rights because of failure to meet an obligation.

Partial eviction: Act that interferes with a tenants possession of a portion of the leased property.

Partition: Court-ordered division of property among tenants.

Patent: Exclusive use of an invention.

Payoff amount: Outstanding amount owed by seller to be paid off by the buyer.

Percentage breakpoint: Type of commercial lease in which the landlord receives a portion of the tenant's gross sales or profits above a set amount.

Percentage rent: Rent based on a percentage of commercial tenant's gross sales.

Percolating water: Ground water.

Periodic tenancy: Tenancy for successive specific periods of time.

Permissive waste: Decrease in value of land due to failure to maintain the property.

Personal property: All property not classified as real property.

Personalty: Personal property.

Plat book: Record maintained at county recorder's office that describes parcels of land.

Plat description: Method of describing property based on a survey.

Pledge: Bailment of property for money.

Possibility of reverter: Automatic reversion of title to grantor in a fee simple determinable.

Premises: Leased realty.

Prime rate: Interest rate banks charge to their best customers.

Principal meridian: Artificial line used to describe rectangular divisions of land; runs north-south.

Prior appropriations doctrine: Water rights determined by historical use.

Private nuisance: Interference with an individual's right of enjoyment of his or her own land.

Promissory note: Evidence of indebtedness.

Proration: Division of rent between the buyer and the seller.

Public nuisance: Interference with the health or safety of the community.

Punch list: Itemized list of remaining problems in newly constructed premises.

Quiet title: Action to have a court decide ownership of property.

Quitclaim deed: Deed in which no covenants are given.

Race: First to record has priority.

Race-notice: To acquire priority, the person must be the first to record without notice of any prior claim.

Radius clause: Provision prohibiting a commercial percentage rent tenant from operating a similar business within a specific geographic area.

Real covenant: Covenant that touches and concerns the land and "runs with the land."

Real Estate Settlement Procedure Act: Federal statute governing real estate closings for all federally guaranteed mortgage loans.

Real property: Land and anything permanently affixed to the land, including vegetation and mineral resources.

Release: Document that relinquishes legal rights.

Realty: Real property.

Reasonable use: Ordinary and foreseeable use.

Reasonable use doctrine: Permits landowner all reasonable use of the property.

Recording act: Statute that establishes the method of acquiring priority with respect to claims against property.

Rectangular survey description: Description of land created by intersection of base and principal meridian lines.

Redemption: Ability of a defaulting mortgagor to reacquire the property.

Redemption in equity: Mortgages may redeem the property at any time prior to the foreclosure sale by satisfying the debt.

Remainderman: Person who ultimately receives a fee interest after intervening estates.

Rent: Fee for use of a property.

Rent escalation clause: Lease provision providing for rent increases over the term of the lease.

Retaliatory eviction: Unlawful eviction of a tenant for asserting legal rights.

Right of entry: Landlord may gain access to premises in the event of a breach of the lease by tenant.

Right of re-entry: Ability of a grantor to regain title to a fee simple subject to a condition subsequent.

Right of survivorship: The right of a joint tenant to succeed to title to property after the death of another joint tenant.

Riparian doctrine: Landowner has unfettered use of watercourse.

Royalty: Fee for use of a copyright, patent, or mark.

Rule Against Perpetuities: All interests must vest, if at all, within 21 years after the death of the lives in being on the date of the initial conveyance.

Salvage doctrines: Statutes enacted to prevent conveyances being found invalid by violating the Rule Against Perpetuities.

Secured investment: Debt with property the bondholder can attach.

Securitization of receivables: Structured finance transaction.

Security deposit: Money given by a tenant to the landlord to be held in a trust account in case of the tenant's default.

Service mark: Trademark that designates a service.

Servient tenement: Property subject to an easement holder's rights.

Settlement: Another name for the closing.

Settlement statement: HUD-1 Statement.

Share: Intangible that represents ownership in a corporation.

Special warranty deed: Deed that only covenants against specific acts of the grantor.

Specific performance: Equitable remedy in which the breaching party is required to perform the contract.

Statutory redemption: Ability to redeem property after a foreclosure sale.

Stock: Another name for a share.

Strict liability: Being held legally responsible for one's actions regardless of any care taken.

Structured finance transaction: Selling shares of mortgages to investors.

Sub-prime mortgage: Mortgage loan to a borrower who is a poor credit risk.

Subjacent support: Anyone who occupies the area beneath the property must support the surface and buildings on the property.

Subject to the mortgage: Transferor remains principally liable on the debt and the property can be attached if the transferor defaults.

Sublease: A transfer of a portion of the tenant's rights under a lease.

Surface rights: Rights to use the land.

Surface water: Water that accumulates on the land.

Survey: Creating a description of a parcel of land.

Tangible property: Personalty that can be touched and moved, and whose value is intrinsic.

Tenancy by the entirety: Joint tenancy for married couples.

Tenancy in common: Multiple ownership of property with transferable interests and no right of survivorship.

Tenancy in partnership: Multiple ownership of property for business partners.

Tenancy in severalty: Title held by only one person.

Tenancy at sufferance: Tenancy resulting when the tenant remains in unlawful possession of the premises.

Tenancy for years: Tenancy for a specific number of years.

Tenancy at will: Tenancy created by agreement of the parties with no specific term.

Tenant: Lessee.

Testamentary gift: Gift made at death by a will.

Time is of the essence: All obligations in a contract must be fulfilled on the dates and times specified or the contract is deemed breached.

Title: Interest in property.

Title insurance: Insurance to protect against a defect in title.

Title search: Making sure the title to property is clear and capable of being transferred.

Touch and concern the land: Requirement to create a real covenant that restricts or requires certain actions.

Tract index: Title recorded by description of the property.

Trademark: Exclusive right to use a name, symbol, or words that designate a product or service.

Trespasser: Person who unlawfully enters onto another's property.

Usual covenants: Common law covenants without the covenant for further assurances.

Variance: Government permission to use property in a manner inconsistent with zoning regulations.

Vendor and Purchaser Risk Act: Statute that passes risk only after the buyer takes possession of the property.

Vertical privity: Necessary relationship from transferor to transferee to create and enforce a real covenant.

Vested remainder subject to complete divestment: Future interest that may be lost due to the happening of a specified event.

Vested remainder subject to a condition subsequent: Future interest that can be lost.

Vested remainder subject to open: Future interest in a class to which members may be added.

Vesting: Having legally enforceable rights.

Voluntary waste: Waste occasioned by deliberate action.

Warranty: Guaranty.

Warranty of habitability: Guaranty that the premises are livable according to local standards.

Waste: Action that lessens the value of the land.

Watercourse: Water on the land coming from rivers, streams, and lakes.

Zoning regulations: Laws designed to limit use of property for governmental geographic design purposes.

Zoning board: Governmental agency that enforces zoning regulations.

Index